-ᴈ Ӗ-

The Quiet Reformation

Muriel C. McClendon

The Quiet Reformation

MAGISTRATES AND THE
EMERGENCE OF PROTESTANTISM
IN TUDOR NORWICH

Stanford University Press, Stanford, California   *1999*

Stanford University Press
Stanford, California
© 1999 by the Board of Trustees of the
Leland Stanford Junior University
Printed in the United States of America
CIP data appear at the end of the book

To Michael

⊰ ⊱

Acknowledgments

The magistrates of Norwich rarely set down in writing their intentions or goals in governing England's second city through the tumultuous years of the Reformation. In the process of trying to unravel and understand their aims and actions, I have benefited from the assistance of a number of individuals and institutions whose help, contrary to the magistrates' practice, I am happy to record here.

This book is a revision of a Ph.D. dissertation completed at Stanford University. As a graduate student, I received generous financial support from the History Department, the Harris Fund, the Weter Fund and a Dorothy Danforth Compton Dissertation Fellowship. The Chancellor's Ethnic Minority Postdoctoral Fellowship Program at the University of California at Berkeley released me from teaching duties at UCLA, and the Academic Senate at the University of California at Los Angeles supported research assistance, both of which allowed me to revise the dissertation into a book.

I carried out most of the research for this book at the Norfolk Record Office, and I would like to thank the staff there, particularly Frank Meeres, for extending their professional expertise and every other possible courtesy to me. I would also like to thank the staffs at the British Library, Lambeth Palace Library, the Local History Department at the Norwich Central Library and the Public Record Office. At Stanford's Green Library, I would also like to extend special thanks to Jim Knox, the Curator of the British and American collections, and to Sonia Moss, the Interlibrary Loan Librarian. At Stanford University Press, I am grateful to Norris Pope, Paul Psoinos, and especially John Feneron for the assistance they have given me.

Paul Seaver was a model dissertation adviser whose example I have tried to emulate. Not only did he teach me a great deal about the study and teaching of history, but his patience, critical rigor, good humor and friendship have been constant sources of support. I would also like to thank Judy Brown, whose door was also always open and who gave generously of her time. And during my years in graduate school and afterwards, I have turned on numerous occasions to Richard Roberts for his wise counsel, which he has never been too busy to give.

I also want to express my gratitude to my graduate student colleagues at Stanford, both for their intellectual support and for their friendship, especially Karen Aschaffenburg, Nancy Berner, Bill Bravman, Nancy Carlston, Monica Chojnacka, David Coe, Pat Hayden-Roy, Priscila Hayden-Roy, Tom Holien, Charles Kimball, Doug Klusmeyer, Naomi Koltun-Fromm, Jim Lance, David Lazar, Wendy Lynch, Laura Mayhall, Thom McClendon, Liz Otero, Penny Russell, Mike Saler, Tom Sanders, Daryl Scott and Bob Shoemaker. I owe very special debts to Sue Grayzel, Tom McCalmont, Deb Rossum, Mark Saltus, Jenny Stine, Katie Swett, Martha Tocco and Joe Ward, who have seen me through the best and worst of times.

My work has benefited from the help of several other scholars. John Pound was kind enough to share material on the Norwich magistrates with me. Charlotte Furth, Tom Sanders, Joe Ward and Bob Woods read earlier drafts of the manuscript and offered constructive criticism. Kirsten Seaver's thoughtfulness has meant a great deal to me. Sears McGee has shared his knowledge about a number of important subjects with me. Marjorie McIntosh has stimulated my thinking on a number of issues in the social history of early modern England and has also shown me many kindnessess.

Part of Chapter 4 first appeared in the *Sixteenth Century Journal* as "'Against God's Word': Government, Religion and the Crisis of Authority in Early Reformation Norwich"; I would like to thank the Journal's publisher for permission to reprint that material here.

At UCLA, my colleagues Joyce Appleby and David Sabean read the entire manuscript and made many useful suggestions. They have also been exceptionally generous with their wisdom, time and encouragement. I am also very pleased to thank Bobby Hill, Jan Reiff and Miriam Silverberg for the support, advice and good humor they offered to me as I struggled through the writing process. It is also a great pleasure for me to thank Amy Davis, Ann Goldberg, Sandie Holguín, Kumar Patel, Shela Patel, Art Stein, Rebecca Winer, Michael Wintroub, Julian Yates, Kariann Yokota and Henry Yu for their friendship, and for the help and advice they have given to me.

A number of friends have kept me in touch with life outside of history. For that, I would like to express my very deepest thanks to Dan Farley, Susan Friedmann, Jessica Hodgins, Paula Krisko, Seth Levenson, Tom Olsen, Mark Schuster, Jeff Webb, Julie Williams and Mike Wolf.

Dean Perton and Emily Woodward offered initial help in drafting the tables in Appendix 6, but more important, they have been very good friends. My next-door neighbor Fred Bradford saved me from computer disaster on too many different occasions. Tom Kennon, Ph.D., read none of manuscript but has offered innumerable insights into the process of writing, for which I am deeply grateful. I would also like to thank Sam Tarica, D.D.S. for his care and concern.

My greatest debts are the ones that are the most difficult to put into words. My sister, Margot McClendon Pinto, has helped me in more ways than I can possibly count but that I will always remember. And words are truly inadequate to express my gratitude to my husband, Michael Salman, who has done more than anyone else to see this project to completion. In the very difficult circumstances that have been our lives over the last several years, Michael took an enormous amount of time away from his own scholarship to read, edit, re-read and re-edit every page of this book. He also pushed me to think, re-think and re-think again every idea contained in it. This is a much better book than it would have been without his considerable input. I hope he will accept it as a very small part of the great affection I have for him.

Contents

Appendixes

1. Aldermen in Office in 1524 and 1535   261
2. Aldermanic Wills Written 1530–January 1547   262
3. Aldermanic Wills Written During the Reign of Edward
      VI   264
4. Aldermanic Wills Written During the Reign of Mary   265
5. Aldermen Who Died During the 1558–59 Influenza
      Epidemic   266
6. Offenses Punished in the Mayor's Court, 1540–41 to
      1580–81   267

Conventions and Abbreviations

Spelling, punctuation and capitalization have been modernized in all quotations and abbreviations extended. Dates are given in the old-style calendar, where the year is taken to begin on January 1. The following abbeviations are used:

AB Norwich Assembly Minute Book.

APC *Acts of the Privy Council of England*, ed. J. R. Dasent, 9 vols. (London, 1890–1907).

BL British Library.

DNB *Dictionary of National Biography*, 63 vols. (London, 1885–1900).

L&P *Letters & Papers, Foreign and Domestic, of Henry VIII*, ed. J. S. Brewer, J. Gairdner and R. S. Brodie, 21 vols. (London, 1862–1932).

MCB Norwich Mayor's Court Book.

NRO Norfolk Record Office.

NCC Norwich Consistory Court Wills.

PCC Prerogative Court of Canterbury Wills.

PMA Proceedings of the Norwich Municipal Assembly.

PRO Public Record Office.

REED *Records of Early English Drama.*

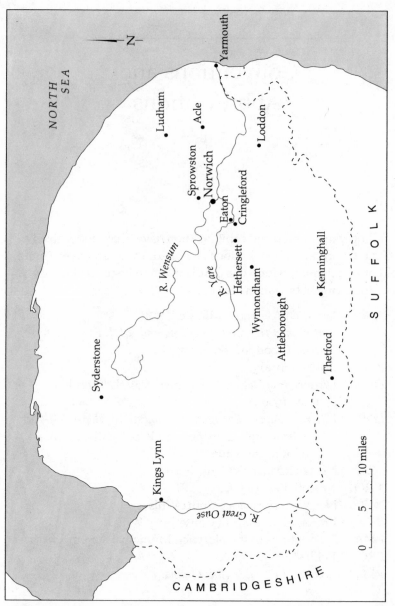

Norfolk

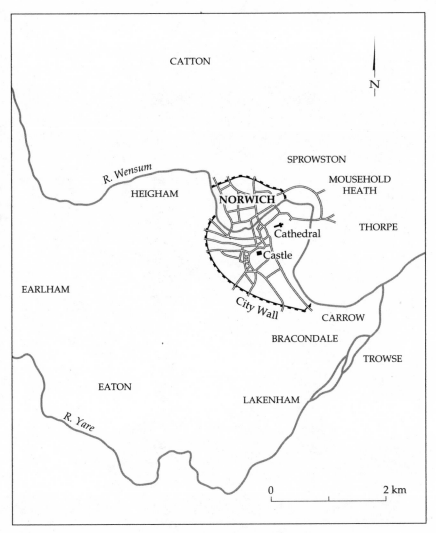

Norwich and its suburbs

The Quiet Reformation

-ːㅓ ㅑː-

Introduction

RELIGION, POLITICS AND THE
POSSIBILITY OF TOLERATION IN THE
ENGLISH REFORMATION

This book explains the unusual course of the Reformation in Norwich, early modern England's second city. As all historians of early modern England know, Norwich was an important religious center, the seat of one of the largest dioceses in late medieval and early modern England and a hub of Puritan activity in the Elizabethan era. When beginning this project, I expected to find widespread conflict over religion, because such conflict has been a major theme of the recent historiography of the English Reformation.[1] My research in the extant records relating to Norwich uncovered many more instances of religious strife in the city than historians had previously known. Moreover, I found that the ruling group of the city was itself religiously divided through almost all of the Reformation period. Yet, for all of the obvious importance of religion in sixteenth-century Norwich, open conflicts over religion were fewer in number and lesser in intensity than I had anticipated. Disputes over religion were, it seemed, actively contained by the city's magistrates.[2]

While a genuine Reformation certainly occurred in Norwich, its course appears unusually quiet compared to what we know about other English towns. How this happened and its significance for our understanding of the Reformation, its relationship to politics and the changing position of religion in society, are the central questions I address in this book.

-≒ II ⊱-

In order to understand the unusual significance and meaning of religious change in Norwich, it is important to be familiar with the life of the city and its relationship to other early modern towns. Norwich's early sixteenth-century population of about 8,500 did not place it among the 150 or so cities in western and central Europe which, according to one recent estimate, had populations of 10,000 and above in 1500, among which were Paris, Venice, Naples and Milan.[3] Small by Continental standards, Norwich was a major urban center in England, second only to London, which was home to between 50,000 and 60,000 of the King's subjects in the early Tudor period.[4] Norwich thus stood at the top of the provincial urban hierarchy that included the smaller towns of Bristol, Exeter, Salisbury and York.[5]

As well as being the most populous city outside of London, Norwich also had the largest economy of any provincial city in the sixteenth century. According to the subsidy returns of 1524–25, 1,423 of the city's inhabitants were assessed a total of £749, the most money paid out by any provincial town. Norwich residents paid a little more than one and a half times what their counterparts at Bristol did, who paid the second highest assessment, £479.[6] As in virtually all Tudor towns, a small number of people in Norwich controlled a majority of the city's actual wealth. In 1525, about 6 percent of the taxpaying population owned over 60 percent of the city's lands and goods, a proportion similar to London's.[7] The source of much of Norwich's prosperity lay in its involvement with the clothing trade, which had flourished since the Middle Ages. In 1525, 30 percent of those identifiable as freemen on the subsidy return made their living working in that industry. Yet, as well known as Norwich was as a center of the textile trade, its economy was not solely dependent on that industry for its affluence. Those in the distributive trades—which included mercers, grocers and drapers—comprised another 17 percent of freemen from the 1525 subsidy rolls and provided Norwich with some of its wealthiest individuals. By the last third of the sixteenth century, the city's economy had come to depend more heavily on these activities, which employed a slightly higher percentage of Norwich's freemen than did the declining textile trade—21.44 percent and 21.28 percent, respectively.[8]

Norwich also stood out as one of the few provincial communities that was self-governing. In 1404, a charter from Henry IV separated Norwich from the jurisdiction of the county of Norfolk and made the city a county in its own right, a status enjoyed by only four other communities in England—London, Bristol, York and Newcastle—at that time.[9] Since 1404, most aspects of daily administration of the city had been in the hands of twenty-four aldermen, from whom a mayor was elected annually, and two sheriffs. Two aldermen were elected from each of the city's twelve petty wards by the city's freemen.[10] The aldermen in turn elected one of the city's sheriffs, while the freemen chose the other. The aldermen and sheriffs annually elected a mayor from among the former group. In 1415, sixty common councilmen were added to the roster of civic governors to assist the mayor and aldermen periodically when they all met together as the city Assembly.[11] Aldermanic tenure was normally for life. Between 1517 and the death of Elizabeth in 1603, there were 167 elections and 158 different men occupied the office of alderman. On average, fewer than two elections to that post were held annually.[12] There was substantial turnover on the aldermanic bench only once during the century, when, in 1558–59, ten aldermen died in an influenza epidemic that swept the city, killing hundreds. Thus, there was great overlap, consistency and stability among the aldermen over the course of the century.

In addition to their executive and legislative duties, the mayor and aldermen also staffed the three main secular courts that administered justice in the city.[13] The sitting mayor and all aldermen who had previously served as mayor acted as the Justices of the Peace who staffed the court of Quarter Sessions. All sitting aldermen served on the court of aldermen, and also on the mayor's court. Boundaries between these bodies were porous: cases presented to the mayor's court and the Quarter Sessions were heard

by the identical people, and the distinction between meetings of
the mayor's court and the full court of aldermen was not always
clear and their records were not kept separately. The men who
ruled Norwich in the sixteenth century composed a tightly knit
group: their jurisdictions overlapped as did their aldermanic tenures. They tended to be among the wealthiest residents of the
city, could be found in large numbers among a few select occupations and were also tied to each other by apprenticeship and
marriage.[14]

The leaders of Tudor Norwich faced difficult problems of governance on several fronts. Dislocations in England's cloth industry in the first half of the sixteenth century had serious repercussions in Norwich. Many textile workers descended into poverty,
contributing to social tensions in the city. Vagrancy posed an increasing problem in Norwich from the 1540's, as it did in other
towns in the sixteenth century. Most famously of all, in the summer of 1549 Norwich was overrun and local government overthrown by Robert Kett and his rebels from rural Norfolk. Unlike
the rebellion in the West Country that had erupted earlier that
year in opposition to First Edwardian Book of Common Prayer,
Kett and his followers made a point of using the new Prayer
Book. The grievances that led to Kett's rebellion were largely
economic in nature. When Kett and his followers marched on
Norwich they found considerable sympathy for their cause
among many of the city's inhabitants, much to the dismay of the
magistrates, whose control of the city they briefly usurped. For all
of its danger and disruption, Kett's presence in Norwich was not
the occasion for any religious conflict. In other spheres of urban
life, however, quarrels involving religion and the Church had
long preoccupied the city's rulers.

Because of the Church's substantial territorial presence in Norwich, until the Reformation periodic jurisdictional disputes flared
between the Benedictine priory attached to the great Norman
Cathedral and the city.[15] Two of the most serious clashes took
place in 1272 and 1443. In 1272, a riot erupted after a fracas between some townsmen and residents of the priory. That assault

left thirteen dead and destroyed several monastic buildings and parts of the Cathedral. As a result, the lay ringleaders of the attack were executed, others were excommunicated and Henry III fined the citizens and revoked the city's liberties for four years. In 1443, citizens launched another offensive against the priory monks that had grown out of conflicts over the right to control long-contested areas around the Cathedral. No one died in this assault, but as in 1272, leaders were fined and excommunicated, and Henry VI's government rescinded the city's charter for four years.[16] A third showdown between the city and priory occurred on the eve of the Reformation. This one was not violent, but involved a tangled Star Chamber lawsuit over jurisdictional claims that eventually brought Cardinal Thomas Wolsey, who sought a settlement of the case, to Norwich in 1517. The matter was only concluded in 1524 when the Cardinal, weary from years of unproductive bickering between the city and priory, simply imposed his own resolution. He removed the Cathedral, which lay inside the city walls, from Norwich's jurisdiction and placed it under the control of the county of Norfolk. It was a decision that city magistrates found intolerable because it permitted Norfolk authorities to exercise jurisdiction inside city walls. Yet as bitter as these and other clashes between city and priory were, religious life in the late medieval city appears to have been both vital and orthodox.

Virtually every outlet of medieval piety was available to Norwich's residents. In the 1520's, forty-six parish churches dotted the city, many of which had been extensively reconstructed in a flurry of ecclesiastical building activity in the fifteenth century.[17] Confraternities were also plentiful in late medieval Norwich: twelve guilds submitted returns in response to the Guild Ordinance of 1389 and wills provide information about thirty-six more. Others undoubtedly existed, but have left no trace in the records. Citizens supported numerous votive lights in the city's parishes, as their wills reveal. Hermits and anchorites lived in Norwich, along with communities of women that resembled Continental *béguinages*. The Franciscan, Dominican, Carmelite and Augustinian friars all had houses in Norwich, and two colleges of secular priests survived into the sixteenth century as well. A Benedictine nunnery, two cells of the Cathedral monastery and two hospitals, all on the outskirts of the city, completed the array of institutions from which the inhabitants of Norwich and the surrounding area could draw spiritual comfort. The friaries and the parishes and their clergy were particularly popular beneficiaries of charitable giving among late medieval testators in Norwich. Between 1370 and 1532 nearly half of all city testators (lay and clerical) left bequests to the four houses. Ninety-five percent of lay men and women bequeathed money to at least one parish church.[18] Thus, the tensions between the city and priory do not appear to have had any theological basis.

In fact, the citizenry seems to have shown little interest in heretical movements and hardly figured in the trials held by Bishop William Alnwick between 1428 and 1431 to eradicate Lollardy, the sole heresy native to medieval England. Of the approximately fifty men and women who were convicted in those trials and for whom sufficient biographical information exists, only two were known to have come from Norwich. In contrast, there were much smaller villages and towns in the diocese that produced a half-dozen or so each who were condemned on such charges.[19] Not only did Norwich residents appear infrequently in the Lollard trials of the fifteenth century, but they were similarly absent in the flurry of activity against heresy in Norwich diocese undertaken by Bishop Richard Nix in the early sixteenth. A priest who might have been from Norwich was burnt in 1510, but few, if any, others from Norwich appear in the extant records.[20]

All of this would seem to suggest that the Reformation would bring dramatic changes to Norwich. On the one hand, the city could have become a staunch defender of traditional religion, given the citizens' extensive participation in religious life on the eve of the Reformation. On the other hand, given the long history of animosity between the city and Cathedral priory, the very size and power of the Church in Norwich could have provided fuel for explosive confrontations with a newly Protestant populace. In fact, Norwich did experience an authentic Reformation in the sixteenth century, which, in some ways, was quicker and ultimately more far reaching than in other communities. By the middle years of Elizabeth's reign, the city had earned a reputation as an important hub of Puritan activity in East Anglia and recusancy presented only a minor problem. This transformation was by no means smooth.

⊰ III ⊱

One of the techniques that historians have used to assess the strength and timing of Protestantism in different communities is to analyze the preambles of wills made during the Reformation era, sorting them into categories meant to reflect traditional or nontraditional beliefs. As all students of the English Reformation know, the confessional categorization of wills is fraught with pitfalls. Among other problems, will preambles were often formulaic, and wills themselves were frequently written by scribes according to their own model. Recent research has shown that a testator's declaration of reliance on Christ for salvation, often assumed to indicate a testator's inclination towards Protestantism, can be found in pre-Reformation wills.[21] Will preambles can still be informative, if read with care and the understanding that they do not often fall into neat categories of Protestant and Catholic.

By this rough measure, Protestantism did take root in Norwich earlier and more widely than in many other communities around England. Many testators there quickly abandoned the traditional Catholic formula, in which they committed their souls to the Virgin and the saints. In the last year of Edward's reign, for example, only 5–6 percent of Norwich testators made the traditional reference to the Virgin and the saints, compared to 61 percent in the city of York.[22]

The fact that the Reformation found early success in Norwich should come as no surprise. Most historians agree that Protestantism made inroads in urban communities earlier and with greater ease than it did in the countryside, although there were important exceptions such as York.[23] Higher levels of literacy among the tradesmen, artisans and merchants who inhabited towns enabled Protestantism, a religion of the word, to enjoy better success in those places. Reform-minded clergy also took their message to towns, where they had the opportunity to reach many more people than they did in rural enclaves. Many towns were also exposed to Continental Protestantism when they received visitors from abroad and when their own residents traveled to the Continent, as merchants often did.[24]

The introduction of the Henrician reforms and subsequent changing religious practice in the city soon brought cases of conflict and disorder before the magistrates in the mayor's court. They heard complaints concerning public denunciations of traditional religious ceremonies and the priesthood, as well as comparable verbal assaults against Martin Luther, Thomas Cromwell and Robert Barnes. Norwich residents engaged in a bout of iconoclastic activity in the early years of Edward VI's reign, when Catholicism was banished and England officially became a Protestant country for the first time, and several cases had to be resolved by the mayor's court. In another instance, several parishioners' defilement of holy bread and water led to an altercation in the church of St. Peter Mancroft. In addition to quarrels such as these that directly threatened public order, Edward's Protestant reforms called for the abolition of religious guilds, which had long been an integral part of the city's public culture. When the magistrates attempted to salvage one of the confraternities, the great civic guild of St. George, they fell into open conflict among themselves. Thus the magistrates themselves were not immune to the disruptions of Protestantism's emphasis on individual conscience, as three of them refused to take part in the annual guild feast in 1548, saying that it was "against God's word." The Reformation was permeating virtually every aspect of public life in Norwich, altering the social and political landscape, as well as religious belief and practice.

The disruptions of the Reformation continued as Queen Mary took the throne upon Edward's death in the summer of 1553. She

restored Catholicism as the official religion of England, by re-
pealing Edward's Protestant legislation. Given the early popularity of Protestantism in Norwich, that is, before 1553, Mary's
reign must have been a tense time there, especially during the trials and executions of Protestant heretics conducted by her government and Church.

Mary's restoration of Catholicism ended upon her death in
November 1558 and the open practice of Protestantism returned
to Norwich as Queen Elizabeth reinstated a Protestant church in
England. In the ensuing decade it put down even deeper roots in
the city, and Norwich developed into a center of Puritan enterprise, but not one immune to fears of popish plots, including a
real planned Catholic uprising in 1570. Prophesyings—confer-
ences of clergy devoted to biblical expositions that were often attended by lay spectators—were under way as early as 1564 and a
number of Puritan clergy began to cluster in the city not long afterwards.[25] Among them was the famed John More, widely
known as "the apostle of Norwich." It was also during these
years that the magistrates launched what historians have come to
call a "reformation of manners," a campaign against vices, such
as drunkenness, illicit sexuality, gambling and idleness, that were
seen as threats to godly and civic order. This campaign prompted
civic leaders to scrutinize the lives and behavior of their neighbors with a previously unseen intensity at a time when poverty
and vagrancy were reaching alarmingly high levels.[26]

The early years of the Reformation in Norwich set in motion a
long period in which problems of authority, both religious and
political, became chronic. Despite the eventual consolidation of
Protestantism in the middle of Elizabeth's reign, English Puritanism's implications for popular politics, changing views of authority and everyday social relations could be intense, most obviously
during the Civil War and Interregnum.[27] We need to remember
that the shift to Protestantism involved much more than the rejection of certain doctrines and practices and the adoption of others in their place. For the citizens and rulers of Norwich, the Reformation was a trying time, fraught with the potential for violent

conflicts, retribution and the loss of the special civic autonomy that Norwich had enjoyed since 1404.

What is so surprising and unusual then about the course of the Reformation in Norwich is the fact that, for all of the potentially explosive conditions, there were no great religious conflagrations. As I will show in the chapters that follow, conflicts erupted over unorthodox religious opinions, behavior and preaching (both traditional and reform), but rarely were outside authorities called in to mediate and settle them. Iconoclasts looted some city churches, but not as extensively and violently as did their counterparts in other towns, where rulers feared that these activities would have deleterious repercussions in the social and political order. The apprehension and execution of Protestant heretics under Mary took a much different course in Norwich than it did in other parts of England. Even when a Catholic conspiracy came to light during Elizabeth's reign, no large-scale persecution of Catholics followed. Norwich's magistrates were religiously divided during most of the sixteenth century, but there is no evidence that they split into factions along religious lines, nor did they attempt to impose religious uniformity in the city.

⊰ IV ⊱

As Martha Skeeters has said about her study of the clergy in Bristol, "until other urban ecclesiastical studies of the period are conducted in depth, we cannot know how representative Bristol and its experience of the Reformation were."[28] The same is true for this study of government, religion and authority in Norwich. While there have been studies of numerous English towns during the Reformation, none has addressed the fate of municipal government in a sustained analysis and few, as I will show, have explored the ramifications of religious change for social and political relations. Sufficient information about other towns exists to suggest that Norwich's experience was special and to raise important new questions that need to be asked in detailed studies of other towns.

The religious controversies that did not escalate in Norwich often erupted into open and dangerous conflict in other towns. While unorthodox preaching did not become the occasion of serious conflicts in Norwich, in Bristol it became the subject of protracted and noisy disturbances. In March 1533, at the invitation of Bristol's mayor and aldermen, Hugh Latimer delivered two well-received sermons in which he strongly supported the new religious order. To retaliate, Bristol conservatives invited three clerics distinguished for their loyalty to the old order to preach at Easter. That was enough to divide the town. From that time, the two camps exchanged allegations of sedition and heresy. The Chancellor of Worcester diocese forbade both Latimer and William Hubberdine, the most dramatic and inflammatory of the three conservatives, from continued preaching. But the ban was lifted from Latimer when Thomas Cromwell intervened in the matter. Partisans on both sides collected articles detailing various wrongdoings by their opponents and sent them to London. As a result, Hubberdine was committed to the Tower, where he remained for about five years; Latimer abandoned his work at Bristol and moved on to London. Religious conflict continued, prompting a commission of city officials to interview over a hundred witnesses concerning charges of "seditious preaching, seditious and slanderous bills, and attacks" against Latimer, who had been elevated to the Bishopric of Worcester in 1535. In 1540, the mayor and aldermen invited Cromwell's representative to the city to balance and stabilize the contending religious factions.[29] In striking contrast, the rulers of Norwich never formed commissions of investigation into religious practice and they typically tried to discourage the intervention of outsiders in the early Tudor period.

Iconoclasm was a problem that came late and not as seriously to Norwich as it did to other English communities. The "wave" or "minor epidemic" that swept East Anglia in 1530–31 completely bypassed the city, while images and roods were destroyed at Ipswich, Great Horkesley, Stoke by Nayland, Stoke and at Dovercourt and Coggeshall in Essex. In 1538 a "group of radical vigilantes" in London pulled down the rood at the parish of St. Mar-

garet Pattens, a popular destination for pilgrims. There were incidents at Chichester and Coventry as well.[30] The capital was
again the site of serious iconoclastic activity in the first months of
Edward's reign. The Privy Council took steps to curb the destruction of images that had resulted from the overzealous response
on the part of London's citizens to the 1547 Injunctions dictating
the confiscation of abused images. In addition, the mayor and aldermen resolved to keep the doors of all City churches closed in
order to prevent further damage and ruin.[31] In 1548, an appalled
Bishop of Winchester, Stephen Gardiner, watched as a Portsmouth mob pulled down and abused several religious images. In
complaining to the local military commander (for neither he nor
any civic authority had intervened in the tumult) Gardiner
warned that such disdain for traditional religious authority
would have similar results in the civil sphere.[32] Neither royal officials nor members of the ecclesiastical hierarchy engaged in any
of the incidents of iconoclasm in Edwardian Norwich.

In the following reign, England underwent one of the most intense religious persecutions in its history. Nearly three hundred
men and women went to the stake as Protestant heretics, most of
humble origins. According to Philip Hughes, who analyzed the circumstances of their arrest, a majority of those for whom evidence is
available—close to 60 percent—were apprehended through the efforts of lay justices, constables or sworn inquest. Many more—close
to another 13 percent—were turned in to the authorities by their
friends and family.[33] In London, thirty-two people were arrested
and executed in the Marian burnings. In Colchester, a town much
smaller than Norwich, where the population had probably not
much deviated from its 1524–25 level of about 4,500, fifteen residents were put to death.[34] These communities stood in marked
contrast to Norwich, where only two people died as heretics. Norwich also stood outside the general pattern of persecution that
Hughes has identified. The two women who went to the stake were
arrested after making public statements declaring their commitment to Protestantism and thus incriminated themselves. Neither

city magistrates nor family members or neighbors were responsible for their arrests. Not all who were arrested in the persecution were sent to the stake; many people were jailed and recanted their opinions. In Norwich, only one person was so punished and there is no evidence that anyone else was accused or tried for Protestant beliefs or activities.

Conflicts over religion during the Reformation had the potential to factionalize governments. Henry VIII's court was dominated by factional intrigue during the last decade of his reign between those who wished to see further doctrinal reform in the Church and those who did not.[35] Such factional disputes were not confined to the court and sometimes dominated local governments, as they did in the 1530's and 1540's at Canterbury, where religious conservatives and radicals vied for control of local government. In 1536, conservatives assailed radical leaders, who were still smarting from a Parliamentary defeat a month earlier. A year later one of the chief targets of the conservative attack had regained the town clerkship of which he had previously been deprived. Religious radicals gained control of the city government at that time, and gave their vigorous support to the Protestant cause. They had images removed from churches and suppressed the annual pageant of St. Thomas. However, upon the death in 1540 of Thomas Cromwell, who had done much to advance the reformers' cause in Kent, the conservative opposition renewed its attack on the radical group. Although successful in retarding the pace of Protestant reform in the city, the group was unable to eradicate it entirely.[36] There is no evidence that the rulers of Norwich ever participated in such internecine struggles.

⊰ V ⊱

Why was Norwich's experience of religious change so different from that of other communities around England? There is ample evidence that religious differences were meaningful and troubling to the city's residents. The key to understanding the un-

usual unfolding of the Reformation in the city revolves around
the ways in which religious conflicts and tensions were handled.
The course and outcome of Norwich's Reformation were shaped
in important ways by the city's magistrates, the mayor and aldermen who were responsible for maintaining local peace and prosperity. In coping with the conflicts that erupted over religion during these years, they did not seek to adopt and enforce Catholicism or Protestantism exclusively. Rather, they enforced none of
the official Tudor religious settlements strictly, and while en-
dorsing each change in official religion in a formal sense, they
failed to enforce conformity with the rigor required by official
policy. The mayors and aldermen who ruled Norwich, it seems,
were willing to tolerate a measure of spiritual diversity among
themselves and the residents of the city.

As I found in my research in the records, the magistrates repeatedly failed to alert outside authorities about the activities of
religious dissidents in their jurisdiction or to punish religious offenders as required by statute. They dismissed cases or took no
action against numerous others involved in conflicts over religion. The sources are largely silent on the reasons for the magistrates' course of action. No policy statements from the mayor's
court, or diaries, letters or memoirs written by any of the aldermen have survived that speak to this problem.

There were only a few occasions on which the magistrates had
to explain their actions to outsiders. In 1535, Edmund Harcocke,
the Prior of the Blackfriars, preached a sermon in which he came
close to condemning the royal supremacy. Cromwell got wind of
his potentially treasonous words and sent Sir Roger Townsend, a
Norfolk JP, to apprehend him. But when Townsend arrived in the
city he and mayor Augustine Styward made a bargain: Harcocke
would remain in Norwich and the magistrates would guarantee
his accessibility to Cromwell indefinitely. As a result, Harcocke
was never incarcerated and lived for close to another thirty years.
He died early in Elizabeth's reign as the rector of the city parish
of St. Michael Coslany.[37] Incidents such as this one pose the prob-

lem of how to interpret the consistent pattern of surprising behavior—de facto religious toleration—revealed in the records.

Much evidence points to magisterial concerns about civic
autonomy and authority as an answer to this question. A coun-
terpoint to magisterial lenience in matters concerning religious
practice and division can be found in cases that involved their
own rule directly. As I will show, local residents were dealt with
severely with fines and imprisonment when they defied civic
authority by disobedience, open criticism or even just failing to
show proper respect for the magistrates as a corporate body.

The encounter with Wolsey between 1517 and 1524 is also in-
dicative of a concern for civic autonomy and authority and, I believe, it proved instructive to the magistrates as well. When the
Cardinal joined the Cathedral to the county of Norfolk, city magistrates strenuously objected to the notion that Norfolk officials
would be able to exercise any jurisdiction inside the Norwich city
walls. The clash with Wolsey was the third time in eighty years
that civic autonomy had been so seriously undermined. In 1437,
riots at the election of civic officers had resulted in the suspension
of civic liberties, as had the attack against the priory in 1443.
These incidents took place, it is important to remember, before
the Reformation when religious allegiance in Norwich was
largely uncontested. In the much tenser atmosphere of the Reformation, such eruptions did not happen again, because sixteenth-century magistrates repeatedly found local and peaceful
solutions to the kinds of problems that proved uncontrollable
elsewhere, as the case of Edmund Harcocke demonstrates. Their
unusual mode of behavior must be understood against the background of these earlier crises of civic authority, particularly the
incident with Wolsey, which happened on the eve of the Reformation.

There is good reason to believe that memory of the Wolsey episode remained influential among the magistrates for quite a long
time. Sixteen of the twenty-four sitting aldermen in 1535, when
Harcocke preached his inflammatory sermon, either had been al-

dermen or common councilors in 1524, when Wolsey made his
judgment in the case with the priory.[38] In addition, the corporation was consciously concerned with historical memory, as reflected in the sixteenth-century practice of displaying paintings of
deceased mayors in the Guildhall and the maintenance of several
books of historical record apart from the regular records of the
mayor's court and like bodies.[39] For example, in 1426 mayor
Thomas Ingham first commissioned the compilation of documents relating to important affairs into a volume called the *Liber
Albus* after a similar book maintained in London since 1419. Like
the London *Liber Albus*, the Norwich version included copies of
civic officials' oaths of office.[40]

The Norwich *Liber Albus* was updated periodically with new
documents, including some pertaining to the Wolsey affair, as
well as to incidents related to the charter revocations of 1437 and
1443. The original pages of the *Liber Albus* also included a calendar of festivals and saints' days. Some of the saints' names were
obliterated during the Reformation, demonstrating that the book
was considered a live and meaningful document, likely to be
read or referenced.[41]

The corporation maintained three other books of historical records, the "Book of Pleas," the "Mayor's Book" and the "Old Free
Book." The "Book of Pleas" primarily contained copies of legal
proceedings in the city's history dating back to the twelfth century. Its compilation was begun around 1454. The "Old Free
Book" is the oldest of these books of historical record, having
been begun in the reign of Edward III. It includes civic memoranda, including lists of civic officers, admissions to the freedom
and notes relating to civic pageantry. The "Mayor's Book" was
given to the city in 1526 by alderman Augustine Styward. It contained lists of civic officials and also chronicled the city's history
into the nineteenth century, when it was last updated. These examples of city officials' overlapping tenures and their historical
consciousness point to a transmission of governing knowledge
that explains how the magistrates could have practiced such a
consistent strategy over the course of the sixteenth century.[42]

In a process that historians have traditionally identified with very different kinds of developments in the seventeenth and eighteenth centuries, the sixteenth-century Norwich magistrates learned to compartmentalize their religious beliefs, effectively creating a distinction between private religious belief on the one hand, and public action and civic loyalty on the other.

⊰ VI ⊱

There is little in the recent historiography of the English Reformation that prepares one to understand the direction that the Reformation took in Norwich. With few exceptions, the preoccupations of most recent writers on the Reformation have been to investigate how much English communities accepted or resisted changes in religious doctrine and practice initiated by the central government. A related issue in the debate has been whether reformed religion was predominant in the country by the mid-sixteenth century, or whether it made its major gains only in the 1570's and 1580's, during the reign of Queen Elizabeth. In other words, historians have been asking if the English Reformation was fast or slow, and whether it came from above, imposed by the monarchy, or below, through voluntary conversions at the popular level.[43] Few scholars have asked questions about the role of religion in society, the changing effects of religious practice and belief and the nature of Catholicism or Protestantism.

Thirty years ago, A. G. Dickens depicted England's Protestantization as a relatively quick one, achieved largely by midcentury and mostly through grassroots efforts.[44] Lollardy laid important groundwork for Protestantism with its antagonism to clerical pretensions and emphasis on Bible reading.[45] When Protestantism burst onto the scene in the 1520's, Dickens argued, its message attracted considerable popular support, often through the efforts of itinerant preachers. Dickens was not inattentive to the political dimensions of the Reformation and was aware of the important support that it received from Westminster. Yet he suggested that even in the absence of Henry VIII's marital problems that had led to the decisive confrontation with the Pope, it would have been difficult for England to remain an orthodox Catholic nation in the face of evangelical Calvinism and the political dominance of Spain on the Continent.[46]

After the publication of Dickens's work, local history has dominated the study of the Reformation. The research of a number of historians into the Reformation in southeastern England has supported Dickens's findings of a lay population primed by late medieval Lollardy to embrace the Protestant message. John Davis, for example, located three areas there that had well-developed Lollard traditions in the early sixteenth century: northern Essex, the Kentish Weald and the northwestern areas of metropolitan London. In his investigation of heresy proceedings in these areas, Davis has argued for a potent link between Lollardy and Protestantism. While he sees "no straightforward move from pre-Reformation dissent into the post-Reformation Church," he nevertheless asserts that later strands of English Protestantism—Puritanism, Anglicanism and Arminianism—"all . . . drew on native pre-Reformation dissent."[47] Other historians who have studied the region, such as G. R. Elton and Peter Clark, have argued for a quick Reformation, although one motivated and imposed by the central government.[48]

In recent years however, an increasing number of historians have criticized this vision of a "rapid reformation." These scholars, the so-called "revisionists," have charged that the voluntary religious change for which Dickens and those who followed him argued could only have occurred among a small minority of English men and women. Rather, they have argued that the Protestantization of England was imposed on a mostly unwilling population and accomplished chiefly through the coercive powers of the monarchy. The broad outline of the revisionist argument is neatly summarized in the opening of J. J. Scarisbrick's *The Reformation and the English People*: "on the whole, English men and women did not want the Reformation and most of them were slow to accept it when it came."[49] These contentions have been based on research undertaken in previously unexploited archives in areas distant from London, such as the far north and south-west, where it was more difficult for Tudor governments to enforce their policies. Using local ecclesiastical records and church-wardens' accounts instead of documents produced by the central government, the revisionists have found little evidence of a groundswell of acceptance of the Protestant message and government religious reforms and much more evidence of open opposition to them.

In his study of Lancashire, Christopher Haigh uncovered substantial pockets of active resistance among local residents to Tudor commands to abandon traditional religious practices and doctrines. Itinerant Protestant preachers made few converts on their northern sojourns and were greeted with hostility more often than not.[50] In his study of the Reformation in the southwest, Robert Whiting has found that inhabitants usually complied rapidly with Tudor religious dictates, but he has nevertheless concluded that they did not embrace the new religion. He has argued instead that their cooperation stemmed from "a sense of duty, xenophobia, a desire for moral freedom, financial calculation, or even physical fear." For the majority of residents of this region, Whiting believes, "the Reformation may thus have been less a transition from Catholicism to Protestantism than a decline from religious commitment into conformism or indifference."[51]

In addition to striking at the heart of the previously conventional wisdom that the shift to Protestantism had been voluntary by bringing to light new evidence of resistance to it, the revisionists have also altered the traditional chronology of religious change. Dickens's story of the English Reformation concluded with the ascension of Elizabeth; with the renunciation of the Marian past and the official re-establishment of Protestant liturgy, the advance of Protestantism was assured, and the Reformation was over. For the revisionists, the reformation in religion of the English people only began in earnest during the reign of Elizabeth. At Queen Mary's death in 1558, they contend, England was not inhabited by a population ready to throw off the "Roman yoke" and aching for a return of the Protestant Church of Eng-

land. Protestantism commanded little support at the popular
level and many people were simply weary and confused by the
successive changes in official religious policy. While the Henrician and Edwardian governments had done much to alter the official face of English religion, they had not succeeded in winning
the hearts of their subjects away from Catholicism. It was Elizabeth's longevity (and thus that of her Settlement) that permitted
Protestantism to take root, at least in part by reducing the number
of people who harbored memories of traditional religious practices before Henry VIII's assault against them began.

Another component of the revisionist interpretation of the Reformation concerns the spiritual health of the late medieval
Church that eventually fell to the forces of Protestantism. Dickens
had characterized the Church in England as a decaying and
moribund institution that had lost much of its former vitality and
thus much of its deliberate and enthusiastic support from the
English people. Mysticism, Lollardy and an increasingly literate
laity were among the forces that had exposed weaknesses in the
Church that later made it so vulnerable to the attacks of Protestant reformers. But Eamon Duffy's recent study of the late medieval Church has offered an explicit and detailed rejection of
that picture, one that reinforces the contentions of Haigh and
Scarisbrick. Duffy contends first "that no substantial gulf existed
between the religion of the clergy and educated élite on the one
hand and that of the people on the other." Orthodoxy was not
"the peculiar preserve of the well-educated and well-to-do." He
accords little importance to the beliefs and activities of England's
"relatively small number of Lollards" and they are largely absent
from his book. Duffy further argues for a robust and vigorous
Church whose constituents were familiar with the tenets of their
faith, and who were also deeply committed to the institution. The
late medieval Church thus enjoyed the broad support of the English population. Finally, Duffy maintains that given the popularity of the Church, the Reformation was unwelcome and its success was ultimately due to the greater power of the Tudor monarchy to coerce than the power of its subjects to resist.[52]

Revisionist historians have made significant contributions to the study of the English Reformation. They have located and highlighted significant opposition and active resistance to the religious policies of the Tudors among ordinary men and women. They have also rescued the late medieval Church from too-ready charges of corruption and deterioration that were rooted in Protestant ideology. While neither the institutional Church nor its clerical members always lived up to Christian ideals, the laity apparently accepted their foibles. No longer is it possible to think of the Reformation as a "walkover for the Protestants,"[53] during which a passive population swiftly abandoned traditional religion at the command of successive monarchs. Revisionist historiography has also rightly stressed the difficulties faced by Tudor governments in enforcing their religious prescriptions. Nevertheless, revisionist historiography has proven less successful in differentiating among the groups and communities in English society who opposed religious innovation and those who embraced it. In addition, the revisionists' stress on continuity has caused them to devote less attention to the impact of Protestantism, especially during the early phases of the Reformation. These issues are now beginning to concern some scholars.

Tessa Watt and Peter Lake have made important contributions on the impact of Protestantism on popular culture. Watt's study of popular literature during the century after 1550 has shown how traditional tunes printed as broadsides with new godly lyrics enjoyed a considerable commercial success and traditional images of Christ resurfaced accompanied by new Protestant texts. In his exploration of murder pamphlets published in the 1570's and 1580's, Lake demonstrates that some of these stories linked divine providence, individual conscience and salvation, thus offering "Protestants an opening or series of openings which they could use to bring the Protestant message to a wider audience." He concludes "that it is a mistake to see the relationship between the 'popular' and the puritan or zealously Protestant as simply adversarial or anti-pathetic."[54]

Working in the enormously rich archives of the capital city, Susan Brigden's *London and the Reformation* offers an engaging and nuanced narrative of the official and popular Reformations through the reign of Queen Mary. She has established that Protestantism had early support in London, producing tensions and confrontations with the large numbers of people who defended traditional religion. Using sermons, wills, letters, chronicles, commonplace books and other sources, Brigden excels at identifying and exploring the meaning of religion for the advocates of traditional and reformed faiths. The main thrust of Brigden's study investigates the pace and intensity of religious reform within the terms laid out by the debate between Dickens and the revisionists. However, her recognition that, at midcentury, "many—perhaps even most—Londoners still lingered in a religious half-world" and often felt "confusion" in the face of the religious changes and conflicts going on around them, points us towards the real flux of religious beliefs and practices during the early Reformation.[55] This suggests that we can go beyond the confines of the debate over the relative strengths of Protestantism and Catholicism by understanding that these terms themselves were fluid in meaning at the time. By grappling with the spiritual meaning of the Reformation for such a wide variety of Londoners, Brigden gives us a vivid sense of the religious matters at stake during decades of vituperative and often violent conflict.

Brigden's findings are obviously different from mine in Norwich. She describes a nearly constant state of open conflict in London. Beginning with Thomas More's campaign of 1529 and continuing through the 1530's, Brigden reminds us that England's "most furious quest for heretics" took place in London. The City's prisons filled with over five hundred suspected heretics who had been betrayed by friends and neighbors after Parliament's conservative Six Articles of 1539, in stark contrast to the absence of any such arrests in Norwich. Retribution and recriminations stemming from religious divisions were routine in London, as citizens and authorities turned the tables on whoever was newly out of favor throughout the period.[56]

London and Norwich were very different places. London was

by far England's most cosmopolitan city, the seat of royal government, "the capital of the printing trade" and the focal point of England's intellectual and economic life.[57] Despite these differences, my study of Norwich suggests some new questions that should be asked of London as well. When religious division itself is the focal point of a study it can become difficult to see how people may have tried to cope with these divisions in different areas of social, economic and political life. Therefore, in conjunction with religious change, it is necessary to study specific institutions, groups and practices, such as town corporations, occupational guilds and ritual life, because these elements of society continued to function throughout the Reformation period. Whereas Brigden's narrative pivots on the breakdown of shared community and its replacement by competing religious communities, the survival of these other institutions and practices of urban life suggests that there must have been be more to the story. As Peter Lake and Mark Kishlansky have shown in a later context, the rhetoric of factional discord as well as that of consensus was often inflated and cannot always be taken at face value.[58]

For Brigden, "when one faith was evangelical, determined that the Word should go forth, whatever the risk and the other rested upon authority, giving all power in the determination of doctrine to the church, there could hardly be peace." So, while it may be correct to say, as she does, that "at the Reformation, because of the Reformation, division in religion was inevitable because everyone agreed that anyone not of their Church was against it, heretic and schismatic," her equation of this division with open and virtually ceaseless conflict may blind us to other possibilities. Brigden tells us that religion divided families and that "[t]he choices made in faith were as likely to have brought divisions within as between the social orders." Indeed her own analysis of wills made by members of London's occupational guilds, known as livery companies, reveals those divisions. However, because she does not inquire into the life and activities of the companies and only mentions them insofar as they had notable evangelical or conservative members, she cannot explain how they managed to survive intact despite the religious differences that she always credits with rending communities. Throughout the Reformation, the companies continued to meet regularly, elect officers and concern themselves with the operation of their businesses and trades. At least sometimes, company members of different religious persuasions managed somehow to maintain their associations with each other. When Brigden writes that Protestants and Catholics "both seemed then to see only the perversion and traduction of the truth by the other," she posits an all-encompassing and totalizing worldview which my study of religion, politics and society in Norwich suggests we need to reconsider.[59]

The consequences of the Reformation for the ecclesiastical community of Bristol, England's third largest urban center, is the focus of Martha Skeeters's *Community and Clergy*. Skeeters argues that the Reformation had a devastating effect on Bristol's clergy and transformed it from a large and complex group "into a simple configuration comprising the Cathedral elite and the clergy of the parishes." She combines attention to the way "Protestant theology itself reduced the power of the clergy" in lieu of the individual conscience with an examination of how institutional changes in the Bristol Church further weakened its authority through internal and external conflicts. Skeeters notes that although she does not "examine in detail the relationship between changes in religion and ecclesiastical structures and those in other areas of life in Bristol," her work does point towards important related changes in politics and society.

Skeeters's account of the fate of the clergy requires her to touch upon the role of town's governors in Bristol's religious crisis. Like the magistrates of Norwich, the mayor and aldermen of Bristol were concerned to protect civic authority and urban stability during the Reformation, when religious conflict revealed its potential to undermine both. However, these concerns led them to very different courses of action than those adopted by Norwich magistrates. Skeeters shows that the magistrates of Bristol divided into religious factions, attempted to impose religious uniformity and repeatedly called on outside authorities to rebalance and defuse religious conflicts that proved to be beyond their control. In fact, she concludes in her discussion of the Latimer affair that the magistrates' "efforts were, in fact, rather clumsy, and they must have felt very deeply their dependence upon Cromwell," whose help they later learned was an "unreliable crutch during further conflict over local pulpits." This subsidiary thread of her ecclesiastical history of Bristol suggests the need for, as she writes, "its integration into the whole of urban history."[60]

⊰ VII ⊱

Just as urban history can inform the study of the Reformation, so can the Reformation contribute to the study of early modern English towns. As Patrick Collinson noted in 1988, the Reformation is fleetingly referenced in urban historiography, but remains "peripheral" to the study of English towns.[61] Through the 1970's and 1980's, the literature was framed by a debate over urban decline. The debate was originally defined by the works of Peter Clark, Paul Slack and Charles Phythian-Adams, and argued that the fifteenth and sixteenth centuries were a time of protracted crisis for England's towns.[62] The ills that afflicted the entire country were acutely magnified there. Towns were plagued by contracting economies, shrinking populations and increasing social tensions born of swelling poverty and vagrancy. The Reformation's chief importance in these studies has been as a double-edged sword that freed townsmen from the burden of expensive ceremonies on the one hand, but sharply attenuated the dominant cultural role of towns, on the other. The abolition of plays, processions and other religious celebrations reduced the expenses shouldered by urban officeholders, but at the same time brought fewer visitors to towns, exacerbating the decline already under way. Some contributions to this school have noted that new and sometimes strengthened forms of civic authority and ceremony did emerge out of the Reformation, but largely in the later decades of the sixteenth century after a preliminary period that is still seen as largely negative and destructive.[63]

Early responses to the theorists of urban decline tended to focus on the pre-Reformation period, challenging the use and meaning of economic data, bypassing questions of Reformation religion and culture.[64] Since the 1980's, historians have been working to expand the scope of early modern urban studies in several directions, often challenging historians' earlier arguments for decline. Some, notably Patrick Collinson, have called for the integration of the Reformation into the whole of urban history. In his brief but suggestive chapter "The Protestant Town" in *The Birthpangs of Protestant England*, Collinson has insisted "that the Reformation was much more than a side-show: that it was as central to the urban history of the period as religious change has traditionally been to the national history of England under the Tudors."

Given that English towns were early sites of Protestant activity and emerged as important centers of Puritanism later in the sixteenth century, historians should be careful in advancing claims of dwindling urban influence in English society and in concentrating on the damaging effects of the Reformation. Collinson has observed that the rich culture of late medieval towns, "inextricably involved with religion as it was," gave way to an urban life in the late seventeenth and eighteenth centuries that possessed "a new richness, solemnity and style." A critical link between these two cultures, according to Collinson, was "the Protestant Reformation, which destroyed so much and limited and restricted what was left, but which acted as a kind of midwife for the future." Thus, in contrast to the understanding of "social history . . . as the application of economics to every aspect of shared communal existence," Collinson asks us to reflect on the Reformation as a creative process that helped to reconstruct the urban religious, social, cultural, political and material landscape.[65]

Collinson's call to include the Reformation as a central theme in urban history is, in his words, a move to "redress the historiographical balance." While my study is aimed explicitly in this direction, I understand the larger importance of this as broadening both the study of the Reformation and English urban history to include a more nuanced and complex sense of society and politics. In this vein, David Harris Sacks's work on Bristol is exemplary. Concentrated on the dramatic economic transformation in a burgeoning world economy, Sacks traces the diverse interactions of Bristolians' economic activities with affairs that are all too often seen separately by historians as social, cultural, political or simply beyond the confines of the supposedly self-contained early modern town. It should be understood that if we integrate the previously separate studies of the Reformation, economic transformation or other phenomena with a broader view of society, the resulting history can never be complete and total, nor can this be the aim without paying a substantial cost in analytical clarity and power. Sacks's main interests, as wide-ranging as they are, nevertheless require him, as he acknowledges, to give "primacy to the long-term economic history of Bristol, while omitting to mention the Exclusion Crisis and the Glorious Revolution and relegating the Civil War and the Reformation to a secondary position." While my topic places the Reformation at the center of my study, I share Sacks's interests in the relationship of urban centers to a wider world as well as the problems of social order, changing modes of authority and the meaning and uses of ritual.[66]

The relationship of urban politics and economic conditions is also the subject of Ian Archer's *The Pursuit of Stability: Social Relations in Elizabethan London*. Archer's work builds upon the debates over urban decline. Whereas Peter Clark ventured that in many late sixteenth-century towns, "as in London in 1595, it seemed as if the whole fabric of the urban community might be about to disintegrate," Steve Rappaport replied by arguing that economic conditions, while occasionally causing disturbances, did not seriously undermine London's fundamental stability. Despite this disagreement, Rappaport concurred with Clark and Slack that "local government in the metropolis remained chaotic."[67] Archer has responded by agreeing with Clark on the reality of socioeconomic tensions and with Rappaport on the fact that they were often defused before escalating out of control, but disagreeing with both in their assumptions about urban government in London. The stability of Elizabethan London was a consequence not merely of impersonal social forces, but of the ways in which politics mediated the outcomes of social conflicts and economic distress, organizing the relationship between the governors and the governed. Archer highlights the importance of elite solidarity and their ability to address popular grievances within the terms of a widely shared urban political culture. The solidarity of London's elite drew strength, according to Archer, from a "relative homogeneity" that was based upon common business interests and religious uniformity.[68] Archer's ideas about the importance of elite solidarity also apply to Norwich, where, in contrast to London, religious uniformity was not a cornerstone of magisterial cohesion.

⊰ VIII ⊱

Elite solidarity functioned in Norwich because magistrates of different religious views managed to coexist by compartmentalizing religion in relation to other political concerns. This process points to the emergence of a practical secularization and a practical toleration in the sixteenth century. Historians have placed both of these developments much later in English and European history, generally beginning at the end of the seventeenth century. Both the causes and the timing of secularization have recently been treated in C. John Sommerville's *The Secularization of Early Modern England*. While I agree with Sommerville that secularization has an earlier than expected history in the sixteenth century and that Tudor politics and "a Protestant spirituality which wanted to distinguish essentials from non-essentials and redrew the line between the sacred and the profane" were important ingredients in these developments, I must emphasize that my study is in many ways different from his.[69] Where I examine the process of secularization in depth as it unfolded in a specific community, Sommerville ranges broadly over two centuries of English history covering topics such as time, work, art, scholarship and science as well as politics. His discussion therefore tends to be summary and dependent on secondary sources. His emphasis on the importance of politics as the motor of secularization is also largely restricted to the central government and, as he puts it, "an aggrandizing nation-state." Most importantly, we differ on what happens to religion and thus, ultimately, on our understandings of secularization. Sommerville proposed to examine England's shift from "religious culture," in which religion permeated virtually every area of life, to "religious faith," in which religion was mostly differentiated from those other areas. In fact, his study mostly chronicles the elimination of religion from other institutions and practices, or as he says, "the fading of religious significance from common activities." This problem in Sommerville's work, perhaps reflecting ambivalences and contradictions in his understanding of religion, is very difficult to track. For example, he describes Protestantism as a "simplification of religion" and, in his conclusion, credits Max Weber with recognizing the Protestant "roots of secularization" while somehow overlooking Weber's exposition of Protestantism's continuing significance in areas not expressly religious, most famously capitalist enterprise.[70] In contrast, my study of Norwich shows that religion did not fade in significance. Although many explicit religious signs and symbols tended to disappear in the Reformation, religious beliefs and values continued to inform public life in various ways as new challenges to authority and new modes its imposition, such as "the reformation of manners."

The historiography of religious toleration and intolerance is considerably more extensive than the literature on secularization. Historians have often begun their investigations of religious toleration in the sixteenth century. Early reformers, such as Luther and Castellio, penned what seem to be the first tracts advancing the concept of toleration, if not without severe qualifications and contradictions. The course of the Reformation also included some well-known official expressions of religious toleration, such as the 1598 Edict of Nantes in France. In England, triumphant Protestantism, in conjunction with skepticism and the politics of the Glorious Revolution, is traditionally seen as the source of modern liberal religious freedoms as delineated by John Locke's 1689 *Letter Concerning Toleration*. It is for these reasons, as Heiko Oberman has pointed out, that "[t]he history of tolerance and toleration is one of the last preserves still firmly in the grasp of intellectual historians," by which he means those who engage in the history-of-ideas approach.[71] In concentrating on ideas, this literature suggests that toleration was the product of the thought and experience of a few intellectuals and princes. It also has shaped, and reflects, our colloquial understanding of toleration by defining it as a (positive) value and ideal, rather than as a practice. But some scholars working in the early modern period, represented in a recent volume of essays edited by Ole Peter Grell and Bob Scribner, have sought to understand toleration's practical dimensions and even to raise questions about its very definition.

Contributors to *Tolerance and Intolerance in the European Reformation* have endeavored to place toleration in its local, political, social and religious contexts in order to understand it as a practice. From varying perspectives, they take as their subject the practice of religious coexistence during the Reformation, which, they all agree, never approximated the very modern ideas of full religious freedom and appreciation of religious diversity for its own sake. The kinds of toleration examined typically developed out of the experience of weak religious minorities or for reasons of state or, as Diarmaid MacCulloch shows, a strategy for achieving religious concord (i.e. religious uniformity) through persuasion rather than persecution.[72] Contextualized in this way, the authors have demonstrated that religious toleration was often malleable, impermanent and erratic, and not simply an idea that unfolded gradually and consistently in European society.

In cities, social stability had always been a significant concern to local magistrates; the religious divisions of the Reformation rendered the achievement of that important goal much more difficult. The extension of some form of religious toleration sometimes proved to be a way to turn back threats of popular disorder. Bob Scribner's early research on Erfurt revealed how concerns about popular disorder motivated the magisterial extension of toleration there. In 1530 local magistrates sanctioned a treaty of state that permitted both Catholic and Protestant worship in the city. Scribner's findings there have led him to reflect more broadly on the issue of religious toleration and to identify several different manifestations of it in sixteenth-century Germany, from the neglect to mete out severe penalties for religious deviance, to the inability to enforce religious uniformity, to the toleration of religious minorities whose services proved economically beneficial to a community. He also points to the existence of what he calls "the tolerance of practical rationality," a phenomenon of daily life among ordinary people who, Scribner suggests, frequently "made little fuss about difference in belief and accepted it as a normal state of affairs." Recognizing the possibility of different measures of toleration and coexistence, Scribner then sees the need to question received interpretations of the sixteenth century as "the age of a 'persecuting society.'" Just as toleration depended upon contingent circumstances, so too did persecution.[73]

Lorna Jane Abray, in her essay on Strassburg, seeks to reexamine the reputation that the city has as a model of religious toleration in a Europe that was otherwise largely intolerant of religious diversity. Local magistrates indeed feared that such diversity imperiled the peace and stability of the city. Abray emphasizes that "toleration in the sixteenth century could not coexist with ease of mind and in Strassburg it was never the policy of choice, but always one undertaken to stave off a larger disaster." Still, Abray notes that while Strassburg's magistrates did not vigorously pursue confessional unity, neither did they "recoil from what they understood to be legitimate violence in defence of right religion." Religious toleration had its limits in Strassburg and the magistrates passed laws that did indeed bear on religion, prohibiting blasphemy and religious argument and forbidding local residents from attending (and presumably disrupting) the services of rival confessions. Strassburg's magistrates executed those who violated these laws or committed other moral breaches. Thus, Abray's study highlights a significant feature of religious toleration as a historical phenomenon: it was neither total nor the equivalent of complete religious freedom.[74]

The essays of Heiko Oberman and Philip Benedict point to the importance of the law and legal institutions in expressions of toleration. In his examination of three case studies from sixteenth-century Germany, Oberman shows that some of the legal structures and procedures necessary for toleration predated the Reformation. He nevertheless cautions against a view of "the organic growth of toleration from the fifteenth century to the seventeenth," as at least some procedures were not permanent ones.[75] Philip Benedict's essay on the coexistence between Catholics and Protestants in sixteenth- and seventeenth-century France also highlights the mutability of legal toleration. He notes that royal ordinances concerning toleration "provided only a general framework for the law in early modern France." Other legal bodies had the ability to adapt those laws to local conditions, which included in some places a relatively high rate of intermarriage between Protestants and Catholics. However, the course of the Wars of Religion and "continuing interconfessional competition for souls" also affected the possibility and practice of coexistence. The extension of religious toleration thus entailed more than the promulgation of a royal decree. As Benedict insists, "[a] full picture of Protestant-Catholic relations needs to make room at once for the evidence of frequent, cordial interaction between members of the two faiths and for the recognition that a continuing sense of difference set them apart—differences that could, in certain situations, spark violence or panic."[76]

Beyond reconfiguring our understanding of toleration and intolerance during the Reformation, Grell and Scribner's volume suggests important questions for our contemporary era. Several of the authors link their reevaluation of early modern toleration to problems in present understandings of the subject. For example, Benedict reminds us that "[t]oleration is a quality that most members of modern liberal societies prize—until they have to put up with something truly intolerable. Where they might draw the line is infinitely varied." Considered as a practice shaped and determined by historical context, he argues that "[t]here can be no unified history of toleration, except perhaps a history of the idea itself."[77] Scribner notes that "a long-standing liberal consensus" is reflected in historical work that has attempted to define medieval Europe, and more recently early modern Europe, as a "persecuting society." But he responds that "we might be tempted to argue that the classification, exclusion and persecution of deviant groups as a response to problems caused by social or economic change is an issue that transcends both the Middle Ages and the early modern period to remain a major dilemma of our own age."[78] Grell and Scribner's preface refers to the conflicts in the former Yugoslavia and asks "whether any progress towards greater tolerance has really been achieved in Europe since the sixteenth century, and whether the liberal tradition of tolerance and respect for others which we consider a central part of our cultural heritage is, in fact, only a paper-thin veneer which given the right, or rather wrong, social and political conditions might quickly be discarded and replaced by violence and bigotry."[79]

The history of toleration in Norwich during the Reformation is not one of heroic triumph. It should be emphasized that I am not concerned with arguing that the magistrates or other residents of Norwich were tolerant people, something quite different and irrelevant to the analysis of toleration as a social and political practice. Toleration in the city was never theorized by an intellectual or codified in law. It remained unstable and could not be fully enforced in the city at all times. During the reign of Mary Tudor, most notably, two Norwich residents went to their deaths as Protestant heretics despite the magistrates' unwillingness to take the initiative rooting out heretics. Although there is no evidence that they desired to stop it, the burning in their city of several more from the surrounding diocese was completely out of their control. When compared with our own faith in the value of religious freedom and diversity, toleration in Norwich seems highly contingent and undeveloped. However, we should remember that even the history of toleration, when monumentalized, can create its own others. For example, when G. R. Elton modified an earlier celebratory historiography that located the roots of modern toleration in humanism as well as the Protestant Reformation, he nevertheless concluded that Protestantism "did not preclude genuine toleration for varieties of the faith, whereas the attitudes of Catholics did."[80] Considered in this light, the history of toleration in Norwich, practiced by both Catholics and Protestants, might speak to us in important ways.

⊰ IX ⊱

The sources for the study of sixteenth-century Norwich are largely unexploited and extensive in many areas. The diocesan archives in the Norfolk Record Office contain long runs of consistory court deposition and act books, episcopal registers, visitation records, probate records, churchwardens' accounts, parish registers, books of the Norwich archdeaconry court and other records relating to diocesan administration. Many records produced by the Dean and Chapter of Norwich Cathedral are also extant. Norwich's civic records include the books of the mayor's court, city Assembly, Quarter Sessions and sheriffs' courts, chamberlains' and clavors' accounts, charity books, Great Hospital rolls, the minutes and financial records of St. George's Guild and Company and the *Liber Albus*, a record of important events in the city's history. There are also some miscellaneous records from specific events, such as the dispute between the city and priory and the arrival of Dutch and Walloon Strangers in 1564. Several collections housed in London contain material relating to state, Church and provincial affairs, including Norwich. The Public Record Office holds the archives of the central government, including State Papers Domestic and lay subsidies, as well as the probate records of the Prerogative Court of Canterbury. Among the records relating to ecclesiastical matters at the PRO, which have been used by other scholars working on the Reformation in England, is a manuscript copy of the 1535 sermon given by Edmund Harcocke, the prior of the Norwich Blackfriars; it is one of the few extant sermons preached in Norwich that I have been able to locate. At the British Library, the Harleian collections contain the manuscripts of Foxe's *Book of Martyrs* and Nicholas Sotherton's description of Kett's rebellion.

When I began my research for this study, I first consulted the records of the diocesan Church courts, expecting them to be an important source for the study of religious change and conflict. While the citizens of Norwich appeared in these records for various causes, cases of unorthodoxy and direct conflicts over religious doctrine and practice were, surprisingly, not among them. The city records, on the other hand, revealed many more instances of unorthodoxy and conflict than had come to light in other studies of the Reformation.[81] The mayor's court, whose records are extant in an almost unbroken series from 1510, heard a variety of such cases. In addition to the pattern of resolution in these cases, which I will discuss in the chapters following, the very fact that they ended up in a lay court and not an ecclesiastical one is not without meaning. Civic authorities in some other towns, including London, also had charge of a significant share of the disputes resulting from local religious conflict. But they differed from Norwich in that, in practice, the Norwich magistrates exercised almost exclusive jurisdiction and, unlike the magistrates of London and Bristol, it does not seem that they actively pursued religious dissidents through inquiries, commissions or investigations. Finally, the Norwich magistrates were peculiarly successful at containing religious divisions and quarrels so they neither escalated out of control nor drew in outside powers of Church or state. Based on the current historiography, Norwich appears to stand out in these respects. Understanding how and why are, of course, the major interpretative problems of this book.

⊰ 1 ⊱

Feuds and Factions

DISCORD AND DISRUPTION IN PRE-
REFORMATION NORWICH

The wide-ranging instability in Norwich politics during the fifteenth century presents a sharp contrast to the maintenance of
civic order in the city in the sixteenth. Internal factionalism and
conflicts with neighboring powers, including the monks of the
Cathedral priory, the Bishop of Norwich and the Earl of Suffolk
disturbed the peace and threatened civic independence. Norwich's citizens quarreled with the Crown as well, which twice revoked the city's charter. The disagreements revolved chiefly
around the extent of political jurisdiction and economic rights.
Competing factions in Norwich frequently called in outside allies
to support their cause and, on several occasions, royal authority
finally had to step in to restore order. Jurisdictional disagreements and disputed elections troubled other English towns, but
few suffered the intense and protracted struggles that Norwich
did.[1]

Norwich's political tribulations of the fifteenth century provide
important background and can help to explain the unusual
course of the Reformation in the sixteenth century. Vaguely defined territorial and jurisdictional boundaries in the city's charter
provided repeated occasions for conflict with the Crown and the
Cathedral priory throughout the century and into the next. When
a minority faction of citizens led by outgoing mayor Thomas
Wetherby tried to manipulate civic elections in 1433 to retain

power, the divisions of city politics combined with the ongoing jurisdictional disputes to place Norwich at the mercy of royal, ecclesiastical and aristocratic outsiders for almost two decades. The scars of the midcentury upheavals were vividly remembered not only because the city twice lost its charter, but also because the underlying jurisdictional quarrels and their costs remained unresolved until the early sixteenth century. This long fifteenth century of turbulence in Norwich concluded with the seven-year-long personal intervention of Cardinal and Lord Chancellor Thomas Wolsey that began in 1517. Exasperated with the uncompromising corporation and Cathedral priory of Norwich, the Cardinal finally imposed his own resolution to the disputes in 1524, threatening along the way to challenge the city's liberties yet again. One might think that such bickering among Church, state and internal factions in fifteenth-century Norwich would have only intensified during the Reformation, when the escalating competition between faiths added a new spiritual dimension to church-related conflicts, but, as this book will show, it did not.

From the contrast between fifteenth-century politics in Norwich and the puzzle of its unusually quiet Reformation in the sixteenth century, it appears that civic leaders may have drawn some lessons about the dangers of factionalism, unbridled conflict and outside intervention in local affairs. Indeed, a close examination of the events following the crises of the 1430's and 1440's reveals that civic leaders crafted an instructive memory of those times and began to practice a more unified city governance.

Something of the late fifteenth-century turn in memory and city governance can be seen in a 1482 suit brought against the city by the Abbot of St. Benet Holme in rural Norfolk. The Abbot tried to collect on a bond guaranteeing the destruction of city mills sealed during Norwich's nadir in 1443, when the rightfully elected mayor was lingering in a London jail and Thomas Wetherby's faction ruled the city. To defend itself, the city government composed a history of those crisis years that showed the illegitimacy of Wetherby's usurpation of city rule through deceit and reliance on outside powers. In addition to protecting its economic

interest by repudiating the Abbot's claim, this narrative also re-
constructs the history of factionalism in Norwich by describing
Wetherby as the mastermind of an ongoing conspiracy to destroy
the city. By juxtaposing Wetherby against the city in this way he
no longer appears as the leader of a faction within city government, but rather another in a series of ill-intentioned interlopers
in Norwich politics. This ideal of civic unity appears to have been
put into practice in the decades following the Wetherby debacle.

The city had been free of serious factional struggles for more
than half a century by the time Wolsey arrived in Norwich in
1517, but the Cardinal and Lord Chancellor's intervention demonstrated that the persistent controversies with the Cathedral priory remained a magnet for royal intervention. While Norwich's
records speak to the citizens' perceptions of danger in Wolsey's
mediation, they do not show the formulation of any policy to
avoid further incursions of outsiders into local matters. Nevertheless, when the social and religious conflicts of the Reformation
began to erupt in Norwich in the 1530's, citizens' memories of
Wolsey's imposition were scarcely a decade old. As the history of
Reformation Norwich makes clear, city rulers must have learned
at about this time how to maintain their autonomy by carefully
managing local conflicts.

⫷ II ⫸

Some of the city's difficulties in the fifteenth century stemmed
from the terms of a charter granted to its citizens by Henry IV. In
1404, the King separated Norwich from the county of Norfolk
and accorded it shire status in its own right. Only four other
communities around England—London, Bristol, York and Newcastle—had attained such standing at that time. From 1404, the
city was formally known as the "county of the City of Norwich."
The charter had given a legal personality to the city that allowed
the corporation to hold land, have a common seal, sue and be
sued, issue bylaws and exclude officials from other shires from its
jurisdiction. Norwich's citizens were now also entitled to hold

their own courts and have their own JP's. The charter also altered
the structure of local government, permitting the citizens to elect
a mayor and two sheriffs annually in place of the four bailiffs
who had previously served as executives. The "Composition of
1415," which was a written agreement among the citizens of Norwich, fine-tuned the city's constitution further and was ratified
by a 1417 charter from Henry V. The Composition and charter set
out the duties of the city's aldermen and sixty common councilors
and fixed the annual election dates for various city officials. It
was an arrangement that lasted well into the seventeenth century.[2]

While Henry IV had conferred enhanced status on the city of
Norwich and its citizens, he failed to define the limits of the new
county clearly, an omission that does not appear to have been a
feature of other charters granted during his reign.[3] In the charter,
the King declared that "[w]e have granted . . . that the said city
and all the land within the said City and the Liberty thereof with
its suburbs and hamlets and their precinct and the land in the circuit of our said City of Norwich (the Castle and the Shirehouse
excepted) shall be separated from the said County of Norfolk."[4]
But he did not enumerate the liberties, suburbs and hamlets specifically. Boundary disputes placed the citizens of Norwich at the
center of a number of controversies as they assumed, incorrectly
as it turned out, that the new county's boundaries would be recognized as extending further (both within and outside the city
walls) than those of the old city.

One of the first such conflicts came in 1417, when Henry V accused a number of citizens of encroaching on royal jurisdiction in
several hamlets and suburbs that lay outside the city walls.
Among numerous charges were that city officials had conducted
an illegal inquest in 1415 on the body of a man murdered in the
hamlet of Bracondale, that in 1416 they had arrested a man living
in nearby Sprowston for debt and that in 1417 the mayor, sheriffs
and a number of others had illegally fished in the Trowse River.
All of these areas and others, the King claimed, were not part of
the county of the City of Norwich. An Inquisition into the charges

began at Cringleford, Norfolk, in the fall of 1417 and the case dragged on for almost fifteen years. Those named in the original indictment were found guilty of violating royal jurisdiction and in 1431 two former sheriffs were fined £4 6s. 8d. and £3 respectively, and a number of others were assessed smaller sums of money. In addition to individual levies, a fine of £12 was imposed on the "present Mayor [John Cambridge] and Commonalty," which points to the acceptance and operation of corporate identity. Cambridge paid the fine as mayor for the actions taken by the city before his term. The decision against the corporation and individual residents of Norwich thus limited the scope of civic authority for the governors of the new county.[5]

Challenges to corporate authority did not come only from outside city government. Shortly after the conclusion of the conflict with Henry V, factional fighting engulfed local government. Factional division both became entangled with the city's quarrels over jurisdiction with outside authorities and worked to preoccupy Norwich's citizens for well over a decade. The result was that political conflict was virtually ceaseless in Norwich throughout the 1430's and 1440's.

The disruptions at Norwich began with a disputed mayoral election. Electoral disturbances were common in late medieval towns and often reflected contests between wealthier and less prosperous townsmen for domination of local government. At Lynn, for example, Henry V had personally intervened in local conflicts and granted the citizens a new constitution in 1416 designed to defuse tensions between the wealthy merchants who monopolized higher civic offices and the rest of the community. Elections at London were also disturbed several times during the 1440's as City aldermen clashed with segments of the electorate. At Hereford, tensions developed between newcomers to the city who were excluded from participation in government and longer established interests and exploded into violence at the mayoral elections in 1448 and 1450.[6] But the discord at Norwich proved lengthier and more virulent than anywhere else.

In the spring of 1433, Thomas Wetherby, a wealthy merchant

who also owned property outside the city, completed his second term as mayor of Norwich. Wetherby and a bloc of his supporters in city government attempted to manipulate the May 1 election to name the next mayor. The regulations for the mayor's election had been precisely laid out in the Composition of 1415. On election day the outgoing mayor, aldermen, sheriffs and common councilmen were to assemble at the Guildhall, along with Norwich's freemen. The mayor, aldermen and sheriffs were then to withdraw to their chamber while the city Recorder was to call upon those remaining to nominate two aldermen who had already served as sheriff as mayoral candidates. The two men who received the largest number of votes became the official candidates for mayor. Those names were delivered to the sequestered magistrates, who voted by secret ballot to elect one of those as the next mayor.[7] In 1433, the names of Richard Purdance and John Gerard were submitted to the magistrates as candidates for mayor. Defying the city's election laws, Wetherby substituted the name of his hand-picked successor—William Grey—for that of Richard Purdance. Finding himself in a minority among the citizens, he had to pressure a sufficient number of the aldermen to vote for Grey to ensure his election. The Recorder, a supporter of Wetherby, announced that William Grey had been selected as the new mayor. Wetherby emerged from the voting chamber and proclaimed to the assembled citizenry, "Sirs, ye have named [two] worthy persons and of them we choose one, William Grey." The crowd reacted angrily, calling out, "Nay, Nay, Nay, we never named Grey but Purdance and Gerard." Wetherby led William Grey home, while the majority of the crowd remained behind and elected Richard Purdance.[8] The citizens who now opposed Wetherby and his allies called upon an outside authority, William Alnwick, the Bishop of Norwich, to negotiate a settlement. The Bishop ruled in favor of the majority faction of city governors and in June 1433, their candidate, Richard Purdance, took office as mayor. Not surprisingly, the new city government stripped Wetherby of his aldermanic office and fined the former mayor the considerable sum of £100. Five of Wetherby's confederates were forbidden from ever holding civic office again and from "pleading in city courts and participating in city assemblies."[9]

Such a setback apparently did not dampen Wetherby's enthusiasm for meddling in civic affairs or his determination to regain influence and power in the city. For the next several years, the former mayor schemed to return to power. To aid him in that effort, he sought and gained the support of a powerful outsider, William de la Pole, the Earl of Suffolk, and also of two of the Earl's retainers, John Heydon and Thomas Tuddenham. Wetherby's association with the Earl dates from about 1435 when both men became members of the Norwich guild of St. George, although their tie would not become evident until two years later. Suffolk was one of the most powerful peers in East Anglia, having succeeded to his title in 1417 on the death of his brother, the third Earl. He was also gaining considerable political influence at the court of Henry VI, having been admitted to Henry VI's Council in 1431.

Wetherby and his allies came close to recovering their authority and influence in 1436 when Robert Chapleyn, who was sympathetic to the group, was elected mayor. Chapleyn sought to restore members of the banned faction to their former offices and privileges. He appointed one of them as city undersheriff. Chapleyn also made an unsuccessful bid to reinstate Wetherby to the aldermanic post that he had lost in 1433. However, Wetherby did become a city Justice and John Heydon, one of the Earl of Suffolk's retainers, served as city Recorder.[10] The restoration of the outlawed bloc was of serious concern to the majority of city governors in Norwich. Their objections to the restoration of Wetherby and his supporters to civic office led the Earl of Suffolk to offer mediation, and it was with great hope that city governors accepted his help. In 1436, the Earl's association with Thomas Wetherby was not common knowledge. Suffolk was best known in Norwich as an influential local magnate whose tie to the city was chiefly as a member of one of the city's important religious confraternities, the guild of St. George.[11]

Suffolk's ruling on the political situation in Norwich, which he gave at a meeting of the city Assembly in March 1437, proved to

be a great disappointment to the majority faction. The Earl nulli-
fied all of the penalties against Wetherby and his allies that had
resulted from the disturbances at the 1433 mayoral election. He
also decreed that their civic offices be restored and that Wetherby
should be reinstated to aldermanic office. The Earl's decision pat-
ently exposed his enmeshment in city politics and, more importantly, his link to the Wetherby group.

In an atmosphere of increasing tension Wetherby's enemies
sought to find their own powerful patron to support their cause
in local politics. They turned to another outsider, Humphrey, the
Duke of Gloucester, asking him to support a petition to the King
and his Council against Wetherby. Gloucester was uncle to the
young Henry VI and his heir-apparent. He was thus a powerful
presence at court, especially as the King was only entering his
majority in 1437.[12] Perhaps more important to the anti-Wetherby
group at Norwich who hoped that he would be their patron was
the fact that Gloucester was the Earl of Suffolk's chief rival at
court. Gloucester was an ardent supporter of continued military
expeditions against France, while Suffolk favored peace.[13] Wetherby's enemies thus hoped to turn this animosity, rooted in national political developments, to their local advantage. Gloucester
forwarded the petition to the Council, and Wetherby was summoned to Westminster.

Norwich's mayoral election was drawing closer and there was
concern at Westminster that it would be contentious. In an attempt to avert unrest and tampering and preserve order, the
King's Council dispatched two commissioners to oversee the
election, at least one of whom had links to the Earl of Suffolk.[14]
But that effort proved unsuccessful. The scene on election day has
been aptly described by one historian as "a showdown."[15] On
May 1, 1437, a large crowd—perhaps two thousand strong—
gathered in the Norwich marketplace, in front of the Guildhall. It
was headed by a number of aldermen, including Robert Toppes,
William Ashwell, John Cambridge and William Hempsted, and
other prominent citizens.[16] When Wetherby and his minority faction approached the marketplace on their way to the Guildhall

where the election was to take place, they were blocked by the assembled crowd and perhaps even beaten. It is not clear whether the election ever took place.[17]

Two months later, in July, the King's Council suspended Norwich's liberties. Wetherby's schemes to reclaim power, his appeal to a powerful outsider for support and the corresponding entreaty that his opponents had made to another outsider, the Duke of Gloucester, had all ended in disaster for the city. The Council appointed John Welles, an alderman from London, as warden of the city. It also banished nine of Wetherby's opponents, giving the appearance of royal sympathy for Wetherby and his supporters.

Welles remained in his post until November of that year, when, citing the high cost of supporting a warden, the Council replaced him with a mayor of its own choosing, John Cambridge, a member of the anti-Wetherby group. This change suggests that the Council had revised its understanding of the circumstances at Norwich. If the initial decision to take control of Norwich's government away from local politicians had been largely based on Wetherby's account of election day, the Council's subsequent appointment of John Cambridge as mayor indicates that Wetherby's account was no longer taken quite so seriously. Still, the new mayor governed Norwich at the will of the King and his Council, which preserved good order at the expense of civic autonomy.

Two years later, in 1439, the citizens of Norwich successfully petitioned the King for a restoration of their liberties. In May, the citizens of Norwich voted in the first election since the disaster of 1437. They selected John Toppes, a Wetherby opponent and former exile, as their new mayor.[18] But peace proved to be short-lived in Norwich. Soon after the restoration of city liberties, the citizens were at odds with the inmates of the Cathedral priory.

⊰ III ⊱

The fifteenth century was not the first time of hostilities between the inhabitants of Norwich and the monks at the Cathedral. There had been difficulties between the two groups almost continuously since the late eleventh-century construction of the Cathedral and monastery. The erection of the church buildings separated formerly contiguous districts of Norwich and thus created something of a nuisance to local residents.[19] In addition, the fact that the majority of the monks came from outside of Norwich during the later Middle Ages might have made the priory appear to local residents as an alien institution.[20] Tensions also flared frequently during the Middle Ages as the expanding scope and authority of civic government came into conflict with that of the Cathedral priory. Although citizens and monks quarreled about several different issues, jurisdictional matters were chief among them. There was nearly continuous disagreement over three problems: the right to control the areas of Tombland, Ratonrowe and Holmstreet, which lay just outside the priory precincts and other areas in the city; the priory's right to hold an annual Pentecost fair; and the rights to grazing lands in the southwestern suburbs of Eaton and Lakenham.[21]

The most notorious expression of animosity between the citizens and monks of Norwich—and perhaps between lay and clerical neighbors anywhere in medieval England—came in 1272. A skirmish between some residents of the priory and townsmen in Tombland had culminated in a full-scale attack against the monastery, which was noted by a number of medieval chroniclers.[22] While it is not clear what led to the initial fracas, tensions between citizens and the monks intensified afterwards until a group of citizens marched on and stormed the Cathedral priory. That assault left thirteen people dead and several Cathedral and priory buildings damaged. Both Church and Crown stepped in to punish the citizens. About thirty lay ringleaders among them were executed and others were excommunicated by Roger Skening, the Bishop of Norwich, and by the Pope. Henry III fined the citizens £2,000. He also went personally to Norwich in order to seize the city's liberties. They were only restored four years later, by Henry's successor, Edward I.[23] Those punishments did little to stem the hostilities between the municipality and the monastery and frictions continued to simmer between them almost without intermission after the thirteenth century. James Campbell has alluded to "recurrent lesser clashes" after 1272 and Norman Tanner has written about conflict between the city and the monastery from 1370.[24] In 1373 jurisdictional squabbles were ignited when city bailiffs arrested a woman in St. Paul's parish in the city's northern ward, only to have her seized by a group of monks who claimed the right to arrest her. In 1380, citizens were threatened with disenfranchisement if they took any pleas to the court held by the Prior. In a bizarre 1436 incident, the Prior cut down and took away twenty willow trees at the house of mayor Robert Chapleyn.[25]

In the fifteenth century, the charter of 1404 served to exacerbate the jurisdictional disputes between the city and the monastery when it neglected to delineate the borders of the new county of Norwich. In particular, the charter's ambiguity reanimated the thorny question of control over long-disputed areas surrounding the Cathedral, especially Tombland, Ratonrowe, Holmstreet, Eaton and Lakenham.

There was little open and direct conflict between the city and priory while Norwich's citizens were absorbed by factional politics and their disputes with the Crown. As soon as the city's liberties were restored in 1439, however, the mayor and other local officials began to exercise authority in some of the contested areas. In 1429, the city and priory had signed an accord in which the corporation had conceded jurisdiction over areas outside the monastery precincts and in Eaton, Lakenham and other Norwich suburbs, but that agreement did not appear to be enduring.[26] Norwich coroners conducted an inquest on a body in Holmstreet; city sheriffs had also arrested defendants in debt, trespass and other civil cases in Lakenham, Ratonrowe, at Magdalen Hospital and in the priory precincts themselves. In response, John Heverlond, who served as the Prior of Norwich from 1436 to 1454, brought legal action against the city in 1441. He charged that the inquests, arrests and other actions taken by civic officers represented violations of the monastery's jurisdiction. While these is-

sues of contested jurisdiction were certainly not new ones between the city government and priory, the timing of the allegations was not coincidental. By 1441, the Prior had become an ally
of Thomas Wetherby's. It seems likely that the Prior's accusations
had become enmeshed in Wetherby's efforts to harass his enemies in civic government.[27]

With new charges pending against them, members of city government once again sought the support of the Duke of Gloucester, but he proved to be of little help. Gloucester's influence at
court was on the wane, no doubt tied to his wife's condemnation
on charges that she conspired at the King's death through witch-
craft.[28]

While city governors were unable to enlist the aid of an outside
patron, it seems that the Prior succeeded. A royal commission
was appointed to inquire into his charges against the city and
other offenses, and the commission's composition indicated the
continuing influence of Thomas Wetherby on local affairs. Included on the commission were Thomas Brown, the Bishop of
Norwich, the Duke of Norfolk, the Earl of Suffolk and Thomas
Tuddenham. Tuddenham and the Earl were known supporters of
Wetherby and Wetherby had also apparently won the patronage
of the Duke of Norfolk as well.[29] Bishop Brown might have been a
supporter of Wetherby, but in any case, he had a number complaints of his own—albeit minor—against the corporation that
were heard at the commission.[30]

The commission sat at Thetford, Norfolk, in July 1441. The
Prior presented his charges against the city, as did the Abbots of
Wendling and St. Benet Holme, who had also become allies of
Wetherby, although there is no record of any decision regarding
the Abbot of Wendling's charges. The Prior's case against the
corporation was transferred to Westminster, where accusations
of encroachment on royal authority—many of them the same as
in 1417—were also being brought against the city by Henry VI.
These two cases would linger on for two more years. In addition,
the charges brought by the Abbot of St. Benet Holme, which concerned mills recently built in Norwich that he claimed obstructed

water passage from his lands, were submitted to the sole consideration of the Earl of Suffolk, an arrangement that inspired little hope in the city for a favorable judgment. The list of adversaries faced by the corporation in 1441 was both long and formidable.

Sometime during the following year, the Earl of Suffolk predictably ruled against the corporation in the matter concerning the Abbot of St. Benet Holme. He ordered the destruction of the controversial mills and required the corporation to enter into bonds with the Abbot, the Bishop of Norwich and the Prior of Norwich to ensure that the decision was carried out. So unpopular was the Earl's ruling that the city government refused to accept it, despite the pressure placed on it to do so. In late 1442, Thomas Wetherby was openly espousing the Abbot of St. Benet's cause, persevering in his campaign against his enemies in city government. On January 22, 1443, Wetherby even attended a meeting of the city Assembly at the Guildhall where he urged members to seal bonds to guarantee the completion of the Earl's decree, but the Assembly rejected Wetherby's exhortation. In addition, some of the members of a crowd that had gathered outside the Guildhall during the meeting broke into the building and removed the city's common seal, possibly prompted by aldermen Robert Toppes and William Ashwell, to ensure that no bonds were sealed.[31]

Disappointment and anger over the city's defeats in the recent legal actions were heightened when, on the day following the Assembly meeting, the Prior arrested and imprisoned two city residents on pleas of debt.[32] Those tensions erupted into violence on January 25, when a local procession ended in a riot. January 25 was the church feast of the Conversion of St. Paul, which commemorated the story told in Acts 9:1–27. Saul, a persecutor of Christians, was converted to Christianity on his way to Damascus and baptized Paul. In Norwich, the feast day was marked by a procession. That year it was led by John Gladman, a local merchant, who rode on horseback wearing a paper crown and was attended by a large crowd of local residents. Three men bearing a sword, crown and scepter marched in front of Gladman. Two dozen more rode on horseback behind him, and they carried bows and arrows. Other marchers followed that group, also out fited with bows, arrows and swords.[33] It is not clear what ignited the tumult, but in the tense atmosphere of early 1443 and the presence of hundreds of people in the streets of Norwich, little provocation was necessary. The procession ended with hundreds of people marching on the Cathedral, who then laid siege to the priory. During the siege, the assailants pointed cannons at the Cathedral and began to tunnel under its walls. They also removed and presumably destroyed a copy of the 1429 agreement. The attack and general unrest lasted for over a week, until the King reestablished peace by dispatching a military force commanded by the Duke of Norfolk and the Earl of Oxford.

After order had been restored in Norwich, the response to the attack against the priory from the Church and Crown was swift and harsh. The Archbishop of Canterbury, Henry Chichele, ordered the excommunication of a number of Norwich's citizens.[34] The Duke of Norfolk and Earl of Oxford arrested leaders of the assault, including the mayor of Norwich, William Hempsted, and sent them to London for imprisonment. Hempsted appealed to the Duke of Gloucester for aid, but was once again unable to secure his support. In February 1443, he appeared before the King's Council and was subsequently imprisoned in the Fleet for his role in the siege. Hempsted languished there until the end of March, when he paid a hefty £50 fine for his release.[35]

The period of the mayor's imprisonment offered Thomas Wetherby and his allies the opportunity to rule Norwich as they chose and to vanquish their enemies. Wetherby, who simply took control of city government, carried out the Earl of Suffolk's decree concerning the city's dispute with the Abbot of St. Benet Holme. He sealed bonds with the Abbot, the Bishop of Norwich and the Prior, as the Earl had instructed. He furthermore oversaw the destruction of the city's mills, which citizens were helpless to prevent. Wetherby's final act against the citizens of Norwich came in March 1443, at the meeting of a commission that had been appointed by the King to investigate the assault against the

Cathedral priory further. Wetherby assumed the responsibility of securing legal counsel for the city. He then instructed that attorney, Thomas del Rowe, simply to throw the city on the King's mercy, rather than to provide any defense. As a result, the commission's judges levied a very substantial collective fine on the citizens of £2,000, which was later reduced by over half to 1,000 marks, and another £1,500 on over 120 individual rioters.[36] More seriously, they seized the city's franchises into the King's hands. They then appointed Sir John Clifton warden of Norwich, perhaps with the hope and expectation that Clifton's Norfolk origins would work to his advantage in ruling the recalcitrant city.

In 1443 Norwich city government stood in ruins. Thomas Wetherby's bid for power had plagued the city government for a decade and was inextricably linked to the violent outbursts that resulted in the first suspension of civic liberties. He was also responsible for the Earl of Suffolk's interference in affairs in Norwich. Of course, Wetherby's opponents in city government had also sought a powerful outsider to champion their cause in the ongoing local conflicts. But they had found the Duke of Gloucester to be an unreliable ally. In addition to the quarrels concerning Wetherby and the disposition of local government, unresolved conflicts between the citizens of Norwich and the inmates of the Cathedral priory had exploded into violence that had prompted a second confiscation of civic liberties. The citizens had also fared poorly in their disputes with the Crown. They had lost the 1417 confrontation with Henry V concerning the boundaries of the new county of the City of Norwich. And in the fall of 1443, they learned that another case concerning charges of jurisdictional encroachment that had been lodged by Henry VI and by the Prior in 1441 had gone against them as well.[37] The Crown had also intervened in the corporation's disputes with Thomas Wetherby and with the Cathedral priory, never to the corporation's advantage. As a result of these combined problems, the mayor lay in prison, city government was in the hands of an outsider and no one knew if or when the political privileges that Norwich's citizens had been so eager to exercise would be restored.

⊰ IV ⊱

Outsiders continued to govern Norwich in the King's name for the four years after the disaster of 1443.[38] Political life in Norwich was more tranquil not only because of the King's might, but also because of the disintegration of the faction led by Thomas Wetherby. Wetherby died in 1444 or 1445. Consequently, the Earl of Suffolk disappeared from Norwich political life. He became increasingly enmeshed in the national politics that would claim his life in 1450.[39] No longer plagued by the Wetherby faction, the Norwich citizens inaugurated what would become a long period of civic unity. In late 1447, they petitioned King's Bench for the restoration of civic liberties, which they received upon paying the reduced fine of 1,000 marks.[40] The citizens promptly reelected William Hempsted, the former mayor who had been imprisoned for his role in the assault against the Cathedral priory, as if to restore the continuity of autonomous corporate identity disrupted by the affair with Wetherby and outside intervention.

In 1450, a royal commission appointed to investigate abuses of law in Norwich questioned Wetherby's allies Thomas Tuddenham and John Heydon along with others about allegations of treason, extortion and other damages to the city amounting to the extraordinary sum of £20,000. Although no actions resulted from this inquiry, the King did act on behalf of the citizens of Norwich. In 1452 Henry VI issued a new charter which, in addition to adjusting the city's constitution, included a pardon to the citizens for the offenses that led to the 1443 suspension of their liberties.[41] But despite the King's now friendly demeanor, the events of the 1430's and 1440's were not easily forgotten. Internal factionalism aside, many of the internal disputes that fueled the troubles of that period continued unresolved into the next century.

The extent of the city's jurisdiction over the Cathedral precincts and the scope of civic privileges remained contentious. In 1481, a new Abbot of St. Benet Holme in the Norfolk countryside asked the judges of the Courts of Common Pleas and King's Bench to call in the £100 bond he claimed the city of Norwich promised during Thomas Wetherby's brief rule in early 1443. The bond was intended to ensure the destruction of city mills that the Abbot said would flood the monastery's lands in Heigham, a north-western suburb of the city. Wetherby sealed the bond and then destroyed the mills, so the £100 was never actually paid. The city rebuilt the mills after the restoration of liberties in 1447, which produced the grounds for the new Abbot's belated claim against the city.

The city responded successfully, as it turned out, by arguing that the bond was invalid because the city government in 1443 was illegitimate and therefore had no authority to seal bonds, no less destroy mills.[42] To bolster its defense against the Abbot, the city government produced a narrative history of Norwich's tribulations during the 1430's and 1440's. This account, along with supporting documents from the 1482 legal contest with the Abbot, was then entered into the city's *Liber Albus*, an ongoing compilation of documents relating to the city's history begun in 1426.[43] As such, this brief contemporary history composed in 1482 is noteworthy evidence of an active historical memory of the searing events from the first half of the fifteenth century, as well as an indication of the solidification of civic unity in Norwich.

The city's chief purpose in constructing its history of the 1430's and 1440's was, of course, to invalidate the Abbot's claim by showing that Thomas Wetherby had usurped civic authority. To this end, the account vilified the former mayor, holding him responsible for the city's afflictions during the time. It characterized Wetherby as a man of "great goods and great pride" and "great wrath and pride," implying that he was greedy for wealth and power. In particular, the narrative blamed Wetherby for the damaging consequences of the intervention of outsiders in local affairs.

According to the Norwich city history, Wetherby "caused great trouble at every election" after his failed bid to install William Grey as mayor, which was "not good unto them [the aldermen and commons] nor profitable to the city." He then prompted Henry VI to dispatch a commission, at his own expense, that ultimately recommended the first suspension of civic liberties in 1437. Wetherby was said to have "continued in his malice greatly" by inducing the Abbot of St. Benet Holme to bring legal action against the citizens over the mills in 1441. In this case, the history held Wetherby responsible for drawing in the Earl of Suffolk, whose partisan mediation caused such a reaction among the citizens that Wetherby informed Westminster that mayor William Hempsted and his followers were "risers against the King." This led to Hempsted's arrest and the second suspension of civic liberties. Conveniently, the city's version of the story omitted the assault against the Cathedral priory on the Conversion of St. Paul.[44]

The 1482 history does not dwell on the immediate effects of losing the city's liberties, no doubt because its main concern was the conflict with the Abbot of St. Benet Holme over the mills. In this respect, the Norwich city government account was not shy about the damage done by Wetherby. For example, it explained that when the Earl of Suffolk's initial favorable award to the Abbot of St. Benet Holme was read in the city Assembly, its members were "further out with the said Thomas Wetherby than ever they were before" because "his untrue dealing" seemed to have prejudiced the Earl against the city. When they tried to inform the Earl that he had been misled by Wetherby and the Earl refused to make any changes, the citizens "thereby understood that his intent was for to destroy them for they understood by the award that they should lose the mills, which should be an utter desolation for the city and should cause the people to go out of the city."

Although the Assembly resisted sealing the bond, reportedly telling the Abbot that he "should never have their obligation under the common seal in destruction of the King's city," Wetherby proceeded to destroy the mills. According to the narrative he "decayed them so that the bakers were full fain to seek mills sometime in the year [ten] mile[s] about Norwich, to the great hurt and scarceness of the city. And so it [the mills] stood decayed many years."[45] This tale of economic woe inflicted by Wetherby's use of outside intervention not only won the case against the Abbot, but also seems to have influenced Edward IV, who granted the city a charter during his visit to Norwich in the fall of 1482. The King was predisposed to show favor to the city because it supported him in the Wars of the Roses that brought him to the throne in 1461 and again in 1471, but this specific charter was likely shaped by the city's emphasis on economic harm in the case before his courts. The 1482 charter permitted the citizens of Norwich to hold two fairs annually, one during Lent and the other at the feast of St. Paul in late June. These fairs provided the city an opportunity to make money, perhaps in compensation for the losses suffered over the mid-fifteenth century.[46]

In addition to inscribing for posterity the memory of damages caused by internal division, the 1482 narrative's depiction of Wetherby is significant for what it reveals about the citizens' sense of themselves in the late fifteenth century. In the 1430's and 1440's, Norwich suffered from factional strife. Wetherby, in fact, had minority support among the aldermen and was able somehow to persuade at least some other aldermen to go along with him in the disputed election of 1433. However, in the 1482 history Wetherby was depicted as an outlaw, an enemy of the city rather than part of it. His followers were not then named nor even recognized as citizens of the city, but only referred to as his "adherents." In contrast, the narrative begins by contrasting Wetherby to "the commonalty and the great part of the aldermen and of the commons" of Norwich. The royal commissioners Wetherby supported in 1441 were said to be "feigning themselves to be friends of the city." And, in the end, the history virtually erased his membership in the citizenry by describing him simply as an enemy and destroyer of the city rather than as the leader of a faction.

As represented in the history of 1482, memory of the faction-ridden 1430's and 1440's reconstructed an ideal of civic unity in which city government, citizens and commonalty stood together as one. In practice, the Abbot of St. Benet Holme does not seem to have received any support from Norwich during the court case of 1481–82. A jurisdictional dispute in 1486 also demonstrated the increasing solidarity and self-control of civic authority. When the mayor and aldermen attempted to assert their authority over Rat-

onrowe and Holmstreet, two of the long-contested areas around
the Cathedral, by building wooden posts at one end of Holmstreet, some of the priory's tenants removed the posts. In the past,
such provocative behavior might well have led to open and violent confrontations in the streets, but the city instead responded
by indicting the tenants for riot.[47] Only once after the death of
Thomas Wetherby did a member of civic government—and a
former member at that—seek to trouble his colleagues in a similarly public fashion. In 1489 William Curteys, who had served as
sheriff in 1484, championed the cause of William Spynke, the
Prior of Norwich, in a dispute with the city government. Curteys's support, however, appears to have made little difference in
the progress of the dispute. There is no evidence that any single
citizen sought or was able to provoke the deep divisions among
the body politic that Thomas Wetherby's activities had.

⊰ V ⊱

While the increase in civic unity helped to protect the city from
unbridled internal disturbances, external intervention was still a
danger. Disputes with the priory had been involved in many of
the quarrels of the fifteenth century. The failure to resolve those
differences posed a continual threat to the city's autonomy. In
1491, the city and priory renewed their dispute in a lawsuit before the court of Star Chamber, the judicial incarnation of the
King's Council.[48] The Council referred the matter to two East Anglian magnates for a decision, and they ruled that the priory was
indeed within the jurisdiction of the city. The Council then directed the city to exclude the priory from its jurisdiction, an order
that the corporation refused. The case remained before the Star
Chamber and no further action was taken on it.[49] Thus, when the
King died in 1509, two decades after Prior William Spynke had
brought suit against the citizens of Norwich, the citizens and
monks were no closer to a resolution of the divisive disputes that
had been the source of so much disorder and chaos for much of
the fifteenth century.[50]

The lawsuit between the priory and corporation of Norwich lingered in the court of Star Chamber for almost a decade after Henry VII's death before it received any attention. The case attracted the attention of Cardinal Wolsey shortly after he became Lord Chancellor in 1515. In the fifteenth century, the court was recognized as "a forum for litigation and arbitration, especially that which could be set into a context of local disorder, perversion of justice or official maladministration."[51] In the sixteenth century, under Wolsey in his capacity as Chancellor, the court expanded the volume and scope of its business as the Cardinal also used it to increase his personal power. During the reign of Henry VII, members of the King's Council heard approximately 300 suits in Star Chamber; during Wolsey's ascendancy that number climbed to as many as 1,685. Of the 473 cases for which sufficient evidence exists to determine their cause, only eight concerned municipal disputes.[52]

The Cardinal had been known to boast of the court as a place where justice might be better served than elsewhere in England's legal system.[53] Perhaps it was this exalted claim that led Wolsey to intervene in the case between the corporation of Norwich and the city's Cathedral monastery. The Cardinal's direct involvement in the dispute began with a trip to Norwich in the summer of 1517. The city Assembly minutes recorded that aldermen Thomas Aldrich and John Marsham and town clerk Leonard Spencer would serve as representatives of the corporation and would "give attendance upon the reverend father in God" upon his arrival in the city.[54]

The issues at stake in the dispute between the city and priory when Wolsey arrived in Norwich were the same ones that had already kept the two parties at loggerheads for years. Both sides continued to claim jurisdiction over Tombland, Holmstreet and Ratonrowe, as well as over other neighboring districts such as Eaton and Lakenham. Wolsey visited the contested sites and had the details of disagreement recorded in a "book," and began his efforts to mediate an agreement that would be acceptable to both the citizens and the Cathedral monks.[55]

The intervention of an exalted figure such as Cardinal Wolsey did little to hasten the pace of negotiation, however. The citizens and monks haggled back and forth after Wolsey's departure from the city without reaching an agreement, because each side refused to relinquish claims to long-contested areas. Preserved among the city records are many drafts of potential agreements that were drawn up and apparently rejected.[56] There were two particularly serious stumbling blocks to reaching an agreement from the city's point of view. One was the Cardinal's proposal that the priory and its environs be alienated from the city of Norwich and be joined to the county of Norfolk instead. The other unacceptable provision of Wolsey was that the city renounce its rights to pastureland in the suburbs of Lakenham and Eaton and also to lands outside St. Stephen's gate. Wolsey tried unsuccessfully to persuade the city Assembly to agree to his terms. In 1522, the Cardinal warned that if the corporation and priory did not agree on a settlement he would allow a royal commission to initiate *quo warranto* proceedings, which would have required the surrender of the city's charter for royal investigation.[57] That ultimatum prompted the city Assembly to send representatives to London and to the Assize judges at Thetford on several occasions to argue the corporation's case, but did not result in an immediate agreement.[58]

In 1523 a thoroughly frustrated Wolsey announced that he was simply going to impose his solution formally. Still, the corporation resisted and as late as March 1524 the matter was still under discussion in the Assembly. Members were especially vigorous in their denunciation of Wolsey's recommendation that the priory and its precincts be placed under the jurisdiction of the county of Norfolk. They charged that "it should be to the great destruction, in time to come, of the city forever if we should agree that [two] shires should be within the closure of the city." They also cited a charter of Edward I that had granted that "no foreign officer should enter to do any service within the same [city]."[59] Assembly members did not elaborate on their opposition to Wolsey's plan, but if jurisdictional questions could not be resolved between two parties, the introduction of a third—the county of Norfolk—would potentially make things worse. Although the terms of Wolsey's proposal would permit Norfolk officials to exercise their authority only in the priory precincts, they would always have to travel through the city to reach there. It was possible that the alien sheriffs of Norfolk might try to extend their jurisdiction inside Norwich city walls, subverting civic authority.

Despite the strenuous objections raised by the Norwich Assembly, Wolsey imposed his proposed settlement of the dispute between the corporation and the priory. In August 1524, an excruciatingly detailed indenture was drawn up and sealed by the city at the Norwich Guildhall. As he had promised, Wolsey gave the area inside the priory walls to the county of Norfolk, and he placed Tombland, Ratonrowe and Holmstreet under civic jurisdiction. Furthermore, the priory surrendered to the corporation the lucrative right to hold a fair during Pentecost, for the fairs Edward IV granted to the citizens in 1482 had not been successful. The monks also ceded eighty acres of pasturelands in Eaton and Lakenham to the city, which were to be surrounded by a ditch. In return, the citizens agreed to pay the priory 20s. a year and they surrendered their claim to lands elsewhere in the two suburbs.[60] When the still suspicious citizens and monks raised the question of financial responsibility for digging the ditch, an irritated Wolsey assumed the cost personally, lending credence to his claim that his "charitable disposition" had driven him to take an interest in the whole matter in the first place.[61] Henry VIII ratified the indenture with two royal charters in 1524 and 1525.[62]

Wolsey's intervention brought an end to the disputes that had afflicted the corporation and priory for at least a century, but, like most compromises, in a way that was not fully satisfactory to either side. Many of the city's economic concerns were answered at the cost of civic autonomy. The imaginative geography of the Cardinal's solution effectively plucked the Cathedral precincts out of the city and put them under the jurisdiction of Norfolk county. Since the Cathedral itself was not physically moved, this meant that the "foreign" authority of Norfolk county officers would exercise power on an island within city walls. This was what the Norwich Assembly feared would cause the "great destruction, in time to come, of the city."

As in Norwich's troubles of the fifteenth century, Wolsey's intervention in the quarrel with the Cathedral priory placed the fate of the corporation in the hands of an outsider. Over the course of Wolsey's seven-year-long involvement in their affairs, the citizens of Norwich had to plead before the Cardinal for their interests and ran the risk of once again losing their liberties. The documents from these disrupting events in the life of the city were entered into the *Liber Albus*, alongside the 1482 history of Thomas Wetherby's assault on Norwich. On the eve of the Reformation, the civic leaders of Norwich were acutely aware of the dangers posed by internal factionalism and unbridled local conflicts that could draw in outside intervention.

2

Handling Heresies

THE EMERGENCE OF TOLERATION
IN HENRICIAN NORWICH

For almost a decade after the beginning of Luther's schism with the Roman Catholic Church in 1517, the ecclesiastical and city records of Norwich offer no indication that religious innovation had surfaced there.[1] There must certainly have been some supporters of Lutheran ideas in Norwich, for it was England's second most important urban center and it had an active trade with the Continent. We know, for example, that the itinerant bookseller Robert Necton, whose brother Thomas became a Norwich alderman in 1530, was arrested in London in 1528 and 1531, for the sale of illicit books, including Tyndale's English New Testament, in Norfolk, Suffolk and London.[2] It is striking that neither Necton, his clients nor any other religious nonconformists in Norwich during this period ever appeared in local records.

There is ample evidence that Lutheran and other reformist ideas were gaining currency and vocal enemies elsewhere in England, most prominently in London and the southeast. In the early 1520's, a group that included future Archbishop of Canterbury Thomas Cranmer and several others later renowned as religious reformers, began to meet in Cambridge to discuss Lutheran ideas at the White Horse Tavern, dubbed "Little Germany."[3] In 1521, Cardinal Wolsey presided over the public burning of Luther's writings in London.[4] Even when the Parliament of 1529 opened with vituperative attacks against clerical abuses,

much to the delight of Henry VIII, who was two years into his ef-
forts to secure an annulment from the Pope of his marriage to
Catherine of Aragon, no immediate reaction was recorded by the
Norwich city government. This was a situation that could not last
for long in England's second largest city, given that the Henrician
Reformation would soon begin to shake the foundations of the
Church and its relationship to secular power from the King down
to the smallest rural communities.

Indeed, by the mid-1530's, city magistrates were beginning to
hear cases concerning conflicts over religion in the mayor's court.
However, while some local residents criticized traditional religious ceremonies and practices and others denounced sympathizers of reform, religious controversies did not escalate in Norwich
to the levels that they did in other towns that have been the focus
of recent studies. In Bristol, the intensification of religious tensions that erupted in the wake of Hugh Latimer's reformist
preaching eventually prompted the mayor and aldermen to in-
vite one of Cromwell's representatives to the city to mediate between opposing blocs. The town government of Canterbury was
a site of intense factional fighting over religion, as reforming and
traditionalist groups battled for dominance. And in London, City
prisons were crowded with those suspected of violating the Six
Articles of 1539. In Norwich, there were no similar outbursts. The
magistrates did not call in outside authorities to settle disputes
over religion or seek out the religiously unorthodox. Nor did they
themselves succumb to factional fighting over religion.

In contrast to the histories of these other towns and to the recent historiography of the Reformation, which has highlighted
conflict and disorder, the magistrates of Norwich handled religious controversies in an unusual way. They did not enforce Henrician religious dictates strictly, apparently releasing a number of
religious offenders from the mayor's court without any punishment. Although there is no discussion of the reason for such actions in the records, it seems likely that the magistrates' recent
brush with Cardinal Wolsey and their subsequent involvement in

the 1531 execution of the heretic Thomas Bilney served as potent reminders of the dangers posed by political and religious divisions.

The magistrates' consistent failure to punish religious offenders harshly—the extension of de facto toleration—served not only to defuse religious tensions among residents, but also to maintain civic order and stability in a way that would not attract the attention of outsiders who might interfere with civic autonomy and authority. Of course, all sixteenth-century urban governors were concerned to maintain order and civic authority, particularly during the uncertain years of the Reformation. However, the magistrates of Norwich took what appear to have been some rather unconventional steps to achieve that goal.

-᷇ II ᷄-

The first glimmer of new religious ideas reflected in the city and diocesan records in Norwich comes from a now often-quoted letter written by Bishop Richard Nix of Norwich to William Warham, the Archbishop of Canterbury, in May 1530. A staunch Roman Catholic who would later recognize royal supremacy reluctantly, Nix had a reputation as a tireless crusader against unorthodoxy in his diocese, which covered the counties of Norfolk and Suffolk and a small part of Cambridgeshire.[5] He complained that his diocese was being contaminated by "erroneous books in English," about which "divers saith openly in my diocese that the King's grace would that they should have." The Bishop was particularly concerned that he could not dissuade people in the diocese from their opinion that "the King's pleasure is that the New Testament in English should go forth and men should have it and read it."[6]

Bishop Nix called upon the Archbishop to request the King's attention and speedy action to correct the opinions of certain vocal and erroneous innovators. If they were allowed to continue with their "erroneous opinions," Nix feared, "they shall undo us all." Nix argued timing was crucial, for the majority of his diocese's inhabitants were not yet "greatly infected" by unorthodox beliefs, except for "merchants and such that hath their abiding not far from the sea" and clerical graduates of Gonville Hall, Cambridge, who "savoreth of the frying pan though they speak never so holy."[7] Although the Bishop did not mention Norwich by name, he may very well have had his episcopal city in mind when referring to merchants and others who lived near the sea, as Norwich was the major mercantile center in East Anglia. Nix's letter highlights the destabilizing nature of the early Reformation. As some provincial inhabitants tried to justify the circulation and reading of the vernacular New Testament by claiming it was the King's will, the Bishop found that he had lost his power to convince them otherwise. Consequently, the religious changes of the early Reformation created crises for local ecclesiastical authorities who, when pressed, would be tempted to call for outside intervention.

Nothing came of Nix's call for royal assistance in stamping out the vernacular New Testament in the diocese, and no one in the episcopal city of Norwich was prosecuted in connection with the Bishop's complaint. Perhaps the lack of action by Church and Crown was partly due to the fact that, just two months later, Henry charged Nix and several other prominent clergymen with *praemunire* for having aided Cardinal Wolsey in the use of his legatine powers.[8] By the end of the year, the King had indicted the entire English clergy on a similar charge. As the power of the ecclesiastical hierarchy came under increasing attack, the line between orthodoxy and heresy became more uncertain, creating greater potential for conflict and upheaval that would draw in secular, as well as religious, authorities.

Norwich's mayor and aldermen did become involved in the well-known 1531 case of the itinerant preacher Thomas Bilney. Bilney was born in Norfolk and rose to some prominence as a reformer while at Cambridge. He was influenced by Lutheran doctrines, although modern historians agree that he was neither a Protestant nor particularly heretical by contemporary standards.[9] In 1527, after a preaching tour that began in Norfolk, of which there are no records in Norwich, he was tried in London before Wolsey, Warham and Bishops Tunstall of London, West of Ely, Fisher of Rochester and Nix of Norwich. Convicted of heresy, he was held in the Tower for almost a year and then released by Wolsey. He took up preaching again, inveighing in his sermons against the invocation of saints and veneration of images, violating the prohibition against preaching without episcopal license handed down at his 1527 trial.[10] He also reputedly gave a copy of Tyndale's New Testament to Katherine Manne, an anchoress at the Dominican friary in Norwich. He was arrested again in 1531 in Norwich by the Bishop's officers and convicted as a relapsed heretic by Norwich Chancellor Thomas Pelles. The ecclesiastical court then turned him over to city authorities for execution, as prescribed by the heresy statutes.[11]

Although much of the celebrity surrounding Bilney's case derived from the highly conflicting eyewitness accounts of his trial and execution, it is clear that Norwich civic officials and the politics of state were already intertwined at his trial. As mayor Edward Rede was later forced to admit in his examination before Lord Chancellor Sir Thomas More, Bilney appealed at his trial to the authority of Henry VIII to adjudicate his case in the King's new capacity as Supreme Head of the Church in England. While certain onlookers reportedly shouted, "Mr. Mayor, you are bound to take him away," Rede asked Pelles to explain the meaning of the King's new title, since the Chancellor had been present at the Convocation of the Clergy that had conceded it earlier in the year.[12]

From the evidence of Bilney's trial it seems residents of Norwich were following events in London. They certainly harbored some distaste for the local ecclesiastical authorities persecuting Bilney, with whom they had quarreled so often in the past. Bilney's manner also earned him some personal support and his ideas, which he had preached in Norwich in the past, must have attracted at least some supporters.[13] Whatever the magistrates' feelings about Bilney's reformist ideas, they now found themselves caught up in the heightening battle between Church and Crown. On the execution of his sentence the law was clear; city officials duly put Bilney to death on August 17, 1531.

Mayor Rede and some of the aldermen soon found themselves in a dangerous situation after Bilney's execution when Chancellor Pelles asked the city to put their seal to the recantation read out by Bilney at the stake. When the aldermen perused the document at a meeting at the Guildhall, all—with the possible exception of alderman John Curat, who later told differing stories about the event—agreed that it did not correspond to the speech Bilney made before his death. Instead, the aldermen put the city's seal to a copy of notes taken by Rede at the execution, which did not mention any recantation by Bilney. According to Curat's later testimony before More, the aldermen did this to prepare the mayor to speak at the upcoming Parliament, where Rede would represent Norwich. We know that the mayor sent his account of Bilney's execution and Bilney's prison writings to the Duke of Norfolk.[14]

News of the controversy over whether Bilney recanted soon reached London, prompting Thomas More to launch his investigation into the matter in Star Chamber. More's investigation was unusual, for such inquiries customarily originated with a bill of complaint from outside the Star Chamber.[15] This only served to highlight the increasingly unpredictable behavior of Church and state in what we now understand as the early years of the Henrician Reformation. These were times when local conflicts could be injected into a wider national arena and escalate out of control to the great peril of those involved.

On November 25, 1531, the first day day his testimony before More, Rede stuck by the story that Bilney had not recanted at the stake, delivering to the Star Chamber his written account with the seal of the city. He even went so far as to suggest, in a line of testimony that was later stricken out, that Bilney did not hold the heretical opinions for which he was condemned and thus had nothing to recant. As for alderman Curat, who was already telling More that Bilney had in fact recanted, Rede insisted that Curat initially doubted the veracity of the bill of recantation that Pelles had put before the city government.[16] But, in the face of More's fierce investigation, the once confident Rede began to back away from the account that had been sealed by the city government.

By Rede's second examination on December 1, the mayor was beginning to waffle, saying he thought that the bill of revocation shown to him by Pelles was the one read by Bilney but that he could not be certain. Apparently protecting his townsmen as well as himself, Rede also claimed he received no assistance drafting his own account, except for some prefatory passages whose authors he could no longer remember.[17] At his third and final examination on December 5, Rede was in fairly full retreat. In addition to claiming lack of memory on a number of crucial points, he admitted that he witnessed the revocation Bilney wrote before his execution and then handed to Chancellor Pelles. This admission confirmed that Bilney had recanted and was exactly what More wanted. It was at this interview that Rede also confessed that he did not act on Bilney's request to be placed in the King's jurisdiction. Not surprisingly, More and his court trumpeted the veracity of Bilney's recantation as a triumph of the true faith.[18]

In his biography of Thomas More, Richard Marius suggests that in examining Edward Rede, the Lord Chancellor "very probably threatened the unfortunate mayor with the same fire that had consumed the subject of the investigation."[19] By intimating that Chancellor Pelles dissembled and denying that Bilney—a convicted, burned and reputedly repentant heretic—held no erroneous opinions, mayor Rede must have been flirting with a heresy charge himself. If so, then Rede may have managed to save himself and some townsmen as he equivocated and lost his memory. Perhaps this was why the line of testimony in which Rede doubted Bilney's heresy was stricken from the record of his first deposition. The dangerous line Rede and the aldermen walked could only have been made clearer when Sir Thomas More's conflicts with Henry VIII led to his resignation in 1532 and his execution three years later.

⊰ III ⊱

It is impossible to know the full extent of influence of early reformers such as Thomas Bilney in Norwich. Some people responded positively to the Henrician Reformation and to Protestant reformers such as the former Carmelite friar John Barret,
who joined the Cathedral staff in the mid-1530's. But early Protestant reformers who preached in Norwich, as Barret and others
would find, had their detractors also. The citizens of Norwich
were divided about religious change in the early sixteenth century and, as city records show, they periodically clashed over
these differences. The available evidence indicates that city leaders also held varying religious views after about 1530.

Except when specific individuals in Norwich were contestants
in the religious disputes that revealed their spiritual beliefs, it is
difficult to identify residents' religious proclivities. One might
expect that since the aldermen were the elite of the city, their religious views were the most likely to be recorded. But this was
generally not the case. Because none left writings and their official records rarely noted disagreements among them about religion, wills are the only surviving personal documents from
which their religious sentiments may be detected.

Seventeen aldermanic wills survive that were written between
1530 and Henry VIII's death in January 1547.[20] These can, with
some important qualifications, be sorted simply into traditional
and nontraditional categories. Traditional wills typically included invocations to the Virgin and saints in the preamble and
provisions for Masses to be said for the soul of the testator after
death. In the sixteenth century, some English testators began to
break from traditional forms by making no mention of saints and
Masses. A few went so far as to renounce the traditional Catholic
doctrine of works in favor of salvation by faith, a clear indication
that the testator had embraced some type of religious reform.
However, the analysis of wills is fraught with difficulties. Wills
were legal documents often composed by scriveners or clerics, so
they tended to be formulaic and potentially expressed the relig-

ious convictions of the scribe as much as the testator. In addition, since wills were proved in ecclesiastical courts, the public reading of unconventional ones could raise the fear of persecution. Even when testators seem to openly display their religious beliefs in preambles, there can be no way to know when or how many times a testator might have modified religious beliefs. It would also be a mistake for modern historians to think the wills can be cleanly divided into Protestant and Catholic categories, since the boundaries between religious camps were not fully formed during Henry VIII's reign.[21]

Even though there are problems involved in analyzing wills, those of Norwich aldermen during Henry's reign still offer some insight into magisterial religious sentiments. Fifteen of the surviving seventeen wills written between 1530 and Henry VIII's death in 1547 fit the pattern of traditional wills by calling on the intercession of the saints and/or bequeathing money for Masses. For example, Robert Hemmyng's will, written and proved in April 1541, committed his soul to "Almighty God, to Our Blessed Lady Saint Mary Virgin Saint, Saint Margaret mine advow and to all the holy company of heaven." Like five other aldermen who wrote wills during this period, Hemmyng's called upon a specific patron saint, in his case, St. Margaret. His will also provided money for "an honest secular priest" to sing and pray for his soul, and those of his parents, friends and benefactors for a year after his death. Nine other aldermen made similar provisions.[22]

Two wills did not fit the traditional pattern because they neither invoked the saints nor bequeathed money for anniversary Masses. Alderman William Rogers, who penned a will in 1542 that was proved in 1553, opened his testament with a long preamble in which he committed his soul to Christ alone and renounced "all my good works" as well, a clear rejection of traditional religion. He also left behind a sum of money for a preacher who would give sermons in and around Norwich for five years following his death while receiving room and board from Rogers's widow, Katherine. Alderman John Trace died in 1544, shortly after drafting a will in which he tendered his soul to Christ and left no money for Masses. However, he did leave a sum for sermons to be preached around the city for two years after his death. Among those who witnessed Trace's will was the ex-Carmelite and early Protestant John Barret.

Admittedly fragmentary and difficult to interpret, the evidence from the surviving magisterial wills written between 1530 and 1547 shows a religiously divided, although predominantly traditional, group.[23] Two aldermen wrote unconventional wills, only one of which reflected a discernibly Protestant theology in its reference to the doctrine of justification by faith alone. The great majority of the wills lay well within the Catholic tradition of seeking the intercession of saints and securing prayers for their souls after death. This traditional form, however, also generally fell safely within the scope of the Henrician Reformation, which, while rejecting the Pope and dissolving the monasteries among other changes, accepted the intercession of saints and prayers for the dead except for a brief period between 1536 and 1539. Consequently, the traditional form does not necessarily indicate whether testators held to traditional practices or participated in some of the dramatic Henrician reforms such as the Dissolution of the monasteries. Mayor Edward Rede's traditional will, which included a provision for Masses, is a good example of how such testaments might not completely reflect a testator's religious views. We know that Rede came perilously close to facing heresy charges in 1531 when he questioned whether Thomas Bilney was a heretic.

The religious differences among the aldermen did not prevent them from acting together as a corporation in the 1530's. Neither did the majority's apparently traditional religious leanings keep them from taking advantage of the assault on the Church when they thought they could benefit from it. For example, the Norwich magistrates found an opportunity to try to reverse the most grating aspect of Wolsey's 1524 settlement with the Cathedral priory. This followed upon Parliament's increasing attacks against the Church, the elevation of Thomas Cranmer to the

Archbishopric of Canterbury and Thomas Cromwell's rise to influence in the early 1530's.

At a time when the Cathedral monks could not expect much support from a beleaguered Church, not to mention an antagonistic Crown, the aldermen tried to pressure them into rejoining the city's jurisdiction. In late 1533, members of the city Assembly ceased what appears to have been their custom of attending Sunday sermons at the Cathedral. In January 1534, the mayor informed the Prior that the mayor, aldermen, sheriffs and commonalty would not attend sermons at the Cathedral unless the monks agreed to restore the Cathedral priory to the liberties of the city. Until then, the mayor said the Assemblymen "shall in the meantime repair to the services of the White [Carmelite] friars" in the city, with whom they had a special relationship. The Prior did not consent to these terms so, it appears, the Assemblymen began to attend sermons at the White Friars.[24]

The priory remained a thorn in the city's side until the Dissolution of the monasteries, begun in 1536, reached Norwich in 1538. Alderman Augustine Styward wrote directly to Cromwell in May 1537, on behalf of the corporation, requesting aid in overturning Wolsey's judgment.[25] As the city prepared the case that it would bring before the Privy Council, the King's program of dissolving monasteries took up the problem of Norwich Cathedral. This made it the first monastic cathedral in England to be refounded and converted into a secular community controlled by a Dean and Chapter. In May 1538, the Prior and twenty-one monks and another from outside the Cathedral were dispensed from the monastic Rule and translated into a secular Dean, six prebendaries and sixteen canons. The magistrates dutifully logged a copy of this royal charter in the *Liber Albus*.[26]

In the following year, Styward and Edmund Grey, Norwich's Steward, argued the city's case for the restoration of the Cathedral to its jurisdiction before the Council, which ruled in the corporation's favor. On April 6, 1539, Henry VIII issued letters patent that separated the Cathedral from the county of Norfolk and made it once again a part of the city of Norwich.[27] This was an important victory for the magistrates. It brought the entire area inside the city walls under civic jurisdiction, overturning Wolsey's unsatisfactory 1524 judgment.

While city magistrates were still engaged in their efforts to have the Cathedral returned to civic jurisdiction, they also sought to take advantage of the dissolution of friaries. In August 1538, the house of the Norwich Augustinian friars was dissolved. A week later, after having consulted the Duke of Norfolk, the corporation wrote to Cromwell to request his assistance in securing the house of the Norwich Blackfriars for the city at its surrender.[28] On June 1, 1540, the Blackfriars' house and lands were granted to the citizens of Norwich for £81, which Augustine Styward paid personally.[29]

The magistrates' eagerness to snap up monastic property and take advantage of the Dissolution to regain control over the Cathedral precincts does not necessarily mean they that they were equally enthusiastic about church reform. The disputes with the Cathedral priory, it should be remembered, were of very long standing, predating the Reformation. Some well-known religious conservatives around England, such as the Duke of Norfolk and the Earl of Shrewsbury, also acquired former monastic lands, sometimes claiming they wanted to prevent the lands from falling into the clutches of their religious antagonists as they added property to their patrimony.[30] The religious profile of the Norwich magistracy available from this evidence remains inconclusive.

≒ IV ≒

When compared to other urban ruling groups in Reformation England, the primary reason for the lack of more definitive evidence of the Norwich magistracy's religious leanings becomes clear. In Bristol, London and some Kentish towns, the magistrates tried at various times to impose religious uniformity through the regulation of religious practice, the appointment of sympathetic clerics and the prosecution of religious nonconformists.[31] When magistrates did these things, they made their prevailing religious point of view quite plain. In Norwich, however, the magistrates made no attempt to impose religious uniformity through the regulation of religious practice or the exercise of great concern in the appointment of clergy. Religious nonconformists were prosecuted in Norwich, but in a way that formed a peculiar pattern.

The Norwich magistrates almost never sought to arrest and prosecute religious dissidents, whether they were religious traditionalists opposed to Henrician reforms or advocates of greater reform of the Church. Consequently, few cases involving religious conflict came before the magistrates and nearly all of these resulted from complaints brought by local residents. When the magistrates did examine religious conflicts, they typically punished the accused wrongdoers lightly or not at all. Only once during the reign of Henry VIII did the mayor's court refer a case to diocesan authorities and they rarely notified the central government about local religious trouble. The records of the diocesan courts reveal that Norwich residents were rarely prosecuted there. The authority of Church courts was weakened during the Reformation by Parliamentary statute and, sometimes, by confusion over exactly what conformity to enforce.[32] Furthermore, diocesan courts often depended upon civil authorities to identify cases for their consideration, so the Norwich diocese was also effectively deprived of a potentially important investigative arm.

The first case of a religious dispute in which the magistrates became involved happened in June 1534. Alderman Reginald Littleprowe wrote to Cromwell to report on the activities of the rector of Norwich's St. Augustine parish, William Isabells. According to the alderman, one of Isabells's parishioners complained to Norwich's mayor and aldermen about words spoken by the priest from his pulpit and also in private. Although Littleprowe's letter did not detail the priest's words and there are no surviving depositions in the case, it is likely that Isabells's offending remarks included some condemnation of recent royal policy, such as the King's divorce and remarriage in 1533, or his formal acquisition of control over canon law conferred by Parliament in 1534. What-

ever the priest's remarks, they had resulted in his examination
before the mayor and aldermen, his imprisonment in Norwich
and a report to Cromwell. Littleprowe also asked how the priest's
£40 worth of movable goods should be treated, as he was currently languishing in the Norwich jail.[33]

No reply to Littleprowe survives and Professor Elton has explained Cromwell's failure to take any further action in his case
by noting that Isabells's words, whatever they were and however
inflammatory, did not constitute treason under existing statutes.
Isabells escaped serious harm in Norwich as well. He appeared
before the Norwich Quarter Sessions, where he was bound in recognizance to keep the King's peace. He was never called to return to the Quarter Sessions or any other branch of the city government again. Shortly afterwards, Isabells became rector of a
parish outside Norwich, undoubtedly taking his £40 in movables
with him, and died about 1540.[34]

The magistrates also prosecuted those who were perhaps too
exuberant in their desire for religious reform. Over the course of
two sessions of the mayor's court in July 1535, the magistrates
heard complaints against Thomas Myles, a Norwich capper. It is
not clear that they ever arrested Myles and there is no indication
that he was present at the sessions in which accusations were
made against him. Six men, two of whom were fellow cappers,
reported Myles's public criticisms of traditional religious doctrines
and practices. Myles "rebuked the priesthood and spake against
images and saints [and] pilgrimages." He rejected the sacrament
of confirmation, saying, "If I had anymore children they should
not be confirmed," expressed disbelief in the Creed, and asserted
that "Our Lady of Grace and Our Lady of Walsingham were
strong whores and bawdy whores . . . [and] that Saint Peter and
Saint Gregory were knaves." Myles also condemned the Norwich
church hierarchy, calling the Bishop "a blind knave." Even
worse, he declared that "the sacrament of the altar is or was as
much in his cap press as it is . . . in the church" and that "the Sacrament of the altar was as well on the [Norwich] Castle ditch as in
the church."[35]

Myles's remarks placed him squarely outside the mainstream of traditional religion and were so recognized by the six accusers who reported them to the mayor's court. His pronouncements on the "sacrament of the altar" cast doubt on the efficacy of the Mass, the centerpiece of orthodox Catholicism in which lay "the redemption of the world."[36] Myles's comments seemed to reject almost all of the intercessory powers of the Church, not just the intervention of saints and the efficacy of pilgrimages and images, which would be vital to traditionalists, but also the role of priests and the special sanctity of church buildings. This put Myles's beliefs well beyond the bounds of the Henrician Reformation. Despite this, the mayor and aldermen appear to have taken no action against him. No judgment was recorded in the court book and his name never appeared in connection with this incident again.

The records offer no insight into the mayor's and aldermen's decision not to act against Myles after hearing the statements against him. They might not have taken his remarks very seriously because he was alleged to be drunk when making some of them. However, they treated the next case concerning controversial religious remarks that they encountered in the same fashion.

In November 1535 William Thakker, a Norwich marble worker, appeared in the mayor's court. Before the assembled magistrates Thakker declared "that a cartload of bread shall or cannot stop the mouths of them that hath called Mr. Dr. Barret apostate and worse within the city."[37] "Mr. Dr. Barret" was John Barret, then a divinity lecturer at Norwich Cathedral, where Thakker probably heard him preach an offending sermon. Barret was a close friend of the Protestant reformer John Bale and has been credited with playing an influential role in Bale's conversion.[38] Thakker further told the magistrates that "certain preachers at London hath been plucked out of the pulpit for making of their sermons," which he said he could prove. It appears Thakker felt it necessary to prod the magistrates to act by warning them that if they failed to do so, angry residents would take matters into their own hands. Nevertheless, the mayor and aldermen took no action against Barret and Thakker's name disappears from the record. Furthermore, John Barret remained in Norwich for the rest of his life and there is no indication that his sermons were ever forcibly halted.[39]

Not all entries in the court books concerning religious conflict were so opaque; judgments were recorded in some. In May 1536, for example, the court examined one Gilmyn, a surgeon, "concerning the having of books suspected," giving credence to the late Bishop Nix's anxiety about the circulation of proscribed books in his diocese. Although the record did not name the books found in Gilmyn's possession, it is likely that they were religious works. Unorthodox religious books were seen as a potent source of heretical infection and in some places their possession could have serious consequences.[40] In the case against the surgeon Gilmyn, however, there is no indication that Norwich magistrates attempted to learn the provenance of the books or sought to confiscate them. Neither did they inform religious authorities about the case. Rather, after having questioned Gilmyn, the mayor and aldermen decided that "upon trust of amendment" he should be "set at large."[41]

The next case in the mayor's court that involved religion also had its outcome noted. In September 1537, Harry Niker "confesseth" to the mayor and aldermen that on the previous Saturday, "being one of [the] ember days," he "and Roger Angell did break their fast at one John Sterylyng's house with bread and butter and herring broiled." The three men consumed more broiled herring on the following day at a fourth man's home. Fasting on the ember days, which fell once in each of the four liturgical seasons, was obligatory, so the consumption of broiled herring and butter during those times was "contrary to the ordinance of the holy church," as the court record observed.[42] The mayor and aldermen committed Niker to prison for this infraction, probably for brief duration since nothing further was recorded in the case.[43]

The Henrician Church never eliminated fasting entirely and did not abrogate a Lenten fast until 1538 nor the fasts on the feasts of St. Mark and St. Lawrence until 1541.[44] Still, the Ten Articles of 1536, intended to resolve questions of doctrine and practice, decreed that the Church's "laudable customs, rites and ceremonies be not to be contemned and cast away," but instructed that "none of these ceremonies have power to remit sin, but only to stir and lift up our minds unto God, by whom only our sins be forgiven. . . ."[45] Not surprisingly, there had been rumors before the promulgation of the Ten Articles that they would include a denial of the efficacy of fasting. Confusion about religious rituals and practices likely increased when, in 1537, Cromwell called on the House of Lords to discuss the validity of "any articles or doctrine not contained in the Scripture, but approved only by continuance of time and old custom."[46]

The disregard of fasts might have reflected the influence of reformed teaching, especially that of a Lutheran bent. It is also possible that Niker and his companions had never been particularly observant Christians; in the tense and confusing religious atmosphere it could sometimes be difficult to differentiate between a lapse in practice and a deliberate rejection of authorized ceremony. Indeed, the diocesan courts of Norwich and Winchester had reduced their once vigorous investigations of such infractions to the imposition of simple penances.[47] In this light, it seems curious that the magistrates punished Niker at all, more so since it appears he freely confessed his transgression without protestation. And it is peculiar, too, that the magistrates did not prosecute any of Niker's three fellow offenders. Perhaps Niker had antagonized the magistrates in some other way.

Challenges to the old order could not easily be contained and attempts, such as the Ten Articles, to resolve all of the outstanding questions about belief and practice were only followed by more controversy. The third article reiterated the necessity of the sacrament of penance, and committed "all bishops and preachers" to instruct the people "that they ought and must certainly believe that the words of absolution pronounced by the priest be spoken by authority given to him by Christ in the Gospel."[48] In Norwich, the butcher Robert Coly complained to the mayor's

court in February 1538 that fellow butcher Geoffrey Rede had declared that "if he had been with [twenty] men he would not be
shriven of [i.e. confessed by] none priest." Furthermore, according
to Coly, Rede said that if he had "stolen an horse I would not be
shriven of a priest for I had as lief be shriven of a plowman. . . ."
Geoffrey Rede denied these were his words. On the contrary, he
maintained, that "if he were in necessity and need he might be
shriven of a plowman as well as of a priest," but Coly was apparently not mollified by Rede's concession. The mayor and aldermen decided to send both depositions to "Mr. Godsalve," by
whom they probably meant Thomas Godsalve, the diocesan registrar to Bishop William Rugge. There is no indication why the
magistrates chose this course of action rather than disciplining
Rede themselves. No more word was recorded by the mayor's
court concerning Rede's religious views. He did, however, go on
to lead a long and fairly prosperous life, punctuated by several
appearances before the court as a representative of the butcher's
guild.[49]

The magistrates' last prosecution of a religious offender before
the passage of the Six Articles of 1539 concerned a local priest
named Thomas Wells, apparently arrested and brought to prison
in January 1538 by a city constable who had found a seditious bill
in his chamber. Another Norwich priest, John Neel, told the
magistrates that Agnes Cooper "brought to him a bill containing
misbehaviors and sedition," and told him that Wells had sent it to
her. The mayor's court did not record or summarize the content
of the bill, but decided that Wells be "remitted to prison until he
find surety to be of good behavior and bearing." No amount was
stipulated for his bond and the court book never recorded its re-
ceipt. Nevertheless, he clearly was not held in prison long, for he
continued in his post as the parson of St. Margaret Westwick until 1544.[50]

John Neel appeared before the Norwich magistrates again in
June 1538, this time as the subject of an unusual investigation. For
reasons that are not entirely clear, the magistrates heard testimony from two aldermen and the suffragan Bishop of Thetford.

They then apparently decided to send the deponents to testify in Thetford at the Norwich Assizes, a circuit court with royal commission to hold sessions twice a year in each county. Sometime in 1538, perhaps about this time, Professor Elton tells us that Neel was arrested on suspicion of treason and bound to appear before the King and Council, but then "he disappears from the record."[51]

Much is irregular about the depositions, both as concerns their content and the way in which they were recorded. Many words and phrases were stricken out and replaced with others throughout the depositions. And sometime after the depositions were given the entire record was crossed out, seemingly in the same clerk's pen. The testimony was odd in that it began with alderman Nicholas Sywhat's recollections of an encounter with Neel four years previously, after Sywhat had returned from London on the eve of Parliament's rejection of papal supremacy. In the first version of the story, Sywhat said that he was telling Neel and another priest, Doctor Buckingham, while all were in the church of St. Michael Coslany, about the impending royal supremacy. Neel reacted by saying that "this is a new thing, it will not last long; the King will not live [for]ever." Part of this was then stricken in the record and replaced by another version that had Sywhat talking only with Buckingham before Neel overheard them and injected his opinion about the royal supremacy.

The second deponent, suffragan Bishop of Thetford John Salisbury, told of a more recent encounter with Neel. Salisbury had attended a sermon at Norwich Cathedral during Pentecost week, where one Doctor Giles had preached favorably on the royal supremacy and the need to resist the usurped authority of the Bishop of Rome, as well as on the correct worship of saints and the abrogation of certain holy days. Salisbury said he heard Neel grumble "they then liest" in response to the sermon. Also confirming Neel's words was city alderman Thomas Codde, who had been in close proximity to him during Giles's sermon.[52]

Neel's fate remains a mystery. He disappears from the Norwich records as well as from the records of the King's Bench used by Elton. The Norwich magistrates' actions are equally difficult to determine. Higher clergy typically did not testify in the mayor's court. Salisbury's association with Thetford suggests, perhaps, that he went before the mayor's court to inform the magistrates of proceedings already under way and vouch for the charges pending against Neel. We do know that Salisbury, after an early bout with a heresy charge while a student at Oxford, became an eager conformist to successive religious regimes, from his promotion under Cromwell to Mary to Elizabeth.[53] It is possible that his presence before the magistrates compelled them to put their recollections of Neel's blunt opinions on record. Notably, no proceedings against Neel had ever been taken before. Looked at from this perspective, the deletions and replacements of words and phrases in the depositions indicate that the magistrates must have been quite concerned about their expression in this matter. While some of the corrections seem minor, the rearrangement of Sywhat's story went so far as to deny effectively even a conversational relationship with Neel. And, in the end, when the clerk crossed out the entire entry, it is tempting to think that the magistrates wanted to wash their hands of the whole matter and expunge it from their official records. There is no evidence that any deponents or depositions ever found their way to Thetford.

There was another case in which the magistrates were clearly made to act by an outside authority. In 1535, Edmund Harcocke, the Prior of the Norwich Blackfriars, delivered a sermon in which he came perilously close to denouncing the royal supremacy. News of the Prior's words reached Cromwell through the Prior of King's Langley. Cromwell then directed Sir Roger Townsend, a member of the Norfolk bench, to arrest the friar. When Sir Roger arrived in Norwich, mayor Augustine Styward struck a deal with him that was clearly intended to keep the central authorities distant from religious controversy in the city: Harcocke would remain in the city and Styward would guarantee his availability to Cromwell indefinitely. Sir Roger accepted the proposition, as Cromwell must have, and Harcocke survived his imprudent sermon and remained Prior for another three years.

Harcocke got into trouble a second time, as Professor Elton tells us. In 1537, the Bishop of Rochester, formerly the Provincial of the Blackfriars, complained to Cromwell about Harcocke's seditious preaching and alleged sexual impropriety. Elton's research in the State Papers does not show "what happened next, but Harcocke may at last have lost the immunity which attended him in 1535; by 1538 another man was Prior of the house. Perhaps he was deposed, perhaps he died; people did, after all, even without assistance from the government." In this case the local records show conclusively that Elton was right. We still do not know what happened to Harcocke in 1538 or after the dissolution of the Blackfriars, because the Norwich city and diocesan records contain no reference to him at this time. In fact, no proceedings had ever been taken against Harcocke in the Norwich city courts. However, Harcocke resurfaced in Norwich in Mary's reign as the rector of the parish of St. Michael Coslany, remained a free man and died peacefully in the early years of Elizabeth's reign.[54]

⊰ V ⊱

The pattern of refraining from vigorous prosecution of religious offenders found in the mayor's court book becomes quite striking after 1539, when Parliament's Act of the Six Articles prescribed harsh penalties for six religious offenses. Hanging or life imprisonment was now warranted for denying the efficacy of auricular confession and votive Masses, questioning the imperative of clerical celibacy and chastity to God, and asserting the necessity of communion both kinds. The sixth offense, denying transubstantiation, was punishable by burning. The Act created commissions to seek out and punish religious heterodoxy and also gave broad power of inquiry to a variety of officials, including mayors and sheriffs.[55] While in London, an eager City government led the investigations that resulted in the imprisonment of hundreds of suspected heretics, Norwich city magistrates did not make a single arrest for violations of the Act.[56]

However, three cases concerning religion that fell outside the scope of the Six Articles came before the Norwich mayor's court in the year following the Act's passage. On the eve of Pentecost in 1540, the priest Robert Spurgeon came before the court after having spent the night in the city's jail. Spurgeon had been found in possession of a Mass book from which the name of Thomas Becket had not been stricken although several references to the Pope had been deleted. Thomas Becket's feast day had been abrogated in the purge of the liturgical calendar that had taken place in 1536.[57] A royal proclamation of 1538 that had declared the priest to have been not a saint, but rather "a rebel and traitor to his prince." It seems that Spurgeon stood in violation of that part of the proclamation that dictated that Becket's name was to be "erased and put out of all books. . . ."[58] The priest claimed "that he had the book of the parson of Saint Michael's of Mustowe [at-Plea] [and] that he used it not this quarter of a year." Still, the magistrates intended to bind Spurgeon over to appear before the Norwich Assizes, but allowed a local tailor, John Pettons, to stand surety for him and nothing further is recorded about the case in city records.[59]

In August 1540, two priests and a layman complained to the mayor's court about Bachelor Newman, the priest of one of the wealthiest parishes in city, St. Peter Mancroft. The priest John Kempe told the mayor and aldermen that Newman denounced Protestant reformer Martin Luther, Robert Barnes and Thomas Cromwell, the last two of whom had been recently executed in London. Kempe said he heard Newman proclaim that "Doctor Barnes was an heretic . . . and that Luther and he brought all the heresies into England." As for Cromwell, Newman reportedly said "this great heretic and traitor . . . is dead, which commanded that we should not sense none images," but, he added in a spirit of Christian charity, that he would pray for him. The second priest, Nicholas Thorp, also heard Newman call Barnes "an heretic" and Cromwell "a traitor and a heretic." John White testified that he overheard Newman proclaim in conversation with fellow priest Robert Sexten that "it was never merry in England since the King had such knaves and young boys to his counsel."

The witnesses Kempe, Thorpe and White obviously found all

of Newman's words inflammatory; however, none but the last reported by White could be actionable at that time. Barnes and Cromwell had been put to death by the Crown as heretics and traitors, and Luther never enjoyed immunity in England. Indeed it is to be wondered what recourse Kempe and Thorpe expected as well as why they felt safe in bringing these charges which potentially identified them as Protestant sympathizers and critics of the King's justice. In this sense, their complaints were as potentially dangerous as Newman's alleged denunciation of the King's selection of counsel. From the magistrates' perspective, this was a highly volatile situation during a dangerous time, for the accusations tarnished all parties and threatened to implicate others. In response, the magistrates appear to have taken no action, recording none in the court book and never seeing any of the contestants again.[60]

The third matter the magistrates heard between the passage of the Six Articles and Henry VIII's death came before them in the spring of 1546. The mayor's court heard the case of Edward Breten, a shoemaker, Alen Gifford and William Grey, all from the Norfolk village of East Bergholt. The three had been sent to the mayor's court for punishment by Sir Roger Townsend, the Norfolk gentleman who, at Cromwell's bidding a decade before, involved the magistrates in action against the Blackfriar Edmund Harcocke. Townsend was in Norwich Cathedral while on a visit to the city when he heard Breten "openly read upon the Bible" to Gifford and Grey, contrary to the 1543 Act for the Advancement of True Religion, which prohibited women and the lower orders from reading the Bible.[61] Once again forced to act by Sir Roger, the magistrates held them in prison until their court appearance. The magistrates heard them "confesseth the matter and thereupon they are dismissed out of prison whereunto they were committed."[62]

During the years in which the Six Articles provoked a vigorous assault against Protestantism and heterodoxy across England, the only instance in which the magistrates of Norwich imprisoned anyone for a religious offense took place at the insistence and un-

der the watchful eye of Sir Roger Townsend, a Norfolk country
gentleman. In that case, a lowly shoemaker and his two friends,
all from a village fifty miles outside Norwich, were briefly imprisoned for Bible reading. The other two cases involved prelates
who longed for the old order, one indiscreet in denouncing the
King's executed counsel and the other unlucky in having his un-
expurgated Mass book discovered by an unsympathetic observer.
The priest who flirted with criticism of the King was let go and
the admirer of Becket was also released upon finding surety for
good behavior. The magistrates were clearly reluctant to punish
religious offenses harshly or even to hear them, no matter whether they stemmed from traditional or reformist heterodoxies.

The magistrates' lack of action did not reflect a lack of continuing religious division and conflict in Norwich. Rather, the
magistrates repeatedly defused and deflected religious tensions
before they escalated. This was not satisfactory to everyone in
Norwich, as demonstrated by the continued complaints lodged
by residents. It may not have been fully satisfactory to the Norwich diocesan authorities either, since they were led by a Bishop
with conservative leanings. However, the diocese prosecuted
only one offender in Norwich in connection with the Six Articles
during these years. In December 1540, they detained Thomas
Walpole in Norwich for circulating "a naughty book made by
[German Lutheran] Philip Melancthon against the King's acts of
Christian religion," by which they meant Melancthon's letter arguing against the Six Articles. Walpole was dispatched to London, where he confessed to his crime, implicated others outside
Norwich in the dissemination of the seditious epistle and was
committed to the Fleet.[63]

Another account of religious persecution in Norwich comes to
us from the Protestant reformer John Bale, an ex-Carmelite of the
Norwich house whose conversion was accompanied by his marriage around 1536. He had fled to the Continent with his family
in 1540 after the passage of the Six Articles and the executions of
Thomas Cromwell and Robert Barnes. Bale's polemical and colorful *The Actes of Englyshe Votaryes*, a book that gave "unchaste ex-

amples" from the history of English monasticism, told the story of his wife's detention in Norwich.

In 1545, Bale's wife, Dorothy, visited Norwich to attend to her son, who was apprenticed "to one which was neither honest nor godly." She was apprehended by a "cruel" Justice and "wicked" mayor, namely Norwich's Steward John Corbet and Robert Rugge, who was the Norwich Bishop's brother. According to Bale, they "imprisoned a faithful woman, and sought to put her to most shameful and cruel death, having none other matter against her but only she had been the wife of a priest, which had been (well bestowed) a preacher among them." The "false justice" and "frantic" mayor "laid unto her charge both felony and treason." They questioned her about her marriage, belief in the sacrament, and then, "to bring her into more deep danger of death," they called her husband's beliefs "erroneous, heretical, and seditious doctrine." But she was saved from further harm because, according to Bale, "God in conclusion provided a learned lawyer and a righteous judge for her deliverance."[64]

No mention of Dorothy Bale appears in the Norwich city records, so it does not seem that she was ever formally charged or tried for any offense. However, John Bale's correct identification of mayor Rugge and Steward Corbet lends some credence to the story.[65] Despite Bale's hyperbole, perhaps in this case the product of his own legitimate fear for his life, and his polemical desire to discredit the institution of clerical celibacy, something probably did happen to his wife. Some evidence suggests both Corbet, a prominent local gentleman, and mayor Rugge probably held conservative religious views, making them likely candidates to be upset by Dorothy Bale's presence in Norwich.[66] While there was no prosecution or appearance before the mayor's court, perhaps Corbet and Rugge harassed her on their own. As was so often the case in Norwich, everyone seems to have gone their way in the end. Dorothy Bale returned safely to her husband in exile.

⊰ VI ⊱

As the example of Dorothy Bale's adventures in Norwich highlights, certain magistrates might have held strong religious convictions even if the magistracy as a whole tended to avoid intervention in religious conflict. Like the city they governed, the magistrates were divided in their religious sentiments and allegiances. Unlike the magistrates who seem to have maintained a unified front in the face of division, the city's laity and clergy tried to resolve some of their religious conflicts by bringing complaints that often could have escalated to charges of heresy.

The complaints filed both by and against religious conservatives and those who seemed to favor reform demonstrate that emergent religious divisions were intolerable to many residents. These changes were confusing, too, as can be seen in cases such as that of Bachelor Newman, who was brought into court in 1540 by two clergymen upset that Newman called Luther and the executed Thomas Cromwell and Robert Barnes heretics and traitors. In this time of rapid religious change and retrenchment, even clergy could not always grasp the shape of the established Church. Furthermore, the royal supremacy made heresy and treason impossible to unravel. Thus, Cromwell, who was condemned as a heretic, could easily become "a traitor and a heretic" in Bachelor Newman's eyes, and so too could many others be labeled whose religious views did not conform with the established Church of the moment.

In the face of the dangers posed by the Reformation, the Norwich magistrates acted in a peculiar way. The evidence from city records shows that they did not attempt to impose religious homogeneity. They did not seek out the religiously unorthodox, avoided prosecutions for religious offenses when they could and punished those offenses lightly when they punished them at all. From this pattern, which, as will be seen, continued throughout the Reformation era, it is difficult not to conclude that the magistrates deliberately abstained from taking decisive action in religious disputes.

The magistrates' restraint in handling religious tensions may well have served to defuse them before conflicts escalated out of control. This did not happen in other towns, where magistrates fell into open controversy over religion by sponsoring specific preachers, engaging in heresy hunts and raising the stakes of the game by punishing nonconformists severely. While the evidence of the Norwich magistrates' actions is clear, the sources do not speak expressly to their motives. But there is good reason to believe that the Norwich magistrates better appreciated than most the dangers posed by the religious and political divisions of the Reformation. They had seen Thomas Bilney burnt as a heretic and then mayor Edward Rede almost face heresy charges himself for defending him. Two-thirds of the aldermen in 1534 were serving in city government in 1524 when Cardinal Wolsey dictated the settlement that took the Cathedral and its precincts out of Norwich's jurisdiction.[67] And the city's *Liber Albus*, a living history updated during this period, would have reminded all of them of the perils and consequences of factional dispute.

3

Symbolism Without Saints

THE REINVENTION OF CIVIC RITUAL

The impact of the Reformation was not limited in Norwich, or elsewhere, to conflict over the doctrinal position of the Church or the devotions of individual laymen and clergy. Nor was the religious turmoil of the period the only problem confronting England's cities and towns. As Norwich's magistrates endeavored to cope with turmoil over the changing posture of the Church, controversial sermons, illicit Bible reading and imputations of treason, they were also beset by contemporaneous economic dislocations and the broader ramifications of religious change. This was particularly true for the city's public culture, which was thrown into crisis by the combination of economic pressures and the Reformation's assault on traditional ritual.

In pre-Reformation Norwich, the rounds of pageants, plays, processions and feasts celebrated on holy days were an integral part of the civic calendar that displayed and actualized the social and political structure in the city. The mayor and aldermen, members of the occupational guilds and institutions of the Church became visible as corporate bodies on these days that brought large numbers of people together from across urban social strata and the countryside. By participating in these rituals, they honored God, the saints and the Church while also cementing the bonds of civic institutions. Not unimportantly, the preparations for these celebrations, the fairs that sometimes accompanied them and the opportunity to provision large numbers of visitors often gave the city's economy a boost. However, economic changes in the early sixteenth century also made the financial support of plays, pageants and processions more burdensome for guilds and civic leaders. It was against this background that the official Reformation under Henry VIII suppressed or altered many of the traditional rituals that composed public culture in England's cities, towns and villages.

Some urban historians, most prominently Charles Phythian-Adams, have argued that the official Reformation's elimination of numerous feast days represented a "release from the burdens of pageantry" for the inhabitants of England's cities and towns. Civic ceremony, they maintain, had become too expensive, too constraining and too much of an illusion for many of the guild members and local officials who funded them.[1] As with A. G. Dickens's functionalist explanation of the Reformation's necessity, these urban historians seem to argue that since traditional civic ritual was swept away it must have been untenable.[2] Phythian-Adams, for example, "traces the manner in which the images and the realities of late medieval urban community finally contradicted each other," laying the groundwork for the demise of an "ideal of community" in the early Reformation that was "already irrelevant." He concludes that the new, more open, "pluralistic" and rational society emerging in Coventry had "lost many of the advantages of medieval community life in the process of change, but it had also cast off its shackles."[3]

In contrast, revisionist historians of the Reformation have argued for the great popularity of the confraternities and occupational guilds that were the locus of vital ceremony and pageantry across late medieval England. The suppression of holy days, they conclude, was imposed on a population well served by traditional religion. Consequently, many clergy and laity resisted reform of the Church and continued to observe the abrogated days in breach of official mandates. Eamon Duffy, for example, found "many clergy continued to announce the abrogated days, or celebrated them with ostentation, like the parish priest of Rye, who kept 'high and holy in the church' the feasts of St. Anne, the

Transfiguration, and the Holy Name, with 'solemn singing, procession, decking of the churches.'" Duffy also recounts the Bishop of Exeter's 1539 "admonition to the clergy of his diocese complaining not only of the people's continued observance of the abrogated days, but of the widespread abstention from work from noon on the eves of feast days, and the observance by fishermen, blacksmiths, and other craftsmen of the feast days of their occupational patrons, a practice which had of course been implicitly condemned by the Ten Articles [of 1536]."[4]

Despite their differences, revisionist historians of the Reformation and the urban historians who chart the demise of late medieval ritual culture all agree that the Reformation era's streamlining of the ritual calendar caused dislocation and conflict. The revisionists emphasize the open conflict and dissension provoked by Henrician reform of the liturgical calendar. Urban historians of the type considered here paint a gloomy portrait of sixteenth-century English towns, depicting the end of traditional ritual as part of a general crisis that attenuated urban cultural dominance.[5]

However, the course of ritual life in Norwich does not conform to any of the patterns outlined by these urban historians and Reformation revisionists. Guild members and civic leaders did not cling to the old celebrations in steadfast opposition to official reform, nor did they jettison them simply to rid themselves of a financially oppressive dimension of urban residence. They did not reject traditional ceremony out of reformed religious enthusiasm and there is no evidence of open conflict about the public performance of ritual celebrations among the magistrates or the populace until the reign of Edward VI. To understand the history of ritual life in Norwich, it is necessary to realize that late medieval public ceremony produced meanings and functioned in ways that were not entirely religious, as the revisionists would have it, nor was it just a representation of a false ideal of community, as Phythian-Adams maintains. In early Reformation Norwich, the ceremonial calendar was not so much simplified as a result of official change as it was reworked and reinvented. As economic and religious difficulties afflicted the city, Norwich magistrates searched for means by which they might support the local economy, their own authority and civic order.

The revival of old rituals, the reinvention of others and the addition of new observances that highlighted temporal events, rather than traditional religious ones, provided a way to strengthen the economy and preserve local order and magisterial authority. The city's reinvented public culture was not based on unity in religion, in keeping with the magistrates' practice of not imposing religious homogeneity. Instead, the new civic rituals allowed Norwich residents to come together to celebrate the civic body and the triumphs of Tudor government with little or no reference to traditional religious doctrines and practices.

⊰ II ⊱

On the eve of the Reformation, Norwich magistrates had reason to worry about the condition of the local economy and its impact on city inhabitants. The early sixteenth century saw a number of bad harvests and there were riots over high grain prices in some English towns. In 1520, grain prices reached an eighty-year high in Norwich.[6] Bad harvests returned at the end of the decade in 1527, 1528 and 1529.[7] Local records also reveal that grain was scarce in the city again in 1532. Compounding the difficulties caused by food shortages were dislocations in England's textile industry, which employed a significant proportion of Norwich's freemen in the sixteenth century.

After disruptions caused by Henry's 1528 threat to declare war against Emperor Charles V, foreign exports of Norwich worsteds revived, fluctuating between 1,000 and 3,000 cloths annually in the early 1530's. After 1535, however, the export trade in textiles dwindled, affecting the chain of producers from shepherds in the countryside to shearmen, spinners and weavers in the city, up to the merchants who participated in overseas trade. Cloth exports steadily declined until, by 1561, only thirty-eight cloths left the city for the Continent.[8] Increased competition from foreign producers contributed to the decline of Norwich's major export commodity. So too did the period's great currency inflation as well as the economic and diplomatic costs of Henry VIII's many foreign military conflicts, which adversely gripped England's economy as a whole.

Like the leaders of other early modern towns, Norwich's leaders moved proactively to alleviate economic distress, especially grain shortages, and preserve order.[9] In 1521, they began the accumulation of a stock of grain to be sold in the city in an effort to circumvent discontent over high prices. The mayor and aldermen reacted to another bad harvest in September 1527 by arranging for the provision of grain to be sold in the city market at a set price. But their attempts were not sufficient to prevent disturbances. A 1527 entry in the "Mayor's Book," a manuscript chronicle of the city's history that was begun and presented to the corporation in 1526 by alderman Augustine Styward and updated into the nineteenth century, notes that "this year was so great a scarceness of corn about Christmas, that the commons of the city were ready to rise upon the rich men."[10] The disruption of the textile trade due to the threat of war in the following year apparently did cause some local disturbance, precipitating action to restore order by the Duke of Norfolk.[11]

When grain was again scarce in 1532, the mayor and aldermen ordered a search of the city early in the year to establish available quantities and also arranged to supply the market with grain to be sold at a set price. In July of that year, the city Assembly took a further step to ensure that grain would be available to "the poor people" by prohibiting tradesmen—"common victualler[s] . . . common bakers, brewers of ale or brewers of beer, oatmeal makers [and] innkeepers"—from buying any grain in the Norwich marketplace.[12] Despite these attempts, unrest over grain prices soon erupted.

On July 20, St. Margaret's day, a group of women commandeered a cartload of wheat brought for sale by a woman from Conisford ward in the city. They proceeded to sell the wheat at 4s. per comb, which was below the 4s. 8d. price that the magistrates had set during the dearth of 1527. One woman gave money from the sales to a friend asking that it be delivered to John Rede, a city sergeant-at-mace monitoring the market, for "she thought if she had put it in her purse it should have been [considered] stolen."[13] Eleven women were brought before the mayor's court in early August for causing this "late insurrection." They were convicted of "selling of divers men's corns against their wills and setting of prices thereof at their own minds contrary to such prices as the mayor of the city had set before that time." The court sentenced the members of the group, except for one who was infirm, to be "tied at the cart's tail and whipped surely with whips round about the market"—a harsh penalty compared to what was typically meted out to the religious offenders discussed in the previous chapter. They reduced that penalty for six to payment of a fine, but the remaining four appear to have been whipped in the market, as per their sentence.[14]

The magistrates probably punished these women so severely because of the nature of their offense. Not only had they flouted the authority of the mayor and aldermen to set grain prices, but the fact that they took the solution of the grain shortage into their own hands must have been a serious insult to the competence and responsibility of the ruling elite. Nevertheless, the magistrates did recognize the particular economic distress of women as they had when they took action to stabilize grain prices. Later, in December 1532, the Assembly passed an ordinance designed to promote employment among the many poor women who had been forced into begging by the seasonal decline in spinning yarns. The Assembly decreed that between the "feast of All Saints" on November 1, and the annual spring sheepshearing, Norwich butchers would now be compelled to sell their mutton skins to "poor women" exclusively during morning market hours. White leather workers, glovers and lacemakers would have to wait until the afternoon to make their purchases.[15]

Although the magistrates had some ready traditional means of alleviating and coping with economic distress, their efforts were no more than partially successful. Complaints about the city's economy continued to come in along with threats to magisterial rule. In 1537, for example, Bernard Utberd openly lamented his recent purchase of the city's freedom; he pointed to the way in which "the guild hall is so ordered" to explain his desire "to have my money again in my purse."[16] That same year, weaver John Cokke confided to a friend that only an uprising would remedy the poverty that left him unable to satisfy the subsidy collector. The magistrates took Cokke into custody and sent his deposition to London, something they rarely did in cases of religious conflict.[17]

The contrast between the magistrates' handling of economic troubles and religious disputes is noteworthy. While the state of the city's economy set residents on edge and sometimes led them to challenge magisterial authority and competence, Norwich's magistrates managed to contain religious dissension more effectively and with less open conflict between themselves and city inhabitants. This is all the more remarkable because the urban economy and religious life were not mutually exclusive spheres. They overlapped, together with city politics, in the organization of the occupational guilds and the occasions for fairs, pageants and celebrations.

⊰ III ⊱

The guilds and magistrates of Norwich felt the increasing burden of supporting feast days when the city economy faltered in the later 1520's, much as leading urban historians such as Charles Phythian-Adams have argued.[18] The economic problem, however, was not so simple, nor was it separate from politics and religion. Magistrates and the guilds did not just jump at opportunities to suspend traditional celebrations. In fact, during the hard times on the eve and through early years of the Reformation, they actually took pains to revive a lapsed festivity and expand another. Even when the official Reformation proscribed a number of traditional ceremonies and weakened others, Norwich magistrates looked for ways to reinvent them, redirecting their practice toward civic ends.

In September 1527, just a week before the magistrates would arrange for the provision of grain to alleviate the effects of a bad harvest, St. Luke's guild (a craft guild composed of pewterers, braziers, plumbers and other occupations) complained to the Norwich Assembly about its responsibility for the annual Whit Monday and Tuesday pageants during Pentecost week. The guild's petition rehearsed how St. Luke's alone among the city's guilds presented "many and divers disguisings and pageants, as well of the lives and martyrdoms of divers and many holy saints, as also many other light and feigned figures and pictures of other persons and beasts." These pageants were "sore coveted, especially by the people of the country." The arrival of so many people in the city, the guild's members hastened to remind Assembly members, effected a dramatic increase in sales of goods and services, "more at that time than any other time of year . . . to the great relief, succor, aid, and comfort of the said citizens and inhabitants." The spectacle thus edified the residents of Norwich and their rural neighbors by presenting scenes from the lives and martyrdoms of saints, while boosting the local economy at the same time.

As instructive and profitable as the Whit Monday pageants were for the city, however, the members of St. Luke's claimed that the costs associated with them were proving ruinous to the guild. They were so "sore charged with reparations, and finding and setting forth of the said pageants and disguisings" that "the said guild is almost fully decayed, and not like in none wise but to remain in decay." The petition concluded with the request that the Assembly "enact, ordain and establish . . . that every occupation within the said city may yearly at the procession upon Monday in Pentecost Week set forth one pageant." Such an order would "be to the worship of the said city, profit of the citizens and inhabitants in the same, and also to the great sustentation, comfort and relief, as well of the said guild and brethren of the same."[19]

The Assembly responded to St. Luke's petition favorably, decreeing that "every occupation within the said city shall yearly from thenceforth find and set forth in the said procession one such pageant as shall be assigned and appointed by Master Mayor and his brethren aldermen as more plainly appeareth in a book thereof made." A list of those pageants was recorded, probably around 1530, in the city's "Old Free Book."[20] It is not clear whether the list represents an expansion in the total number of pageants performed on Whit Monday—twelve were recorded—or an increase in the number of crafts participating in their production. But the list does indicate that the Assembly assigned pageants to the city's various crafts and that they were, in all likelihood, being performed.[21]

City leaders' interest in the economic rewards of civic pageantry is also evident in their treatment of the feast of St. Mary Magdalen, which fell annually on July 22. Magdalen Hospital, just outside the city gates, held a fair and religious services on this saint's day, its annual dedication feast. At a meeting of the city Assembly in December 1532, the same day on which members passed the ordinance mandating the sale of mutton skins to poor women, they also lamented that the "old, ancient and laudable" celebration of St. Mary Magdalen's day in Norwich "hath been discontinued." In the past, through "all the time whereof the remembrance of man is not had to the contrary," the mayor, sheriffs and aldermen put on the city's armor and rode together to the fair "in harness."[22]

There are no extant records concerning the magistrates' participation in St. Mary Magdalen's day proceedings before 1532. We do know that Magdalen Hospital was decisively removed from civic jurisdiction during the tumultuous factionalism of 1443.[23] The corporation probably ceased its customary riding in armor to the fair at that time. If so, the years before 1443 were the ones from which "the remembrance of man is not had to the contrary," marking a corporate horizon of memory more than a century old. Whether they were remembering an old ritual practice or, quite possibly, creating a new one, they decided to reinvent the traditions of St. Mary Magdalen's day celebrations.[24]

On the next St. Mary Magdalen's day and all those after, the

Assembly decreed that the governors of Norwich should celebrate the feast as of old. The aldermen and sheriffs, dressed in
harness, as custom dictated, would wait upon the mayor at his
home. Together they would all ride to the fair, stopping at St.
Mary Magdalen's chapel for a service. Then they were to proceed
to the "wrestling place," an area constructed for exhibitions of
military ability "at the cost and charge of the said mayor." Finally, the group was to return to the city. Any mayor who failed
to comply with this new ordinance would be fined £10. Only rain,
other "troublous weather," or some other impediment approved
by six "substantial commoners" would prove sufficient reason to
cancel any future celebration.[25]

Interpreting the magistrates' reasons for reviving and reinventing their celebration of the feast of St. Mary Magdalen provides a good illustration of the multiple meanings and uses of
ritual in early modern towns. Obviously, the day itself was dedicated to the memory of the saint and this would be further
marked by the city rulers' devotions and offerings at her chapel.
But it would be a mistake to see the celebration of the saint's day
solely in those narrowly religious terms. The magistrates themselves expressly argued that in the past, their procession led to
"the great laud, praise and worship of the said city," as well as
producing "the great aid, succor and comfort of poor handi-
craftsmen" hired to clean and repair the harness. These, no
doubt, were effects the magistrates hoped to produce again during a time of economic downturn and social turmoil. It also seems
reasonable to think that the magistrates must have contemplated
this ritual within the context of their century-long jurisdictional
disputes. Riding out together in military regalia to Magdalen
Hospital, taken away from the corporation during the magistracy's nadir of political division, would be a powerful symbolic
statement of their continuing claim to the suburb.

This reinvention of the celebration of St. Mary Magdalen's feast
proved short-lived despite the Assembly's intention to commemorate it "forevermore." St. Mary Magdalen's day was one of
the numerous holy days abrogated in 1536 when Henry VIII

moved in the direction of Thomas Cromwell and other reformers who held that salvation came through faith alone and not through "works," such as the observance of saints' feasts.[26] The Ten Articles, Convocation's restriction of saints' days and the Injunctions, all of 1536, opened the official Reformation's attack on traditional doctrines and practices of the Church, including the belief in the intercessory powers of saints which lay at the foundation of so many feast days.

Tracing the unfolding of official policy on the worship of saints through the 1536 articles and Injunctions allows us to see the multiple sides of reaction against traditional religious rituals. The Ten Articles, issued by the King as Supreme Head of the Church, insisted on the subordination of saints to God, thereby limiting their powers and the expectations that Christians should place upon them. The Convocation of the Clergy under Henry then drastically curtailed the number of saints' days by consolidating the many parish dedication feasts onto a single day and by prohibiting the celebration of patron saints' days from interfering with work. Furthermore, Convocation decried the idleness and disorder that too often accompanied the celebrations of church feasts and the reduction of holy days also was intended to limit the number of occasions on which the important work of bringing in the harvest was laid aside. Royal Injunctions to the clergy reinforced "the abrogation of certain superfluous holy days" and reiterated the Ten Articles' limitations of pilgrimages and prayers to saints' images, relics and shrines. The Injunctions prohibited the celebration of all holy days except for the feasts of the Apostles, the Blessed Virgin, St. George, the Nativity, Easter, St. John the Baptist and St. Michael the Archangel. They also reminded clergy that unrestrained worship of the saints diverted Christians from pleasing "God more by the true exercising of their bodily labor, travail or occupation."[27]

Like the magistrates' in Norwich, Henry's attitude toward traditional ritual combined religious and economic considerations, but in rather different ways. The King, of course, unlike the Norwich magistrates, who did not seek religious uniformity, was engaged in theological and institutional reform of the English Church. The King's and Cromwell's conceptions of the intersection of religious and economic considerations were different, too. They juxtaposed a general command to labor and good order against the undisciplined celebrations on saints' days. As Convocation put it, the multiplication of feast days was "not only prejudicial to the common weal, by reason that it is occasion as well of much sloth and idleness, the very nurse of thieves, vagabonds, and divers other unthriftiness and inconveniences . . . but also pernicious to the souls of many men, who, being enticed by the licentious vacation and liberty of those holy days, do upon the same commonly use and practice more excess, riot, and superfluity, then upon any other days."[28] In contrast, the Norwich Assembly was sometimes concerned with the cost of putting on pageants, but they were even more interested in ritual celebrations' contributions to the city's economy and their own prestige.

Despite the clarity of royal Injunctions, the Norwich magistrates were reluctant to abandon their recently reconstructed observance of St. Mary Magdalen's day. The city chamberlains' records for 1537–38 list payments for the construction of a booth at Magdalen fair.[29] It was not until mid-July 1539 that we know for sure that the reputedly traditional celebration of St. Mary Magdalen's day had come to an end in Norwich. An Assembly meeting then noted that no "citizen shall go to Magdalen fair in harness for the consideration of the King's grace have commanded all his true and loving subjects as they will have his gracious favor and avoid his high displeasure that no man shall solemnize nor hallow the day of Mary Magdalen, but that they shall and may do all manner of good and lawful work according to his gracious commandment."[30]

Still unwilling to forsake the civic ritual that featured city rulers parading on horseback in armor, Assembly members took steps to reinvent the ceremony yet again. They established a similar festival that would be celebrated in the religiously less suspect Pentecost week, thereby divorcing it from the feast of St. Mary Magdalen and the fair at the Hospital. By this time, Norwich Cathedral had been translated and the city had received royal letters patent returning the long-disputed Cathedral precincts and lands to its jurisdiction.[31] It was no longer necessary for the magistrates to stake a symbolic claim by riding out to Magdalen Hospital and, of course, there would be no more stopping for devotions at the chapel since the religious basis for the ritual had been removed. Instead, the city leaders would carry out a "like watch within the said city to be ordered in such wise as the mayor and his brethren aldermen shall think most convenient and seeming for the honor and worship and defense of the same."[32]

From a holy feast day ritual that honored a saint and also served economic and political purposes, the magistrates' procession in armor became a wholly secular civic occasion within the city walls. Although St. Mary Magdalen's day was one of the three abrogated feast days Henry officially reinstated to the liturgical calendar in 1541, it was never again celebrated in Norwich.[33] The new "watch" in Pentecost week served to enhance the image of the city's ruling group, symbolizing military strength and cohesion. In 1541–42, rather than restoring the original saint's day, the corporation invested money from the city treasury to improve the "wrestling place" and construct spectator areas, suggesting that the magistrates continued to take advantage of the opportunity to display their martial authority.[34]

A pattern of emphasizing civic dimensions of ritual can also be detected in the history of the feast of Corpus Christi in Norwich. The feast of Corpus Christi, celebrating the Eucharist, survived the purge of holy days in 1536 because the Henrician Reformation did not openly challenge the doctrine of transubstantiation that lay at the heart of the Mass.[35] And so the ritual observance of Corpus Christi day in Norwich appears to have continued in its late fifteenth-century form through the early 1540's.[36]

The earliest reference to the celebration of Corpus Christi day in Norwich comes from the 1389 returns made to the Chancery from the Norwich Guild of the Assumption and another unnamed confraternity that might have been the priests' Corpus

Christi guild. Both were associated with the college of secular priests at the church of St. Mary in the Fields. An entry in the "Old Free Book," most likely from 1449, the year the city issued extensive ordinances regulating the craft guilds, listed the sequence of crafts and civic officials in the Corpus Christi day procession. We know from this document that the procession ended at the church of St. Mary in the Fields, which had also been used for civic assemblies in the early fifteenth century before the completion of the city's own Guildhall. The Host, surrounded by light-bearers, headed the procession and thirty-one crafts followed in precise hierarchical order, each bearing a banner. The mayor, sheriffs and aldermen came last, carrying either a book or rosary beads.[37] It is not entirely clear whether the inclusion of the crafts and corporation in the celebration marked an innovation. But, following so soon upon the crises earlier in the decade, the magistrates' concern for the display of civic order and unity on this important religious feast is manifest.

Corpus Christi's combined spiritual and civic functions persisted into the sixteenth century until about 1543, when the magistrates acted on their own to reorganize the celebration. An ordinance composed that year codified a new sequence in which the craft guilds would march and also noted that the procession should now to advance "from the Common Hall by Cutlerrowe about the Market by Holter and so directly [back] to the said Hall."[38] Although Corpus Christi was still celebrated in mostly the traditional fashion, the focus of its elaborate procession was no longer a religious site—the church of St. Mary in the Fields—but a civic one. The Common (or New) Hall was the former house of the Blackfriars, acquired by the corporation in 1540 and since then used as a meeting place for craft guilds, a storehouse for grain and a venue for companies of travelling players.[39] The magistrates also converted the monastic church's choir into St. John's chapel, but there is no indication that the Corpus Christi procession entered the chapel. The close connection between city and Church made so visible by the old procession's path to the Church in the Fields had been considerably muted. Where the procession formerly ended at a college for secular priests, now it reached its finale at a city-owned building with a city-maintained chapel.

The 1543 revision of the Corpus Christi day celebration appears related to a reorganization of the guilds ordered by the city Assembly at about the same time.[40] These reforms also involved use of the Common Hall as a new center for many guild activities. Unlike their counterparts in London, none of the occupational guilds in Norwich had their own halls. It is not known where most held their feasts and meetings prior to the Reformation. Extant records reveal that on at least one occasion the grocers' guild held an assembly at the Guildhall. Religious services on the guilds' annual days appear to have been held at a number of religious sites around the city, including the Cathedral, Carrow priory, the house of the Blackfriars, the colleges of secular priests and St. Michael's chapel, a suburban nonparochial chapel.[41] In addition, as the ordinance of 1543 noted, the guilds "have not hitherto grown or risen any profit or commodity either to the politic body of this city or to the corporations of fellowships of any of the said crafts or occupations, for that there hath not been had nor used hitherto any profit, order nor rule among the brethren and sisters of the same fraternities and fellowships."[42]

The magistrates sought to correct a number of faults involving the election of guild officers, the maintenance of apprentices and the performance of religious services, such as the failure to light candles on guild days and attend funeral diriges and Masses. This perceived laxity in performing religious duties might have partially resulted from the 1536 reduction of holy days and restrictions on traditional religious practices, which would have eliminated the days on which guilds formerly held their annual feasts. In addition, a second set of royal Injunctions, issued in 1538, sharply curtailed the use of candles, although a proclamation issued by the King later that year sanctioned their use "before the Corpus Christi" and at Candlemas ceremonies.[43] Except for the abrogated holy days many traditional religious practices were tolerated again after the passage of the Six Articles of

1539. Unfortunately, there are few surviving records for Norwich guilds and none that offer insight into their inner workings at this time.[44] It seems likely that guild members were divided in their religious sentiments just as the magistrates were. We do know that the economic troubles of the period taxed some guilds' ability to perform public pageants, but there are no specific sources on wider guild activities. Nevertheless, guild practices continued to be unsatisfactory in the eyes of the magistrates in 1543, leading them to attempt to regularize guild practices.

The 1543 ordinances called upon each craft to hold its annual feast and meeting at the Common Hall. In place of meeting on the old patron saints' days, which had been prohibited since 1536, the Assembly now stipulated new days for the performance of guild services and elections. The magistrates consolidated the guild days by assigning groups of crafts to worship, feast and elect new officers together on the same days, most often on specific Sundays falling after Trinity.[45] Religious services on the guild days were to be held at St. John's chapel at the Common Hall, according to "certain godly orders and rules to and for the maintenance of divine service."[46] They also ordered that the crafts use the chapel for the funeral diriges and Masses celebrated for their members.

To staff St. John's chapel, the corporation had hired and maintained the priest John Kempe since March 1541. This was the same John Kempe who had complained to the mayor's court in November 1540 that Bachelor Newman, the priest of St. Peter Mancroft, had called Martin Luther, Robert Barnes and Thomas Cromwell heretics—a likely indication that Kempe harbored reforming sympathies. All crafts were now required to help maintain the Common Hall priest. While the guilds were therefore compelled to support Kempe, who remained the chapel's priest until Mary's reign, the 1543 ordinances' injunction to light candles might well have helped to mitigate any hard feelings about the employment of a likely Protestant.[47] There is, in any case, no record of complaints or questions from the guilds about either instruction.

By making the Common Hall the locus of important civic rituals such as Corpus Christi day and the occupational guild days, all of these celebrations came to have a larger civic dimension. Robert Tittler has argued that many of the town halls acquired by urban communities, often in the wake of the Dissolution, operated not only as administrative centers, but also as the "'tangible formulation' of the notion of civic authority."[48] While Tittler is mainly concerned with towns that were newly incorporated in the sixteenth century and whose new ruling groups were eager to distinguish themselves from a former seigneurial authority, much in his argument has merit for the case of a newly acquired civic building in an established community like Norwich, which had a longer tradition of self-government. The Common Hall was an imposing building, considerably larger than the city's Guildhall, the seat of municipal government.[49] The former friary also stood closer to the geographic center of Norwich, although the Guildhall overlooked the city marketplace, always a center of activity. The corporation's takeover of the Blackfriars' house thus gave local authorities an added and weighty presence in the city, especially when civic ritual was redirected there and away from traditional religious centers.

⊰ IV ⊱

Although economic difficulties sometimes led to the cancellation of a celebration in a given year, guilds' complaints about the cost of pageantry were virtually routine and, as Ronald Hutton has correctly observed, no "municipality before the Reformation deal[t] with economic pressures by abolishing a single ceremony."[50] Such abolitions only occurred when the centrally directed Henrician Reformation abrogated most holy days, including the patron saints' days that craft guilds typically celebrated. As we have seen, however, the abolition of holy days did not necessarily entail the eradication of all the various rituals performed on them. Late medieval and early Reformation rituals changed over time and served multiple purposes for different groups.[51] If the Henrician Reformation spurred the Norwich magistrates and guilds to end some celebrations and reinvent others, this was not just a case of provincial reaction to innovations imposed by a dominant central government that defined the meaning of all ritual observance. We know that communities around England responded very differently to the changes emanating from the central government, so local contexts must have always played some role in shaping ritual observances. In between the dictates of the central government and the powerful meanings derived from religion, the pattern of evidence suggests that Norwich magistrates had their own agenda regarding civic ritual.

Not only did the Norwich magistrates reinvent certain rituals in response to official proscription, they also took it wholly upon themselves to invent new ceremonial occasions that had not existed before. New ceremonials were invented in other towns as well, but the flurry of such activity in Norwich appears to have been unmatched. The kinds of new ceremonies introduced in early Reformation Norwich would only become widespread in England during the Elizabethan period, highlighting the importance of studying ritual in local context.[52]

The first new ceremony in Norwich took place in October 1537, when the city held a splendid triumph to mark the birth of Prince Edward, Henry VIII's long-awaited male heir. The celebration featured cannon fire, paid for by the corporation, and pageants performed by the grocers' and tailors' guilds, perhaps the same ones used on Corpus Christi.[53] Such a festivity was not a regular feature of public culture in Tudor Norwich. Members of the royal family were grandly feted when they visited the city, as Henry VII was in 1486 and 1490, and as Henry VIII's sister and brother-in-law, the Duke and Duchess of Suffolk, were in 1515.[54] But their birthdays had not before been the subject of a public festival in the city. Nor was Prince Edward's birth the occasion of many similar celebrations around England, as happy an occasion as it was. Henry VIII's pursuit of a legitimate male successor was a decade old in 1537. Edward's birth would hopefully secure a peaceful succession for England on Henry's death and, equally important, the survival of the House of Tudor. At court, Henry himself launched a series of triumphs and banquets to celebrate the delivery of his son.[55] But there is no evidence that England's major towns, besides Norwich, mounted spectacles in recognition of the birth of the future King.[56]

In the years following Edward's birth, Henry returned his attention to foreign affairs and his military engagements provided the corporation of Norwich with new occasions for ceremonial activity. In 1542, the King renewed hostilities against the Scots. The damage English forces inflicted on the Scots, combined with the fallout from the unexpected death of King James V, resulted in the Treaty of Greenwich, signed in July 1543. It included a proviso for the marriage of Prince Edward and the infant Queen Mary, meant to unite the crowns of England and Scotland in the future. But the Scots were slow to implement the terms of the treaty and in December 1543 went as far as to annul it. Henry responded by dispatching a military force led by Edward Seymour, Earl of Hertford and maternal uncle to Prince Edward, to Scotland. In May 1544, Seymour sacked the capital city of Edinburgh and the port of Leith with efficient ruthlessness. By that time, however, Henry had become involved in another military entanglement, wrongly believing that matters in Scotland had been concluded. The King entered into an alliance with Emperor Charles V early in 1543 for a joint invasion of England's old enemy, France. The Emperor also committed to defend the English King against attacks by any temporal princes. Henry landed at Calais in July 1544 and began a siege of Boulogne shortly afterwards. The city surrendered to him in September, but the victory was dampened by the news that the Emperor had come to terms with the French, leaving Henry to face them—and the recalcitrant Scots—alone.[57]

It does not appear that Henry celebrated his accomplishments abroad with triumphs and banquets, as he did at the birth of his son. In Norwich, however, two triumphs are noted in the city records for 1544. The first, held on May 30, was "to have lauds and praisings to almighty God for his [the King's] victory had in Scotland," and specifically honored the sack and burning of Edinburgh and Leith by Edward Seymour.[58] This celebration featured a procession and the corporation paid for bonfires and music performed by the waits, musicians employed by the corporation. A second triumph marked "the obtaining of Boulogne," also with a procession, bonfires and music.[59]

No reason is given in the records why Norwich magistrates chose to commemorate these particular military victories with processions, bonfires and music. The celebrations are especially noteworthy because on May 17, two weeks before the Scottish triumph, the mayor's court had canceled the annual Whit Monday observance.[60] The mayor and aldermen cited the cost incurred by the city in furnishing men for the King's wars, paying its MP's and "other urgent causes apparent" in their decision to suspend the pageants "for ease of poor people" in the city.[61] The two Norwich triumphs are also interesting because the raids on Edinburgh and Leith and the capture of Boulogne do not appear to have been the cause of widespread celebrations in many other English towns.[62] The surrender of Boulogne was marked by a triumph in Plymouth, but that West Country town had endured recurrent raids originating from the French port, making the celebration there more understandable.[63] Norwich, situated in East Anglia, never faced any such danger.

Nevertheless, the French town's fall to the English and the despoliation of Edinburgh and Leith, were exploits that all in Norwich could cheerfully applaud. While foreign affairs certainly had a religious dimension in the 1540's, satisfaction over defeats wreaked on England's traditional enemies was not the sole preserve of religious reformers or conservatives, or those in between. At a time when religion remained a contentious issue in Norwich and the local economy was in some disarray, military victories at Edinburgh, Leith and Boulogne were uncontroversial subjects for public celebration.

Norwich's magistrates seized another such opportunity when Henry signed a treaty with the French at Ardres in the summer of

1546 that ended the war upon which he had embarked in conjunction with his erstwhile ally, the Emperor. By the terms of that
agreement, England would keep Boulogne until 1554, when
France would pay £600,000 for its return. Henry would again receive his annual pension of £35,000 from King Francis, the payment of which had been suspended in 1534. As Professor Guy has
pointed out, this arrangement was not as advantageous as it first
appeared, given that Henry had already spent over £1 million on
the siege and garrisoning of the city. The total sum spent on the
French and Scottish campaigns was over £2 million. To meet
those exorbitant costs, Henry imposed heavy taxes, collected
forced loans, sold monastic lands still in his possession, borrowed
on the Antwerp money market and debased English coinage.[64]
The last measure was particularly immiserating, driving prices
up to nearly unprecedented levels.[65]

Norwich marked the 1546 Treaty of Ardres with another civic
triumph, apparently alone among English towns.[66] There was
cannon fire and three bonfires were lit, two in the market and one
at Tombland. The city waits performed, as did three minstrels,
professional entertainers who were not employees of civic government. This celebration also coincided with the city's observance of Corpus Christi, layering the recently reinvented Corpus
Christi tradition with an additional coat of civic meaning.[67]

Norwich magistrates' experience with the reconfiguration of
old rituals and the inventions of new ones during the reign of
Henry VIII proved valuable to them during the even more tur-
bulent years of his successor, Edward VI. In February 1547, an
elaborate civic triumph commemorated the new King's corona-
tion. The town of Plymouth was also the site of such a triumph,
although there are no extant details of that celebration.[68] In Norwich, city waits and minstrels performed and spectators saw a
pageant of King Solomon and one of a mermaid, which had been
given to the corporation in 1540 by a local resident. The feasts of
Corpus Christi and St. George were then routinely observed in
the spring. However, in May the magistrates suspended the Whit
Monday pageants again for unknown reasons.[69] By the end of

1547 the new central government, headed by Edward Seymour, now Duke of Somerset and Lord Protector, had outlawed all processions and abolished all intercessory institutions.

As we shall see in the next chapter, the definitively Protestant Reformation under King Edward would produce an increase in religious conflict in Norwich, including in 1548 the first open dispute about a major ritual event, the annual celebration of the feast of St. George. The middle of his reign would also see the corporation of Norwich beset by Robert Kett and his rebels from rural Norfolk, who overran the city in the summer of 1549. The magistrates faced these threats to civic unity, order and autonomy at the very time when traditional ritual culture was being all but destroyed by the Edwardian Reformation. Continuing the practice established during Henry's reign, Norwich's leaders proceeded to reinvent civic rituals when possible and create new ones when needed. After the defeat of Kett's rebels and the restoration of civic government, the Assembly ordered shops to close "from henceforth forever" on August 27 for thanksgiving services held in all the parish churches, creating a new local holiday marked annually for more than a hundred years.[70]

While it is easy to see why Norwich's civic leaders would be eager to give thanks for the defeat of Kett's rebels, their holding of another triumph defies such easy explanation. In 1550, the city celebrated the Treaty of Boulogne, the nadir of sixteenth-century English diplomacy and thus an event that was no cause for celebration anywhere else in England. By terms of that treaty, the Duke of Northumberland, head of royal government after the fall of Protector Somerset in 1549, sought to cut the considerable losses suffered through Somerset's pursuit of an ill-fated foreign policy. England surrendered Boulogne to France, forgoing the £600,000 compensation called for in the Treaty of Ardres. The English also had to remove their troops from Scotland and, consequently, abandon the proposed marriage of Edward VI to Mary, Queen of Scots, that would have secured the union of English and Scottish crowns.[71] The magistrates of Norwich had no special attachment to the terms of the treaty, so one can only sup-

pose that the act of civic celebration had meanings with little relation to the event being honored. The fate of ritual in Reformation Norwich did not follow directly from the decrees of the central authorities or the Supreme Head of the Church of England,
nor did it even always depend upon royal successes in the world
of politics and diplomacy. Instead, Norwich's public culture persisted and changed throughout the period in a process that linked
local problems and imperatives to the wider worlds of state politics, the international economy and the contests of faiths spanning England and the Continent.

❧ 4 ❧

Protestantism Without Purity

CONFESSIONAL DIVISION, CRISIS AND
TOLERATION IN EDWARDIAN NORWICH

The previous chapters have shown how, during the early years of the Reformation, the leaders of Norwich sought to contain the conflicts that were emerging out of religious fragmentation by tolerating religious diversity and sustaining, inventing and reinventing civic ritual. While these measures proved largely successful in defusing local conflicts and deflecting official attention away from matters in Norwich, the risk that religious turmoil could become uncontrollable and result in outside intervention increased markedly during the reign of Edward VI. This chapter will examine and analyze the factors that led to the disruption of civic order and autonomy that the magistrates had worked so hard to build.

The brief reign of Edward VI witnessed the rapid advance of the Reformation. The religious innovations of Edward's government are well known. Images were banned, and Edward's first Parliament overturned the Six Articles, legislation restricting access to the Bible and the heresy statutes, and also suppressed chantries, confraternities and all other intercessory institutions at whose foundation lay the doctrine of purgatory. Many traditional Church ceremonies, such as the use of ashes and holy water, were also prohibited. In addition, Parliament permitted the marriage of priests and passed two Acts of Uniformity in 1549 and 1552, which authorized and imposed the First and Second Books of

Common Prayer, respectively. The Prayer Books provided the English people with Protestant forms of worship. The 1549 Book introduced an English Mass service for the first time, but did not repudiate transubstantiation. The 1552 Prayer Book abolished the Mass altogether, replacing it with a Holy Communion service. The Communion service lost the sacrificial character of the Mass; it was now simply a memorial of Christ's original sacrifice. The doctrine of transubstantiation was rejected and the priest no longer performed the miracle that had been at the heart of the Mass. Christ was present in the Eucharist for believing communicants. Finally, in 1553, Edward gave his assent to the 42 Articles of Faith, which enumerated the key points of religious doctrine. All of these measures served to create an official Protestant church for the first time in England.

In Norwich, the central government's imposition of official Protestantism provoked a variety of responses from residents motivated by varying religious beliefs. Some Protestants engaged in iconoclasm, attacks against church buildings and furniture, ignored traditional fasts, disturbed religious services and dishonored holy objects. While the Edwardian reforms triggered such actions, the King's government did not support or condone them. Attacks on objects and practices still considered holy by the official Church (as well as religious traditionalists) dramatized some Protestants' belief that the Reformation had not gone far enough. On the other hand, Norwich traditionalists vocally expressed their hostility to Protestant preachers in the city, to married clergy and to the innovations imposed on religious worship. Catholics, and some mainstream Protestants, reported on the actions and statements of their radical neighbors.

When these controversies surfaced, the magistrates continued their attempts to mitigate the resulting contention, but that proved an especially difficult strategy during Edward's reign. The changes to religious doctrine and practice imposed by Edward's government solidified and hardened divisions between Protestants and Catholics. Furthermore, Protestantism's call for Christians to read and interpret the Word of God for themselves and to act on their interpretations created a potentially dangerous challenge to traditional authority, secular as well as religious. This was a point raised by contemporary critics of religious reform. In the aftermath of an iconoclastic riot that he witnessed in Portsmouth in 1548, Stephen Gardiner, the Bishop of Winchester, voiced his fear that such activities "containeth an enterprise to subvert religion, and the state of the world with it," pointing to Germany, where attacks against traditional religion in 1525 had led to civil disturbances. Gardiner went on to assert that those who exhibited so little respect for religion, especially the lower orders, would have concomitantly little regard for civil government. He predicted that the destruction of the Church and its liturgy would have profound and deleterious repercussions in the social and political order.[1]

If Gardiner's rhetoric was overblown, embedded as it was in the Reformation era's apocalyptic fears and accusations, he still recognized incipient changes in the nature of authority and obedience which were already challenging the Norwich magistrates. Religious diversity among the magistrates persisted throughout Edward's reign; for example, most of the mayors, at least four of seven during the period, were probably Catholic.[2] However, religious differences among them also increased as they did among the populace of their city. Divisions between the now more explicitly Catholic and Protestant magistrates were further exacerbated by the actions of some radical Protestant dissenters. For the first time, religious differences among city rulers developed into an open conflict, with serious repercussions for the authority and stability of civic rule.

In addition to the increased number of religious cases heard in the mayor's court, the magistrates had to adjudicate cases involving civic officials. For example, five civic officials and four others who had or would occupy civic office were examined in December 1547 for engaging in a fight over holy bread and holy water in the parish church of St. Peter Mancroft. A year later, one of these men, common councilor Andrew Quasshe, led two others in breaking their oath to hold the annual feast for the civic guild of St. George, which had been newly reinvented to satisfy the demands of the Edwardian Church. Quasshe not only broke ranks from the civic elite and disrupted what was arguably their most important annual festivity, but he also compounded this by repeatedly defying magisterial authority and justifying his actions by appealing to "God's word" and the central government.

Although the magistrates managed to ride out this incident, which concluded only with Protector Somerset's intervention, in the aftermath they were beset by accelerating challenges to their authority that were only stopped by the still greater calamity of Kett's rebellion. Kett's rebels were agrarian protesters from rural East Anglia with no initial ax to grind against Norwich. They tried to achieve their primarily economic and political objectives by appealing to royal authority from the encampment they made on Mousehold Heath outside Norwich. When events led them to invade the city, both their occupation of Norwich and the royal forces sent to restore order resulted in the brief, but effective, dissolution of city government.

Despite these challenges, the magistrates quickly reestablished civic rule without wreaking vengeance on residents who had cooperated with or supported Kett. The magistrates only heard a handful of cases involving religious disputes during the last three years of Edward's reign. This perhaps suggests that Norwich's residents might have grown weary of so much conflict. At the same time, the magistrates regained enough composure and sufficient authority to resume handling cases of religious conflict in their typical fashion.

The reign of Edward, albeit brief, threw into sharp relief the threats that the Reformation posed to civic autonomy and authority. Events that unfolded in Norwich during that short time revealed not only the contingent nature of magisterial power, but also the limits of magisterial tolerance. The course of the Reformation in Edwardian Norwich serves as an important reminder that the toleration extended by city magistrates was not the product of a theorized ideal, but a practice that was often unstable.

⊰ II ⊱

Although Henrician religious legislation was not swept away until Edward's first Parliament convened in the fall of 1547, it must have seemed likely to some people that the new government intended some kind of religious innovation. Somerset and the other royal councilors who ruled in King Edward's name were known to favor reform. The Protector had welcomed the Protestant Hugh Latimer into his home in 1539 when Latimer resigned the Bishopric of Worcester to protest the passage of the Six Articles. He also ran a Protestant household and corresponded with Calvin.[3] Thus, in London, the Lenten fast was disregarded in 1547 and scurrilous rhymes lampooned it. During a Mass celebrated at St. Paul's Cathedral, one Thomas Dobbe urged the assembled congregation not to offer the customary reverence to the elevated Host at the consecration. Official response to such transgressions gave little comfort to religious conservatives. Dobbe was arrested for his outburst, but the Protector pardoned him. However, Dobbe died in prison before the news reached him.[4] Perhaps it was anticipation of the continuation of such official reaction to violations of traditional religious practice that explains the reappearance of religious conflict as a matter to be considered by Norwich's mayor's court in the spring of 1547.

In May of that year Ralph Gilmyn, who had appeared before the mayor and aldermen in 1536, was there again and confessed to holding unorthodox beliefs about the Eucharist. Gilmyn told the mayor and alderman that "there is not in the sacrament of the altar the very body of our Savior Jesus Christ that was contained in the Virgin Mary; that it is a signification and a commemoration of it." That admission was consistent with testimony given by John Wulf concerning a conversation that Wulf had with Gilmyn the previous day in a local tavern. Gilmyn's renunciation of the real presence was grounds for a death sentence under the terms of the Six Articles, which would not be repealed by Parliament until November. But no harm came to him. The court clerk entered a recognizance into the record for Gilmyn that bound him to good behavior and he was never called before the mayor and aldermen again in relation to that matter.[5]

There are no indications in the court books or in other records of any more religious disturbances in the city until the early fall of 1547. In September the mayor and aldermen discussed and condemned a recent wave of iconoclastic activity in the city, although they provided no details about it. The origins of that disruption could surely be attributed to the Injunctions that had been issued by Edward's government in July. The Injunctions were based and expanded on those of 1538 and had, among other things, prohibited the veneration of images and commanded the destruction of abused ones. While there was opposition to the order in some places, in London it was carried out with such enthusiasm that the mayor and aldermen decided to shut church doors in the City to prevent further loss and destruction.[6] In Norwich, city leaders took no such steps to curtail the problem. Believing that "divers curates and other idle persons" had gone into churches around the city "pulling down images" and then taken those images away, on September 27 they merely called upon Thomas Conyers, the parish priest of St. Martin-at-Palace, and Richard Debney, a Norwich beer brewer, neither of whom appears to have been present, to "surcease of such unlawful doings." At the same court session the beer brewer was the subject of additional testimony. Robert Echard testified how he had recently heard Debney say, one morning at the parish of St. Martin-at-Palace, "we shook on Saturday last past for we were afore Annas, Caiaphus, Herod and Pilate and more knaves than they," but no action appears to have been taken against him.[7]

At the following court session a few days later, the mayor and aldermen took no action when William Tyller reported to the court Edward Greene's comment that "the Bishop of Norwich and Doctor Parker were idols and hypocrites and that the same Parker a blasphemer of the word of God." Bishop Rugge, who had been elevated to Norwich after the death of Richard Nix, was known both for his pastoral ineffectiveness and his antagonism to religious reform. Greene also denounced the future Archbishop of Canterbury, Matthew Parker, a Norwich native and brother of a future city alderman. From 1535 to its dissolution ten years later, Parker had been the Dean of the College of Stoke-by-Clare in Suffolk, which he used, as Diarmaid MacCulloch has shown, as a haven for religious reformers.[8] Parker had recently criticized a sermon preached in one of the city churches by Dr. Henry King, who would be appointed a Cathedral prebendary in 1548. Parker's criticism of King's sermon apparently provoked Greene's anger. The record contains no further information about King or his sermon's content, but evidence from an incident in 1549 suggests that King might have been a reformer.[9] Greene's simultaneous condemnation of Rugge and Parker may suggest that he found the future Archbishop's "gentle version of the reformed faith" insufficiently vigorous and thus saw little difference between him and the traditionalist Bishop. Greene was at the court session and denied the words attributed to him and the case ended there.[10]

In December 1547, the court heard a case concerning the mistreatment of holy bread and water that had taken place at St. Peter Mancroft church. On a recent Sunday "a variance" had erupted among nine parishioners, resulting in their appearance before city magistrates. Five currently occupied positions in civic government: John Bengemyn (common councilor for Mancroft ward), John Blome (common councilor for Mancroft ward), Thomas Elsay (constable for St. Peter petty ward), Andrew Quasshe (common councilor for Mancroft ward), Robert Reynbald (city Chamberlain). The other four either had or would later serve in city office: Robert Barnard, Richard Rudd, Leonard Yonges and John Carre.[11] Some had taken the church's holy bread and water, "casting" and "dealing" them, and the other defendants had taken great offense at the defilement and an altercation ensued. The record does not recount who took which side, but later evidence finds Barnard, Bengeymyn, Quasshe and Yonges involved in or accused of activities that branded them as Protestants.

Such scenes were becoming increasingly common in places

around England where emboldened religious radicals displayed their contempt for the sacrament and other holy objects. To handle holy bread so irreverently and to say that a priest "joggle[d] the water" to make it holy was to reject ostentatiously the sacramental character still attributed to them by the official Church and religious traditionalists alike.[12] After debating a course of action, the mayor and aldermen decided that each of the nine men was simply to "bear his goodwill and favor to others accordingly as God's law."

A tenth man, however, was committed to ward (i.e. to prison) for his role in the incident. Harry Swetman, who never occupied any civic office in Norwich, had not been among those mishandling the sacraments but he had said during the incident, among other things, that "one Sir Thomas Rose which preached at St. Andrew's was a knave." Rose was a priest who had converted to Protestantism in the 1530's and had, according to the martyrologist John Foxe, preached against the Six Articles in Norwich in 1539. He also spent part of Edward's reign near Norwich. Swetman was bound to appear at the next Norwich Sessions, which took place three days later. Two more witnesses gave depositions at that meeting, but Swetman himself was not present and his case never appeared in city records again.[13]

In the first year of Edward's reign then, early religious initiatives from the central government had sparked some contention in Norwich. City leaders were able to defuse those conflicts as they had done in the past by refusing to persecute or punish. But as they were considering the incident of St. Peter Mancroft, important religious legislation was being debated in Parliament, which would ignite a controversy in Norwich that the magistrates were unable to control.

Parliament passed the Chantries Act in December 1547, thereby suppressing all institutions based on the doctrine of purgatory. Orthodox Catholics believed that the souls of the dead lingered in purgatory before attaining their final redemption and that prayers and Masses for those souls decreased their time there. Convinced Protestants denied the existence of purgatory, arguing that it was a human invention with no basis in Scripture. To them, chantries, guilds and other intercessory institutions were superfluous. The Chantries Act's preamble condemned the great "superstition and errors in Christian religion" into which many had fallen "by devising and fantasying vain opinions of purgatory and Masses satisfactory to be done for them which be departed."[14] It dissolved all colleges, free chapels, chantries, fraternities, guilds and all goods and plate belonging to them, dealing a death blow to most of England's remaining traditional religious ritual. The legislation also put a great deal of money into the hands of Protector Somerset's cash-strapped government, which was again prosecuting a war against Scotland. It claimed for the King all lands whose profits had been used to fund a priest in perpetuity or for a term of years, all rents that had been paid to stipendiary priests and all lands and rents that had supported lights, lamps, obits and anniversaries.[15]

The Chantries Act set Easter Sunday 1548 (which fell on April 1) as the date by which all the targeted institutions were to be put down. Commissions were dispatched around the country to survey all chantry possessions. In Norwich, the dismantling of most of the city's intercessory institutions appears to have proceeded without incident. Some chantry endowments were sold, such as the one attached to the parish of St. Michael Coslany. Alderman Richard Catlyn and Edward Warner, a Norfolk gentleman, purchased it in 1548.[16] The city bought the revenues of John Cosyn's and Lettice Payne's chantries, both of which had been founded in the fourteenth century in the church at St. Peter Mancroft.[17] By July 1548 the city Assembly could order that the monies previously belonging to local guilds would be used to clean the river Wensum, which ran through the city.[18]

The magistrates continued to conduct routine business during the initial dissolution of chantries and guilds, which in 1548 included contending with increasing levels of religious discord. In March, three disturbances came to the court's attention. A pair of eager proponents of the Reformation named Dobleday and Derme (or Derne) stood accused of throwing stones at the east window of St. Andrew's church, leaving it "sore broken." The two other cases concerned hostilities expressed against the preacher Thomas Rose, who was the target of verbal abuse, such as that heaped on him by Harry Swetman, and ugly rumors about his personal life. His sermons also inflamed hostility among a number of Norwich residents.

Robert Barman was heard to have declared that "he had rather go to a bear baiting as to Mr. Rose's sermon and that he should find [a hundred] to say the same." Nicholas Waleys testified that Thomas Brygges had lamented "that it was pity that Mr Rose was not hangen when he was [three] days old," words that Richard Bety confirmed. Thomas Brygges might have been the same Thomas Brygges who served as alderman for a year in 1542.[19] Their outbursts reveal that Protestant preaching was not warmly embraced by all in Norwich. The magistrates' response to each of these incidents was characteristic. The iconoclast Derme was committed to prison, although the lack of any further account of this sentence in the court books makes the outcome of his case uncertain. His partner Dobleday paid a fine of 12d. Robert Barman was bound to good behavior, after which his case disappeared from the record. In the case of Thomas Brygges, no outcome of any kind was recorded.[20]

No matter what motivated religious offenders in Norwich—the reforming enthusiasms of Dobleday and Derme or the more traditional outlook of Robert Barman and Thomas Brygges—they received the same type of treatment at the hands of city officials. As the mayor and aldermen decided these cases, they were complying with the terms of the Chantries Act by reorganizing the civic guild devoted to St. George. Guild members fell into open conflict over the process, the only time during the sixteenth-century Reformation that city governors failed to conceal and manage their religious differences.

⊰ III ⊱

The guild of St. George was one of the oldest confraternities in Norwich. The earliest record of its existence is a certificate returned to the Chancery in 1389, which put the foundation date at 1385. The purpose of the guild was to honor its patron saint, venerate God and pray for living and dead members of the fraternity and all men in the King's service. Initially, St. George's did not hold as exalted a position as did another local confraternity, Le Bachelery (also called guild of the Annunciation), but by the sixteenth century it had become the preeminent guild in the city.[21] Many of the guild's activities were indistinguishable from those of other guilds around the city: members gave alms, supported a light, made offerings and participated in various religious services. An exceptional feature of the guild was its membership, as scions of leading county families and eminent ecclesiastics figured prominently. The guild rose to prominence in 1417 when Henry V granted members a charter of incorporation, making St. George's the only fraternity in Norwich to secure one.[22] That charter rendered the guild a permanent body which later assured its survival during the Reformation. St. George's consolidated a dominant position in Norwich in 1452 when it was united to the city government, part of the settlement of the earlier disturbances in Norwich. According to the agreement, each year the outgoing mayor of Norwich would become the alderman, or chief officer, of the guild. All city aldermen were to receive automatic membership in the guild, and the option to join was extended to all common councilors.[23] Hence St. George's guild became an institution barely distinct from the ruling body, although county and ecclesiastical notables continued to be offered membership. The guild's activities thus underscored the inextricable link between the temporal and spiritual spheres before the Reformation.

The high point of the guild's annual activities was the celebration of the feast of its patron saint on April 23, which combined religious services spanning two days, a procession and a feast.[24]

Neither the procession nor the feast was mentioned in the guild return of 1389; they seem to have been incorporated into the guild celebration before the second decade of the fifteenth century. Observances began on the twenty-second, with an evensong service at the Cathedral. On the saint's day there was a splendid procession, only a few details of which are known. Each year the guild selected a member to play the role of the saint and another to portray the dragon. Others, dressed in the guild's livery, carried colorful banners and a cross and were accompanied by two dozen secular priests and four poor men carrying torches. Finally came Norwich's mayor and aldermen clad in their scarlet robes of office. The marchers assembled at the parish church of St. Peter Mancroft and then processed through St. William's Wood in the nearby hamlet of Thorpe St. Andrew on their way to the procession's conclusion at Norwich Cathedral.

At the Cathedral, the guild offered up wax to the High Altar in honor of the Trinity, Our Lady and St. George himself. Then the brethren heard a Mass in honor of the King, St. George and the guild. After these services came the annual dinner, financed by four members of the guild chosen for this purpose each year. Before 1473 the guild dined in the Blackfriars' Hall, and in that year members decided to hold the feast in the hall of the Bishop's palace whenever possible. At the conclusion of the feast, guild members returned to the Cathedral for more prayers. On the following day, there were additional religious services at the Cathedral and at another predetermined location, the election of guild officers for the next year and the conduct of other guild business. The magistrates participated in a ritual heavily imbued with religious meaning.[25]

St. George's day was one of the feasts not purged from England's liturgical calendar in 1536 and so the Norwich guild's annual celebration continued without incident through the end of Henry VIII's reign. The guild should have been suppressed by the terms of the Chantries Act, but it escaped dissolution because of the permanence accorded it by Henry V's charter.[26] It could no longer serve as an institution committed to traditional Roman

Catholic doctrines and practices, however. In March 1548, just before the Act was to take effect, the members of St. George's, most of them associated with Norwich city government, moved to reinvent the guild and its ceremonies along lines that would be acceptable under the new religious regime.

They began by changing the guild's name: the guild minutes for March 16 noted that "this company of the citizens elected into the same from henceforth shall be called and known by the name of the Company and Citizens of St. George, and by none other name."[27] Members rewrote the oath to be sworn by new members, eliminating the reference to the "guild" and substituting the term "company."[28] The members of St. George's also set down new ordinances for the Company that maintained its fundamental structure but omitted all ceremonial elements that were now defined as Catholic in nature. There would be no procession, no prayers for St. George, Our Lady or any departed guild members nor a Mass attended by all of the members. All that was left of the annual celebration was the evensong service the night before, a church service and the annual dinner on the feast day and a service with a sermon and the election of officers on the following day.[29]

It is noteworthy that guild members sought to ensure St. George's continued existence at all, given that the theological foundations of intercessory institutions had been so badly impugned by the Chantries Act. The fact that its members bothered to rewrite the regulations suggests that even in its attenuated form the institution still held some meaning for them. Thus, what remained of the annual observance, the church services, feast and election of officers, represented not only what was legally permissible for the new Company, but perhaps some of also what members cherished most about the celebration. While these changes might have saved the guild and its civic functions, they provoked considerable controversy.

The trouble began when the three members who had been chosen to act as feastmakers for that year—Thomas Quarles, Andrew Quasshe and Richard Tompson—refused to honor that commitment. All three were members of Norwich's common council and thus had voluntarily joined the old guild. Quarles had served the Northern ward since 1542 and Tompson had been a council member for the Northern ward only since 1546. Quasshe had represented Mancroft ward since 1540. He was also one of the nine men involved in the debate over holy bread and water at St. Peter Mancroft in 1547, and so he was no stranger to religious conflict. The fourth and compliant feastmaker was the Wymer ward councilor Thomas Gray, serving in that post since 1543.[30] At first only Quasshe expressed his opposition to holding the feast, appearing before the mayor's court on March 19, where he declared that "for his part he will not perform the same," referring to his responsibility as feastmaker.[31]

At a city Assembly meeting on April 4, Quarles and then Tompson joined with Quasshe in refusing to provide the Company dinner. Initially, only Thomas Quarles voiced his intention to side with Quasshe. But sometime during the meeting, Richard Tompson declared his unwillingness to hold the feast as well. He then retreated from this position, indicated by the fact that his name is stricken through in that portion of the Assembly minutes, before adopting it again once and for all. No reason was given for the three men's resistance. The meeting was a remarkably heated one for Norwich. The Assembly record noted that "[w]hereas the Citizens in this house the time of the Assembly hath heretofore risen up and stand out of order and spoken divers of them together so that any one could not conveniently be heard," and continued that in the future each common councilor who spoke out of turn would forfeit 12d., an alderman 2s. Furthermore, the mayor was given the authority "to compel the offender to pay the same or else to be committed to ward there to remain until it be paid."[32]

At the conclusion of that meeting, the trio were ejected from the Company, dismissed from their posts as civic officials and then stripped of their franchises, which deprived them of political and economic privileges in the city. Tompson's disenfranchisement is recorded separately from Quasshe's and Quarles's, giving further evidence of his initial indecision about refusing to serve as feastmaker: "And afterward [i.e. after Quasshe and Quarles had been disenfranchised] the said Richard Tompson offered himself and desireth before the whole house likewise to be defranchised and discommoned. By reason whereof he shall henceforth accounted and taken as a foreigner." Such wholesale withdrawal of offices and liberties was in accordance with both the former guild and civic regulations.[33]

The matter did not end there. Sometime after Quasshe's disenfranchisement, it seems he engaged one Robert Watson as his lawyer. With two local gentlemen, Sir John Robsart of Syderstone and Sir John Clere of Ormesby, both in Norfolk, Watson brought Quasshe's case to the attention of the Privy Council, hoping that the Protestant Protector Somerset would side with Quasshe and restore his liberties. No direct evidence of this original solicitation survives. It is only referred to in the later correspondence from Somerset to the mayor and aldermen that ultimately concluded the case.[34] It is also not clear when the magistrates first learned of Quasshe's petition to Council, but this news was surely received poorly. In the meantime, the nature of the case compounded because Andrew Quasshe continued to conduct his grocer's business in the city in clear violation of his disenfranchisement.

For his open defiance of the mayor and aldermen, Quasshe was summoned to the mayor's court on April 14, where members rehearsed his, Quarles's and Tompson's offenses. The magistrates reminded Quasshe that he and the other two feastmakers had freely agreed to serve as feastmakers when they were elected. They further emphasized that their noncompliance was contrary to the oath of obedience that they had sworn both before the Company of St. George and before the mayor and his council. Their behavior stood in marked contrast to that of Thomas Gray, whom the record described in civic rather than religious language as a "tractable and obedient citizen" who stood ready to honor his commitment as feastmaker. The magistrates demanded an explanation for Quasshe's actions. Quasshe proclaimed his punishment unjustified and therefore denied the magistrates' authority to impose his disenfranchisement. Nevertheless, the magistrates committed Quasshe "to the free prison of the Guild-hall."[35]

Seeing Quasshe go to jail for practicing his trade without proper liberties, his accomplices Quarles and Tompson submitted themselves to the city Assembly to regain their franchises upon payment of a small fine. Yet, even these proceedings were not without incident. Quarles and Tompson submitted themselves to the Company on April 18, and a few days later to the city Assembly.[36] Their request to have their franchises restored was granted and each one was fined £5, though that amount was promptly reduced to 5s. "by the good consideration of this house." But Tompson evidently balked at the terms at the last moment during the Assembly meeting, which resulted in his imprisonment. His name is crossed off the original entry when he apparently decided that he did not like the terms of the submission. A subsequent entry for the same meeting reads: "Whereas agreement was and is made for Thomas Quarles and Richard Tompson with him and the same Richard is not pleased upon the declaration thereof to him with the same order, it is ordered and decreed by the whole assembly that he be committed to the jail until it be otherwise considered & c."[37]

Reconsidering his position from jail, Tompson returned to the Company on April 22 and to the Assembly on May 3.[38] At the Assembly meeting, he was fined £5, which was then reduced only to 10s., perhaps a penalty for his earlier recalcitrance. This time Tompson was also ordered to bring a quantity of grain to the marketplace to sell to the poor at a discounted price.[39] Quarles and Tompson were readmitted to the Company in time to select the feastmakers for the following year. Both men served again briefly on the common council in the 1550's before disappearing permanently from the list of civic officials.[40]

Six weeks after Quasshe's imprisonment, a longer term than anyone in Norwich seems to have been imprisoned for a religious offense, Robert Watson appeared before the mayor's court arguing for his client's release. He contended that the magistrates' reasons for the initial action against Quasshe were "against God's word." Thus, he went on, "the disobedience of the same law is lawful and the imprisonment of the said Andrew for disobeying the same law is not lawful." Quasshe's and Watson's invocation of "God's word" highlighted the compounding problems of religious and civil authority at the heart of the case. The Protestant emphasis on individual reading of Scripture as the source of knowledge of true faith was here used to justify Quasshe's original objections to the reinvented St. George's Company and thereby invalidate the successive penalties imposed for his defiance of city magistrates. From Quasshe's point of view, this was a religious issue to be decided by a correct understanding of "God's word." For the magistrates, the issue involved the fulfillment of an oath to perform a civic function and then their authority to impose penalties for civil disobedience and practicing a trade illegally. The court now agreed to release Quasshe from prison on the substantial bond of £40 that he not do business in the city.[41]

During Quasshe's incarceration, Watson and his associates must have apprised the Lord Protector of this new state of affairs. On June 4, the mayor's court was read a letter from Somerset to Sir John Robsart voicing his support for the "discharge of his [Quasshe's] imprisonment."[42] The magistrates followed suit, which at this time probably entailed the return of his £40 bond. A month later, on July 7, the mayor's court read a letter sent to them by the Protector, written on June 15.[43] Quasshe was directed to appear at the next Assembly meeting, on July 12, when the letter was read again and entered into city records.[44]

Somerset's letter directed Quasshe to accept his imprisonment "in just part" for his disobedience so that it would not give "example to further misorder." In return, the magistrates were ordered, "in consideration of his acceptance of his punishment herein we will that ye renew to him your favor and restore him to his former franchisement." The Protector also asked the magistrates to declare that they "punished him not for disallowing of any abuse in the said guild, but for the manner of his disallowing." Quasshe "might have secretly declared his mind although

not openly declared his obstinacy." Despite Somerset's endorsement of a "godly and seemly order" that might have appealed to
Quasshe's Protestant sensibilities, he nevertheless elevated the
imperative of government authority over the claims of individual
conscience, no matter how well founded. "Thus," declared Somerset, "would we [want] all others to take example of his disorder
and learn that in a commonwealth no private man may further
withstand a common consent."[45] Like the Norwich magistrates,
Somerset had parceled out the religious elements of the dispute
and subordinated them to the needs of state.

If Somerset and the magistrates saw the Quasshe case primarily as a test of government authority, Quasshe, Quarles and
Tompson almost certainly instigated the matter for spiritual reasons. The available evidence suggests that something about the
new St. George's Company tweaked the feastmakers' Protestant
consciences.[46] Even though the former guild had been purged of
its conspicuously Catholic features, it still contained elements
that Protestants could find objectionable. The new Company remained dedicated to St. George. Its annual celebration, of which
the feast was a part, was still observed according to the Catholic
liturgical calendar, all of which squared poorly with Protestantism's rejection of the saints. Questions concerning feastmaking
for the new Company did not end there. In February 1549, the
four feastmakers chosen for that year were called before the
Company "to know and hear their intents and opinions concerning their election and keeping of the feast, and after much
communication and debating the same cause, it is deferred till a
new day."[47]

There can be little doubt that Quasshe and his defenders harbored a strong commitment to Protestantism. Quasshe's history
of defiling the sacraments, his appeal to "God's word" and his
selection of Robert Watson to represent him in the matter all suggest that his Protestantism was probably of a fairly radical nature.[48] In addition, Quasshe's and Watson's religious sensibilities
are suggested by their turning to the central government for help,

a government whose recent actions had concentrated on undermining Catholic religion in England. Watson was a long-known
and vocal supporter of Protestantism. In 1539, he had challenged
the position on free will expressed by Bishop Rugge in a sermon.
As a result, Watson had come to the attention of Thomas Cromwell, who, intrigued by what appeared to be Watson's "soundly
Protestant view," summoned Watson to court for an interview.
The matter ended with Cromwell writing to the mayor and aldermen of Norwich to recommend him for a position in the city.[49]
Watson and his associate Sir John Clere later fell victim to anti-
Protestant persecution during the reign of Catholic Queen Mary.[50]

Sometime after his liberation from jail, Quasshe rejoined the
Company, but remained a figure of controversy. On July 4, 1548,
a week before his formal submission to the Assembly, he was the
subject of a complaint in the mayor's court. Alderman Richard
Davy told how on the previous Sunday, poor-relief gatherers had
approached Quasshe in the church of St. Peter Mancroft and
asked for a donation. Quasshe asked them how much they
wanted, to which they replied 2d. Quasshe responded by offering
only a penny, "and thereupon contemptuously threw out and
shook his hand, saying, so tell your alderman." The mayor and
aldermen took no action, but Quasshe's retort to the poor-relief
gatherers reveals that his conflict with city government had developed a strongly personal dimension.[51] After several more run-
ins with the mayor's court Quasshe was again disenfranchised
and ejected from St. George's Company in 1551, having "openly
spoken and declared certain unfitting words upon the magistrates of this city." Twice burned, St. George's readmitted him yet
again in 1554, when the restoration of Catholicism under Queen
Mary would have made it easy to exclude a Protestant troublemaker, had its members so desired.[52] Quasshe was reelected to
the common council in 1558, elevated to alderman the following
year and died a respectable citizen in about 1563.[53]

⊰ IV ⊱

The commotion over the new St. George's Company and the conflict over holy bread and water in St. Peter Mancroft shows that religious differences persisted among city leaders in Edward's reign. It also demonstrates that Protestant magistrates were divided over religious issues among themselves as well as being divided from Catholics. Most Protestants among the Company's members were apparently willing to accept the reinvention of the old guild, but Thomas Quarles, Richard Tompson and especially Andrew Quasshe were not.

Some evidence of the religious heterogeneity of city rulers during Edward's reign can also be found in wills, although their analysis in this period presents even greater difficulties than in Henry VIII's reign. Nine city aldermen wrote wills during Edward's reign and another seventeen who served between 1547 and 1553 composed their testaments later in the sixteenth century.[54] As Eamon Duffy has pointed out, Edwardian testators had to take into account the official proscription against traditional religious doctrines and practices, such as Masses for the dead and the veneration of the saints, and wrote their wills accordingly. The omission of saints and intercessory provisions did not necessarily indicate a renunciation of traditional Catholicism, but might rather reflect testators' concerns about the precarious nature of Tudor religious settlements. Many Catholic testators during Edward's reign adopted phrasing that was uncontroversial and would not make their wills likely targets of special scrutiny.[55] Similar problems affect the interpretation of wills written after Edward's short reign, whether under the Catholic Queen Mary or the Protestant Queen Elizabeth. In addition, wills written ten or twenty years after the Edwardian period, spanning one or more dramatic reversals in official religion, might not accurately reflect testators' past spiritual beliefs. For all of wills' shortcomings as accurate evidence of individuals' religious belief, the testaments of Norwich magistrates are nevertheless sufficient to show the continued existence of religious diversity.

The majority of the nine will preambles written during Edward's reign are of completely indeterminate religious affiliation. Four testators committed their souls to God alone, with no mention of the Virgin, saints, Christ or good works. The commitment of a soul to God alone could have been associated with a variety of religious beliefs that remained known only to the testator. A fifth testator did not commit his soul to anyone at all; alderman Henry Dunham began his 1552 will with "I bequeath my soul & c," phrasing that certainly concealed his sentiments. The remaining four will preambles mention Christ, but make no reference to the Virgin or saints. Some historians would classify these testators as likely Protestants. However, as Eamon Duffy has argued, and as a closer look at some of these wills demonstrates, such a conclusion is not always warranted.

Wills sometimes contain bequests that provide clues to religious allegiance. In the nine wills written during Edward's reign, this information offers evidence of religious diversity among the magistrates.[56] Two wills' bequests show commitments to well-known Protestant clergy. Another two reveal continued adherence to traditional Catholic religious practices and objects.

For example, Richard Suckling, who wrote a preamble in September 1551 committing his soul to God alone, also made bequests to known Protestants John Barret and Thomas Rose and two other clergymen to "preach three godly sermons to the edifying of the people." Edmund Wood, who died in 1548 during his mayoral term, left money to Matthew Parker and also to the Common Hall priest John Kempe, but only if another priest, Roger Cockson, did not survive to collect Wood's bequest. These legacies suggest that Wood had embraced Protestantism.

A contrasting example comes from the 1550 will of Felix Puttock, who later died while serving as Norwich's mayor in 1555, during Mary's reign. While Puttock trusted his soul to Christ in the preamble—sometimes taken inadequately at face value as an indication of Protestantism—he then directed his executors, if no heirs survived him, to use his goods "in deeds of piety and charity for my soul, to the most pleasure of God." This indicates traditional Catholic devotion to good works. Thomas Grewe's 1549 will had an indeterminate preamble committing his soul to God, but he also bequeathed to his daughter Alice "a pair of beads of coral with pater nosters silver and gilt." The use of rosary beads had been energetically discouraged by the Church since Edward's accession in its effort to eradicate traditional practices and devotions, so Grewe's willingness to bequeath this proscribed religious article demonstrates an avowal of Catholic faith.[57]

The continued, and perhaps even increased, diversity of religious opinion among the magistrates during Edward's reign did not change their fundamental approach to handling religious conflict in the city. It did, however, sorely tax their abilities, especially after the calamity of the St. George's celebration of 1548. The falling out among the magistrates over the reorganization of the guild of St. George disrupted the ritual life of the city in which they had invested so much effort. More importantly, it exposed religious and political divisions among the magistrates in the form of open conflict and disobedience that could only raise questions about magisterial ability to maintain peace and order.

As Andrew Quasshe languished in jail and then was released on the Protector's orders, the magistrates tried to cope with accelerating religious strife in the city. In May 1548, alderman Thomas Grewe accused the butcher Thomas Toly in the mayor's court of declaring "that we have a popish priest and if he [Toly] might have two more with him he would pull the popish priest out of his fool's coat." Toly was also in court and confessed to the words attributed to him. He was bound over to appear again before the court but was never called.[58]

This case was an unusual one in that a Norwich alderman acted as a witness against a religious offender and is worth a closer examination for that reason. It is not possible to know what motivated Toly's tirade—aversion to a certain priest, a more general dislike of the priesthood rooted in a commitment to Protestantism or something else—for there is not sufficient information in the record. Nor is it possible to know why Thomas Grewe took the uncommon step of testifying in a case concerning religion before his colleagues. Perhaps Grewe sought to protect the reputation of a local Protestant priest whom he felt that Toly had maligned as "popish." Given that Grewe would draft a will revealing Catholic sympathies less than a year after this incident, such a possibility seems remote.

A more plausible explanation is that Grewe wanted to see Toly punished for vilifying a conservative priest whose beliefs Grewe shared. Perhaps Andrew Quasshe's recent and dramatic strong stand on Protestant religious principle encouraged Grewe to make a public show of support for his own Catholic convictions. Alternatively, Grewe might simply have been concerned to suppress a public expression of religious discord. The location and circumstances of Toly's outburst are not noted, but maybe they took place in the city market, where the two men, both butchers, might have interacted. Yet, whatever lay behind Toly's diatribe and Grewe's involvement in the court case that resulted from it, the matter was resolved in the way that was, by 1548, typical in Norwich. No action was ultimately taken against Toly.

Like Toly's outburst, verbal attacks against clergy were the subject of the overwhelming majority of the cases of religious conflict heard in the mayor's court for the rest of 1548. In June four examinations resulted from the preaching and presence of the Protestant Thomas Rose in the city. The mayor and aldermen committed Thomas Bedys to ward after they learned that he had said "that Mr. Rose is a false knave and here like a false preacher." But on the following day they decided that "upon trust of amendment he is this day discharged."[59] A man named Jobson was commanded to confess to the preacher that he had deemed Rose unfit "to eat cats and dogs," but there is no record that Jobson ever submitted himself.[60] The court took no action against Robert Emons of nearby Felthorpe after William Morley's report that Emons had declared "that Mr. Rose should have been rung out of town."[61]

Similarly, no punishment appears to have been meted out when John Grace complained to the court in late June about a recent conversation with a Heigham tanner named Bonyng. Bonyng claimed "that Rose of late came home . . . and found another man in bed with his wife, for which cause he hath now made a sermon. And after [he] will go to London and leave his wife behind him." Parliamentary-sanctioned clerical marriage was still a year away in 1548 and to many, like Bonyng, Rose's marriage was a scandal. A woman who married a priest was thought little better than a harlot and would surely behave like one. Grace expressed his disbelief to the tanner, but Bonyng maintained the rumor's truth, citing a local carpenter and shoemaker as his reliable sources. The hostile and divided response to Rose and his sermons among Norwich's inhabitants helps to explain why Edward's government considered sermons so disruptive that a proclamation was issued in September 1548 that prohibited all preaching.[62]

Perhaps Thomas Rose curtailed his preaching in Norwich after the cold reception of his Protestant message in certain quarters of the city, as the avalanche of criticism against him largely subsided. If so, his absence did nothing to stem the tide of criticism against local clergymen. In July 1548, Robert Tryll came to the court to complain about Robert Leman. According to Tryll, Leman had defamed Dr. Henry King, calling him "Doctor knave and Doctor thief." Henry King was the same man who had been reproached by Matthew Parker for a sermon he preached in 1547. By 1548, King had become a prebendary at Norwich Cathedral, but was still a source of irritation to at least one person in Norwich. The fact that Leman struck Tryll must have been part of the reason why Tryll "came personally before Mr. Mayor," but he did not detail what about King Leman found so offensive or why Leman's remarks were sufficiently upsetting that Tryll would report them to the court.[63] Leman was brought into the court by alderman Hamon Linsted but apparently did not respond to the charges against him and the case ended after that.[64]

Criticism of clergymen did not come only from the laity, as a case from August 1548 demonstrates. The butcher Thomas Hoberd recounted to civic rulers "that on Sunday last past about three of the clock in the afternoon . . . Philip Curston, clerk, said

these words following: 'fie on preachers, arrant knaves and renegades and heretic knaves.'" Ecclesiastical records from the next
reign, that of Queen Mary, would reveal that Philip Curston was
a chantry priest in the nearby village of Hellesdon from 1541 to
1548, when the chantry must have been suppressed. Those records also noted that in 1555, Curston "was never married" and
that he was "an honest Catholic man."[65] Curston was thus a traditional priest who rejected the innovations to religious doctrine
and practice promulgated by Edward's government. In particular, as Thomas Hoberd had protested, Curston was hostile to
preachers such as, and perhaps even including, Thomas Rose,
whose Protestant theology was responsible for the suppression of
the Hellesdon chantry. Protestant preachers were thus, in his
eyes, "arrant knaves and renegades and heretic knaves." The
court committed Curston to ward until he found surety, and no
more is recorded about his case.

Threats against the clergy were the subject of two cases in
September 1548, although with a twist not seen before in the
mayor's court. On the tenth, Robert Barnard, who had been
brought to court for his involvement in the fight about holy bread
and water at St. Peter Mancroft the year before, came before the
mayor and aldermen as an accuser. Barnard told how a shoemaker named Thomas Dynglove had reported that he had been
pressured by the mayor to name Barnard as "a captain with the
said Dynglove and others to pull a priest at Mass out of his
clothes," a charge that Barnard presumably denied. If Dynglove
did not confess to that conspiracy, the mayor had allegedly
threatened that Dynglove "should be set on the pillory or else
whipped at the cart's arse." A tailor named James Reder was also
implicated. Not surprisingly, mayor Edmund Wood does not appear to have admitted to making any such threats. Instead, he
and his brethren directed Dynglove and Reder to come before
them again at the next court meeting, but the minutes of that session show no record of any such appearance.[66]

Reder himself was the focus of a case on September 26. The
ever-quarrelsome Andrew Quasshe and John Bengemyn, both of

whom were involved in the St. Peter Mancroft conflict of 1547, made an accusation against the tailor Reder similar to their compatriot Robert Barnard's. According to Quasshe and Bengemyn, Reder had gone about saying that "Mr. Mayor and other of his council threatened him that if he would not confess that Bengemyn and Quasshe were counsellors and aiders of them to pull a priest being at Mass out of his clothes that he [Reder] should be set upon the pillory or whipped at a cart's arse." Leonard Yonges, yet another participant in the St. Peter Mancroft affair of 1547, confirmed Quasshe's and Bengemyn's testimony. If Quasshe hoped that these charges would result in some action against "Mr. Mayor and other of his council," then he was soon disappointed, for it was Reder who was slated for punishment. The court committed Reder to the stocks, but on his "humble submission" and confession that he had slandered the mayor and aldermen he was released. On the same day, a Christopher Billings was examined for "setting up a bill of arrest against [Thomas] Rose, preacher." Billings denied the charges, claiming that the handwriting on the bill was not his, and the investigation ended there.[67]

The Dynglove and Reder cases provide special insight into the magistrates' practice of handling religious conflict and also the great potential danger that they faced in late 1548 and early 1549. The four accusers in these cases—Barnard, Bengemyn, Quasshe and Yonges—had three things in common. All had served or would serve in city office, all had participated in the fight over holy objects at St. Peter Mancroft and all therefore appear to have been militantly Protestant. Their seemingly sequenced participation in the Dynglove and Reder cases, both of which really sought to destroy the mayor (the likely Protestant Edmund Wood) by impugning his justice, smacked of an incipient factional politics aimed at upending local government.[68] If this was indeed their goal, they failed. But their effort, like the quarrel over St. George's day, must have taken a toll on the magistrates' ability to command implicit respect. This can be seen in the contemporary upsurge of religious conflict which the magistrates could not stem as well as in a number of cases, like Reder's, in which even common folk did not always answer to magisterial command.

Later in 1548 or early in 1549, the priest Philip Curston also fell into trouble with the mayor and aldermen. An undated court book entry that comes from around that time records that the mayor had dispatched one of the city constables to deliver Curston to the Guildhall, for what purpose the account does not note. The priest responded to the summons by telling the constable "that he had nothing to do with Mr. Mayor and . . . would not come." The magistrates committed Curston to prison and also warned him "that while he is in the city that [he] shall use him[self] as other priests [do]." After this, Curston's name did not appear again in city records.[69]

On the same day that Curston was committed to jail, the mayor and aldermen disciplined two other local priests. Thomas Seman, the priest of St. John Sepulchre, was committed to ward because on Christmas morning he "disobeyed Mr. Mayor's commandment in using certain ceremonies contrary to the King's [order]." John Floraunce, whom Marian ecclesiastical records later identified as the former priest of Lettice Payne's chantry in St. Peter Mancroft, "living continently and Catholicly," was also committed to ward because he too had conducted "communion contrary to the book sent . . . by the King's majesty."[70]

What is notable about these two cases is that the exact nature of the offense in question was not given. Seman's and Floraunce's deviations in the conduct of religious services might have violated a February 1548 royal proclamation prohibiting all "private innovations in ceremonies." Or the two priests could have breached the "Order of Communion" that had been authored by Archbishop Cranmer, introducing the novelty of English prayers into the Latin Mass along with communion in both kinds also by proclamation in March 1548.[71] Given later references to Floraunce as a steadfast Catholic, he probably ignored Edwardian innovations to religious services, but this is nowhere noted in the records. This patent lack of regard for the details of religious strife underscores that Norwich magistrates were less concerned with the content of religious discord than with its very existence and potential for stirring public controversy.

A variety of religious conflicts continued to erupt among Norwich's residents during the third year of Edward VI's reign and the court still took little punitive action against defendants. On March 2, 1549, Robert Osbern reported to the court that he had recently overheard a group of men—"Nicholas Coke, a keelman, Richard Debney and Mutton's man [and] young Oldman"—boast about their recent disruptive activities in two villages near the city and future plans for further disturbances. First they had threatened "to pull the parson of Rockland out of his clothes," and they had bragged that they had broken windows at the church at Bramerton and pulled down a cross there and at Rockland also. Richard Debney was the beer brewer who had been charged with iconoclasm in Norwich in 1547. He, like the rest of those whom Osbern named, was not punished.[72] One week later, on March 9, 1549, William Goose and Roger Greensmith confessed in open court that they and Roger Ives, the shoemaker Blewet and Richard Debney went to an alehouse in Kirby and "did eat upon a Friday a swine's cheek [and] a cold pie," violating the prescribed abstention from flesh on that day. Only Goose and Greensmith were bound to appear before the mayor again, while no action was taken against the others.[73]

In the days after the case of William Goose and his partners had been considered, the mayor and aldermen became aware of the circulation of scurrilous tracts in the city that "mainteneth any part of the usurped power of the Bishop of Rome or any popishness disproved by public authority." The handbills, "commonly called Eccho or Nemo or Vincent Verity," were "set forth in rhyme" and combined attacks against "the King's majesty," specifically the royal supremacy and Thomas Rose, with "unseeming terms of railing against the governance of Mr. mayor [William Rogers] within this city."[74] City leaders suspected that the tracts' author or authors must be among the inmates of Norwich Cathedral, which would potentially rekindle long-standing friction between city government and the local Church. Members of the mayor's court wrote to Dean and suffragan Bishop of Thetford John Salisbury to demand that seven occupants of the Cathedral be sent to the mayor's court for examination.[75] Salisbury quickly agreed to dispatch the seven men in question to the court, only on the explicit condition "that you examine them no further than the importance of the King's majesty's cause requireth, and that you do not meddle with any other matter or matters being prejudicial to our composition and liberties."[76]

That interrogation does not appear to have taken place, as there is no account of it in municipal records. The Dean examined the Cathedral's five petty canons and two singing men himself, but learned nothing about the authorship of handbills. He did find, however, that Dr. King was also a target of a derogatory handbill. Given that the other individuals who were derided in the handbills for their religious sentiments were Thomas Rose and the Protestant mayor William Rogers, King's inclusion in that group suggests that he too harbored Protestant sympathies. However, not all of the bills disseminated around the Cathedral lampooned Protestants or Protestant doctrine; one mocked the Latin Mass.[77]

Despite the magistrates' initial concern and their intention to question suspects themselves—they warned the Dean that if he failed to send the men "we require you to advertise us thereof by your letters to the end that we may proceed further therein as the cause and justice requireth"—they ultimately abandoned their investigation. Perhaps they feared that such a challenge to the Dean and Chapter would end with another assault on magisterial authority, much as the incident with St. George's Company and Andrew Quasshe had. Although they did not pursue the origins of the offensive bills, they were not troubled by the circulation of those tracts again.

If the circulation of handbills ceased, other religious disturbances did not. The shoemaker Thomas Hardy admitted to the mayor and aldermen in early May 1549 that he and two others "did throw a stone at the glass window of the parish church of Saint Julian," but that he could not "declare any manner cause why he should do the same." Hardy was bound over to appear again, although his accomplices never appeared before the court at all. Perhaps because "there have been like trespasses committed within the city by whom it is unknown," the mayor and aldermen took the novel step of calling Hardy back to court in June. They bound him to good behavior until Michaelmas, but did not recall him a second time.[78]

No such penalty was meted out to the cordwainer Peter Lynage, who was in court on May 8, 1549, shortly after Hardy. Thomas Keswik reported to the mayor and aldermen that on May day, mayoral election day in Norwich, he saw Lynage walking with a group of people. As Keswik passed them by, he heard Lynage declare that "Mr. New Elect was a popish knave." "Mr. New Elect" was alderman Thomas Codde, who was to be installed as the new mayor the following month. His will, drafted in 1558 while Mary was still Queen, indeed revealed Codde to be a Catholic. But Lynage denied having said anything at all about Codde and his case ended there.[79]

Neither was there much in the way of punishment ordered for William Stampe, the rector of the city parish of St. Augustine, who was in court on the same day as Lynage. One night in May 1549 at about ten o'clock, according to the court records, the priest along with his "adherents" entered the church and "brake down the altar called the high altar of the said church of his own froward mind without the assent of the parishioners and against their wills and minds." Reforming Protestants rejected traditional altars, charging that their continued existence lent credence to the belief in the Mass as a sacrifice. Edward's government would dictate the removal of altars and their replacement with communion tables, but before the official order, there were enthusiasts, like Stampe and his "adherents," who took matters into their own hands.[80] Stampe confessed to the court and apologized for his transgression, after which the magistrates sentenced him to rebuild the altar. There is no record that they ever verified his completion of the task.[81]

In addition to his troubles with the mayor's court, William

Stampe was also cited in a Norwich Archdeaconry inquisition of 1551 for wearing his cope inside out and in 1554 he was deprived as a married priest under Queen Mary.[82] In early 1549, Parliament had authorized the marriage of priests, ending the requirement for clerical celibacy that had been in place since the end of the eleventh century. It is not known how many clergy in the city of Norwich took wives, although those associated with seven parishes were deprived of their posts when the Marian regime repealed that act, as well as some members of the Cathedral staff.[83] In 1549, however, one Norwich resident expressed his deep antipathy to the relaxation of the standard of clerical celibacy. In June the mayor examined a man named Thurston who had been heard to say that "all priests' wives were whores." Thurston denied that statement and he was released from court with a warning to hold his tongue.[84]

The marriage of priests was not the only controversial legislation that Parliament passed in 1549. It also passed the Act of Uniformity that authorized the use of the first Edwardian Prayer Book, which was greeted with hostility in some places around England, most famously in the southwest.[85] In Norwich, the mayor and aldermen handled two cases in which use of the Prayer Book was at issue. In early July, John Beston, the priest of St. Paul's parish, was brought to court where he was charged with failing to use the Prayer Book properly, although once again the record did not indicate the precise nature of his transgression. Beston replied that he was indeed conducting services according to the Prayer Book and his case ended there.[86]

On the same day, the mayor and aldermen reprimanded Andrew Colby (or Coby), a nonbeneficed priest who served at the parish of St. Michael Berstreet. According to the court book, Colby "useth not and order himself in his church according to the King's majesty's book concerning an altar." The altar had been destroyed, presumably by Protestant enthusiasts in the parish, among whom might have been the priest himself, leaving nothing in its place. Colby replied that if his parishioners cared to erect another altar, he could "accept the same." But the court, for reasons that are not clear, also began to doubt whether Colby was a priest at all. After "long debating" of the matter, they sentenced Colby to prison until he produced witnesses to confirm his clerical status and in the meantime forbade him to serve as a priest. They entered a recognizance to that effect, committing him to the mayor and, unusually, the diocesan Chancellor, but they did not pursue his case further.[87]

⊰ V ⊱

Although the volume and intensity of religious discord among Norwich residents increased during the early years of Edward's reign, spilling over into the magistracy for the first time, the rulers of Norwich prevented the city from becoming engulfed by religious conflict. Still, they could hardly have predicted or been prepared for the calamity of Kett's rebellion. The uprising began on June 20, 1549, when villagers in Attleborough, Norfolk, threw down hedges of a landlord who had enclosed portions of the local common land and culminated, before its suppression by the central government, with the invasion of Norwich and deposition of city government.

Kett's rebellion has traditionally occupied only a small place in the history of the English Reformation. It is best remembered in this context for the support Kett's rebels exhibited for the official Reformation when they used the newly imposed Prayer Book to conduct services at their camp on Mousehold Heath, just outside Norwich on the city's northeast side.[88] Thomas Conyers, the priest of St. Martin-at-Palace in Norwich, read morning and evening prayer to the rebels and Robert Watson, who, in addition to having served as Andrew Quasshe's lawyer was also known as "a preacher . . . of good estimation," sermonized the rebel camp. Matthew Parker and John Barret also preached there at various times with the intent of moderating the rebels' actions, which was apparently also the goal of Watson and Conyers.[89] In contrast to the Western Rising on the other side of England, the other famous rebellion of 1549, religious issues did not play a major role in mo-

tivating Kett's rebels. Famous as it is, the literature on Kett's rebellion is built on a slender base of primary sources, especially
concerning the rebels' actions in and around Norwich.[90] But the
available evidence does show that Kett and his rural followers
from the Norfolk countryside were primarily concerned with
agrarian issues such as enclosures and unreceptive local government in East Anglia. Although they marched on Norwich because it was the provincial capital, Kett's rebels did not perceive
the city as a cause of their economic problems and there is no indication of any religious dispute between the rebels and the city.

Kett's rebellion is important for this study because it raised issues that paralleled and intensified those that Norwich magistrates were already confronting in the context of the Reformation.
When the rebels camped outside the city, the magistrates faced
the familiar problems of maneuvering between provincial politics
and the central government, as well as the potential of disturbances' spreading and disrupting civic order. The attack on Norwich, during which some urban support for the rebels was evident, exposed the serious socioeconomic tensions that racked the
city.[91] The overthrow of civic government marked the ultimate
breakdown of magisterial authority, which could then only be restored by the intervention of the central government.

In many ways, the course of action adopted by the magistrates
in the face of the advancing rebel army was consistent with how
they had coped with religious conflict in the city. From its begin-
nings in Attleborough, the rebellion gained strength when Robert
Kett, a local landowner, agreed to serve as its leader, even though
his own best interests lay with the landlords whose hedges were
being destroyed. Kett decided to take the rebels to Norwich, but,
it appears, not with the initial intention of overrunning the city.
The group arrived outside Norwich's gates on July 9 or 10, and
one secondary source claims Norwich mayor Thomas Codde visited their encampment on that day.[92] City records for July 10
show that two messengers from the rebel camp, Lawrence Dek-
erell and Nicholas Lane, came before the mayor's court, asking
permission to buy supplies in the city and to pass through Nor-

wich on their way to Mousehold Heath, where they planned to make camp.[93] The mayor and aldermen denied both requests, forcing the rebels to march around the city to reach Mousehold Heath. But they also tried to maintain cordial relations with the rebels in order to avert conflict while waiting for royal advice and support.

Through early July, "much matter" was "moved, reasoned and debated" among the aldermen about the rebel camp, "but nothing determined nor concluded."[94] They finally resolved to accede to several of Kett's requests, allowing the rebels to secure provisions in the city and to send their prisoners for confinement in the city jail. Mayor Thomas Codde and Thomas Aldrich, a gentleman "of Mangrene, a two mile from Norwich," visited the rebel camp and signed their names next to Kett's on a list of the rebels' demands and, perhaps as one secondary source claims, several other documents as well.[95] This association between civic leaders and the rebels is suggestive on several levels. Kett must have held them in some esteem or thought highly of their influence since he had them sign their names next to his in a place more prominent than the leaders of his rebel councils. Mayor Codde, a Catholic, put aside his religious sensibilities in order to sustain amicable relations with the avowedly Protestant rebels. Codde's religion seems to have neither hindered his efforts nor excited animosity from Kett's camp. Lastly, the civic leaders' cooperation with the rebels was both a courageous and a desperate move. They had few alternative ways to protect the ill-defended city from the rebels, who outnumbered their total urban population, but signing rebel documents must have caused at least some suspicion as to their motives and backbone.[96]

The conciliatory relationship with the rebel camp persisted until July 20, when a royal messenger arrived at Norwich to offer the King's pardon if the rebels disbanded, an offer that "the said camp wholly refused."[97] With that rejection, the magistrates understood that the central government and rebels would engage in the kind of direct conflict which they had tried to avoid. Only now did the magistrates decide to fortify their ill-positioned city against a rebel attack. By July 23 the attack was over and Norwich had fallen readily into the hands of the rebels, in part because of the assistance offered by some of Norwich's lower orders who had their own socioeconomic grievances. The city government was promptly overthrown. Kett took mayor Codde, Thomas Aldrich and aldermen William Rogers and John Homerston prisoner, bringing them out of the city to his camp, "where they remained in chains and fetters unto the last day that some by God's provision was saved and some died."[98] Some sacking of the city by Norfolk rebels and local sympathizers ensued, despite Kett's attempts to defend property. Norwich's aldermen appear to have kept a low profile during the month-long occupation of their city.

The story of the defeat of the rebellion is a familiar one. Protector Somerset dispatched the Marquis of Northampton and an army of nearly 1,500 to Norwich to conquer the rebel forces. The arrival of royal troops invalidated the city's charter. Alderman Augustine Styward, standing in for the incarcerated Thomas Codde, surrendered the city's sword of state to the Marquis, symbolizing Norwich's submission to the Crown.[99] Northampton was a man of little military experience and his army was routed by the rebels, who had again refused the King's pardon. For three more weeks, Norwich remained in rebel hands, as citizens awaited additional help from the central government. That relief finally arrived on August 23 when an army led by John Dudley, Earl of Warwick (the future Duke of Northumberland), arrived outside Norwich. Four days later, over 3,000 lay dead and the rebellion was over. Robert Kett escaped capture that day, but was soon apprehended, convicted of treason and hanged at Norwich castle on December 7.[100]

Kett's rebellion was a catastrophe for the rulers of Norwich. It was a local disorder that had escalated beyond their control, in spite of their early efforts to appease the rebels at Mousehold. They had been unable to prevent the complete capitulation of civic government, an outcome they had clearly wished to avoid. The assault on, and liberation of, Norwich had resulted in the nullification of civic authority. It must have been a humiliating experience for the aldermen who were present to witness Augustine Styward's surrender of the civic sword of state to the Marquis of Northampton, even though the city received a new charter from King Edward soon after the rebellion that restored its former franchises.[101] Moreover, the rebellion had taken the life of John Homerston, one of the aldermen who was imprisoned in the rebel camp.[102]

Not surprisingly, in the months immediately following the rebellion the magistrates were more preoccupied with those who expressed their lingering support for the rebellion than with religious conflict. But they punished few of Kett's supporters, apparently not retaliating against them. The mayor and aldermen listened to testimony such as that given against Burnham, the parish clerk of St. Gregory, on September 21, 1549, whom two witnesses heard remark that "there are too many gentlemen in England by five hundred," drawing on the rebels' distaste for and distrust of the gentry. Burnham, who was in court, in an exchange with the mayor exclaimed, "Ye scribes and pharisees; ye seek innocents' blood. But if I cannot have justice here, I shall have it of better men and I ask no favor at your hands." No judgment was recorded in the case.[103] In an undated entry in the court book from just after Burnham's appearance, Edmund Johnson, identified as a laborer, related to the mayor and aldermen one Bossewell's assertion "that it should cost a thousand men's lives first," before Kett was hanged. The record ended there.[104] On November 23, John Rook was reported to have predicted that "except for the mercy of God, before Christmas, you shall see as great a camp upon Mousehold as ever was." Rook was bound to appear again before the court, but never called. On the same day, a man named Claxton declared that he thought "nothing but well" of Kett, and that he "trusted to see a new day" for men like himself.[105] The mayor and aldermen took a number of other depositions related to Kett's rebellion, but took no action on them.[106]

In keeping with their inclination for adding new celebrations to the civic calendar, sometime after the rebellion's end, the city Assembly declared that each August 27 would be kept annually in

Norwich as a day of thanksgiving. All shops were to close and all city residents were to "repair to their parish churches" to remember how the Earl of Warwick "vanquished Robert Kett and his whole number of adherents of their most wicked rebellion, and did suppress them, and delivered this city from the great danger, trouble and peril it was in, [and] like to have been lost forever."[107]

Despite the serious blow to civic authority, the magistrates emerged from the great upheaval of Kett's rebellion still committed to their strategy of disregarding religious differences when the temptation to crack down on all dissenters must have been great. Religion still proved a divisive issue and one that continued to demand magisterial attention, although they considered only a few more cases between the end of the rebellion and Edward's death. In December 1549, they examined Robert Warden and John Florens. Florens was not attending the proper parish church and was also encouraging others to do the same. The magistrates committed him to jail, but the record does not indicate if he ever served the sentence. Warden was a parishioner at St. Augustine's church and an apparent opponent of traditional religious devotions. During a recent service he "went up to the high altar there and took away the wax candles being light upon the same, by reason whereof many of the parishioners were greatly offended and grieved with the same and some well contented." The mayor and aldermen at first decided to send Warden to jail until they contemplated his case further, but then changed their minds. Upon further consideration they released him, as they had other such offenders.[108]

There was not another matter concerning religion in the mayor's court books until early 1551, when testimony was given about a carpenter from King's Lynn, Norfolk, who had apparently criticized the Church. It is not clear who spoke at the hearing, but the court book noted that Thomas Derling was heard to say "there is no thing set forth this day in the Church in this realm of England that is justly agreeable to God's word," an inflammatory assertion that surely marked Derling as a progressive or radical Protestant.[109]

The hearing on Derling was an unusual session of the mayor's court in that only four city officials were present: mayor Robert Rugge, alderman Thomas Morley, town clerk Henry Ward and city Recorder Thomas Gawdy. Also in attendance was former Recorder John Corbet, who had harassed Dorothy Bale in 1545 and, as we shall see in the next chapter, would be instrumental in the arrest of a Norwich Protestant during Mary's reign. It seems possible that Corbet, a zealous religious conservative by Norwich's standards, could have been the one responsible for bringing the outsider Derling into court.

The mayor took no action against Derling at his first hearing, but Derling apparently continued to frequent Norwich and make provocative comments while in the city. In April 1551 Derling was again a subject of a mayor's court session, this time for reportedly saying that "if prayer and supplication be not made, the realm of England will come to destruction and my Lord Rich [England's Lord Chancellor] and his company will make the King his majesty a poor King and deceive him if the King do not take heed."[110] Derling might have singled out Lord Chancellor Rich in his dire predictions for England because the Chancellor played a role in the fall of the Protector Somerset, who had a popular reputation as a defender of Protestantism and the poor, such as carpenters like Derling. Lord Rich was also a known religious conservative who avoided the fate of most members of the conservative faction at court at the end of Henry VIII's reign by deftly allying with the reformers at the last moment.[111] As Lord Chancellor under Edward, he had helped pilot the Lord Protector's religious legislation through Parliament. Yet he turned against his onetime friend Somerset when the opportunity for a coup was provided by the unrest throughout England in the summer of 1549.[112] For these reasons, Derling might have perceived Rich as a dangerous deceiver and enemy of Protestantism.

The magistrates did not record any action against Derling at the hearing on April 18, but news of Derling's words somehow reached the Lord Chancellor. Three weeks later mayor Rugge received a letter from Lord Chancellor Rich requesting that Derling, apparently imprisoned in Norwich according to the letter, be conveyed to the Privy Council at Westminster. A plot to restore the deposed Somerset had been uncovered in London during April, likely causing official alarm over comments like Derling's.[113] Rugge followed Rich's orders quickly. The Chancellor's letter was dated May 6 and Rugge replied on May 10 that Derling was on his way to London. Rugge added that since Derling's imprisonment the carpenter had been praying for Lord Rich's preservation. Derling did not appear again in city records.[114]

While it is unclear why or for how long Derling was in Norwich or under what circumstances he made his various remarks, it is not difficult to see why city magistrates could have been particularly glad to comply promptly with Lord Rich's command. Derling was an outsider and sending him to Westminster posed little threat to local autonomy. The magistrates might also have understood Derling's comments about Lord Rich as an implied expression of support for the fallen Somerset and hope for his restoration. Somerset had become unpopular around England after the summer of 1549, blamed by many for not responding more quickly and severely to the uprisings. Such sentiments were surely quite strong among Norwich's civic elite.

Shortly after the beginning of the Derling matter, in March 1551, Alice Fylby appeared in court to give an account of a conversation she had recently heard in Henry Holden's shop.[115] John Holden (whose relationship to Henry was not given) had commented, upon hearing a story of a local clergyman sent to London to be examined by Archbishop Cranmer, "that the bishop [of Norwich] was a popish bishop and that his preachers did preach false doctrine." Holden referred to new Bishop Thomas Thirlby, who had been translated to Norwich after William Rugge's resignation in 1550. Thirlby was a diplomat who only once visited his diocese.[116] Another witness corroborated Fylby's testimony. The magistrates bound Holden over to reappear before them at their convenience and also ordered him to ask the Bishop of Norwich for forgiveness in the presence of the aldermen. Holden was not called to court again, and given that Thirlby only visited Norwich diocese once during his episcopate, it seems unlikely that Holden ever saw the Bishop.[117]

Finally, in June 1553 the mayor and aldermen committed John Dyxe to jail until he could find sureties to be bound over for a later appearance before the court.[118] When the curate of Dyxe's parish, St. Martin-at-Oak, had proclaimed on the previous Sunday that the feast of St. John the Baptist should be kept with fasting, "the said Dyxe immediately by divers ways and means in words moved and stirred the people there to dissension, saying that the curate had not done well therein, and that it was not so used in other places." Dyxe never appeared in court again, and it is unclear whether he served his jail sentence or whether he found sureties. But the magistrates showed their concern for religious upheaval by seeing Dyxe in court shortly after the disturbance.

⊰ VI ⊱

The case against John Dyxe was the last one of Edward's reign for a religious offense in Norwich, as the young King died two weeks after Dyxe's appearance in the mayor's court. Edward's brief reign had been an eventful and disturbing one for city magistrates. Conflict over religious doctrines and practices among Norwich's inhabitants had appeared more frequently in the pages of the mayor's court books than it had in the past. Those records revealed that the Edwardian Reformation elicited a variety of responses among the city's residents. There was neither universal acceptance nor rejection of religious change, but the contours of religious difference in the city had clearly changed. Most importantly, during Edward's reign the lines had become more clearly drawn between Catholics and Protestants. In Norwich, one can also see the emergence of substantial religious diversity within Protestantism itself as Protestants began to dispute with each other as much as with Catholics over the course of religious change.

If religion was becoming a more divisive issue among Norwich's governed, the incident concerning St. George's guild had publicly exposed deep religious divisions among the magistrates that they had worked so long to disguise. The intervention of the Duke of Somerset into the affair had compromised magisterial authority, but it was a setback that proved temporary. Despite that misadventure, and the even greater assault on civic authority of Kett's rebellion, the magistrates persisted in their strategy for handling religious dissension. Whether offenders had demonstrated Catholic antagonism to the Edwardian settlement or had shown their willingness to accelerate the pace of religious change, the mayor and aldermen refused to punish them severely. Andrew Quasshe had even been reincorporated into the body politic after his obnoxious outbursts. The magistrates remained willing to tolerate religious differences as a means of maintaining civic order and stability, but the success of that practice had been shown to rest on somewhat fragile foundations. As agitated as they had become over the refusal of St. George's feastmakers to furnish the annual dinner, they managed to prevent those deeply held religious sentiments from overwhelming and undermining civic government.

5

The Quiet Restoration

NORWICH AND THE RETURN OF
CATHOLICISM UNDER QUEEN MARY

Even though there were significant disruptions to civic rule during Edward's reign, Norwich magistrates had largely managed to contain religious conflict and shield the community from outside inquiry into its conformity with the official Reformation. With the sole exception of the St. George's Company incident, neither the Bishop of Norwich nor the Somerset and Northumberland regimes had found cause for concern about religious affairs in England's second city. In the exceptional instance of the St. George's Company, Andrew Quasshe had been responsible for drawing the attention of the central government, for Somerset had no other reason to be concerned with the reorganization of a local religious guild. If city magistrates' practice of managing local religious differences through Henry's and Edward's reigns was unusually effective, then at no time would their success be more striking than under Queen Mary.

Mary Tudor, of course, restored Roman Catholicism as the official religion of England after succeeding to the throne on the death of her half-brother Edward in 1553. Mary was widely known to be a committed Catholic, having openly refused to use the two Protestant Prayer Books during her brother's reign. Consequently, many Catholics anticipated a return to official sanction upon Mary's ascension and in Melton Mowbray, Oxford and some parishes in London and around Yorkshire, for example,

Mass was celebrated again soon after the new Queen's accession.[1] Mary first showed the direction in which her government would move in a proclamation issued on August 18, 1553, expressing her desire that her subjects should follow her in the practice of the religion that "she has ever professed from her infancy hitherto." If the return of Catholicism was now certain, the persecution for which Mary's reign is often remembered was not, for she also promised, for the meantime, not to compel her subjects in the matter of religion.[2]

Mary's first Parliament made the Queen's intentions in the realm of religion considerably clearer when it met in October 1553. With the First Act of Repeal, it rescinded Edwardian religious legislation, including the statute sanctioning clerical marriage, and reinstated Henrician religious worship. In July 1554, the Queen married Philip of Spain, in the face of strong opposition from Parliament. Philip was the heir to the Spanish throne, to which he would succeed in 1556, and also to the vast Hapsburg dominions that stretched across Europe and to the Americas. A delegation from the House of Commons expressed fears to the Queen that such a union would force England to become involved in Spanish military conflicts and eventually render England a mere Spanish satellite. But Mary remained firmly committed to her Spanish cousin and the marriage took place on schedule. In late 1554, the Queen received Reginald Pole into England as a papal legate, sent to reconcile England to Rome. That reconciliation was made official by Mary's third Parliament in early 1555: it restored papal supremacy, while maintaining possession of former church lands for their current lay owners, rather than requiring them to return those properties to the Church. The third Parliament also passed a law against heresy that set the stage for the trial and execution of close to 300 Protestants that began in 1555 and only ceased with Mary's death in 1558.[3] That legislation also helped to encourage the self-imposed exile of nearly 800 English Protestants that was already under way.

In Norwich, the religiously diverse magistrates pursued a fa-

miliar course of action in response to the new religious regime.
They complied with religious directives that fell within their pur-
view but did not enforce the new settlement in the mayor's court,
with a few notable exceptions. Thus, aldermen called together
families in the wards they represented in March 1554 to charge
them to observe the new religious mandates and, in 1555, they restored the St. George's day ceremony to its Henrician form.[4] In
the mayor's court they persisted in treating lightly most of the
cases of religious conflict that continued to erupt in the city early
in the Queen's reign. However, when the heresy law passed
through Parliament in January 1555, religious conflict virtually
vanished from the pages of the mayor's court books, much as it
had after the passage of the draconian Six Articles during Henry
VIII's reign.

If Norwich's Protestant inhabitants were not often punished
for religious nonconformity in the mayor's court during Mary's
reign, they also largely evaded prosecution by central and diocesan authorities. In so doing, they surprisingly escaped execution
under the heresy statutes that claimed the lives of nearly 300
people across England, 85 percent of whom came from the southeastern dioceses of London, Canterbury, Chichester and Norwich.[5] The city of Norwich, as the seat of the diocese covering
Norfolk, Suffolk and parts of Cambridgeshire, was the site for
some of the diocese's more than 40 burnings. Witnessing executions must have made an impression on Norwich's inhabitants, as
it did in other communities throughout the country. Indeed, as
we shall see, far fewer residents of Norwich, both in absolute
numbers and as a proportion of the population, met their deaths
at the stake than in other towns. Almost all of the Protestant
heretics executed in Norwich were from towns and villages outside the city. Only two Norwich residents died in the flames, and
both of them were only arrested because of self-incrimination.

Neither did a significant number of Norwich's Protestants go
into Continental exile to escape capture and punishment. Of the
roughly 800 Marian exiles, Christina Hallowell Garrett's study
could identify 472, but she noted that a good number of those

identifications remain uncertain. From Garrett's study, we can identify only four who might have fled from Norwich, while dozens, perhaps as many as one hundred, left London. Two of these names match Norwich priests who were deprived for marriage in 1555, but their identity is doubtful because there is no supporting evidence and their names—John Fisher and William Johnson—were not uncommon ones. A more certain identification is that of John Dodman, who was born in Norwich, but who was, in all likelihood, living in Hadleigh, Suffolk, when he left England. The fourth identification of an exile from Norwich is for Robert Watson. This is the only one that we know is certainly correct. There is no other evidence from city records to indicate that other residents of Norwich fled the country during Mary's reign. It appears that even well-known Protestants in Norwich felt secure enough not to flee to the Continent.[6]

The burnings of the two Norwich residents and the execution of Protestant heretics from around Norwich diocese showed that persecution and delation were possible in Norwich. The persecution of heresy was an accepted part of the Norwich magistrates' world, but it was a part that they tried to restrict as much as they could. The magistrates were required to preside over the diocese's executions when the Church brought the condemned to the city. These were outsiders who did not enjoy the advantages of civic belonging that served to protect Norwich's own residents. Nevertheless, magisterial toleration and protection had its limits. Public self-incrimination by Norwich residents could not be ignored. As we shall see, the two executed residents incriminated themselves so blatantly—the first in church and the second at the first's execution—that the magistrates would have risked drawing the attention of the Church and Crown had they failed to act.

Despite Norwich rulers' long-standing religious differences and the difficulties they had encountered containing religious dissension, the Marian persecution affected the city mostly indirectly. The potential for far worse was certainly there. Norwich had a Catholic population, albeit one whose size is difficult to estimate. Catholics served as aldermen and mayors under Mary, as they had during the preceding Protestant regime. Any one of them, humble resident or civic official, layman or cleric, could have pointed an effectively accusing finger at any number of local Protestants. And, as has been shown in the preceding chapter, Edwardian Norwich was home to many vocal Protestants, including some impolitic radicals for whom King Edward's Reformation had not gone far enough. Clearly, Norwich magistrates' skilled practice of tolerating religious diversity received some crucial support from the broader population, enabling the city to survive the Marian persecution mostly unscathed.

⊰ II ⊱

The rulers of Norwich took a cautious approach to the proclamation of the new sovereign on King Edward's death on July 6, 1553. They did not recognize the Protestant Jane Grey, whom the Duke of Northumberland had attempted to place on the throne instead of the Catholic Mary, as the town of King's Lynn and several members of the ruling group of Great Yarmouth did. Nor did they come out for Mary Tudor. Rather, they waited and watched as Mary installed herself at nearby Kenninghall, only twenty miles southwest of the city. On July 12, Mary sent a messenger to the city so that Norwich might proclaim her Queen. But the mayor and aldermen declined to do so initially, not because they did not support her, they replied to her emissary, but because they claimed to have received no official word of Edward's death. Perhaps they wished to wait in order to see how the forces that Mary had gathered around her would fare in the struggle against Northumberland. If that was the case, they did not wait much longer. On the following day, they claimed to have received whatever assurance they sought and Norwich dutifully declared Mary Tudor the new and rightful monarch, sending a hundred soldiers to meet her at Framlingham castle in Suffolk, where she had moved.[7]

Norwich was calm during the first days of Mary's reign. There is no evidence of popular support for, or opposition to, her succession in the city records. But in the ensuing months the Queen's religious edicts elicited sufficient reaction among some of the city's residents to land them in the mayor's court. While most of these cases from the early part of Mary's reign were characterized by magisterial desire to suppress religious conflict before it attracted extramural attention, three incidents during this period deviated conspicuously from this customary pattern.

In the fall of 1553, before the new Queen's government had begun the repeal of Edwardian religious legislation, the mayor's court apparently took the unusual step of sending John Hallybred, one of the Cathedral prebendaries, to the Privy Council for examination for his "lewd talk . . . contrary to the Queen's Highness' proclamation."[8] That move stirred some controversy in the city, as two men appeared before the court in connection with it. On November 4, Richard Bonyng reported to the court that in London, where it seems he had been not long before, he heard that "a man of worship" expressed surprised that the mayor sent Hallybred to the Council for "so light a matter." Bonyng was apparently released without any further investigation or penalty.[9]

A week later, Nicholas Chapman, mayor Henry Crook's cook, testified that one William Derne had expressed surprise to him about Hallybred's dispatch to the Privy Council. Evidently unaware of the details of the matter, Chapman inquired exactly what Hallybred had done to warrant such a penalty. Derne replied, "the matter was not great; it was but for a service in the church." He added, "I would that they were served here as they be at London," where apparently Derne had heard that the Mass had been restored, "for if I were in London I would no more stick [i.e. be reluctant] to pluck of a priest's clothes over his ears as to drink when I am dry." When Chapman warned that he would have to notify the mayor of Derne's words, Derne replied, "Marry, do if ye will, for I dare as well ride to London as tarry at home." Despite the opposition Derne had voiced for Catholic worship, the magistrates appear to have taken no action against him.[10]

On the same day that Chapman related his conversation with

Derne to the aldermen, a letter from the Privy Council to mayor Crook concerning the Hallybred case was read in open court and entered into the court book. The letter, dated October 31, did not discuss the remarks that had prompted the magistrates to send the priest to Westminster, but gave "hearty thanks" to the mayor "for your travail." The Council noted its decision to return the prebendary to Norwich. The letter further directed mayor Crook "to keep the said Hallybred in safe ward by the space of [five] or [six] days, and then upon some market day or at some open assembly cause him to confess his offense and declare his sorrow therefore to the end he may be example to all such misordered persons as shall so misdemean themselves."[11]

Hallybred's infraction cannot be known for sure. Perhaps he violated a recent proclamation that prohibited preaching about the Scriptures without express license from the Crown, a copy of which the Privy Council had sent directly to the Chancellor of Norwich diocese.[12] If so, it is possible that diocesan authorities were instrumental in bringing Hallybred's misdeeds to the magistrates' attention and, through them, to the Privy Council's. While the mayor's court had disciplined Norwich's parochial clergy on numerous occasions, Hallybred was the first Cathedral prebendary to be so treated. In any case, there is no indication that the magistrates ever carried out the Council's orders to discipline him despite their role in bringing Hallybred's transgressions to the attention of the central government.[13]

The Hallybred matter did not put an end to religious controversy in Norwich. The next incident was treated in a fashion that was more typical for Norwich. On November 25, Thomas Swanne appeared before the mayor and aldermen to complain about words spoken by John Wagstaff. Two days before, Swanne, who was from the village of Acle, almost due east of Norwich, was in the city buying groceries at the shop of George Walden, where Wagstaff was a servant. Perhaps learning that Swanne was from Acle, Wagstaff began to voice his opinion of Thomas Tuddenham (or Tedman), the village parson, who was also a Norwich Cathedral prebendary and apparently a religious conservative.[14] Tuddenham clearly rejoiced in the religious reversal of Mary's reign, while Wagstaff did not. "Doctor Tuddenham had lien in his den this last [seven] years," Wagstaff had complained, "and now did preach upon Sunday last past, and for his preaching had like to have been pulled out of the pulpit. And if he cometh and preacheth so again he shall be pulled down indeed," a threat that Swanne must have found offensive. But Wagstaff had not stopped there and continued that "Mr. Mayor [Henry Crook] was like to have been pulled down at the time of preaching. And said, 'you have Mass up now, God save it. How long it shall hold God knoweth.'" For his outburst Wagstaff was bound to appear in the future before the mayor's court, as was his master George Walden, perhaps for failing to control his servant better. Neither was ever called.[15]

There were more complaints about the restoration of traditional worship that came to the magistrates' attention. On December 1, 1553, they took a deposition from Robert Mason, who recounted a recent conversation with a tailor named Bonor. Bonor told him that "[t]his year will be as troublous a year as ever was," and that he would wager his life on it. When asked why that might be so, the tailor replied that it would be "[f]or the alteration of the service." Bonor went on to suggest that if no way were found to complain to the Queen and the Duke of Norfolk, watch would have to be kept for two years. Bonor's words were certainly ominous, predicting unrest and discord, but the magistrates did not act in his case.[16]

The magistrates did act against Richard Sotherton, a member of a prominent city family, in January 1554.[17] Sotherton was somehow involved in the composition or publication of writings against Stephen Gardiner, the Lord Chancellor and Bishop of Winchester. Gardiner was a religious conservative whom Edward VI had deprived of his see and imprisoned in 1551 and replaced with the radical Protestant John Ponet. On her accession, Queen Mary had released Gardiner, restored him to the bishopric of Winchester on Ponet's resignation and also elevated him to the Chancellorship. No details of Sotherton's undoubtedly uncom-

plimentary writings about Gardiner survive, but the court bound
him to appear before city magistrates in the future with a £20
bond.[18]

Two weeks after Sotherton's recognizance was entered into the
court books, the court examined Robert Watson, in the second
unusually handled case of Mary's reign. Watson had defended
Andrew Quasshe in the St. George's Company incident and
preached to Kett's rebels in 1549. He had occupied a Norwich
Cathedral prebendary's stall from 1549 to 1551, despite his status
as a layman. He also served as a Steward to Archbishop Cranmer
under Edward.[19] In February 1554, Watson had recently returned
to Norwich from London, and was staying at the home of Thomas Beamond, who was either the future alderman of Norwich
or his father.[20] According to the record, Watson attended matins
and evensong the previous Sunday at St. Andrew's, a parish
known in Norwich for its progressive religious complexion.[21]
When mayor Henry Crook asked Watson why he had not attended Mass on Sunday, Watson retorted that "he intendeth not
to be at any Mass, for his presence at the Mass is against his conscience and intendeth never to hear Mass while he liveth by the
grace of God." The magistrates committed Watson to jail where
he was to remain "until further order be taken," but his case did
not conclude there. A letter from the Privy Council to the magistrates that arrived in Norwich later the same month suggests that
city leaders had informed Westminster about Watson's activities.
The Council instructed the mayor and aldermen to deliver Watson to the diocesan Chancellor, who kept him imprisoned for
over a year, after which he fled to the Continent.[22]

Like the Hallybred case, there is no direct evidence to explain
how Watson's activities came to the attention of the magistrates
or why the magistrates informed Westminster of their encounter
him when they usually recoiled from contact with outside authorities over religious matters. However, it is not difficult to see
why they might have been willing to hand Watson to the Privy
Council as a special case. By 1554, Watson was a well-known
Protestant troublemaker in Norwich. In 1539, he had challenged

then-Bishop Rugge's position on free will, acting on the belief that he could justly dispute a bishop's interpretation of religious doctrine based on his own understanding of Scripture. Watson had appealed to the central government and then the authority of "God's word" in arguing for Andrew Quasshe's innocence in 1548, in both instances denying magisterial authority.

Where Watson's religious beliefs, per se, had never provoked magisterial inquiry, his religiously inspired disputation of magisterial authority must have been a sore point. The magistrates' reception of his 1554 declaration that attending Mass was "against his conscience" needs to be understood against this background and their typical reluctance to discipline Protestant enthusiasts during Mary's reign. It seems most likely that the magistrates were less concerned about Watson's religious beliefs than they were about the potentially disruptive nature of his public statements. If the magistrates allowed such highly audible proclamations to proliferate unchecked, then they would have risked drawing attention that would have likely exposed large numbers of Protestants.

On February 16, 1554, two weeks after the magistrates committed Robert Watson to jail, they turned their attention to the activities of John Toppylow, a carpenter, recently arrived in Norwich from London, where he claimed to have taken part in the failed insurrection now known as Wyatt's rebellion. At the end of January, Sir Thomas Wyatt, a Kentish gentleman, led a revolt in his home county against Queen Mary. Wyatt and his followers then marched on London even though the planned concurrent uprisings in the West Country failed to materialize. The rebellion ultimately failed in large part because of the Queen's bold personal appeal to Londoners to turn back the rebels. Wyatt's uprising aimed ostensibly at preventing the impending marriage of Queen Mary to Philip of Spain. But some contemporaries (as some historians have) detected strong Protestant overtones in the rebellion.[23]

The depositions concerning the carpenter Toppylow reflect contemporaries' competing and conflicting understandings of the

motives behind the uprising. According to John Chamber, Toppylow came to the home of Thomas Hammond, where Chamber
was a servant, on the night of February 15. Chamber inquired
from where Toppylow was arriving and the carpenter replied
that he had been in Kent among the rebels. In further conversation, Toppylow defended the insurrection as an attempt to prevent the Queen's marriage to Philip of Spain, arguing that if the
marriage took place, "I should lie in the street for default of
lodging and the Spaniards should have our houses," and also
that "we should drink no drink but water and pay a penny for a
quart pot full." Chamber rejected that contention and asserted his
belief that the rebellion was really "against the Queen and her
proceedings," clearly ascribing Protestant motives to the rebels.

Other witnesses spoke more directly about Toppylow's Protestant convictions, which might have influenced his participation
in Wyatt's rebellion. Thomas Hammond, Chamber's master, testified that Toppylow had asserted before him and others gathered
at his house the intention never to hear Mass again, despite the
group's warning "that whosoever speak against the Queen's proceedings were very traitors." As in his conversation with Chamber, Toppylow also predicted dire consequences if the Queen
married the Spanish prince: "we should lie in swine sties in caves
and the Spaniards should have our houses and we should live
like slaves and be glad to drink a pot with water." Finally, Harry
Darby, one of those at Hammond's house that evening, told the
mayor and aldermen how he had attempted to convince Toppylow of the wickedness of Protestantism by pointing to the ruin of
the Duke of Somerset. Contrarily, God had preserved the Duke of
Norfolk and the Bishop of Winchester, to which Toppylow sourly
responded, "Yea, peradventure to do more mischief."[24]

The testimony against Toppylow reflects the deep divisions
between Protestants and Catholics in mid-Tudor England. To
Toppylow, Hammond, Darby and Chamber were idolaters. And
he steadfastly maintained his intent never to hear Mass, despite
being labeled a traitor and being presented with evidence of
God's judgment against Protestantism by people who were pre-

sumably friends or relatives. (The records did not indicate why Toppylow was in Norwich or at Hammond's house in particular, but it seems that he was known at least to Hammond.) The three men who gave testimony were sufficiently offended by Toppylow's vilification of Catholicism, now the official religion, that they reported his words to the mayor and aldermen immediately. But despite the fact that Toppylow had admitted participation in the recent rebellion and had spoken quite openly and disparagingly against the restoration of Catholicism, the magistrates apparently took no action against him.

The investigation of John Toppylow was the only fallout from Wyatt's rebellion that has left traces in Norwich city records. If other participants fled to Norwich to elude capture after the uprising's collapse, their movements did not come to the magistrates' attention. By March 1554, the aldermen were occupied with another matter. They received a letter from Thomas Howard, the third Duke of Norfolk, complaining about the priest John Barret's dereliction of duty. Shortly after Queen Mary's accession, the Duke had been released from the Tower, where he had spent the entirety of Edward's reign. She restored him to the prominent role in English affairs that he had played under Henry VIII until, as part of the conservative faction at court, he fell from power during the last days of the King's life.[25]

From his East Anglian seat at Kenninghall, the eighty-year-old Duke wrote to the mayor and aldermen that he recently learned that Barret, who had been serving as the rector of the parish of St. Michael-at-Plea since 1550, "should omit either to preach the word of God . . . or to come to his divine service, to the evil example of such other as have him in credit and estimation." Having recently been at Norwich, the Duke continued, "I cannot a little marvel that at my late being among you, you would not declare the same unto me." He concluded the letter by demanding that the magistrates secure the priest's compliance or else commit him to ward.[26] Barret was a known Protestant and had been the target of hostility for his preaching in Norwich as early as 1535.[27] If the Duke's allegations were true, perhaps Barret's aversion to the restoration of Catholicism rendered him less than enthusiastic about the performance of his pastoral responsibilities.

The magistrates replied to the Duke's missive almost immediately and their response combined an effort to avoid conflict with an outside authority of the Duke's stature with a defense of a local clergyman and their own oversight of his activities. They assured the Duke that the allegations against Barret "we do partly know to be untrue," unwilling to contradict Norfolk completely. Barret had preached in the Green Yard at the Cathedral and at St. Michael-at-Plea. The mayor and aldermen had gone so far as to examine some of Barret's parishioners, who reported that the priest did indeed "say Mass and minister the Sacrament according to the Queen's proceedings." If Barret had failed to preach as often as he should have, they added, it was only because of illness. This answer must have satisfied the Duke as there was no further correspondence on the matter.[28]

The magistrates enjoyed a short respite from religious dissension after their correspondence with the Duke, for it was not until May that they confronted religious controversy again. On the twentieth, mayor Henry Crook, six aldermen and former city Recorder John Corbet took a deposition from the minstrel James Wharton, of East Wynch, Norfolk. The inquiry was into "certain unfitting songs unreverently supposed to be sung" by two of Wharton's apprentices. The songs railed "against the Mass and the godly proceedings of the Catholic faith of the Church, touching therein the honor and dignity of the Queen's highness." Wharton denied that his apprentices had sung any such songs, although an examination of some of his belongings found "one very evil and lewd song." Wharton again denied that he or his apprentices had sung the song openly and further contended that they had not even "read it [over] above two . . . times." He told the mayor and aldermen that he did not know the origin of the song, but received it from a minstrel named Robert Gold of Wymondham and also noted that the copy of the song was signed by a William Mason, with whom he was not acquainted.[29]

Wharton was not further detained by the magistrates, but his testimony resulted in action against both Gold and Mason, the third Norwich case with an atypical dimension. On May 26, 1554, Mason, who was a Norwich resident, was "set upon the pillory with a paper upon his head for devising of unfitting songs." Two others, a Norwich blacksmith named Richard Sturmyn and Matthew Harman, a worsted weaver, stood surety to ensure Mason's future appearance before the court, which never occurred. Two weeks later, on June 9, Robert Gold "was set upon the pillory and his ear nailed to the same for devising of unfitting songs against the Queen's majesty."[30]

These were certainly stronger measures than the magistrates had even taken against ordinary religious offenders in Henry's and Edward's reigns. In trying to understand why Mason and Gold were prosecuted at all and then subjected to such comparatively harsh treatment, it is difficult to ignore the presence of John Corbet at James Wharton's deposition. Corbet had harassed Dorothy Bale in 1545, when he was city Steward, and had been present at the initial hearing about Thomas Derling in 1551, when he occupied no civic office.[31] Corbet's presence at the examination of Protestant agitators is striking. It seems likely that he was instrumental in the apprehension and prosecution of Gold and Mason and might also have insisted on their harsh punishment. As Corbet was a prominent Norfolk gentleman, a former Steward and Recorder, as well as Norwich's MP in 1554, it would have been impolitic to disregard his counsel.

After Gold's and Mason's punishments, and what was an apparently quiet summer in Norwich, Richard Sotherton was back in court in September 1554. This time, the court bound him with another £20 bond, requiring that "the said Richard shall not utter or sell any seditious book, but immediately bring them to Mr. Mayor so soon as they shall come to his hands or else know where the same books be."[32] It is not known whether Sotherton ended his participation in the seditious book trade, for he was never called to court again and there is no indication that he ever turned over any treasonous materials to the magistrates.

The magistrates tackled a different issue when they considered the case of Gregory Addinge, Rowland Moore and John Burton on November 6, 1554. The three men stood accused, by whom it is not noted, of eating links on a Friday, contrary to an Edwardian statute. They did not deny the allegations against them and were committed to prison. Four days later, the court records noted that the three men were compelled to acknowledge their offense publicly, wearing papers on their heads, perhaps in place of a longer jail term. They were then discharged from further punishment on account of their poverty and because of their submission.[33] None of the three appeared in city records again.

Religious conflict was thus relatively muted in the first year of Mary's reign, with only a few incidents resulting in cases before the mayor's court. Despite the rather uncommon treatment meted out to John Hallybred, Robert Watson, Robert Gold and William Mason, the magistrates handled the other cases in the same way as they had in Henry's and Edward's reigns and the city was not the target of any scrutiny from the outside.

⇥ III ⇤

In 1554, Mary's government took major steps to complete the reversal of the Reformation. She issued royal Injunctions to the bishops in March, which covered a host of issues, from the suppression of "evil books," to the restoration of traditional clerical discipline, to the reestablishment of "all manner of processions of the Church" and the "laudable and honest ceremonies."[34] In November, the Queen's third Parliament met. Earlier Parliamentary legislation, such as the First Act of Repeal, had rescinded Henrician and Edwardian religious mandates, but did not yet nullify the break with Rome which the Queen so desired. The process of reuniting with the Roman Church picked up speed in 1554, when England received Reginald Pole as a Cardinal of the Roman Church and a papal legate. The staunch English Catholic Pole had opposed the dissolution of Henry VIII's marriage to Catherine of Aragon in the 1530's and gone into exile on the Continent as a result. He now returned ready to lift the papal sentence of excommunication from his native land. To help smooth the way for Parliamentary repeal of all remaining anti-papal legislation, Pole brought with him papal dispensation allowing the current owners of former monastic lands to keep their new properties. With that assurance in hand, Parliament passed the Second Act of Repeal in November 1554, which formally restored papal supremacy in England.[35]

There were no outbursts in Norwich over the return of papal supremacy or any of the other Marian religious directives. In fact, the magistrates of Norwich embraced the Queen's charge to resuscitate abandoned and formerly outlawed rituals and ceremonies. They were not alone, for many communities around England acted quickly to comply with Mary's wish. Corpus Christi plays and pageants, suppressed since 1548, reappeared in Ashburton, Cambridge, Chester, Coventry, Lincoln, Louth, Sherborne, Wakefield, Worcester, and York, as well as in a host of smaller communities. The Corpus Christi pageants also went forward again in Norwich from 1556.[36] At York and Chester, the celebration of St. George's day returned with processions and plays. In 1554, Leicester parishes held their first Whit Monday procession since 1548. The feast commemorating Becket's translation was observed in 1555 in Canterbury for the first time since its suppression in 1538. Churchwardens' accounts for some parishes around the country also reveal the purchase of "cloths" to be used in the formerly forbidden Lent and Palm Sunday ceremonies.[37]

In Norwich, the Queen's Injunctions had a discernible impact on the observance of the feast of St. George. On March 28, 1555, members of St. George's Company determined that "the feast of this company shall from henceforth be had, made, holden and kept, upon the day that it was wont to be holden and kept twenty years past and in like manner and form as it was then used in every condition." Two months later, they restyled the Company a "guild," completing the restoration to pre-Reformation form.[38]

With the reinstatement of the doctrine of purgatory, members were once again permitted to pray for the souls of their deceased brethren at the annual festivity, to light candles at those services and maintain lights at the altar or chapel of St. George at the Cathedral. Also revived was the guild's annual procession, although perhaps without some of its former grandeur. In 1550, St. George's, like so many parishes and guilds around England, had sold much of its ceremonial inventory.[39]

The revived St. George's guild in Norwich did not correspond entirely to its pre-Reformation form, however. In May 1555, guild members decided that "upon divers considerations" they would hold the annual festivity on the Sunday after Trinity, rather than on St. George's day itself. The Sunday after Trinity day remained the regular day for the guild's celebration through the mid-Elizabethan years, permanently decoupling the annual festivity from the April 23 feast of St. George. The guild minutes offer no reason for the shift in dates, but the unusual step indicates that city magistrates did not simply adopt the Queen's prescription for revived rituals wholesale. Rather, they reinvented St. George's Company and its rituals again along lines that would be acceptable to the new religious regime and also to conform to their own agenda.[40]

Not only did the magistrates revive older rituals, but they added new celebrations to the civic calendar, as they had been doing since the reign of Henry VIII. In June 1556 an elaborate three-part show marked alderman Augustine Styward's third election to mayoral office. It included three pageants mounted in the parishes of St. Peter Hungate, St. John Maddermarket and St. Andrew. This production had a more explicit religious dimension than the other celebrations the magistrates added to the civic calendar. In the first pageant, schoolmaster John Bucke, extolled the restoration of Catholicism:

> The ancient use and custom then
> at Rome hath been of old
> to reverence all such worthy men
> As did their wealth uphold

Their glory and their fame was fair
till fortune turned her ways
when worthy men defrauded were
of their deserved praise

But what of Rome since you have brought
whose virtues doth excel
A man in whom what grace hath wrought
unnethe [scarcely] mine tongue can tell.[41]

In late summer 1557, the corporation created a celebration of a kind that would have been more familiar to city residents, one that marked an English military victory at St. Quentin in France.[42] Earlier that year, King Philip persuaded Mary to commit English resources to support Spain in its war with France, news that was greeted with hostility in most corners of England.[43] In August, 5,000 English troops aided a much larger Spanish and Imperial force of about 70,000 in the siege of St. Quentin. Philip sent back an inflated report of the English role in the siege, which was the source of great jubilation at court.[44] The success at St. Quentin perhaps served to distract attention from the adversities that afflicted England at that time.

Recent harvests had been poor and the country was beset by both malnutrition and some starvation. The population was further weakened by epidemic disease, raging since 1555. Executions of Protestant heretics continued and rumors of conspiracy and rebellion were circulating. While the Privy Council found it necessary to command the Lord Mayor of London to celebrate the victory, no such coaching was necessary in Norwich.[45] The magistrates were accustomed to finding reasons to bring city residents together for celebration during difficult times.

Restoring Catholicism, however, could not be as simple as securing the necessary legislation from Parliament or reviving a few abandoned ceremonies. Nor, in important religious and political ways, could simply reestablishing official position of the Roman Catholic Church in England be enough for Mary. In her earliest days on the throne, Mary believed that most English men and women would return voluntarily to Roman Catholicism when given the opportunity. While many had, too many continued their vociferous opposition to the Roman Church, mocking and sometimes physically attacking priests, engaging in iconoclasm, and accusing the Queen of exposing England to depredations by her Spanish allies.[46] Mary's early hope that wayward Christians would be persuaded to accept Roman Catholicism as the one true faith soon wore thin. Her disillusionment with the possibility of persuasion was compounded by the political dimensions of religious opposition. Ever since the break with Rome heresy had been inextricably linked to treason. Papal supremacy could be restored, but the close connection between religious dissent and sedition could not be broken because the country's official religion was now inextricably tied to the monarch's choice of spiritual direction. In Mary's case, the problem of heresy melting into treason was exacerbated by the roots Protestantism had put down in some English communities, its critique of spiritual authority and its ability to ally with English xenophobia, currently directed at Philip of Spain.

The failure of attempts to achieve religious concord through persuasion did not immediately lead to full-blown persecution.[47] In 1554 Parliament did revive the medieval heresy statutes repealed by Edward VI, which enjoined death by burning for convicted heretics, the customary punishment across late medieval Europe.[48] Yet, as Christopher Haigh and Susan Brigden have pointed out, the nearly three hundred executions carried out under that legislation went far beyond the Queen's original expectations.[49] In pre-Reformation England, bishops found that public abjuration and penance combined with the execution of a handful of Lollards served to suppress those heretical communities for years.[50] In 1554, the Queen and her advisers and churchmen undoubtedly believed that the course of persecution would be much the same.[51] A few extremists would be put to death, some more would publicly recant and these demonstrations would serve as a suitable warning of the dangers of religious schism, driving the remaining heretics back to the true faith or, at least, public obedience to authority. From the perspective of contemporary religious and political practice, Mary's initial implementation of the 1554 heresy statute fell within customary usage.

In fact, the Queen and her churchmen hoped for reconciliation much more than for execution and martyrdom. Some persecutors, such as London's Bishop Bonner, later known as "bloody Bonner" for his role in London's 32 executions and countless more examinations, were initially reluctant to carry out their responsibilities.[52] Imprisoned Protestants were exhorted numerous times to abandon their heresy. Sometimes they were visited in jail by theologians, bishops, friends and family, who tried to induce them to accept Catholicism as the one true religion or simply beg them to recant to save their own lives.[53] Some Protestants were initially released from episcopal custody with hopes for future conformity. But obstinate heretics had to be put to death and more than a few loyal Catholics were willing to participate by accusing and testifying against Protestants, sometimes even when they were neighbors, friends or family members.[54]

Soon the persecution developed a dynamic of its own. Unlike the Lollards in the earlier sixteenth century, who had more readily retracted their opinions and disappeared from public life, the Protestants persecuted by Mary did not. They were too widespread and their Church had just recently been England's official religion. The executed became martyrs, known for often being cheerfully willing to die for their beliefs. Their surviving co-religionists were, in fact, driven to worship in secret cells and conventicles, but rather than breaking them this only strengthened their commitment. In addition, the burnings often inspired sympathy for the victims and a reaction against Mary, thus encouraging still more criticism and defiance of her rule. Mary's examiners quickly learned that Protestant disobedience had become more resolute and organized as a subversive underground, and this only magnified the imperative to burn willing and unrepentant heretics. From there the cycle accelerated, taking the initially squeamish like Bishop Bonner and making them eager to perform their pyrotechnical tasks, which only created more martyrs for the Protestant cause. And so the burnings stretched from February 1555 until just before the Queen's death in November 1558.[55]

Norwich remained quiet for some months after the heresy statute went into effect in January 1555, as there were no cases of religious conflict brought to the mayor's court until mid-1555. In the surrounding region, as Ralph Houlbrooke has pointed out, the outbreak of official persecution under the heresy statute was connected to the diocesan visitations of the new Bishop, John Hopton, the first of which occurred in the spring and summer of 1555.[56] The inhabitants of Norwich were not subject to that persecutorial effort because the Bishop directed his attention almost entirely to rural areas, especially in Suffolk. It was not until the summer of 1557 that the first of Norwich's two convicted heretics would be burnt.

The Queen's restoration of Catholicism appears to have proceeded relatively smoothly in Norwich after the passage of the heresy statute, although there were, of course, some tensions. Norwich diocesan officials acted quickly in response to the Queen's March 1554 Injunctions for the deprivation of all English clergymen who had taken wives.[57] With the "celerity and speed" demanded, Miles Spenser and Dr. John Fuller, the Vicar General and the Official Principal to Bishop Hopton, presided over the consistory court specially called to divorce and deprive married priests in the diocese. By the spring of 1555, thirteen priests who served at the Cathedral or in city parishes had been forcibly divorced from their wives and deprived of their livings. Included in that number were William Stampe of St. Augustine, who had destroyed the altar there in 1549, prebendary Henry King, whose preaching had come under attack, Andrew Colby, whose clerical status was doubted by city magistrates, and the Common Hall priest John Kempe.[58] No protests from city residents appear in the records.

In late 1554 and early 1555, Norwich diocesan authorities also turned their attention to the problem of re-equipment of the parishes. The restoration of Catholicism made necessary the reacquisition of chalices, Mass books, candlesticks, altar cloths and other ornaments. Church officials also required the obliteration of Scriptural texts that had been painted on church walls during Edward's reign, a particular preoccupation of Bishop Hopton. These changes appear to have been made without incident at slightly more than half of Norwich's approximately thirty-five parishes.[59] In December 1554, St. Andrew's, a parish of "known radical sympathies" according to Ralph Houlbrooke, was singled out by the consistory court for its failure to obtain the ornaments essential for Catholic worship. In February 1555, the consistory called nineteen city parishes before it, including St. Andrew's again, to inquire into the progress of their re-equipment. The churchwardens from five parishes did not appear. Of the remaining fourteen, only five had made the necessary acquisitions. Failure to furnish churches for the celebration of Catholic services could be evidence of resistance to Marian religious policy, but often it reflected simple parochial poverty. Consistory court records, in which these inquiries are contained, are lost for the last three years of Mary's reign and no other sources indicate conflict over the re-equipment of churches during the period.[60]

The mayor's court of Norwich heard no cases of religious conflict from the passage of the heresy statute until the end of Mary's reign. One case of sedition, possibly with religious content, did appear before the Norwich Quarter Sessions in June 1555. The Justices ordered the punishment of Abraham Martin, who had spoken "certain seditious words" against the Queen. Martin was to be taken from prison, where he presumably was being held, "to the pillory, and have both his ears nailed to the same." Martin's accuser was not named, nor were his "seditious words" detailed. Furthermore, it is not clear why his case was pursued in Quarter Sessions rather than the mayor's court, where Robert Gold's and William Mason's very similar transgressions were handled in mid-1554. Notably, Martin was ordered released after his punishment and was not turned over to ecclesiastical authorities for further examination.[61]

Over a year passed between Abraham Martin's encounter with

the Norwich Quarter Sessions and another instance of religious persecution in the city. In November 1556, the mayor and aldermen received a letter from the Privy Council notifying them that a Richard Vere of Stratbroke, Suffolk would be sent to the city for punishment. Vere, the letter explained, had been discovered circulating a treasonous letter. It is not clear why the Privy Council sent Vere to Norwich for punishment, as he did not appear to have any connection to the city. But when ordered to act by the central authorities, particularly when it concerned an outsider, the mayor and aldermen complied. The court book shows that they duly set Vere on the pillory in February 1557.[62]

The next case of religious conflict concerned one Elizabeth Cooper, who was ultimately burned as a Protestant heretic at the Lollard's pit outside Norwich's Bishopsgate on July 13, 1557. Cooper's execution followed scores of others around England since the implementation of the heresy statute in 1555, but hers, remarkably, was the first of a Norwich resident. Elizabeth Cooper was a pewterer's wife who had earlier forsworn her Protestant beliefs and later became "greatly troubled inwardly" by her actions. One day she interrupted a service at St. Andrew's parish, the scene of her recantation, and publicly revoked it. She told the assembled worshipers that "she was heartily sorry that she ever did it [i.e. recanted], willing the people not to be deceived, neither to take her doings before for an example." An irate member of the congregation, "one Bacon," whose identity cannot be definitely established, insisted that city sheriff Thomas Sotherton, who was present at the service, place Cooper under arrest. He exclaimed, "Master sheriff! will you suffer this?" Sotherton placed Cooper under arrest and she was later condemned to death. She went to the stake along with one Simon Miller of King's Lynn, on July 13, 1557. Miller had been turned over to diocesan authorities by an unnamed "evil disposed papist," according to the martyrologist John Foxe, after he had arrived in Norwich and asked a group of people leaving a church "where he might go to have the communion."[63]

In the crowd that attended Miller's and Cooper's execution was a young woman who exclaimed that "she would pledge them of the same cup that they drank on." That woman was Cicely Ormes, the wife of a worsted weaver from St. Lawrence's parish in Norwich. Also in the crowd was "Master Corbet of Sprowston by Norwich," the former city Recorder. Upon hearing Ormes's remark, Corbet took her and turned her over the Chancellor of Norwich diocese, Michael Dunning.[64] Dunning examined her, inquiring into her views on transubstantiation. In response to the question "What is that that the priest holdeth over his head?" Ormes retorted, "[i]t is bread: and if you make it any better, it is worse." Dunning sent her to the Bishop's prison, where she was subjected to further examinations. Dunning offered Ormes her freedom "if she would go to the church and keep her tongue," but she refused, "for God would surely plague her." Although reluctant to condemn "an ignorant, unlearned, and foolish woman," Dunning sentenced Cicely Ormes to death. He committed her to the custody of sheriffs Thomas Sotherton and Leonard Sotherton, who placed her in the Guildhall prison, where she lingered for over a year. Ormes recanted her beliefs at one point, but recommitted herself to Protestantism. She died bravely, according to Foxe, on September 23, 1558, before a crowd of two hundred.[65]

Cooper and Ormes were the only two Norwich inhabitants put to death in the Marian persecution. A third person was examined for heresy by ecclesiastical authorities in 1558 and then abjured the "errors, heresies and damnable opinions" of which he stood accused. In a signed retraction, the grocer Thomas Wolman, of St. Andrew's parish, repudiated his belief that the Protestant martyr Thomas Carman, who was executed in Norwich along with two others in May 1558, had "died well for that he did affirm and say that he did believe that Christ was not present in the Sacrament of the altar." Carman, a plowright from nearby Heigham, was sentenced to death for pledging support for Richard Crashfield, a Protestant from Wymondham, Norfolk, burnt at Norwich in August 1557. Wolman was released after abjuring his opinions and came to no further harm, dying in the early days of Elizabeth's reign.[66]

These three incidents involving Cooper, Ormes and Wolman occupy little space in John Foxe's *Acts and Monuments*, commonly called the *Book of Martyrs*. Despite East Anglia's reputation for Protestant fervor, none of the three Norwich victims of persecution became well known. Nevertheless, Foxe's narratives of their tribulations, based on correspondence and interviews conducted in the early days of Elizabeth's reign, provide important evidence for understanding the exceptional nature of persecution in Norwich.

A close examination of how each of the three Norwich victims was discovered, accused and then responded to his or her examination reveals the very tenuous structure of the persecutorial apparatus in Norwich. The stories of Cooper's and Ormes's arrests and executions we have from Foxe are highly unusual. In contrast to many other communities where the persecution was more systematic and aggressive, the two executions in Norwich only occurred because of several peculiar contingencies. Indeed, the two victims' public self-incrimination was instrumental in this respect, making it seem that with a little bit more discretion there would have been no execution of Norwich residents.

Elizabeth Cooper and Cicely Ormes were arrested only because they stood up, Cooper in church and Ormes at Cooper's execution, and publicly announced their adherence to Protestantism. No one had betrayed them or reported their heresy to the authorities, nor had the civil or ecclesiastical powers discovered them through an investigation. Cooper was not being examined when she renounced her recantation; she walked into a "popish service," as Foxe called it, and incriminated herself before the entire congregation of her own free will. This was only barely enough to bring her down in Norwich. When the irate Bacon complained and forced sheriff Sotherton to arrest Cooper, Foxe tells us the Protestant sheriff "was very loath to do it" for he and Cooper "had been servants together before in one house, and for the friendship he bare unto her, and the more for the gospel's sake."[67]

Ormes's apprehension was much like Cooper's. She acted in a similar manner, voluntarily announcing her support of Cooper, the outsider Simon Miller and their beliefs in full view of the townspeople, including civil and ecclesiastical officials, assembled for Cooper's and Miller's execution. This public statement must have been heard by a number of people who would want to see her punished. However, it is worth noting that, as Foxe tells the story, former city Steward and Recorder John Corbet was the one who immediately detained Ormes and turned her over to Chancellor Dunning. Corbet had already shown himself exceptionally eager to act against Protestants on three prior occasions. Corbet harassed Dorothy Bale in 1545 on his own initiative and was involved in the investigation of Thomas Derling in 1551, when he occupied no civic office. In 1554, during his term as MP for Norwich, Corbet went beyond his duty to participate in the examination of James Wharton, which ended with the unusually severe punishment of two other men, Robert Gold and William Mason, whose ears were nailed to the pillory. One wonders if Ormes would have met the same fate had Corbet not been present. But, as it happened, Ormes was executed for her indiscreet public remarks about Cooper's execution, which occurred only because Cooper incriminated herself in open church.

The chain of serious persecution under the heresy statute in Norwich depended on the weak links of self-incrimination, bad timing and Ormes's reaction to Cooper's execution. The third victim of persecution at this time, Thomas Wolman, was also detained for his reaction in support of a burned heretic, this time an outsider. In much of England, this kind of chain reaction against executions set in motion more investigations, examinations and executions. This did not happen in Norwich, where no heresy hunt followed Cooper's and Ormes's executions. In fact, Cooper's and Ormes's executions serve to underscore the rarity of such persecution in Norwich. The special contingencies on which their executions depended highlight the problem of understanding how and why Norwich, a well-known home of many Protestants, escaped large-scale persecution.

⊰ IV ⊱

Unlike Elizabeth Cooper and Cicely Ormes, the majority of the Marian martyrs were taken into custody through the efforts of lay authorities. Philip Hughes's analysis of the circumstances surrounding the capture of martyrs listed in Foxe's *Acts and Monuments* reveals that secular officials were responsible for close to 60 percent of those arrests. When secular magistrates were not involved, the next most common way in which Protestant suspects were apprehended was through the betrayal of a family member, friend or neighbor. Hughes found that such betrayals accounted for almost 13 percent of those executed.[68]

If the burnings ultimately had the effect of turning many English people against Mary's religious policies as many historians have claimed, it was nevertheless the case that magistrates and lay people played a critical role in making the Marian persecution possible. As David Loades has commented, "[t]he persecution involved a massive administrative and judicial effort by both the ecclesiastical and secular authorities in East Anglia and the Home Counties, with thousands of detections, investigations, and interrogations behind the hundreds of trials."[69] The system of lay courts, Church courts and royal commissions could be set in motion by just a single accusation against a suspected Protestant.

The diocese of Norwich was active in hunting down and trying heretics throughout Norfolk and Suffolk, but not in Norwich. Ralph Houlbrooke has described the nature of the persecution in Norwich diocese as "spasmodic" and "geographically limited." Official persecution was intermittent, with four major eruptions of activity: the spring and summer of 1555, the spring of 1556, the winter of 1556–57 and the spring of 1558. Houlbrooke relates the first two waves to diocesan and metropolitical visitations, but suggests that the last two were motivated by local concerns. The majority of the diocese's victims were from rural areas. Consequently, Houlbrooke writes, "the major towns of the diocese, with the exception of Ipswich, were hardly affected." Ipswich, he notes, was home to a large number of Protestants, but this leaves us to wonder why other towns with many Protestants did not see nearly as many investigations and executions. Houlbrooke adds that Bishop Hopton, the chief proponent of the diocesan persecution in 1556, even departed from Ipswich before completing his investigations, "much preferring to deal with heretics from rural mid-Suffolk."[70]

Although Houlbrooke's study of church courts does not include detailed histories of the diocese's many villages and towns, he suggests that the persecution's irregular geographical pattern was rooted in local historical circumstances, even during the first two waves of examination sponsored by the Bishop's and Archbishop's office. He observes that "it is significant that according to Foxe's account there were a large number of persecuting justices of the peace in Suffolk," where the suppression of Protestantism was fast and furious. This again highlights the important role of civil authorities and local sociopolitical conditions in the campaign against heresy. Although Norwich was the diocesan seat and known to harbor many Protestants, all of the evidence indicates that the civic authorities who resided in the shadow of the Bishop's palace abstained from participation in the Marian persecution of Protestant heretics.[71]

If one were unfamiliar with the history of religious division among Norwich magistrates and their practice of de facto toleration under Henry VIII and Edward VI, it might be tempting to speculate that a strongly Protestant leadership protected an overwhelmingly Protestant population from persecution during Mary's restoration of Catholicism. Indeed, Norwich's population did become strongly Protestant under Elizabeth and also known for its fervent Puritanism, but this later development and the nature of its effects only followed some dramatic changes which will be discussed in the next chapter. During Mary's reign, both the city's population and its leadership remained religiously divided between Protestants and Catholics. The tinder was there to start the fires burning, but with the exceptions of Elizabeth Cooper and Cicely Ormes, it was never ignited.

Norwich magistrates did not fail to participate in the Marian persecution because there were no Catholics among them. In 1553, then-mayor Henry Crook, who had been elected to his position during the reign of the Protestant Edward VI, publicly expressed his support for the return of the Mass. (Crook remained in civic service until his death in 1565, during the reign of Elizabeth.) His election as mayor under Edward was no anomaly, for there were three others elected who were probably Catholic.[72] In addition, an examination of wills written during the Queen's reign reveals continuing religious diversity among the aldermen.

Thirteen aldermanic wills survive that were written during Mary's reign.[73] Marian wills are subject to many of the same interpretive problems of wills written in Edward's reign. On the one hand, testators who opposed the prevailing religious settlement—in Mary's reign, Protestants—might have been reluctant to declare themselves openly. They might have been even more hesitant to do so once the burnings began. Neutral preambles that committed a soul to God alone or to God and Christ would not have aroused suspicion and potentially exposed family members to persecution. On the other hand, even committed Catholic testators might have been averse to making provisions for traditional services or leaving money for traditional church ornaments in their wills, fearing a future reversal of Mary's religious policies. Despite these inherent difficulties, the wills written during Mary's reign nevertheless indicate that there was not complete agreement among Norwich's magistrates on religious matters.[74] While five wills were indeterminate, the majority clearly reflected an allegiance to restored Catholicism.

Eight of the thirteen offer evidence of Catholicism, with their testators invoking the saints and/or bequeathing money for Masses. Seven aldermen, including Thomas Marsham and Thomas Cock, who wrote their last testaments in September 1557 and August 1558, respectively, committed their souls to "Almighty God, to Our Blessed Lady Saint Mary and to the holy company of heaven." The eighth alderman whose will suggests that he was Catholic was Thomas Malby, alderman for Coslany ward from 1554 until his death in 1558. Malby did not commit his soul to the saints, but to "Almighty God the Father and to his son my Lord and Savior Jesus Christ, throughout whose merits and passion I true to be saved." His Catholicism is clearly revealed by his provision for two perpetual obits to be kept in the Norwich parish of St. Mary Coslany. Malby requested that the mayor, the sheriffs and a few aldermen attend one of those anniversary Masses every year. In all, a total of five aldermen left such intercessory provisions, including Thomas Codde, who was mayor in 1549 during Kett's rebellion.

The religious sentiments of the remaining five testators are more difficult to evaluate, for they neither invoked the saints nor left legacies for anniversary Masses. Four of their preambles resembled the one written by Thomas Gray, who had been the sole compliant feastmaker in the 1548 St. George's Company incident and an alderman since 1550. He also served as Norwich's MP in 1555.[75] He drafted his will in July 1557 as influenza raged through Norwich, but did not succumb until the following year. Gray bequeathed his soul "to Almighty God the Father and to my Savior Jesus Christ through whose merits and death I believe faithfully that I am redeemed and saved and shall live with him forever." The fifth preamble was composed by the city's senior alderman Nicholas Sywhat, who had represented Colegate ward since 1520. It was considerably briefer, simply committing his soul "to God Almighty."

Other provisions in three of these remaining five wills offer small clues to the testators' religious allegiances, suggesting possible traditionalist leanings. John Balle, who wrote his will in 1554, served as alderman of South Conisford ward from 1553 until his death in 1556. His selection of John Corbet as supervisor of his will could suggest Balle's own conservative religious bent, given what is known of Corbet. Or it might simply indicate a tie between men who held lands outside Norwich, which they both did.[76] Perhaps Robert Leche's choice of Thomas Codde as his testament's supervisor was based on a shared religious outlook and/or a link between the two men based on their long years of civic service together. There is no way to know. Thomas Gray left no money for Masses, but he did earmark 10s. for his executrice to "give and dispose in true preaching and setting forth of Word of God in the City of Norwich." He also bequeathed £3 6s. 8d. to John Barret, "to pray for me." Barret was once known as a reforming Protestant, but sometime during Mary's reign he reembraced Catholicism and remained a Catholic until his death in the fifth year of the Protestant Elizabeth's reign. Ralph Houlbrooke notes that Barret was rewarded with a prebend at Norwich Cathedral, probably in 1558. Barret's Catholicism, combined with the fact that Gray was the sole compliant feastmaker during Andrew Quasshe's refusal to serve in 1548, suggests that he might have been of a conservative religious outlook.[77]

The remaining two wills of Nicholas Sywhat and Geoffrey Ward do not provide any hint of religious allegiance, unless one chooses to regard their very reticence as evidence of Protestantism. Sywhat's silence exemplifies the difficulty of discerning magistrates' specific religious beliefs. Sywhat spent close to forty years on the aldermanic bench, including one term as mayor. Yet, despite his long tenure, no trace of his religious affiliation can be found in any city record during the years of his service. While Sywhat's case is extreme because of his longevity, his practice of keeping his religious beliefs to himself was not unusual. In fact, with the exception of those wills that make religious sentiments evident and the public actions of a very few, such as Henry Crook, the great majority of aldermen did not leave a public record of their religious beliefs and sentiments. In the case of someone like Sywhat, who served through so many changes and reversals in official religious policy, such reticence helped to make a long career possible.

Thus, there were Catholic aldermen in Norwich who could have participated in the Marian efforts to eradicate Protestantism had they so desired. The cases of religious conflict that came to the mayor's court in 1553 and 1554 also show that there were indeed Catholic residents of Marian Norwich who also could have taken part in the suppression of Protestantism had they been willing to take the initiative. In addition, the examples of Elizabeth Cooper and Cicely Ormes make clear that, in each case, one person was able to secure the arrest that led to their executions after they incriminated themselves. John Corbet alone took Cicely Ormes off to the Chancellor for examination after her outburst at Elizabeth Cooper's burning. When the St. Andrew's parishioner Bacon insisted that the reluctant sheriff Thomas Sotherton arrest Elizabeth Cooper, the sheriff had to comply or risk serious danger to himself. For the same reason, he and other civic officials would have had to act in response to any credible public accusation of heresy. If the mayor's court book is any indication of the number of such accusations, few or none were made. Thus, not only did the magistrates fail to root out Protestants, but their willingness to accept religious heterogeneity appears to have had some support from the populace.

Norwich residents were certainly not defending some abstract ideal of religious freedom. Rather, it seems they were looking out for themselves both individually and collectively. Protestant protest against Catholicism was muted, especially after 1555. Before that date, as I have shown, there were a few individuals who publicly stated their opposition to the return of Catholicism. For example, Robert Watson told the mayor's court that he would never attend Mass and soon found himself imprisoned. William Derne seemed to promise more dramatic action when he proclaimed his eagerness to pluck a priest out of his clothes, but he was let go without punishment. There is no record of any iconoclasm or attacks on priests or their vestments in Norwich of the kind that occurred in London.[78] By way of contrast, the extraordinary cases of Cooper and Ormes, as well as Simon Miller from distant King's Lynn, show how Norwich Protestants kept a low profile during the years of persecution. Miller, it is worth remembering, was burned along with Cooper because he wandered into the city one day in 1557 and, standing in a crowd of people outside one of the city's churches, inquired into the availability of Protestant services.

Secret Protestant services must have existed in Norwich, as Simon Miller believed. But no underground conventicles seem to have been discovered by the authorities, nor is there any evidence that they even looked for them either before or after Miller's public and ill-advised inquiry. Norwich Protestants appear to have enjoyed a certain level of security against incrimination by simply keeping quiet. Likewise, aside from the peculiar case of John Corbet, who figures as a principal in multiple actions against Protestants, and perhaps the irate but obscure Bacon, Catholics in the city do not appear to have expressed or acted on a desire to extirpate Protestantism. It is difficult to escape the conclusion that Miller was doubly vulnerable because of his indiscretion and his status as an outsider, which denied him the immunity that almost all Norwich Protestants seem to have enjoyed.

The Marian persecution simply did not get off the ground in Norwich. Despite the ample presence of Protestants and Catholics, only two were executed, few were even examined and only one is known for certain to have gone into exile. This epitomizes the success of the Norwich magistrates' emphasis on civic unity and their practice of de facto toleration. Given the Norwich magistrates' quarter-century of highly consistent practice regarding religious conflict and civic unity, it is clear that their failure to participate vigorously in the Marian persecution was deliberate.

The continuity of the Norwich magistrates' practice of toleration was supported by its past success and by the continuity among the practitioners, who were thus enabled to pass down knowledge of their experiences to new generations of aldermen. On January 1, 1558, toward the end of the Marian persecution and at the beginning of the last year of Mary's reign, 17 of Norwich's 24 aldermen had been in service since the time of Edward VI. Thus, more than half of the aldermen who survived in office through the worst of the Marian persecution had served under the previous Protestant regime. Of the total of 30 aldermen who held office at any time during Mary's reign, 14 had also been in office during the time of the Six Articles under Henry VIII. Therefore, almost half of all the aldermen in office under Mary had served on the mayor's court during the years of the draconian Six Articles, when cases of religious conflict could have, but did not, result in serious charges and investigations. There were even four long-lived aldermen who had been in office at the time of Thomas Bilney's execution in 1531. One of these aldermen, Nicholas Sywhat, was a man of extraordinary fortitude, having held office continuously since 1520, after a one-year term in 1517. He served until his death in 1558 at the end of Mary's reign, thus providing a living connection through all of the events since Cardinal Wolsey's visit to Norwich.

Understanding the peculiar course of the Reformation in Norwich is the particular purpose of this book. However, the practice of toleration in Norwich cannot be understood apart from some consideration of the practice of intolerance that affected other parts of England.

⊰ V ⊱

Historians have not yet published extended analyses of urban politics and religion during the Marian persecution, so it is difficult to compare Norwich with many other towns on this point. Indeed, it might be that the Marian persecution was lighter in towns than in the countryside, despite the usual association of Protestantism with urban areas. Ralph Houlbrooke's study suggests that most towns in Norfolk and Suffolk escaped the brunt of the persecution because of reluctant local authorities. In Bristol, Martha Skeeters has found some evidence that the "mayor and aldermen had attempted to dissociate themselves from the burnings" of the four to eight residents put to death there. While this pattern of local magistrates' apparently impeding the course of persecution seems similar to that in Norwich, there are some crucial differences. Skeeters's primary evidence of the magis-

trates' alienation from official policy is chiefly based on their refusal to worship at the Cathedral whose Chancellor directed
Bristol's heresy trials and the consequent reproach they received
from the Privy Council on the eve of the last Marian execution in
the city. As in the past, Bristol's magistrates had taken a decided
position on religious matters, something that Norwich's magistrates did not do.[79]

The city for which we have the most research is, thanks to Susan Brigden, London, the very same city that experienced more
burnings than any place in England. The difference between
Norwich, where there was so little persecution, and London
probably cannot be explained by the depth or intensity of religious belief, for either Catholics or Protestants. We know that there
could not have been a shortage of unhappy Protestants in Norwich during Mary's reign, just as there was no shortage of unhappy Catholics during Edward's. Instead, it is necessary to
identify the conjunctural factors of politics, society and belief that
made persecution—or toleration—possible in a given time and
place. Thinking about persecution and toleration as practices, differences in such local factors as familiarity, trust, civic solidarity,
the presence of central government and the political traditions of
urban ruling groups all help to explain why London and Norwich followed such different courses during the Marian persecution.

In her study of religious conflict in the capital, Susan Brigden
estimates that 32 Londoners died in the fires. Hundreds more
were investigated and examined for heresy.[80] London's population was probably about eight to nine times greater than Norwich's in the mid-Tudor period, but sixteen times the number of
Norwich victims were executed in the persecutions and the proportion arrested for religious reasons was many times greater.[81]
In addition, approximately 40 more men and women from other
parts of England were also put to death in the capital. Still more
were sent there for examination. This illustrates London's central
role in the persecution. The heresy statute originated there, more
victims came from London than any other town and, more im-

portantly, the number of outsiders who met their deaths in the capital exceeded the number of native martyrs. Some of these outsiders had moved to London or were passing through, others were transported to the capital for their interrogation and trial. London attracted many immigrants from around the country because it was England's biggest and most cosmopolitan city, as well as its economic and political center. Because it was the seat of central authority, London also pulled the unwilling into its administrative hands. In both ways, London differed consequentially from Norwich.

Norwich remained a provincial city in which the distinction between city residents and migrants from the countryside appeared sharply maintained in the differential treatment given outsiders brought before the mayor's court. London, on the other hand, could not so readily uphold a similar sense of corporate unity and civic identity. Its population was much more mobile and expanding than Norwich's and, as the seat of the kingdom, London had to play host to visitors from around the country as well as the Continent. Susan Brigden's study of London during the Reformation tells us much about conflict and the breakdown of community caused by confessional division, but, as this study of Norwich and several others of Continental towns show, the fact of confessional division alone cannot fully explain urban disturbance. A more focused study of urban society and its institutions in London, such as Joseph P. Ward's examination of London's livery companies, shows us that the challenges to community were not just religious and that, in some important ways, communal solidarity survived.[82] This could help to explain Brigden's seemingly contradictory conclusions about the pervasiveness of religious conflict during the Reformation and some Londoners' reluctance to delate each other during the Marian persecution.

As the country's administrative center, with heretics from around the provinces being brought there for examination, the anti-heresy campaign could not possibly have bypassed London as it did Norwich. Bonner himself was painfully aware of the expectations placed on him during the persecutions, for as Bishop of London he had to examine large numbers of suspects, many of whom were sent to him directly by the Privy Council. In the early days of the burnings when he was, apparently, still hesitant about his responsibilities in the persecutorial effort, Bishop Bonner lamented to the future martyr John Philpot that the vigilance of the court limited his ability to avoid the unpleasant task of pursuing and punishing heretics. Bonner was right, for he was later officially scolded for allowing too many heretics to slip from his grasp undisciplined.[83]

Bishop Bonner's personal history also illustrates the dynamic cultural process of persecution. From his initial reluctance to burn Protestants, Bonner became a most eager proponent of the practice. First he had been forced to start because of his position in London, then he became the target of Protestant criticism. As Brigden observes, "[t]he wilfulness and obduracy and teasing of the godly goaded him."[84] This same process of constructing a culture of persecution affected many others from the Queen down to some local magistrates and residents. Practicing such a draconian policy inherently tended to raise the stakes of the game for all involved. Once Protestantism was defined as heresy and Protestants were identified and executed, their threat to Church and state only increased. In addition, once the process of apprehending heretics had begun, the failure to follow through would potentially endanger one's own safety. For this reason, the process of hunting heretics was very difficult to stop once it gained momentum. Even the reluctant sheriff Sotherton in Norwich felt compelled to arrest and preside over the July 1557 execution of the unfortunate Elizabeth Cooper, more than two years since the first burning in London and after 28 Londoners had already been consumed by the flames. Perhaps if the Marian burnings had continued, instead of slowing to a halt just before the Queen's death, the pressures to persecute would have become overwhelming in Norwich. As it happened, civil and ecclesiastical officials found the pressure to persecute irresistible in London from an early date, while those in Norwich did not.

London officials and residents may have been more responsive to the Marian call for persecution partly because they had engaged in comparable acts in the past, though with less serious consequences in the cost of human life. London's magistrates had long been involved in efforts to impose religious uniformity. During Henry VIII's reign, they presided over the arrests and imprisonment of hundreds of Londoners under the terms of the Six Articles. Under Mary, hundreds of Protestant suspects were routinely arrested by aldermen's deputies and sergeants.[85]

Brigden's interpretation of the Marian burnings is subtle and often difficult to track, especially on the subject of how heretics were betrayed and how cross-devotional solidarity emerged in the face of the persecution, despite her emphasis on the Reformation's destruction of community. While Brigden notes that Marian persecutors such as Bonner typically took action "upon information given to them rather than searching out and arresting suspects themselves," she reports that the identities of the informants are still mostly unknown. She tells us that certain "Judas-like promoters" of Catholicism were identified as betrayers by chroniclers such as Foxe, but she adds that "of Londoners delating their fellow citizens there is almost no evidence. When Protestants were reported, as during the 1554 visitation, it was often the trouble-makers, disliked for other reasons than their religion alone, who were named."[86] She appears to be distinguishing between common Londoners and the most devoted advocates of Catholicism, between Protestants persecuted only for heresy and those who troubled Catholics in additional ways, as well as between persecution in general and the rash of burnings under Mary. As Brigden explains, "[c]itizens might draw back from accusing their neighbors of heresy" when the punishment was death, "but the old suspicions and grievances harboured against confessional enemies did not go away."[87] Cross-devotional solidarity in London only went so far, as the city still led the country in burnings.

If Catholic Londoners were sometimes reluctant to send their neighbors to the stake, Brigden recounts how they "found other ways of persecuting the gospellers," forcing them, for example, to finance the re-equipment of parish churches for Catholic worship or harassing them with other charges.[88] In the end, Brigden reports that "the Marian persecution, and its aftermath, left much bitterness and much guilt."[89] Persecution once started, institutionalized and sustained in London would not subside so easily. But in Norwich, where there was so little persecution during Mary's reign or before, there were only slight grounds for lingering resentments.

6

Fervor and Forbearance

NORWICH UNDER THE
ELIZABETHAN SETTLEMENT

Unlike many other Protestant communities in England, Norwich survived the Marian persecutions relatively unscathed. The executions did not directly deplete the ranks of Protestants in the city, nor were Norwich's most vocal advocates of reform forced into exile. Consequently, upon the death of Mary and the accession of Elizabeth in November 1558, the restoration of Protestantism in Norwich followed a somewhat different course than in many other parts of England. Except for John Parkhurst, Elizabeth's first Bishop of Norwich, few if any Elizabethan residents of Norwich had experienced Continental exile or severe persecution under Mary.[1] The magistrates' tradition of de facto religious toleration combined with sufficient neighborly forbearance on the part of the wider population to prevent the sowing of persecution's bitter seeds, which were now sprouting a new crop of religious conflict and recrimination in many other communities.

Elizabeth signaled her intention to restore Protestantism in a series of steps soon after coming to the throne. She ended the Marian heresy trials in December 1558 and freed surviving prisoners. At court, Elizabeth replaced Mary's Catholic ladies-in-waiting with Protestant women. She also reorganized the Privy Council, dismissing a number of Mary's Catholic councilors and replacing them with Protestants. In her own chapel, the Queen prohibited the elevation of the Host during Mass and had the words of the consecration spoken in English.[2]

Elizabeth's first Parliament met in January 1559 and soon passed legislation formally creating the official Protestant Church of England that survives, with some modifications, to this day. The Act of Supremacy separated the English Church from the papacy and made Elizabeth its Supreme Governor. The Act of Uniformity abolished the Mass and reimposed the Second Edwardian Prayer Book of 1552 with several important revisions aimed at broadening the appeal of the Church.

By the terms of the Act of Uniformity, the anti-papal entreaty in the litany was removed and the administration of the sacraments was altered to include both the more and the less skeptical interpretations of the real presence in the Eucharist from the 1552 and 1549 Prayer Books. Whereas the Prayer Book of 1552 forbade priests from wearing any of the medieval Mass vestments except the surplice, the Elizabethan Prayer Book restored the use of the cope, which had been permitted in the 1549 Prayer Book. The Act also, as its name implies, demanded uniformity of religion. All clergy were required to perform services only from the Prayer Book and all people were enjoined to respect it on pain of penalties escalating from fines for the first offense to imprisonment for life for a third. Attendance at the newly established Church was mandatory; ecclesiastical and civic officials were authorized to impose fines for nonattendance.

Royal Injunctions for the "suppression of superstition" and "to plant true religion" in the summer of 1559 required the use of an English liturgy and the provision of English Bibles while also demanding the abolition of images, rood screens, the parish procession, the cult of saints and traditional vestments except those authorized by the 1559 Prayer Book. To enforce these Injunctions, Elizabeth appointed commissions to undertake a royal visitation of the dioceses along the lines of Archbishop Cranmer's enforcement of Edwardian reforms in 1548.

The two Acts of 1559 with the supplementary Injunctions and articles which followed are collectively known as the Elizabethan

Settlement. However, as all scholars of the subject know, the Elizabethan Settlement settled very little other than determining that Elizabeth's Church would be Protestant. Given the recent frequent alterations to official religion, few could be confident in the permanence of this arrangement. Moreover, because of the range of strongly held religious beliefs recently fostered by the Marian restoration of Catholicism, the Continental experiences of the returned Marian exiles and the example of the martyrs monumentalized by Foxe in 1563, it was guaranteed to breed conflict. And that it did from the very beginning, when the Queen had to force the 1559 Acts through Parliament by imprisoning some of Mary's bishops who still sat in the House of Lords. When the legislation finally passed, all but one of the bishops resigned in protest. Their replacements, many of whom had been Marian exiles, were soon voicing their own discontent with a Church that they did not think was sufficiently Protestant.

The research of revisionist historians has emphasized the widespread opposition, criticism and, especially, noncompliance with the Elizabethan Settlement in certain regions.[3] Occasions for conflict and recrimination proliferated as the Elizabethan Church attempted to enforce uniformity of religious practice. Ecclesiastical authorities deprived three hundred clergy for refusing to submit to the Elizabethan Settlement at the beginning of the Queen's reign and it appears many others were no less lax in compliance.[4] Although the official confiscation of religious paraphernalia preempted the kind of popular iconoclasm that occurred under Edward, the destruction of holy objects still carried a vengeful streak. In several communities, Catholics were forced, during royal visitations, to heap saints' images, rosaries and the like onto the bonfires, often in retaliation for having hidden such objects. Non-compliance and passive resistance continued for many years, vexing the Queen, her bishops and many committed Protestants.[5] But Protestants also could not agree among themselves. Some committed Protestants who called for further reformation of the Church were derided, from the 1560's, as "Puritans" for their efforts to purify the Church. The range of such critics of the established order grew to include Separatist congregations, whose members felt they could no longer participate in the life of the established Church, as well as those who risked their careers and well-being to reform it from the inside.

Despite the fact that Norwich's population and magistrates became more strongly Protestant after 1558, the magistrates continued to exercise restraint in their handling of religious divisions and tensions among Protestants as well as between Protestants and Catholics. There was no magisterial persecution of Catholics after Mary's reign. There was also virtually none in later years, even as the era's well-known plots against the Queen, including one that failed in Norwich in 1570, excited anti-Catholic sentiment throughout England. Norwich was also home to sometimes factious Protestant groups who became the focal point of controversy when the Queen called for greater religious uniformity on many occasions throughout her reign. But, following their tradition of tolerance, the magistrates took no steps to enforce uniformity on Protestants.

However, it would be a mistake to think that the relationship between politics and society in Norwich was simply static throughout this period. Social and demographic changes combined with the early influence of varieties of strong Protestantism soon to be associated with Puritanism, altering the nature and practice of governance in Norwich. The resulting reformation of manners redefined the problems of poverty, vagrancy and disorderliness, expressing a spiritually inflected imperative to regulate behavior quite different from the magistrates' long-standing practice of accepting confessional heterogeneity. While the magistrates remained tolerant of religious differences, from the early days of Elizabeth's reign they began to demonstrate an increasing intolerance of social transgressions.

⊰ II ⊱

In the last years of Mary's reign and the first of Elizabeth's, outbreaks of disease combined with harvest failures to produce a demographic crisis unseen in England for some time, probably decreasing the country's population by 6 percent. In Norwich, disease inflicted heavy mortality in 1556. Two years later, in 1558–59, an epidemic, probably influenza, swept through the city.[6] Unlike plague or other epidemic diseases that claimed the lion's share of their victims from the poorest and most cramped quarters of the city, influenza made no such distinction between the prosperous and penniless. Disease initiated what Norwich's Catholic and Protestant citizens had refused to do for so long. The epidemic made possible the rapid confessional unification of the magistracy.

The epidemic of 1558–59 took lives from a wide cross-section of the city's inhabitants, including ten of its twenty-four aldermen. The death of so many aldermen was understood as a signal historical event and recorded as such in the "Mayor's Book," a manuscript chronicle of the city's history that was begun in 1526 by alderman Augustine Styward.[7] Sometime shortly after the epidemic's course had been run the names of the recently deceased magistrates—John Atkins, Thomas Cock, Thomas Codde, Thomas Gray, John Howse, Thomas Malby, Alexander Mather, Robert Rugge, Nicholas Sywhat and Geoffrey Ward—were entered on a page of the history.[8] The loss of such a large proportion of the city's governors was unprecedented. The deaths took three of the most experienced aldermen and significantly altered the religious composition of the aldermanic bench.

Nicholas Sywhat, Robert Rugge and Thomas Codde were the three senior aldermen in 1558 and all three had served terms as mayor. When Sywhat wrote his will in May 1558 he was the senior alderman, having served continuously since 1520 with an additional year of aldermanic service before that. Rugge had served first East Wymer and then Middle Wymer ward since 1533, and Codde had represented North Conisford ward since 1538.[9]

At least six stricken aldermen were certainly Catholic and a seventh probably was also. The six aldermen who were definitely Catholic left wills that clearly indicate their religious affiliation. Thomas Cock, Thomas Codde, Thomas Malby and Alexander

Mather all requested that Masses be said for their souls or made other provisions in their wills that leave little doubt about their faith. Although Robert Rugge made no such arrangements, he proclaimed his allegiance to "the true faith of the holy Catholic church." Like Rugge, John Howse made no intercessory provisions, but called on "the holy company of heaven" in his preamble, indicating that he too was probably Catholic.

The religious sentiments of the remaining four aldermen are more difficult to evaluate. Thomas Gray, who did not call on the saints or leave bequests for anniversary Masses, did leave money to John Barret, who re-embraced Catholicism under Mary. For this reason, along with his service as MP under Mary in 1555 and the fact that he was the sole compliant feastmaker in the 1548 incident involving St. George's Company, there is good cause to believe that Gray was a religious conservative. Nicholas Sywhat's will left no clues about his religious affiliation, just as he left no clues during his almost forty-year tenure on the aldermanic bench. Geoffrey Ward's will and one-year tenure as an alderman are similarly devoid of any indications of his religious sentiments. Finally, the alderman John Atkins left no surviving will nor other clues about his religious beliefs.

Christopher Haigh has noted that the epidemic helped Protestants to gain control of the universities early in Elizabeth's reign by eliminating many of the Catholics who then held positions.[10] It seems likely that the influenza epidemic would have had a similar effect on governments in afflicted towns. It certainly did in Norwich. Of the twenty-four aldermen serving in Norwich on January 1, 1558, before the epidemic hit their ranks, ten can be identified with some degree of assurance as probable Catholics. There may have been more, but there is no evidence to identify additional Catholics and it seems highly unlikely that there were many more. Thus it can be estimated that more than one-third of the aldermen at the start of 1558 were Catholic. After the epidemic of 1558–59 only three Catholic aldermen—Robert Leche, Henry Crook and William Mingay—can be identified with any degree of assurance. Leche died in 1559, soon after the epidemic, and both Crook and Mingay would die in 1565.[11] After that date there is no evidence to suggest that any Catholics sat on the aldermanic bench for the rest of Elizabeth's reign. From at least a substantial minority in 1558, the number of Catholic aldermen declined precipitously in just one year and most likely fell to zero within a decade.

It is difficult to identify the religious leanings of most of the ten new aldermen at the time that they entered office in 1558–59 and it is similarly difficult to develop a portrait of the fourteen survivors of the epidemic. Two of the ten new aldermen can be identified as being committed Protestants by 1558. New alderman Andrew Quasshe had made his religious sentiments well known in the 1548 St. George's guild incident, among other episodes. A second new alderman, John Blome, had participated in the 1547 fight over holy bread and water at St. Peter Mancroft, and fellow participants Andrew Quasshe and Thomas Elsay acted as witnesses to his 1561 will.[12] For the other eight aldermen there is little or no evidence of their religious views before 1558.

Wills for seven of the eight remaining new aldermen have survived, but these were written over a nearly forty-year span from 1561 to 1600, so there is no way to know if their beliefs had changed between 1558 and the drafting of their wills later on. All of the will preambles fell within acceptable Protestant parameters for the Elizabethan period. None invoked the saints and all committed their souls to Christ. But this by itself is no guarantee that they were Protestant. Other evidence attests to two of the testators' Protestant leanings. Nicholas Norgate's 1568 will, in addition to its lengthy preamble, bequeathed money to support sermons to be given by four preachers selected by the Bishop of Norwich, who was then John Parkhurst, a moderate Puritan and Marian exile.[13] While alderman and former mayor Thomas Parker was the brother of Elizabeth's first Archbishop of Canterbury and long-time Protestant Matthew Parker, there is no direct evidence of his own religious leanings before 1558. Thomas Parker's 1570 will left bequests to Protestant clergy, including his brother, the "godly divine" Henry Bird, Dean of the Norwich Cathedral

George Gardiner, and Cathedral prebendary John Walker, who would soon make his very vigorous Protestantism known by smashing the organ at Norwich Cathedral.[14] The bequests and witnesses in the remaining five wills offer no additional clues about the testators' religious beliefs.

The ten new aldermen elected in 1558–59 joined fourteen survivors of the epidemic. The probable Catholics Crook, Leche and Mingay account for three of the fourteen survivors. There is no evidence of the pre-1558 religious beliefs of the remaining eleven, ten of whom left surviving wills, composed between 1563 and 1590. All ten fell within the acceptable Protestant parameters for the period. Eight of those wills provide no additional clues to the testators' beliefs. Two wills by aldermen John Aldrich and Richard Fletcher offer further evidence of their Protestant leanings. John Aldrich's 1582 will left sums of money to a number of clergymen, including the Puritans Henry Bird, John More and Thomas Roberts, whom he labeled "faithful workmen in the Lord's business." When Richard Fletcher penned his will in 1570 he left money for George Leeds to preach a sermon. Leeds was the curate of the parish of St. Stephen and one of the group of Puritan clergy in the city that would be suspended for nonconformity in 1576.[15]

From this evidence, we can begin to sketch a portrait of the new magistracy that emerged after 1558. By the end of the epidemic, there were probably three Catholics sitting on the bench, one of whom would die later in 1559. Two aldermen were clearly strong Protestants of long standing and the evidence from wills demonstrates that five more would become strong Protestants, if they were not so already, making a total of seven identifiably fervent reformers. Of the fourteen remaining aldermen, twelve left wills that were at least nominally Protestant, while the final two left no surviving wills. The probably Catholic alderman Robert Leche, who died in 1559, was replaced by Thomas Beamond, almost certainly a Protestant.[16] Although most magistrates' religious affiliations can be surmised only from their wills—notoriously inexact sources in most instances—it does seem that the religious composition of the aldermen had changed in the course of two years to become heavily Protestant, with but two identifiable Catholics and at least twenty probable Protestants.

The firmest and most interesting evidence of the Norwich magistracy's religious reorientation after 1558 comes not from their past proclamations or their often difficult to interpret wills, but from their practice of governance. As we shall see below, the Norwich magistrates continued their practice of tolerating differences between Protestants and Catholics as well as the developing diversity among Protestants. Given their history of religious toleration, this does not seem to reflect a new Protestant solidarity among the magistrates. However, in other areas of governance the magistrates demonstrated a new and strong Protestant influence. Without imposing religious uniformity, the magistrates embarked on a campaign of moral and social discipline closely related to their own religious reorientation. Establishing the magistrates' continued practice of religious toleration and then demonstrating their exertion of a new kind of spiritually inflected social and moral discipline will underscore the magistrates' deepened commitment to religious toleration as a form of governance.

⊰ III ⊱

Norwich was quiet during the first years of Elizabeth's reign. No outpourings of support for or opposition to her regime have left any trace in the city records. Neither is there record of acts of retaliation against Catholics. There is no evidence, for example, that any Norwich Catholics, like some at Exeter, were forced to throw images or other objects sacred to them into fires made to destroy them. Nor is there any record that city Protestants engaged in vengeful iconoclasm, as some did in Bures, Suffolk, where some enthusiastic Protestants cut down rood screens and demolished the Easter Sepulcher canopy.[17] The royal visitation of 1559 was apparently without much incident in Norwich, for no priest in the city was deprived of his living for opposition to the new religious regime. Three hundred priests were deprived in other communities across England.[18]

There were signs of changes in the city related to the alteration of religious regimes. The magistrates themselves sought to conform to the dictates of the Elizabethan Settlement by reorganizing the guild of St. George again. They discreetly renamed it the "Company and Fellowship of Saint George," much as they had in Edward's reign, in order to disconnect the institution from its recent Catholic past. The new Company also made a significant alteration to the annual celebration, deciding in early May 1559 that "there shall be neither George nor Margaret." That resolution eliminated the costumed members who portrayed St. George and the lady Margaret in the annual procession during Mary's reign, which would help to direct attention away from the Company's medieval foundation as a religious confraternity established to pray for souls in purgatory. Nevertheless, members still permitted the dragon that had been part of the procession to remain part of the Company's yearly festivity.[19]

In other changes to ceremonial life in Norwich, the Corpus Christi pageants, revived in 1556, were halted after 1558, even though there was no order mandating their suppression from the central government.[20] Finally, the mayor and aldermen also rehired the priest John Kempe to serve at the Common Hall. Kempe had been the Common Hall priest from 1541, just after the city had purchased the former Blackfriars' building, until 1555, when he was deprived for marriage. Kempe, like the other clergy so deprived, was reinstated at the beginning of Elizabeth's reign. He served for only a year and his name disappears from city records after 1559 when, perhaps, he died.[21]

It was not until 1561 that the mayor and aldermen heard evidence that touched on conflicts over religion. In June of that year, the magistrates took a deposition from Thomas Blome. Blome recounted a recent conversation with Laurence Hodger as they rode to Walsham Market. Blome asked Hodger if the "perk" or rood screen had come down in the latter's parish of St. Andrew. Hodger replied in the affirmative and went on to declare that "you have a sight of rebels' hearts" in Blome's parish of St. Peter, although he did not specify which of the four city parishes with that name he meant. Hodger added that the rood screen at St. Peter's would soon be razed. This incident demonstrates that religious tensions did indeed exist among Norwich's inhabitants, even if there were no explosive conflicts over issues such as the continuing presence of traditional Catholic church furniture. The magistrates did not act in the matter and Thomas Blome apparently returned to his parish church, where a rood screen still stood, two years after their demolition had been demanded in the royal visitation of 1559.[22]

Several weeks later, in early July 1561, the magistrates listened to a series of accounts that focused on recent statements made by a Norwich worsted shearman named John Seman. Edward Boston, a servant to alderman Thomas Parker, testified that during the previous Lent (which in July, when the deposition was being given, was some months previous), he had been sent to Seman's house on an errand. Seman asked Boston about the whereabouts of John Barret, to which the servant had no answer. Seman then continued, recounting a sermon he heard preached by Bishop John Parkhurst. According to Seman, Parkhurst had charged his predecessor with asserting that it was better that poor people starve rather than churches go unadorned. Parkhurst continued in his sermon "that Christ was never no fornicator, whoremaster, nor yet adulterer," but Seman added that he believed that Parkhurst was all of those things. The talkative Seman then offered his own opinion of Parkhurst's sermons, declaring, "I had as lief hear this chair preach as to hear him."[23]

Testimony about John Seman continued a week later, when Robert Munds told the mayor and aldermen of a recent conversation with Edward Boston. Tuning a pair of virginals at the home of Thomas Parker, where Boston served, Munds observed, "[i]t is a wonderful thing to hear men talk nowadays," to which Boston could only reply, "[i]f you had heard as much as I have done it would make the ears burn off your head." He then told Munds how John Seman had complained that the only preachers around were adulterers and fornicators. Finally, George King of St. Lawrence's parish in Norwich reported that Robert Munds told him that John Seman called the Bishop a whoremaster. The magistrates dropped the case against Seman after taking the three depositions and there is no indication that they sent Seman to the Bishop for discipline.[24]

Nearly two months after concluding the depositions about John Seman, the mayor and aldermen received a letter from the Privy Council, encouraging them to enforce a number of different statutes. Among them was one that urged them to have "a special regard that religion be reverently used, and that you admonish all householders that they and their family repair to the church to hear the common prayer." The Council further instructed them to order city churchwardens to collect the 12*d*. fine, imposed by the Act of Uniformity, from all of those who absented themselves from church. Any money collected was to be earmarked for the poor. The mayor and aldermen responded promptly, assuring the Council that all was well in the city and that they were doing their best to see the Queen's laws enforced.[25]

If the magistrates directed local churchwardens to seek out those who did not attend church and collect fines from them, they did not note that charge in the city records. Nor is there evidence that they pursued local residents who refused to attend Queen Elizabeth's church. In fact, no incident of religious conflict appears in city records for three years after the cases about Laurence Hodger and John Seman.

In May 1564, a city tailor named Richard Tanner told the mayor and aldermen how a servant, Jer[e?]my Gardener, had threatened Cathedral prebendary Nicholas Smith with a bow and arrow as Tanner and Smith ambled through the Cathedral two days previously. Gardener was also in the Cathedral, making a lot of noise and preparing to shoot at one of the Cathedral doors with his bow and arrow. When Smith warned that he might hurt someone, Gardener replied, "I will shoot here and axe thee no leave thou old papish knave—I know thee well enough." Tanner intervened, stepping between Smith and Gardener, and saved

Smith from serious injury or death. Gardener's provocative display did not prompt the magistrates to act on Tanner's complaint. Gardener's name did not appear again in city records.[26]

Tanner's testimony was the last complaint concerning religion that would appear in city records until 1570. The lack of recorded religious conflict cases, however, is not an indication of the absence of nonconformists in Norwich, either Catholic or Protestant. For example, the servant Jer[e?]my Gardener was probably not far off the mark when he identified prebendary Nicholas Smith as a Catholic. While there is no other evidence about Smith, a number of his fellow prebendaries at the Cathedral were certainly religious conservatives. Indeed, as Ralph Houlbrooke and Diarmaid MacCulloch have pointed out, much of the diocesan hierarchy of Norwich was dominated by religious conservatives until 1570.

Many of the diocesan officials in the first decade of Elizabeth's reign had been appointed with patents for life during Mary's reign or before, some as early as the 1530's. MacCulloch has shown how the political and familial networks of the late traditionalist Bishop Richard Nix and the Howard Dukes of Norfolk exercised great influence over these appointments at key moments.[27] These lifetime appointments gave the officeholders the opportunity to choose their successors through grants in reversion and grants of next presentation, which they used to pass their offices to relatives or like-minded associates. As a result, numerous traditionalist clergy held positions throughout the diocese at the start of Elizabeth's reign.

The Dean of Norwich Cathedral from 1560 until his death in 1573 was John Salisbury, a political survivor whose "religious views had not moved far beyond Henrician Catholicism," according to MacCulloch.[28] Salisbury had begun his career as a monk and served as Dean of the Cathedral from 1539 until 1554 when he was deprived for marriage, but returned to his former post at the beginning of Elizabeth's reign. Among the prebendaries, as Houlbrooke has noted, there was not a majority of religious reformers until 1570; religious conservatism predominated before that date.[29] John Barret, once known as a Protestant reformer, re-embraced Catholicism under Mary. John Hallybred had also been in trouble at the beginning of Mary's reign for his religious views, but conformed to that Queen's settlement and remained a religious conservative for the rest of his life. Other prebendaries who held traditional religious views included Henry Manuel, a former monk, Nicholas Wendon, Miles Spenser and possibly Nicholas Smith.[30]

In addition to their positions as prebends, Wendon and Spenser also served as heads of two of the four archdeaconries into which the diocese of Norwich was divided. The Archdeacons each presided over a court whose business focused on probate matters and religious discipline. Bishop Parkhurst deemed the four men who served in these posts until the early 1570's as "popish lawyers or unlearned papists."[31] Nicholas Wendon became Archdeacon of Suffolk in 1559, but apparently spent much of his tenure travelling on the Continent. He was ejected from that post and from his prebend's stall in 1570 for never having taken priestly orders. After that, Wendon settled permanently on the Continent, where he at last took orders, but in the Roman Church. Miles Spenser had been the Archdeacon of Sudbury since 1536 and also served as diocesan Chancellor under Bishops Nix and Rugge and acted as a co-Chancellor during the episcopates of Thomas Thirlby and John Hopton. He was a staunch opponent of religious reform, singled out by Foxe for the enthusiasm with which he pursued Protestants during Mary's reign. Richard Underwood, a member of the Duke of Norfolk's religiously conservative household, was appointed to the Archdeaconry of Norwich, which covered Norwich and thirteen parishes outside the city, under Mary. The fourth man, Matthew Carew, Archdeacon of Norfolk, besides being unsympathetic to the Elizabethan Church, also spent much time away from his post.[32]

The dominance of conservatives in important positions in the diocese was certainly a hindrance to Elizabethan religious policy, yet it would be a mistake to understand the lax enforcement of the Elizabethan Settlement simply as a product of conservative

obstruction. Part of the explanation must focus on Bishop Parkhurst, who, almost from the time of his elevation to the see of
Norwich in 1560, was regularly assailed by the Queen, the Privy
Council and the Archbishop of Canterbury for his failure to enforce religious uniformity in the diocese among both religious
conservatives and radicals.

Parkhurst was not indifferent to religious matters. As a fellow at
Oxford in the 1530's he had already shown his inclination toward
Protestant doctrine and established a relationship with the visiting
Rudolph Gwalther, the Zurich reformer Ulrich Zwingli's son-in-
law and the city's future Chief Minister. This connection shaped
the experience of Parkhurst's exile under Mary. Parkhurst first fled
to Strassburg in summer 1554, then he moved to join the English
exile colony in Zurich. He carried with him correspondence for
Chief Minister Heinrich Bullinger, who had raised Gwalther in his
own household. Parkhurst's sojourn to Zurich brought him into
contact with John Calvin, among others, and certainly supported
his theological movement toward a moderate Puritanism.[33] In the
matter of religion, Parkhurst was deeply committed to Protestant
reform long before he became Bishop of Norwich.

Soon after his elevation to Norwich Parkhurst received the first
of many rebukes for not enforcing the Act of Uniformity. On
royal progress through East Anglia during the summer of 1561,
the Queen was shocked and angered by the deportment of ministers. Secretary of State William Cecil lamented Parkhurst's "re-
missness in ordering his clergy" in a letter to Archbishop Parker.
As Cecil explained, Parkhurst "winketh at schismatics and ana-
baptists, as I am informed. Surely I see great variety in ministra-
tion. A surplice may not be borne here. And the ministers follow
the folly of the people, calling it charity to feed their fond hu-
mour."[34] Parkhurst had carried out his primary visitation of the
diocese just a few months earlier and so must have been aware of
the "great variety" in clerical practice of which Cecil complained.[35]

While Parkhurst might have personally supported those clergy
who rejected the surplice, there is no reason to think more radical

or more conservative practices would have received his endorsement. The conflict over the use of the surplice, required by the Act of Uniformity but regarded as improper by many Protestant clergymen, heated up in the mid-1560's. The Queen's growing alarm over neglect of the surplice resulted in Archbishop Parker's publication of *The Advertisements* in 1566, demanding its use. The Vestiarian controversy is well known to historians of Elizabethan England, but its importance here is to be found in the charges that Bishop Parkhurst was allegedly one of the few on the episcopal bench who made no move to see that the vestment was regularly used within his diocese.[36] This charge seems to be supported by a letter from Rudolph Gwalther to Parkhurst, in which Gwalther congratulated the Bishop for refusing to enforce the Archbishop's orders.[37]

Parkhurst's role in the Vestiarian controversy probably prompted Archbishop Parker's metropolitical visitation to press uniformity among the recalcitrant ministers of Norwich diocese in 1567. However, the visitation did not go as planned. As Houlbrooke reports, "perhaps because much more fundamental abuses demanded their attention," the visitors "do not appear to have acted very severely against puritan dissidents." After the visitation, diocesan courts did see a small increase in the number of cases relating to nonconformity among Protestant clergy, but it does not appear that infractions were actually corrected.[38] It is likely that the Archbishop's commissioners and Bishop Parkhurst turned more of their attention toward conservative nonconformity and the shoddy condition of diocesan administration.

The direction of the visitation seems to have been changed by George Gardiner, a prebendary at Norwich Cathedral since 1565. Although Gardiner took the side of reform in the 1560's, he was also known to have been a zealous persecutor of Protestants under Queen Mary, for which he had been rewarded with a fellowship to Queen's College, Cambridge. Through Parkhurst's episcopate, Gardiner continued to build his reputation for divisiveness and opportunistic climbing.[39] In 1567, Gardiner told the metropolitical visitors lurid tales of laxity, waste and indifference to the Elizabethan Settlement at the Cathedral itself. His charges, and the observations of the visitors, were sufficient to initiate a royal visitation of the Cathedral headed by Bishop Parkhurst, which concluded in January 1569. Gardiner then expanded on earlier charges, noting that three of the prebendaries had never taken orders, that religious services and sermons were routinely neglected and that "sin is not punished."[40]

Sadly for Bishop Parkhurst, his late efforts to respond to the disorder revealed by the 1567 and 1569 visitations were not enough to stem the tide of criticism coming from Westminster. In the autumn of 1569, a Privy Council examination of a number of gentlemen from East Anglia had exposed the strength of Catholic recusancy among the gentry of Norwich diocese. Parkhurst received the most severe reprimand of his episcopate in a letter from a number of councilors who wrote to chastise him for the "evil governance" of the diocese.[41] The potential seriousness of the Council's discovery could only have been heightened by the outbreak of the Northern Rebellion, a plot to overthrow the Queen and English Protestantism led by Catholic aristocrats such as the Duke of Norfolk, in November.[42]

The Council's condemnation apparently induced Parkhurst to make some attempt to impose greater discipline on the diocese. The results of those efforts were reflected in the visitation he undertook shortly afterwards. In the city of Norwich, Parkhurst cited the parish of St. Gregory, where, a full decade after its demolition was commanded, the rood loft still stood. In the Norfolk parish of North Walsham, fifteen parents were presented for failing to have their children catechized. Even after the visitation was completed, Parkhurst continued his work. He summoned the priest Peter Kilburne, the rector of Hepworth, Suffolk, before him for interrogation. Kilburne had never subscribed to the royal supremacy and was alleged not to have lived, conducted services or preached in his parish for ten years.[43]

Parkhurst's enthusiasm for more rigorous discipline was short-lived and probably not very strong in the first place. The Bishop seems to have taken little or no additional action against Protestant nonconformists. The rood loft at Norwich St. Gregory's had not yet been taken down as late as 1573. Peter Kilburne continued to hold the living of Hepworth and, in 1573, the Bishop discovered to his chagrin that Kilburne was indeed a committed Catholic and lived in the Norwich Cathedral close, far from his Suffolk benefice.[44]

There is little doubt that Parkhurst was far from the best episcopal administrator who served under Elizabeth. In numerous cases concerning appointments, matrimonial disputes and supervision of episcopal properties it is evident that Parkhurst's competence left something to be desired.[45] It is possible to explain some of his failure to enforce stricter discipline in the diocese in similar terms. However, there is also some evidence that suggests that his inaction against nonconformists, both Protestant and Catholic, stemmed, at least in part, from a strong distaste for persecution and open religious conflict. In the wake of the Vestiarian controversy, friends proudly praised him to Bullinger in 1567 for his "kind forbearance" toward nonconformists.[46]

Parkhurst's Zurich friends no doubt appreciated his tolerance of Protestant nonconformists, but his attitude appears to have extended to Catholics as well. In 1572, after the Northern Rebellion hardened Protestant opinion against Catholics throughout England, Parkhurst still tried to rule his diocese through concord and not deal harshly with recusants. For example, he pleaded with Sir Thomas Cornwallis of Brome Hall, Suffolk, to convince his kinsman, William Hare, to attend church, telling him "[m]y conscience toward God, my duty to the Queen's Majesty, and the sharp rebuking letters which I receive from men of authority, all these do bind me to be more diligent wherein." Parkhurst warned Sir Thomas that if Hare did not go to church, he "must be contented to feel of justice without all farther favour of forbearing." When Parkhurst penned a similar appeal in 1573 to William Plator, a Suffolk recusant, he wrote "although I might justly call you and proceed against you herein, or otherwise cause you to appear before the High Commissioners, yet have I thought good to spare you upon hope of amendment."[47]

Trusting a recusant to reform through "hope of amendment" was very similar to the Norwich magistrates' ruling in several cases of religious conflict over the past few decades. Parkhurst defended his manner of rule in a letter to Archbishop Parker, explaining, "I find by good proof; that the rough and austere form and manner of ruling doth the least good, and on [the other] part the contrary hath and doth daily reclaim and win divers; and therefore do I choose rather to continue my accustomed and natural form and manner, which I know how it hath and doth work, with love and favor, than with others by rigor and extremity to overrule."[48]

Even if in imposing religious uniformity Parkhurst was more stymied by his own incompetence than restrained by his distaste for harsh governance, the same cannot be said of Norwich's magistrates. The magistrates had ample authority to arrest, fine and imprison religious nonconformists for a host of offenses. They also could have notified Westminster or, perhaps, even Archbishop Parker, whose brother sat on the aldermanic bench. But they did none of these things, nor did they ever voice a complaint about Bishop Parkhurst's administration of the diocese. This followed their long-standing practice of not imposing religious conformity. The magistrates continued this practice through the 1560's without discernible alteration, despite their own greater religious unity. If there is any doubt that their inaction resulted from a kind of administrative weakness similar to Parkhurst's, such doubts will be dispelled by an examination of their new mode of governance in a related area, social discipline.

⊰ IV ⊱

Soon after Elizabeth's accession in 1558, the pages of the Norwich mayor's court book began to fill with records of petty criminal and moral offenders for the first time. The magistrates meted out harsh disciplinary actions for theft, vagrancy, illicit sexual behavior and a number of other social transgressions. After 1561, the almost unheard-of crimes of "evil rule" and "ill rule" were commonly recorded in the mayor's court book, often without any additional description of the illicit act committed. While many of these breaches had appeared in the court books intermittently before this time, the correction of such faults became a much more regular and frequent feature of court sessions after 1558. The mayor and aldermen punished these offenses by routine whipping, deportation, setting in the stocks and imprisonment. The timing of the sudden upsurge in punishment points to the beginning of a deliberate effort to impose discipline on the city's inhabitants through the office of the mayor's court, in striking contrast to the magistrates' continued toleration of religious diversity.

Accounting for the causes and timing of such campaigns against disorder has been an important issue in the historiographical debate over Protestantism's effect on social discipline and governance. The thesis of a reformation of manners spurred by Puritanism, most prominently expounded by Keith Wrightson and David Levine in their study of the Essex village of Terling, has recently been challenged by a number of historians. Marjorie McIntosh and Margaret Spufford have identified similar drives against disorder during the fourteenth and fifteenth centuries, when neither Protestantism nor Puritanism could have been an available ideological component. They have further argued that these crusades were responses to socioeconomic dislocations rather than religious change. More recently, Ian Archer has emphasized the multicausal nature of disciplinary campaigns and the ideological dimensions to their intensity, scope and definition. He has also highlighted the issue of timing by tracing London's reformation of manners back to the mid-Tudor years and calling upon historians to examine the towns, where Protestantism took hold considerably earlier than in rural areas like Essex.[49]

The new regime of social discipline in Elizabethan Norwich responded to socioeconomic problems that had been plaguing the city for some time. Norwich's textile industry continued to languish, with broad-reaching effects on the urban and neighboring rural population. The influenza epidemics of 1557 to 1559 set many families adrift, no doubt increasing in-migration from the countryside while also continuing to depress the city's population. There are no precise figures available of the number who died in the epidemic, but it is clear that influenza struck at a broader segment of the city's population than other diseases, such as plague, ever had. Whereas plagues tended to afflict the poor and young with special severity, the influenza of 1557 to 1559 took a heavier toll among elders across social lines. The exact effect on the city's economy is impossible to measure, as is in-migration from the countryside.[50]

Although the epidemic certainly produced some new social and economic problems, it is very difficult to discern exactly how much the overall economic distress centering on the textile industry worsened during the first decade of Elizabeth's reign. In fact, John Pound, in his studies of Norwich's economy, trade structure and population, has argued that some sectors of the city's economy were quite robust during the first decades of Elizabeth's reign even though the textile industry stagnated and the number of poor remained substantial. For example, his analysis of a 1569 muster, which lists the occupations of 1,250 freemen, reveals that about 80 percent of them engaged, directly or indirectly, in the production of consumer goods. Pound concludes that the trade structure of early Elizabethan Norwich indicates a great demand for goods and services, much of which originated from gentry households in the countryside.[51]

The magistrates had also long been active in efforts to boost the local economy and cushion the effects of hard times on the poor. They took a new and more adventurous step in this direction in 1564, when the corporation, led by mayor Thomas Sotherton, consulted the Duke of Norfolk about asking the Queen to permit a number of refugees from the Netherlands to come and live in the city. The mayor and aldermen pointed to the continuing dislocations in the cloth trade that had left many Norwich residents unemployed. Rising unemployment, in turn, had driven many people out of the city, resulting in further decay. The mayor and aldermen hoped that Dutch and Walloon textile workers, Protestants who were fleeing religious persecution in the Netherlands "then raised against them by the power of the Duke of Alva, principal of the King of Spain," would help to revive the sagging local cloth industry by initiating the production of a special cloth in high demand called the "New Draperies." In November 1565, the Queen issued letters patent allowing thirty master craftsmen with their families and servants to settle in Norwich. The initial group of immigrants numbered about three hundred. By the end of the decade that number swelled to 4,000.[52] Their arrival helped to restore the population and, by the 1580's, revive the textile industry, too.[53]

This review of Norwich's economy strongly suggests that the timing of the new campaign for social and moral order cannot be fully accounted for by reference to an objective change in social and economic circumstances. Nor can it be explained by sudden failings on the part of other local courts, such as the Norwich Quarter Sessions, Assizes or consistory courts. Assizes, in theory, were devoted to more serious crimes and felonies, such as murder, highway robbery and treason, and there are few referrals to the Assizes in city records. The Quarter Sessions bench in Norwich, composed of the present and former mayors, who met four times a year, tended to be reserved for only the most serious and propitiously timed cases, because the mayor's court met at least twice a week. The consistory courts did hear cases of sexual misconduct, but Ralph Houlbrooke's sampling of extant and datable records from several deaneries outside Norwich does not show any trend of increase or decrease between 1532 and 1570.[54] There is no evidence indicating that the mayor's court took over areas of the administration of justice from these other courts.

It seems likely that the mayor's court took over some disciplinary responsibilities that were previously exercised informally. For example, Cynthia Herrup and Keith Wrightson have noted the role that magistrates, ministers and other prominent locals were expected to play in resolving disputes, including some criminal matters, before they reached the courtroom.[55] Masters and parents were also expected to supervise and discipline their apprentices, servants and children. Evidence for such informal dispute resolution is often dependent on the survival of diaries and prescriptive literature, of which there is none for Elizabethan Norwich. While there is no direct evidence for such a shift from informal extrajudicial dispute resolution to the mayor's court, the court records for theft certainly support such an explanation.

It is difficult to believe that the dramatic rise in the mayor's court's punishment for theft—from an average of just over one case every two years between 1540 and 1558–59 to an average of eight per year between 1559 and 1569–70—simply reflected a rise in crime.[56] As Cynthia Herrup has noted, "we cannot discriminate between changes in actual illegal behavior and changes in enforcement" based on court records alone; therefore "these shifts are open to several interpretations," such as changes in jurisdiction or the redefinition of crime itself.[57] The relationship between property and theft does not appear to have altered in sixteenth-century Norwich, nor did economic fluctuations reduce the propensity to steal during the 1540's and 1550's, when times were consistently difficult. Therefore, it seems likely that the magistrates supplanted some of the informal extrajudicial mechanisms resorted to in the past. This, together with their forays into punishment for the more novel crime of "evil rule" and other moral offenses, suggests that some changes had occurred in the theory and practice of authority.

The Reformation, of course, had a major impact on the theory and practice of authority in England. Debates about papal and royal supremacy, Scripture, the role of the clergy and ceremonial practice had been gripping the country for about three decades by the time Elizabeth came to the throne. Through this time, the Norwich magistrates faced the challenge of coping with quarreling residents and successive monarchs' drastic alterations to fundamental religious beliefs and practice. Common English men and women also found themselves struggling to cope with the unprecedented changes in religious regimes. Many, as Susan Brigden has suggested, found themselves in between their more committed fellows, not infrequently confused by the official theological shifts. With confessional division, clergy could not expect their voice to be heard by the whole parish, as in times past, but only among their faithful. Familial unity also sometimes fractured along spiritual lines. These disruptions to traditional forms and figures of authority began with religious disputations but did not stop there.

As we have seen in the case of Andrew Quasshe and the Company of St. George, magisterial authority could be challenged directly by "God's word" and indirectly by interrupting the magistrates' performance of public ceremonies that represented communal unity behind their rule. If sources on the informal resolution of civil and criminal disputes were available for sixteenth-century Norwich, it would not be surprising to find priests, parents, masters and maybe even the magistrates losing their power to persuade. Perhaps the splintering of authority could account for some increase of illicit activity in mid-Tudor England. In her article "Youth and the English Reformation," Susan Brigden writes, "[w]ith the new faith had come new opportunities and excuses for disobedience."[58] But such a hypothesis cannot explain the timing of the drive for social and moral discipline by the Norwich magistrates. Nor does it take into account Protestantism's other side. In addition to emphasizing individual reading and interpretation of the Bible, many Protestant theologians expressed heightened concern for hierarchy and order. No less than Martin Luther and John Calvin argued against the idea of free will, and the "apostle of Norwich" John More preached a sermon entitled "declaring first how we may be saved in the day of judgement and so come to life everlasting: secondly, how we ought to live according to God's will during our life."[59]

The timing of the upsurge in discipline in Norwich seems closely related to the dramatic turnover on the aldermanic bench in 1558–59. Not only were close to half of the aldermen replaced in the space of a year, but their successors brought an overwhelming Protestant majority to the bench for the first time in 1559. By 1566, after the deaths of the last two identifiably Catholic aldermen, it is highly likely that the Norwich magistracy was entirely Protestant. It is also important to note that from around the time of the deaths of the last Catholic aldermen there is evidence of growing Puritan influence in Norwich.

The city was, by 1564, a site of "prophesyings," public gatherings at which clergymen engaged in biblical exegesis and discussion. These exercises would become strongly associated with the Puritan emphasis on individual reading and interpretation of Scripture, and thus also with Puritanism's reputation for nonconformity in the eyes of the Queen. She disliked doctrinal disputation because of its potential for division, schism and conflict. Nevertheless, prophesyings continued in Norwich as a number of Puritan clergy from the universities began to settle in the city in the late 1560's. It is possible that some arrived earlier, since we do not know who began the prophesyings in 1564. A connection between the Puritan clergy and city governors appears to have been established as early as 1561, when George Leeds, who would be suspended for nonconformity in 1576, was first hired to preach before the corporation in Rogation week.[60]

A close examination of the patterns of punishment, the categories of crimes and the accounts of particular cases in the Norwich mayor's court between 1540–41 and 1569–70 further supports the link to a Protestantism concerned with social order and obedience. And, as will be shown later in this chapter, the campaign for moral and social discipline expanded in still more novel ways after the discovery and thwarting of a Catholic-inspired plot in 1570, which will be discussed in the next section. While the records very clearly show a significant increase in the magistrates' punishment of social and moral transgressions, they also pose a number of problems for interpretation. The mayor's court books are extant for the sixteenth century in a complete run, except for a gap in the years 1532–34 and a few months in 1581–82. Despite their problems, and maybe even because of them, the court books cry out for a full-scale study of crime and social order for the entire sixteenth century. For the present study, the variable categories of offenses recorded in the mayor's court books serve to highlight magisterial discretion and initiative in punishing residents.

Although the mayor's court met at least twice weekly and
maintained its books consistently, the court records reflect a lo-
cally devised and somewhat informal judicial practice. The court
brought no formal indictments, so criminal charges were never
filed against offenders and there are no records of acquittal. Trial
by jury was not a feature of the court; an offender's guilt and
punishment were determined only by the mayor and present aldermen. Legal codes are seldom mentioned, nor do any appear to
have been regularly consulted in the formulation of magisterial
opinion. Only in a few cases did the magistrates refer to statutes
of the realm or local ordinances. For all of these reasons, the categories of offenses for which residents were punished, especially
the moral ones, were inexact and often overlapping. Only occasionally do the court records include sufficient descriptions to
further identify the offense.

In some cases, the records show that similar illicit acts were
categorized differently. This is evident in the following three
cases concerning sexual misconduct. In a May 1570 case record
that did not utilize any of the common categories of offense, the
parson William Keryn was described as "taken very suspiciously
in the company of one Bach's wife, [and] he and she were both
carried about the market with a basin before them."[61] Another
case of sexual misconduct in July 1562 was recorded as follows,
using the term "abused himself," which appears in the court
book periodically: "This day Henry Pyry was whipped about the
market for that he abused himself toward Elizabeth Riches servant to Roger Munds."[62] Finally, the category "evil rule" seems to
have often included sexual misbehavior, as in the May 1568 case
of Thomas Tyryll and Alys Nesshe, sentenced "for evil rule
committed, he being [a]n apprentice and she being a hired servant are punished, he with whipping with rods and after they
both to ride in a cart about the market."[63]

While offenses like sexual misconduct were often labeled
"abuse" or "evil rule," among other categories, these categories
did not consistently refer to crimes of a sexual nature. For example, in June 1560, city constable Richard Blewett was brought into

court because he "kept ill rule of playing at cards."[64] Many other cases of "evil rule" or "ill rule" did not contain as much description.

The inexact and overlapping categories employed by the mayor's court make the data in their records difficult to tabulate, except in rather general terms. It is possible to tally the total number of cases the court acted upon in each mayoral year and to break them down according to such categorical keywords as "evil rule," "filching and stealing," "vagrancy," "disobedience," "abusing" or "misusing," "fighting and scolding" and "running away." However, only a few of these categories, theft and vagrancy in particular, seem to be reliably consistent indicators of the kind of action punished. For this reason, it is prudent to use this data heuristically only, but that is sufficient to demonstrate the rise in punishment that marks the magistrates' new practice of moral and social discipline.

My count of social and moral cases in the mayor's court encompasses all appearances for which punishment or correction was typically applied. This includes all of the categories discussed above, such as "evil rule" and stealing. But it excludes all cases concerning directly religious disputes of the type treated throughout this book and also all civil and other cases that typically resulted in orders for recompense, such as debt actions and bastardy cases for child support. The cases are divided by mayoral year, which in Norwich began on the Tuesday before Midsummer.

The pattern of increasing punishment after 1558–59 is strong.[65] For the eighteen-year period from 1540–41 to 1557–58, a total of 137 cases were recorded in the mayor's court books. The number of cases heard in each year ranged from a low of 2 in 1553–54 to a high of 30 in 1548–49, which was a year of significant religious turmoil in the city that seems to have spilled over into social and moral areas as well. Only three other years in this period had 10 cases or more, 1544–45 (12), 1549–50 (11) and 1555–56 (10). On average, the court heard almost 8 cases per year.

After hearing only 6 cases in 1557–58, the court heard 19 cases in 1558–59 as the turnover of the aldermen was completed. In the twelve-year period from 1558–59 to 1569–70, a total of 440 cases were heard. The smallest number of cases heard in a year was 14 in 1562–63 and that number increased every year to a high of 87 in 1569–70. On average, the court heard almost 37 cases each year during this period, almost six times the average before the dramatic change on the aldermanic bench.

The cases before 1558 tended to be evenly spread among the different categories, although there was some bunching of cases concerning disobedience to a superior in the mid- to late-1540's. For example, in the particularly quarrelsome year of 1548–49, 10 of the 30 cases concerned such disobedience. The only other notable concentration of cases was in 1555–56, when 7 of the total of 10 for the year concerned the punishment of gaming, an offense which was only rarely specified in other years.

In the period after 1558, there is a marked difference not only in the number of cases heard, but also in the kinds of offenses punished. Cases were fairly evenly distributed among a variety of categories during the first fours years after the turnover of aldermen. Crimes of sexual misconduct were most numerous in 1558–59 (5 of 19), 1559–60 (5 of 16), and 1661–62 (6 of 25), but only slightly so in absolute terms. In 1560–61, cases related to theft were most numerous (7 cases of 15), with sexual misconduct close behind (5 cases). New patterns emerged in the early 1560's, when the magistrates began to punish theft, vagrancy and "evil rule" much more than other offenses.

From hearing just 5 cases of vagrancy during the four years between 1558–59 and 1561–62, the court heard at least 5 each year from 1562–63 through 1569–70. Vagrancy was the most commonly heard offense in the mayor's court in six of the eight years after 1562–63, peaking in 1569–70 with 28 cases. It was the most frequently punished offense in the period from 1558–59 through 1569–70, with a total 117 appearances. Cases of theft numbered in the single digits until 1566–67, when they climbed to 14 and then peaked at 21 in 1568–69. Theft was the second most commonly heard offense in this twelve-year period, with 96 appearances.

The once rare category of offense signaled by the keyword "evil rule" became the third most common cause of punishment in the period, with 51 incidents.

Although there was little or no difference in the way the magistrates recorded cases before and after 1558, offenders do seem to have been punished much more harshly for comparable crimes after that watershed year. The most common penalties in the earlier period were imprisonment, setting in the stocks and fining. For example, in July 1544 servant Margaret Swale was "set in the stocks openly to the example of other ill-doers" for having stolen some of her master's goods and then leaving his service without permission.[66] For "misbehavior committed by her to her husband and among other [of] her neighbors," Alys Millicent was imprisoned in November 1541.[67] In June 1548, Agnes Malet, a servant of alderman Rede's, was brought to the court "for taking a pair of gloves" from Rede's house and then, "upon trust of amendment . . . she shall be delivered without any further" delay, presumably back to her master.[68] Vagrancy, then a rarely heard offense in the mayor's court, was punished lightly in the June 1541 case of Robert Bedom, who only had to agree to leave the city "and not hereafter as a vagabond to come or resort in the same."[69] Whipping, while not unknown in the years before 1558, still was not common. During Mary's reign, in February 1556, one Thomas Pope was "this day whipped about the market as a vagabond and for other misdemeanors approved against him as well touching his mother and another wench."[70] Perhaps Pope's multiple offenses, including one against his own mother, moved the magistrates to take immediate action upon his body.

Sexual misconduct, including "whoredom," did not regularly provoke the magistrates to use the rod or the whip before 1558. During Edward's reign, in June 1550, the court ruled that "Margery Savery, the wife of William Savery, for her misbehaviors and incontinent living with William Bolton and others is enjoined and commanded to depart out of this city betwixt this day and this day seven night."[71] In October 1555, one Margaret Thacker was "enjoined for her vicious and incontinent living to depart out of this town betwixt this [day] and Saturday next. And if she remain here in this city after that day, then she to bring of [two] sufficient sureties for her honest behavior or else she shall remain in prison."[72] Similarly, in February 1557, the mayor's court recorded that "whereas Joan Manton, the wife of John Manton of Yarmouth, hath been apprehended and imprisoned here for her vicious and incontinent living, this day it is ordered by the house that she shall be sent about the market upon Saturday next with a paper upon her head entitled, 'for whoredom.' And that done, to be exempted to this city."[73]

After 1558, corporal punishment was much more commonly used for a wide variety of offenses, including sexual misconduct. In May 1558, for example, Agnes Barker was "whipped for her vicious and incontinent living," then banished "and enjoined to seek her husband and to remain with him." If she were found in Norwich again, the magistrates ordered that she be "whipped again and so forth as often as she is taken here."[74] Thomas Thyrketyll and Margaret Assheforde were brought before the court in March 1560 for consorting as if they were husband and wife; Thyrketyll was "whipped with a paper on his head of fornication" and Assheforde was set in the stocks with a similar paper.[75] In June 1560 Robert Vale and Anne Farror were stocked for their "whoredom," and in October of that year Amy Day was also put in the stocks with a paper on her head that read, "for whoredom."[76] Robert Ancell, evidently a recidivist, and Elizabeth Walker were "taken in bawdry" and brought before the mayor's court in January 1561. The court ruled that since "the said Robert Ancell hath had warning thereof and [was] punished in the stocks and yet, will not leave his ill and naughty behavior, it is agreed that the said Robert Ancell and the said Elizabeth Walker will be whipped about the market with papers on their heads 'for whoredom.'" The magistrates seem to have moderated their view of Elizabeth Walker, for her name was stricken and then listed below with one Alice Keyes to be set in the stocks for their "whoredom" with Robert Ancell.[77] In another case from May 1570, Richard Woodhouse, a servant to the Puritan minister

Nicholas Bownd, was whipped "for evil rule with Frances, wife [of] the mason."[78]

Unlike the few vagrants brought to court before 1558 and some other non-native perpetrators of moral offenses, who were simply deported and sometimes shamed, most of those taken as vagrants by the Elizabethan magistrates of Norwich were whipped before being given passports and ejected from the city. When Gregory Wright was whipped and evicted from Norwich in June 1569, for example, he was sent back to Kersey, near Hadleigh in Suffolk. In September of the same year, Robert Herryng was set in the stocks before being returned to the Norfolk village of Eccles. John Emons was found wandering in Norwich in June 1569. He told the magistrates that his home was in Newcastle, and after whipping him, they issued him a passport to go back there. In July of the same year, Richard Pelfe was sent back to Sandford Ferry in Oxfordshire after being whipped.[79]

The increasingly large number of cases of theft and evil rule were also regularly punished with whippings. John Bell was whipped in April 1564 "for stealing a glass of dates" from his master. When Joseph Harryson took 4d. "from another lad" in December 1569, he too was whipped.[80] John Rolf, "for evil rule and disobeying the constables," received a whipping at a cart's tail in May 1565. Thomas Clarke's offense is not at all clear to the modern reader, for he was whipped in February 1567, "for misdemeanor and evil rule."[81]

Although whipping was much more common after 1558, the magistrates did not use the whip to the exclusion of other punishments. In December 1561, they imprisoned the journeyman Edward Cheney after he confessed that he "did break the said Thomas Jackson's his master's head with a pair of tailor's shears." A few days later, they jailed his master Thomas Jackson because, after the assault, Jackson "did not complain to Mr. Mayor so that justice could not be ministered in due time."[82] John Rolf was imprisoned for three days in April 1563, two years before his 1565 whipping, when constables Thomas Sparrow and Richard Flower complained of his "evil rule and evil behavior as well of his body

as his tongue." Katherine Clere was set in the stocks with a paper
on her head in April 1565 "for that she would have poisoned herself with rat's bane as she doth confess."[83] That was the same
punishment given to Katherine Chandler in October 1569 "for
harboring and lodging of evil people and maintaining of evil
rule."[84]

The records do not often contain profiles of offenders and so it
is very difficult to know the social status of those punished in
Elizabethan Norwich, except, of course, for vagrants, those referred to as servants and occasional cases in which an offender's
occupation is used for identification. However, there are three
cases from this period that show clearly that the offenders were
citizens, as they lost their civic liberties as punishment for their
infractions. John Gorney was disenfranchised by the city Assembly in September 1561 "for the detestable and abominable act"
that he committed with Agnes Leman, whose fate was not set
down at that time. The Assembly also seized the civic privileges
of Robert Kyndersley in June 1562 on account of his "notorious
offense and evil living." The following month, Thomas Steward
was similarly punished after Assembly members learned that he
had "begot his maid servant in [his] house with child, to whom
he made a contract but . . . he married to another woman in the
parish of St Lawrence." Two of these three men were readmitted
to the civic body. In January 1562, Gorney made "humble suit" to
the Assembly and his freedom was restored upon payment of a
40s. fine. Kyndersley received his civic freedom again less than
two weeks after he was first disenfranchised. His fine was a considerably steeper 100s.[85]

Responding to Margaret Spufford's critique of the reformation-
of-manners thesis, Ian Archer has cited the willingness of authorities to punish those higher on the social ladder as an indication of the influence of Protestantism in Elizabethan London's
upsurge in social discipline. Sexual license, for which Gorney,
Steward and probably Kyndersley were disenfranchised, was, of
course, never condoned by the pre-Reformation Church. But one
of the ways in which Protestantism refocused and reformulated

social and moral discipline, according to Archer, was by "ensuring that the offenses of the wealthier sort did not pass unpunished." He has also pointed to London governors' increasing willingness to penalize illicit male sexuality, in contrast to the traditional focus on female behavior, as a mark of Protestant influence.[86] In Norwich, disenfranchisement certainly struck at the more prosperous of the city's residents, for freemen, with their "virtual monopoly over both political and economic affairs," comprised a minority of the total population.[87]

In the case of Robert Kyndersley the magistrates also showed themselves willing to take drastic action against a member of civic government, as he was a common councilor from Mancroft ward. His disenfranchisement also reveals something about the magistrates' notions about the ideal godly community and its members. Because of Kyndersley's offense, he was "not thought a man meet to be in so worshipful a company as the worthiness of this house requireth." Even though Kyndersley was readmitted to the freedom less than two weeks after his initial disenfranchisement, this episode ended his civic career. He lost his office and was never elected to a position again.[88]

The language of Kyndersley's disenfranchisement and the entire campaign for moral and social discipline reflect the influence of Protestantism on the Norwich magistrates' urban governance. As Patrick Collinson has wisely noted in connection with the cleansing of traditional rituals and rhythms from town life in Elizabethan England, this seeming "secularisation . . . paradoxically involved the sacralisation of the town, which now became self-consciously a godly commonwealth, its symbolic and mimetic codes replaced by a literally articulated, didactic religious discipline." Needless to say, town governors had long been concerned to uphold civic order and peace and promote civic harmony. Yet, as Collinson suggests, the goals of civic leaders became "more explicit" with the establishment of Protestantism, connecting order "with obedience, disorder with disobedience, that is to say disobedience to God, sin." These connections were certainly made in Norwich, where they probably account for the emergence of magistrates' great concern about "evil rule." The enforcement of order in Elizabethan Norwich fit the form Collinson described as a "new order," "spelt out in the spoken word and enforced by coercive discipline, not achieved in the charmingly roundabout fashion of 'pastime' and instinctive ritual and carnival."[89] Yet, while the Norwich magistrates imposed moral and social discipline as a kind of "divinely inspired code of conduct," they also continued their traditional practice of religious toleration.[90]

⊰ V ⊱

The magistrates' practice of toleration was tested by events that unfolded in the city in 1570. Elizabeth's attitude toward Catholics hardened after the Northern Rebellion in late 1569. In February 1570 the Pope raised fears of Catholic disobedience within England and hostility from without by issuing a bull that excommunicated and deposed Elizabeth as the legitimate monarch in the eyes of the Church. When a Norfolk gentleman living in London posted a copy of the bull on the Bishop's palace gate in May 1570, he was arrested, put on the rack to discover his accomplices and then executed later that year.[91] While fear of Catholic conspiracies grew and the Duke of Norfolk sat in the Tower for his part in the Northern Rebellion, several Norfolk gentry and a Norwich gentleman of known Catholic sympathies began to frequent Norwich in May and talk openly of rallying the common people to eject the Dutch and Walloon Strangers. The Norwich magistrates and their Norfolk neighbors did not move against these would-be rebels until the end of June, but when they did finally round them up many of the ringleaders betrayed each other's allegedly true desire to free the Duke of Norfolk and overthrow the Queen. This alarmed the central government, with profound consequences for Norwich.

The uprising of 1570 never really got off the ground. When John Appleyard and his fellow rebellious gentry first announced their intent to "raise up the commons and levy a power and beat the strangers out of the city of Norwich" on May 16 they appear to have drawn little support from city residents. The magistrates took no action, either because they did not regard this as a serious threat or, perhaps, as one historian has proposed, "to give them as long a rope as possible." On May 26 the conspirators returned to the city to make another declaration of their designs, this time calling for "but four faithful gentlemen in Norfolk" to take action against the Strangers. In early June they twice more visited the city, both times calling for the commons to rise and assembling small but growing bands of lightly armed men. On June 16 they gathered again in Trowse, just outside the city, and then planned to begin a surprise attack on Norwich from Harleston on June 24, picking up more supporters as they marched to the city. Wind of this reached the magistrates, who joined with Norfolk officers to arrest the leaders and armed bands just outside the city.[92]

In the climate of 1570 news of the foiled plot traveled fast. The Privy Council responded by sending several reliable Protestant gentlemen to live in Norwich, so that they might help city leaders contain the "great multitude of people of mean and base sort" whom sixteenth-century elites always feared might be easily led into rebellion.[93] The principal conspirators and 45 witnesses were sent to Buckinghamshire to be examined by the Council, which drew up charges against them and 14 others. The prisoners were then returned to Norwich for trial at the Assizes and a special tribunal for the most serious charges. Witnesses told of schemes hatched to place the English Crown on the Duke of Norfolk's head. Some of the accused spoke at the trial, hoping to save themselves by implicating the others. It might have worked, for in the end only three were convicted of the most serious crimes and executed, including the Norwich gentleman, John Throgmorton, of whom little is known. Mercy was extended to many of the others, who, although sentenced to life imprisonment, were released a few years later.[94]

At the time of the plot, Bishop Parkhurst was supervising the reform of the staff of the Cathedral Chapter, partially as a result of the pressure put on him by the Council in 1569 to deal more severely with Catholics in Norwich diocese and partially as the fortuitous result of death among the prebendaries. In the summer of 1570, four prebendaries, including the ever enthusiastic George Gardiner and two newly appointed prebendaries, Edmund Chapman and John Walker, decided to take the cause of reform into their own hands. They smashed the organ at the Cathedral and perpetrated "other outrages" there that raised an uproar. The Council dispatched yet another sharp letter to Bishop Parkhurst, instructing him to bind the four men over for examination by Archbishop Parker. Ralph Houlbrooke tells us that Gardiner "learnt his lesson." Detecting the change in wind, Gardiner stopped breaking symbols of Catholicism and turned his attention in later years to combatting further reformist enthusiasms by his erstwhile friends.[95]

Meanwhile, the Council felt the need to badger Parkhurst again in 1571 about his handling of recusancy in the diocese.[96] This led the Bishop to plead with certain gentlemen, as we have already seen, that they should attend the Queen's Church so that he could avoid the kind of prosecution for religious difference that he found distasteful.[97] In connection with a long search for a notorious recusant in London, Parkhurst was ordered to once more examine the Suffolk parson Peter Kilburne in 1573. Kilburne, the Bishop discovered, was now living in the Norwich Cathedral close and, apparently, acting as a connection among diocesan Catholics. Kilburne's examination revealed not only his Catholicism, but also a trunk full of prohibited Catholic paraphernalia, including "an image of Christ with the cross upon his back, three other tables, two of wood and one of alabaster, with gilded images of the Trinity, Christ crucified and of our Lady, a superalter, a Mass book with a *portuus*, and the case of a chalice without a chalice."[98]

Once more, however, despite fears of Catholic conspiracies, practical attention turned to the problem of Protestant nonconformity. In 1573, the central government issued two proclamations calling for religious uniformity in an effort to curtail Protestant nonconformity. They were followed by commissions issued to bishops and local gentlemen to enforce them. As a result, Parkhurst returned lists to Archbishop Parker of clergy who did not wear the surplice in Norwich diocese, although they appear to have been incomplete.[99] Neither fears of Catholic uprisings nor the growing controversy over Puritan demands for reform moved Parkhurst to crack down.

The Norwich magistrates responded to the events of 1570 with even less interest in persecuting local Catholics than exhibited by their Puritan bishop. Given that one of those executed in the failed uprising of 1570 was from Norwich, they might have perceived a reason to apprehend local Catholics before they hatched another plot. The central government's growing alarm over the extent of recusancy since 1569 did move Bishop Parkhurst to take some action against recusancy, as we have seen, but the Norwich magistrates did not.

Nor did the central government's new political fear of Catholicism in the early 1570's prompt Norwich magistrates to pursue Catholics. In London, the 1571 Parliament required all MP's to take the oath of Supremacy and then went on to a series of anti-Catholic measures. The Treasons Act forbade publication or speech that called the Queen a heretic or usurper. The Act Against Bulls prohibited the acquisition or publication of papal documents. Finally, the Act Against Fugitives aimed at Catholic exiles, such as those northern rebels who had fled after the uprising's collapse, by confiscating the goods and lands of anyone who left England for longer than six months without license. Later that year, William Cecil uncovered a plot against Elizabeth's life. The Ridolfi plot, named for the linchpin Roberto di Ridolfi, sought to bring the Pope, Mary, Queen of Scots, and the Duke of Norfolk together in order to depose Elizabeth, with the aid of several thousand troops provided by the King of Spain. Norfolk, who had been released from his earlier imprisonment in August 1570, was sent back to prison and, this time, tried, convicted and executed for treason in June 1572.[100] The Duke was England's premier peer and long the dominant political figure in East Anglia. His execution could not have failed to impress the

Norwich magistrates and other East Anglian officials with the central government's growing anti-Catholicism.

Despite all of these pressures, the Norwich magistrates did not begin pursuit of local recusants. John Throgmorton, executed as one of the 1570 plot's ringleaders, was not the sole city resident with Catholic sympathies. Christopher Haigh has cited the 180 people presented in the archdeaconry of Norwich in 1569 for neglecting to attend church as evidence of growing recusancy.[101] Of course, there were many reasons why people did not go to church and so it is difficult to know exactly how many of those 180 refused out of Catholic loyalties. Surely many did. Given the general picture of Protestantism's slow spread painted by Haigh and other revisionists, Throgmorton and Kilburne must have represented just the most prominent surface of Catholicism in the city.

A good indication of the extent to which the magistrates were willing to abide the presence of local Catholics is suggested by the continued existence of the rood loft, outlawed by the Elizabethan Settlement, at St. Gregory's church. Bishop Parkhurst had ordered the removal of the St. Gregory rood loft during his 1569 visitation, but it was still standing in 1573, as he noted in a September letter to Archbishop Parker. Furthermore, Parkhurst complained to the Archbishop about the "adversaries" of reform, of which "there be many in that parish."[102] St. Gregory's thus appears to have been a parish with a nucleus of Catholic sympathizers known even to Bishop Parkhurst, who spent most of his episcopate living at Ludham, outside Norwich, and who was not known for his zeal in pursuing Catholic recusants either.

Surely the magistrates were aware of the group who belonged to St. Gregory's. But they did not seek out Catholic loyalists at that parish or anywhere else in Norwich. In the mayor's court, they heard no religious cases concerning Catholics in the aftermath of the failed uprising of 1570. No Catholics would appear in the mayor's court for over ten years. In fact, the magistrates heard only a handful of cases of religious conflict in the mayor's court in the 1570's and they all appear to have involved conflicts among Protestants.

The first such case occurred in 1570, while the trials of the conspirators were in progress. On July 27, John Fairchild appeared before the Justices of the Norwich Quarter Sessions "for speaking against nobility and railing against preachers." It is not clear why Fairchild's case was heard in Quarter Sessions rather than the mayor's court. The distinction between those two bodies was not rigid and Fairchild's offense might simply have been more speedily handled at the Sessions meeting. But it could also reflect a greater seriousness ascribed to any threatening outburst given the recent events in the city.[103]

Whatever the reason Fairchild appeared before the Sessions, it seems most likely that his outburst represented an expression of a general, and somewhat vague, animosity. He did not rail against any noble person or clergyman in particular and no other words or actions were attributed to him. The Justices sentenced him "to stand before the pulpit at the Common Place three several Sundays with a paper upon his head 'for railing against preachers,'" but apparently did not punish his outcry against nobility. After Fairchild's case, the magistrates heard no others concerning religion for six years. As we shall see, it would not be until 1576, in the wake of a new bishop's suspension of the Norwich Puritan preachers, that conflict over religion would again be chronicled in city records.

Rather than searching out religious nonconformists, the magistrates responded to the events of 1570 by intensifying their campaign for moral and social order in two different ways. First, soon after the collapse of the 1570 plot, the magistrates responded to Cecil's concern about the loyalty of the "great multitude of people of mean and base sort" by conducting a comprehensive census of Norwich's poor, apparently unprecedented for its time. They then used this information to institute a novel program of reform of the city's poor laws, both more extensive and more systematic than in any other community in England. In 1572,

Norwich MP John Aldrich, the mayor under whom the 1570 census was taken and Norwich poor law instituted, sat on a Parliamentary committee on poor relief which, according to John Pound, "incorporated several aspects of the Norwich scheme" in legislation passed that year.[104]

Second, while the new Norwich poor law delegated authority to a system of deacons and select women charged with the care and correction of the poor, the magistrates themselves continued to punish large numbers of moral and social offenders in the mayor's court. Both responses to the failed plot of 1570 addressed continuing social and economic problems in the city, but, once again, the matter of timing is crucial to our understanding of the causes for this intensification of discipline. In addition to the clear impetus to monitor and control the poor in Cecil's admonition after the failed uprising, it seems likely that the magistrates were also influenced by their relationship with the Puritan clergy settling in the city.

Norwich's census of the poor is unlike any surviving census from the Tudor period. Other towns, such as Ipswich, attempted to count and classify their poor, but none of the surviving evidence suggests that these others were as comprehensive or wideranging as that of Norwich.[105] The magistrates conducted the Norwich census in late 1570 or early 1571. The census uncovered about 2,300 poor people living in the city, out of a total population estimated by John Pound at around 8,000. Information was taken about their sex, age, occupation and family status. Census takers noted the place of residence and length of time in that residence, as well as how long people had lived in Norwich.[106] With this information in hand, mayor John Aldrich appointed three aldermen and a common councilor—Thomas Beamond, Simon Bowde, John Sotherton and John Brerton—to reorganize the city's poor relief system.[107]

The new poverty regulations established regular taxes for the support of the poor, reorganized the city's Bridewell, called for the regular inventory of paupers and authorized a network of deacons and select women to oversee their care and correction.

Deacons were expected to record the number of poor regularly, distribute alms and put the able-bodied to work. The mayor and aldermen also delegated to them the authority to punish vaga- bonds and any other idle or disruptive people. The select women supervised between six and twelve people each, also making sure that the able-bodied worked and they were expected to teach children to read. Pound has highlighted the systematic way in which the scheme's provisions were applied as one of its novel features. The poor relief system remained in effect into the sev- enteenth century.[108]

As the new poor relief scheme was being implemented, the magistrates continued to punish offenders for social and moral infractions in the mayor's court. The number of punishments they meted out in the years after 1570 does not represent the full ex- tent of correction for social and moral offenses in Norwich be- cause, by the terms of the poor relief scheme, deacons were authorized to punish offenses without resort to the mayor's court. The deacons' actions were not recorded. Nevertheless, for the eleven years from 1570–71 to 1580–81, the magistrates heard a total of 595 cases in the mayor's court.[109] The least number of cases heard in the period was 31, in 1573–74, and the most was 70, in 1570–71. The average number of cases heard per year in this pe- riod was 54, substantially higher than the average of almost 37 cases per year heard between 1558–59 and 1569–70, before the failed uprising.

In general, the cases differ only slightly from those in the pe- riod 1558–59 to 1569–70. Despite having shown their ability to collect information systematically in the 1570 census, the magis- trates continued to keep court records in the same terse and in- formal way, without indictments, charges, or, in the overwhelm- ing majority of cases, any description of an offender's defense. The three most commonly punished offenses were still theft, "evil rule" and vagrancy, but now vagrancy ranked third for the eleven-year period from 1570–71 to 1580–81, rather than first, as it had been in 1558–59 and 1569–70.

The number of vagrancy cases the mayor's court heard dropped

from an average of nearly 10 per year in the earlier period to just
over 7 per year between 1570–71 and 1580–81. Two factors account for this change. The first and most important was the census and Norwich poor law of 1570. The new scheme delegated
authority to the deacons to put the poor to work and to punish
the idle and vagabond. There is no way to know how often the
deacons and select women meted out punishments or to discern
exactly how they punished, but it seems clear that they must have
taken over a large share of the aldermen's workload in the area of
vagrancy. If the figure for the year 1570–71 is excluded, the total
number of vagrancy cases for 1571–72 to 1580–81 is 52, or an average of 5 per year, half of the pre-poor law figure. The decline in
vagrancy cases was probably also quickened by a serious outbreak of plague in 1579 and 1580. In 1580–81 the mayor's court
heard no vagrancy cases, perhaps a result of the plague's effect
on population and travel.

Theft was the leading cause for correction between 1570–71
and 1580–81, with 173 incidents punished. The average number
of cases heard by the mayor's court nearly doubled, to almost 16
per year from 8 per year between 1558–59 and 1569–70. The often
ambiguous charge of "evil rule" was the second most common
cause for punishment, with 91 cases during this period. The average number of these cases heard annually by the mayor's court
also doubled, from just over 4 in the early period to just over 8.

The magistrates continued to apply the whip and rod regularly. Almost all theft cases were punished in this way. Thomas
Farror's servant John Docker was whipped in November 1570
"for embezzling his master's goods."[110] Another servant, Rose
Porter, was whipped in August 1575 "for lending certain sheets
and giving certain victuals of her said m[istress] to one Thomas
Cawdell." Her accomplice Cawdell was whipped, in turn, for receiving stolen goods.[111]

The decreasing number of vagrants who came before the court
continued to be whipped and banished. James Stone and Richard
Bridgeham were taken as vagrants at nearby Eaton in November

1579. After being whipped at the Norwich mayor's court, they were simply "commanded to avoid out of this city presently."[112] John King, "being taken in this city as a vagrant" in May 1578, "was whipped about the market and had his passport to go to Rye."[113]

Norwich residents continued to be punished for the often cryptic charge of "evil rule." In October 1572, the tinker Robert Gloser was whipped "for disordering himself and evil rule" but no further details of his transgression were provided.[114] Similarly, Margaret Green was whipped "for evil rule" in January 1578.[115] Thomas Alldred was whipped in December 1579 "for misbehaving himself in this city and for keeping evil rule in the streets."[116] But the accusation was not always so impenetrable. In March 1580, both Robert Middleton and Elizabeth Denton were whipped "for incontinency and evil rule."[117]

The magistrates punished prostitution when they uncovered it, in addition to noncommercial illicit sex. In July 1580, Robert Hastings and Agnes Parker were punished "for committing evil rule." Both were set in the stocks and Hastings, whom the court deemed "a common carrier of lewd women from place to place," was also whipped in the court chamber. He was furthermore bound in recognizance to "see and provide that Agnes Parker be conveyed out of this city to London and that she do not remain in this city after Monday next."[118] If Hastings and Parker left Norwich, Parker returned. In July 1581, when Robert Bayle and Elizabeth Elgar were whipped "for evil rule in committing fornication," Parker was sentenced to be set in the stocks "for concealing the same [and] being suspected to be bawd to them."[119]

The influence of drink was increasingly noted in connection with a variety of cases during this period. In January 1574, the widow Anne Dinge was set in the stocks "for evil rule and maintaining of men's apprentices in the house contrary to order." She was further ordered not to keep a tippling house or sell beer.[120] Richard Long was imprisoned "for taking away a pot of pewter being drunken" in February 1577.[121] The magistrates sent both Edward and Christian Goodale to prison in August 1578 "for keeping of [a] tippling house contrary to the statute and receiving servants into their house."[122] This was one of the few occasions on which the magistrates made reference to legal statutes when meting out punishment. When John Mallerd and Thomas Thetford fell to fighting one evening in July 1580, they confessed, when they came before the court, "that they had been drinking and playing at a house in St. Edmund's [parish]." The magistrates decided that they "shall be set in the stocks with papers on their heads 'for drunkenness and fighting' and that they shall also be committed to prison until they find surety to appear at the next Session and to be of good behavior."[123] In July 1580, the mayor's court closed down the house of innkeeper Thomas Claxton because of the "great disorder and misrule kept and maintained" there, which was "to the high displeasure of Almighty God and slander of this city." To enforce their ruling, the magistrates committed him to prison until he found "surety to perform this order."[124]

The language of the mayor's court's record in the case of Thomas Claxton speaks directly to a link between the reputation of the city and God's will. The large number of punishments for such moral and social offenses as "evil rule," drunkenness and control of the body speak implicitly to such a connection as well. While the stepped-up campaign for discipline continued to address multiple concerns in the 1570's, the influence of a Protestant sacralization of the city seems to have grown.

Norwich in the late 1560's and early 1570's was beginning to develop its early reputation as a center of Puritanism, with a growing demand for hot Protestant preachers. The hottest among them would be John More, who was hired as the curate of St. Andrew's parish in Norwich in 1573. Patrick Collinson has described him as "one of the most celebrated preachers of his time."[125] More was said to have preached daily and three or four times on Sunday in the city and around Norfolk. He became the central figure among the city's Puritan clergy, which included fellow Cambridge graduates Thomas Roberts and Richard Crick and Cathedral prebendary Edmund Chapman. So great was his reputation that he became known as "the apostle of Norwich" and exercised a kind of unofficial superintendency over the clergy throughout much of Norfolk.[126]

The extant Chamberlains' accounts show that John More preached before the corporation on numerous civic occasions, such as Rogation week and the anniversary of Kett's rebellion, at least as early as 1580. The Chamberlains' accounts for the 1570's have not survived, but the magistrates had hired other Puritans to preach before them as early as the 1560's, so it would be surprising if they did not hire the popular and energetic More during his first seven years in Norwich. Certainly, by the end of the 1570's More had established relationships with at least two aldermen. The 1574 will of alderman Ellis Bate provided a small bequest to More, as did that of John Aldrich, who died in 1582. Aldrich, it should be remembered, was the mayor in 1570 who supervised the census of the poor and the implementation of Norwich's new poor scheme.[127]

In the preamble to the new Norwich poor law, the magistrates did not speak directly of a "godly commonwealth" or the extension of a new form of urban authority or even of the need to control a population that might one day prove receptive to the seditious plans of Catholic rebels. Rather, they reported "the great complaint made by divers citizens, who found the going abroad of the poor, not only very chargeable, by reason they came in such numbers but also very hurtful." The problem was not that the poor were hungry, but that Norwich's residents had become so generous in their almsgiving that the indigent threw excess victuals "abroad in the street." To this waste and disorder the poor added dissipation, for "they cared not for any exercise of body, or to work with their hands, to get them clothes or lodging, to keep them warm in the night." Consequently, "they fell into such absurd diseases of the body" and "filthiness of body, as one corrupeth another." Their children were thus rendered "unapt ever after to serve or do good in the commonwealth. And another mischief was, that when their bellies were filled, they fell to lust and concupiscence, and most shamefully abused their bodies, and brought forth bastards in such quantities as it passed."[128]

If the number of poor was a problem in Norwich, it was not because of the depth of their poverty. The preamble to the poor law makes this clear. In addition to the plenitude of food they threw on the street, some among the poor took into their houses "harlots, other scolds and bawds, and such like . . . to help the discharge of their house rent." The magistrates went on to explain that "by their disorder the heads of the city are so troubled with searching and correcting them." The census of the poor and the cases heard in the mayor's court shaped the magistrates' perception. In the mayor's court, as we have seen, the magistrates had just heard a record number of cases. From the census of the poor, John Pound has calculated that more than three-fifths of the 513 poor men counted were gainfully employed in a trade or as common laborers, with no adjustment for the elderly or disabled who were considered deserving of alms. Almost all of the women, he found, reported some form of work or employment.[129]

As John Pound has argued, the implementation of the new city poor laws was not prompted by an explosion of local poverty. Pound has hypothesized that concern about the "great multitude of people of mean and base sort" described by William Cecil after the failed plot of 1570 provided a significant catalyst for embarking upon a major reorganization of poor relief. In support of that contention, he has also noted that Norwich's first major effort at compulsory poor relief came in 1549, the year of Kett's rebellion, when "the local poor had been only too ready to participate."[130] The timing of the census and new poor relief program do suggest they were responses to the failed plot of 1570. However, timing by itself does not fully explain the nature of the response.

The magistrates had been engaged in a campaign for social and moral discipline for a decade, which they intensified in the aftermath of the failed plot through the apparatus of poor relief as well as the mayor's court. The scope of their effort is indicated in the preamble to the poor law's reference to the overburdened magistrates' "searching and correcting" of the poor. But social and moral regulation went beyond the ungodly filthiness, sexual license and disorder of the poor. Even the undisciplined giving of alms by the more prosperous residents of Norwich fell within the magistrates' corrective sight, along with all categories of offense seemingly regardless of social status. This was a new mode of authority dedicated to regulating social life according to a Protestant moral calculus. Despite its religious inspiration, it coexisted with magisterial toleration of religious difference.

⊰ VI ⊱

The success of the magistrates' practice of toleration in the 1570's depended in part on the presence of a cooperative bishop. Until 1575, Bishop Parkhurst provided such cooperation. Like the magistrates themselves, Parkhurst shied away from punishing religious nonconformity, whether Protestant or Catholic. And he did not inquire closely into religious affairs in the city, which allowed the magistrates to handle matters on their own. That situation would change with Parkhurst's death in 1575.

While Parkhurst did not punish religious nonconformity in the diocese, he was a patron of Puritans, advancing them in the diocese.[131] The Bishop was also well known for his reluctance to enforce proper clerical dress among his clergy and he was also known as a warm supporter of the prophesyings with which Puritan clergy were often associated. The Queen, however, was adamant in her views on clerical dress, and she disliked the Puritans' prophesying exercises, perceiving in them the seeds of religious division and conflict. The Bishop protected the exercises as long as he could, but he was forced to suppress them throughout the diocese in a 1574 episode that proved rather embarrassing to him. Parkhurst later learned that he was the only bishop ordered to put down the exercises, although he had been told that the order for their suppression had been dispatched to all of his colleagues on the episcopal bench.[132]

Parkhurst's death in February 1575 brought about a dramatic

change in the climate for Puritan clergy. Such drastic change must not have been anticipated at first, for, shortly after the Bishop's death, Norwich ministers resumed the prophesyings that Parkhurst had been compelled to suppress.[133] Before the year was out, however, Parkhurst was replaced as Bishop of Norwich by Edmund Freke, whom Patrick Collinson has described as a "sometime moderate puritan who had turned his coat." Freke came to his new diocese with orders to bring the recalcitrant Puritan clergy to heel. In his first visitation of the diocese in November 1576, Bishop Freke suspended all of the Norwich Puritan ministers for nonconformity, including their leaders John More and Thomas Roberts. Their suspension was said to have suppressed nineteen or twenty prophesying exercises in the city alone.[134]

Freke replaced More at St. Andrew's parish with a Mr. Holland, apparently in consultation with the mayor of Norwich and the parish's aldermen. Holland's first day at his new job was a disaster. An account of the episode survives in a letter written by Francis Wyndham, the Norwich Recorder, to his brother-in-law Nathaniel Bacon. Wyndham's information came from Bishop Freke. When Holland was ready to give what had been the popular Thursday sermon, the parish clerk refused both to ring the bell to call parishioners to church and to lead them in the singing of the psalm that normally preceded the sermon. When Holland finished preaching, "certain persons . . . namely one Cornewall, a minister, and one Morley, a baker, and one Bruer . . . did call Holland turncoat and said that he preached false doctrine and had betrayed the Word."[135]

An angry Bishop Freke went to the magistrates and demanded they punish those who had treated Holland so badly. But the Bishop, as Wyndham told it, "found the mayor and aldermen very cold in reformation and that their answer always was that they would confer with their learned counsel erst they could do anything." Unlike the magistrates' easy relationship with the tolerant Bishop Parkhurst, their reluctance to punish religious offenders quickly put them at odds with Freke. Consequently, Freke wrote to "their learned counsel" Wyndham and the magistrates threatening an appeal to the Privy Council. This was precisely the kind of external intervention into local religious affairs they routinely tried to avoid.

The magistrates grew more cooperative in the face of the Bishop's threats and arrested Cornewell, Morley and parish clerk Thomas Dix on Wyndham's advice. The mayor's court then sent Dix to prison for "disobeying of Mr. Mayor's commandment" to support More's substitute, while Cornewell and Morley were bound to good behavior for their "contemptuous behavior and other unseemly words spoken against Mr. Holland, a preacher."[136] Wyndham immediately found that this course of action "scarcely satisfieth the Bishop for he would have them bound to appear at the Assizes," where the offenders' fate would be taken out of the magistrates' hands. Wyndham apparently tried to placate the Bishop's desire for sterner punishment. It is doubtful that he could have eased the Bishop's anger at the way the prisoners were treated while awaiting their appearance in the mayor's court, for Wyndham "marveled at how many came to them in prison, and how they were banqueted and wine brought to them."[137]

Bishop Freke's quarrels with the Norwich preachers dragged on for years, as Patrick Collinson has shown.[138] The impact of the new Bishop on the magistrates' jurisprudence was evident again in May 1577, when James Moone was set in the stocks "for speaking slanderous words of the Lord Bishop." Perhaps the magistrates sought to repair their relationship with Freke by demonstrating their unwillingness to tolerate any vilification of the Bishop; perhaps they even stood in fear of Freke and were ready to come down harshly on Moone for that reason. Moone's case is remarkable because similar incidents had not been treated so severely in the past. When John Seman called Bishop Parkhurst a "fornicator, whoremaster . . . [and an] adulterer" in 1561, the magistrates took no action against him, even though they were far more sympathetically disposed to Parkhurst than to Freke.[139]

In other cases concerning religion but not involving Bishop Freke's reputation the magistrates continued to exercise their traditional tolerance. They bound George Smith to good behavior in March 1580 and never recalled him after they learned that he had violated the Lenten fast by allowing meat to be prepared in Thomas Farror's house, where he was apparently a servant.[140] In September 1582 they had required Elizabeth Molle to bring proof of the "slanderous words" she had spoken against the preacher Mr. Barnard, "that he hath a bastard," or else be "ducked in the cart." Three weeks later, Molle, apparently unable to substantiate the charge, asked Barnard's forgiveness in open court. When the minister forgave her, the mayor and aldermen decided that "her punishment is remitted and she [is] discharged."[141] The mayor's court heard no other cases involving religion during this time.

Eventually, Bishop Freke's tireless campaigns against Puritans in Norwich diocese helped to provoke charges that he was soft on Catholic recusancy. Puritans in the diocese accused Freke of taking counsel from recusants and even sheltering some in his household. Hassell Smith has argued that if Puritan charges against Freke were overstated, there is still ample evidence of his leniency toward recusants. The well-known recusant Sir Thomas Cornwallis dined at the Bishop's table. And when Freke did imprison suspected Catholics in the course of carrying out his episcopal duties, he freed them at the earliest possible opportunity, sometimes so early that the Privy Council commanded their reimprisonment.[142]

Allegations about Freke's indulgence of recusants were presented in an unsigned memorandum of early January 1584 outlining the reasons why the Bishop was excluded from the recent commission of the peace.[143] The commission began its work in the wake of the discovery of the Throckmorton plot in November 1583, named for the man who revealed its details under torture when arrested by central government authorities. Like the Ridolfi plot of 1571, the Throckmorton plot aimed to depose Elizabeth and restore Catholicism to England. Official fear of, and hostility toward, Catholicism was already on the increase. In 1581, Parliament had increased the fines for nonattendance at church from 12d. weekly to a hefty £20 per month. The discovery of the plot only hardened attitudes. The Spanish ambassador had given his blessing to the conspiracy and Mary, Queen of Scots, had been implicated as well. After the plot was uncovered, the Privy Council, perceiving a major threat to the Queen's life and English Protestantism, composed the so-called *Bond of Association*. By its terms the members of the Privy Council each vowed to pursue and destroy those responsible for the Queen's assassination in the event of a successful attempt on Elizabeth's life.

The commission excluded Bishop Freke, according to the memorandum of January 1584, because the Bishop had "very rarely" used his authority "against any papist." Furthermore, Freke seldom assisted those secular justices who pursued Catholic suspects and when he did provide evidence to them, "it was slender in regard of the number presented and it was unperfect through want of Christian names, surnames, place of abode and other necessary instructions for indictments." The memorandum also charged that "suspecte[d] persons are his most familiar guests [and] friends." Finally, while the Bishop "could spy out from the furthest of his diocese some ministers of the gospel for omitting the least duty," he had been unable "to spy out any one mass of so many [recusants] in Norfolk and Norwich, some of them being in his own parish almost at his palace gate."[144]

This last charge obviously reflected the anger of Puritans and their sympathizers who felt harassed by Freke. While the Bishop's suppression of Puritan clergy was energetic, his pursuit of Catholics was not. The commission uncovered a sizable group of Catholics just outside Norwich in January 1584. The memorandum maintained that Freke had been apprised of the presence of the recusant group, "wherein nothing was ever done by the Bishop that we know nor the party informing was ever called." Testimony taken during the course of the commission's investigation told of the celebration of Mass in Sprowston, outside Norwich, and of the attendance by one of the Bishop's own servants.[145]

The commission's investigations and increasing fear of Catholicism across England in the wake of the Throckmorton plot's discovery must go a long way in explaining why the magistrates took the unusual steps of apparently arresting a group of Catholic recusants and informing the Privy Council of those arrests in January 1584. In the tense atmosphere of 1584, the habitually tolerant Norwich magistrates could not completely disregard the campaign against Catholic recusants, lest they too be accused of a lax attitude toward Catholicism.

Concerning the recusants, the mayor and five city Justices told the Privy Council, "we, according to our loyal duties, presently apprehended so many of the suspected persons as we could come by." They appended to the letter a list of the people apprehended with the names of their priests, but this list has not survived. In the letter, the magistrates described their offenses as including hearing Mass, absenting themselves from church and wearing "hallowed beads." Some had "been shriven" as well. The magistrates noted that they had turned over the names of other suspects to officials of Norfolk. Having shown themselves to be vigilant in the search for recusants, they closed the letter by asking for mercy for some of the suspects, whom they described as "being poor persons of mean account" and noted that they "seem to be penitent." No reply from the Council survives. The mayor's letter exists only in the State Papers; no mention of these recusants appears in any of the city records. While it is difficult to believe that the magistrates would lie to the Privy Council, especially under such circumstances, the absence of any local record concerning the recusants strongly suggests that the magistrates took no further action against them.[146]

These would not be the last recusants discovered in Norwich. From time to time through the rest of the 1580's and during the following decade, the magistrates examined a few Catholic recusants in the mayor's court. After notifying the Council about local recusants in early 1584, the magistrates returned to their customary methods of handling religious conflict. They heard only one case in the mayor's court during the rest of that year. In November, Robert Crask and David Bulwer protested to the mayor's court that a local minister, Mr. Olyet, "hath spoken unseemly and contemptuous words tending to the discredit and defaming of the preachers of God's word." Olyet was sentenced to jail until he could find sureties, after which his case disappears from the records.[147] The magistrates were not troubled by Bishop Freke, who was busily involved in seeking his escape from the factious Norwich diocese. His liberation came in December when he was translated to Worcester. Freke was replaced by Edmund Scambler, with whom the magistrates appear to have had little contact.

A recusant was discovered again in Norwich in early 1585. The Chamberlains' accounts for that year recorded payment for the dispatch of "letters sent to the Lords of her Majesty's most honorable Privy Council touching certain books found at Mr. Hobart's house." Henry Hobart was a member of a prominent gentry family of Loddon, Norfolk, whose members had served the monarchy for generations as county sheriffs and Justices until the reign of Elizabeth, when their recusancy prompted their exclusion from further service.[148] It is not clear who discovered the books, but the next step in the case was taken by local clergymen. The mayor's court book noted that at the command of the Privy Council, George Gardiner, now Dean of Norwich Cathedral, "with Mr. Paman and Mr. Mosse, preachers," scrutinized books, papers and "other popish stuff" found in Hobart's house. The Council had further ordered the three to burn a number of the items in question, which included a vestment and altar cloth; the burning took place in the Norwich market on January 16. The mayor's court only recorded the incident because the burning took place in the market, which lay in their jurisdiction. There is no record of what happened to Hobart, but he was alive and well three years later, when Bishop Scambler denied him a license to travel.[149]

For the rest of the decade, the magistrates took little action against any more recusants, despite growing fears throughout England of Catholic plots and invasions. Parliament passed the Act Against Jesuits and Seminarists, which mandated hanging, drawing and quartering for any Catholic priests found on English soil, on the grounds that their mere presence constituted treason.[150] The discovery of the Babington Plot in 1586 provided conclusive evidence of the complicity of Mary, Queen of Scots, in an attempt on Elizabeth's throne and life. Mary was executed for her role in early 1587. War erupted between England and Spain and King Philip's Armada set sail for the invasion of England in 1588. But Norwich magistrates did not respond to the threats these events seemed to represent by rooting out local Catholics. In the late 1580's and early 1590's, they took only a handful of Catholics into custody, none, apparently, of the elevated social status of Henry Hobart.

In February 1588, the Council wrote to the mayor and city sheriffs concerning the fate of the recusant Anne Houlet, who was then imprisoned in the city jail. The Council's letter did not discuss the circumstances of her arrest. Houlet's husband apparently informed the Council of her plight and persuaded them that he was "conformable in religion" and could convince her "to like obedience." The letter further instructed the mayor and sheriffs to secure bonds from Houlet "with sufficient sureties" in the amount of £40, after which she could be set free. Only the letter from the Privy Council survives in this matter, for Houlet's case has left no trace in city records. The silence of the records suggests that she came into city custody by the efforts of some other authority, perhaps officials from Norfolk or the diocese. There is no evidence that the magistrates had attempted any further investigation of local recusancy at that time.[151]

It would be more than a year after the Houlet matter before another case involving religion would be recorded in the mayor's court books. In March 1589, Peter Spyuwyn, a Dutchman, confessed that "he hath been beyond the seas and there hath heard Mass," as had his countryman John de Walle. The magistrates resolved to banish Spyuwyn, ordering him "to depart this city on Monday next and be shipped at Yarmouth and so pass over the seas." If he returned to Norwich, they warned him that they would immediately dispatch him "to the Lords of her Majesty's most honorable Privy Council." Spyuwyn was committed to prison until he could find sureties to carry out that decree. John de Walle was also sentenced to be banished from the city with his wife and children. He too was at first committed to prison, but for reasons not specified in the court record, he was released. There is no further account of either man and thus it is impossible to know whether they left Norwich as instructed.[152]

A second religious case was heard in the mayor's court in 1589. This one involved conflict over the preacher John More and demonstrates that his popularity did not extend to all corners of Norwich. In August, six men signed a complaint against the minister of St. Martin-at-Oak, a Mr. Yould, who was apparently not one of the hotter sort of Protestants. The complaint charged Yould with "saying that the preachers be dolts . . . and that the said preachers as Mr. More and others are not worthy to carry their books after them whom he keep company with, with many other unseemly and railing words against the preachers." Yould was committed to prison until he could find sureties for his good behavior and the case ended there.[153]

John More and other Puritan clergy were again the subject of verbal assault in April 1591. The blacksmith Richard Stutter reported a recent conversation with the cordwainer Miles Wyllan. Wyllan asked him "why he resorted to the exercises and preaching of Mr. More, Mr. Flood and other preachers because . . . they do not teach the truth but teach men's fantasies." Wyllan also asked how Stutter liked the minister of his parish, which he did not name, to which Stutter replied that he "liked him very well." That response provoked Wyllan to retort, "I perceive you are ignorant and have no understanding," after which he "turned his back and departed." The magistrates apparently found this insult more serious than others they heard in the mayor's court and bound Miles Wyllan to appear before the next Court of High Commission, the highest ecclesiastical court. Perhaps even more galling for Wyllan—not to mention extraordinary for the aldermen—was the additional order that he should "in the meantime . . . resort to the church to hear sermons or such prayers as are used and set forth by the laws of the realm."[154]

Wyllan's case was the last one concerning religion heard in the mayor's court for the rest of Elizabeth's reign. But, while they listened to Wyllan's insulting remarks about John More, another resident, the scrivener Richard Lasher, languished in the city jail as a recusant. Lasher's case is known only because of the survival of a letter from the Privy Council to Bishop Scambler, the mayor and sheriffs. The Council noted that "he is very poor" and unable to support his family while imprisoned. It seemed convinced that there was "some hope of his conformity if his liberty be granted him," with sufficient sureties for his good behavior. The Council did not offer details of Lasher's arrest, but the fact that the letter was also addressed to the Bishop suggests ecclesiastical involvement in the case. In this instance, not even the Privy Council seemed interested in meting out severe punishment to individual recusants of little stature and with few connections. Presumably Lasher was released and never appeared before the mayor and aldermen as a recusant.[155]

⊰ VII ⊱

In Elizabethan Norwich, a reformation of manners and practical religious toleration coincided. The city's magistrates embarked upon a Protestant-inspired campaign to impose greater social and moral discipline, creating new modes of authority, order and governance. At the same time, they rarely punished religious nonconformity, Protestant or Catholic—in fact, on more than one occasion they appear to have protected it from the prying eyes of more persecutorial authorities. At first glance, this amalgamation of religious fervor and religious forbearance seems contradictory.

In *The Birthpangs of Protestant England*, Patrick Collinson has described the "new order" in Elizabethan and Jacobean towns as a product of a "tight alliance of ministry and magistracy." Citing the 1570 plan of poor relief, he lists Norwich as one of the earliest examples of the Protestant-inspired "coercive discipline" and "determined, rational and, it must be said, enlightened onslaught on social evils and endemic problems" composed by a coalition of magistrates and ministers.[156] In several of his other studies, Collinson refers to Norwich as exemplary in this respect.

Based on his extensive research on East Anglia and Protestantism in Elizabethan and early Stuart England, Collinson begins an essay on "Magistracy and Ministry" in rural Suffolk by asserting that "Elizabethan Norwich provides the paradigm of urban puritanism."[157] In a lecture on "Magistracy and Ministry" devoted to complicating Michael Walzer's and Christopher Hill's claim that "the logic of Protestantism led to an egalitarian individualism," Collinson begins by recounting the thirty-year "tradition of civic godliness at St. Andrew's" church in Norwich, and its crisis in 1607. In that year the diocesan Chancellor excommunicated the churchwardens of St. Andrew's for refusing to remove recently installed seats in which, they explained, "the ministers of the city were placed in one roumethe [place], and in another, next them, the aldermen." Collinson uses this history to illustrate the "paradox" of Protestantism's—and, indeed, Puritanism's—proclivity for the imposition of worldly and spiritual order on the one hand, and the propagation of disorder and dissent, on the other.[158]

Collinson's nuanced view of the generally conservative "new order" of urban rule is highly persuasive. However, his portrait of magisterial religious fervor does not seem to allow any room for the magistrates' religious forbearance. When Collinson describes the union of magistrates and ministers as fitting a "typically Tudor conception of Church and Commonwealth indissolubly one," he is in line with the opinion of most scholars of the period.[159] There does not seem to be any space for religious diversity in this assessment of religion and politics, let alone religious toleration on the part of "the protestant governing class."[160] This study of Elizabethan Norwich suggests that the magistrates' and ministers' "tight alliance" in religion and politics was not always so tight or indissoluble.

If the Norwich magistrates became more solidly Protestant after 1558, the ministry of Norwich remained divided throughout the Elizabethan period and the magistrates never seem to have complained about it. In matters of religion as well as social and moral discipline, the Norwich magistrates seemed to care only about how people behaved and not what they thought. Moreover, they seem to have averted their eyes whenever possible from religious nonconformity, thus tolerating the practice of Catholicism and Protestant dissent in their city so long as it did not seriously threaten civic order or provoke the intervention of external powers.

Norwich magistrates did indeed go to some lengths to practice religious toleration, as their clash with Bishop Freke in 1576 clearly demonstrates. When Freke directed them to punish the men who had scorned and mocked the substitute preacher Mr. Holland, the magistrates initially balked, causing the Bishop to reportedly say that he "found the mayor and aldermen very cold in reformation and that their answer always was that they would confer with their learned counsel erst they could do anything." When Bishop Freke threatened to call on the Privy Council, the magistrates moved first to punish the offenders as lightly as possible and then to placate the still angry Bishop, whom the mild penalty "scarcely satisfieth."

The stakes of religious conflict were high in the Elizabethan era. Local records reveal that at least four people—Matthew Hammond, Abdyall Lewis, Peter Cole and Francis Ket alias Knight—were burnt as heretics in Norwich. However, none appear to have been from the city. All four executions were recorded in the "Mayor's Book," but did not include the victims' places of residence. Other records reveal that three of the four were from outside of Norwich, suggesting that city rulers did not feel it necessary to note the residence of outsiders. It thus seems likely that the fourth, Lewis, was an outsider as well.

Two were executed while Freke was still bishop. In 1579, the wheelwright Hammond of Hethersett was executed for denying the divinity of Christ. A week before his May 20 death, his ears had been cut off as a result of his conviction at the Norwich Quarter Sessions for speaking "seditious and slanderous words ... against the Queen's Majesty."[161] Abydall Lewis went to the stake in September 1583, "most obstinately without repentance or any speech," also for denying the divinity of Christ.[162] The last two died as heretics during Edmund Scambler's episcopate, both also for denying the divinity of Christ. Peter Cole, a native of Ipswich, went to the stake in 1587 and Francis Ket alias Knight, from Norfolk, was burnt in January 1589.[163]

While none were executed, the now well-known Norwich Separatists known as "Brownists" fled the city after the leader from whom they took their name, Robert Browne, was harassed and imprisoned, probably more than once, by ecclesiastical authorities in 1581. Browne settled in Norwich in 1580 or 1581, joining his friend from Cambridge days, Robert Harrison, who served as master as one of the Norwich hospitals. Browne subscribed to Presbyterian views in the 1570's and by 1581 moved in a more radical direction. The two formally organized a Separatist congregation by April 1581. Local ministers complained about the Brownists to Bishop Freke, leading to Browne's arrests. Browne's troubles with the Bishop convinced the congregation to leave Norwich and they settled in Middleburg in the Netherlands in 1582. There is no evidence in city records that the magistrates were aware of the existence of this Separatist congregation and if they were, they were not among those who complained about it to Bishop Freke.[164]

The Bishop's reputation for protecting Catholics while persecuting godly ministers produced hostile feelings toward him on the part of some Norwich Protestants. Notably, however, the unsigned memorandum from the time of the 1584 recusancy commission assailed Freke for this improper discrimination and not his toleration of Catholics per se. This well illustrates an aspect of toleration and persecution that the Norwich magistrates apparently understood since at least the time of Queen Mary: accusations breed counter-accusations and persecutions breed counterpersecutions, sometimes merely out of self-defense rather than a desire to suppress difference.

The Norwich magistrates' relationships with their ministers were obviously complex. The magistrates stood in one relationship to Bishop Parkhurst and quite another to Bishop Freke. Like the magistrates, Bishop Parkhurst was thoroughly reluctant to seek out and punish religious nonconformists of all stripes. He spent most, and perhaps all, of his fifteen-year episcopate in Norwich quite aware of the presence of numerous Catholics throughout the diocese and even in his own Cathedral, not to mention the nonconforming Puritan ministers whom he tried to support and protect. Unlike the magistrates, Parkhurst appears to have believed in concord through persuasion, that is to say, the creation of religious uniformity through persuasion rather than persecution.[165] There is practically no evidence that the magistrates were interested in concord. That is why the punishment they inflicted on Miles Wyllan in 1591—"to resort to the church to hear sermons or such prayers as are used and set forth by the laws of the realm"—was so exceptional. In no other case in the seventy years between 1530 and 1600 did they ever force anyone to attend church as a penalty or correction.

When the magistrates were forced by external powers and circumstances to punish religious nonconformists, they did so in a telling way. Not only did they punish as few as possible, and these as lightly as they could, but they also restricted their search for such sacrificial offerings to the lower orders of society. For example, when the magistrates rounded up some Catholics to appease central authorities in 1584, they described them as "poor persons of mean account," for whom they then sought clemency.

There is no way to know exactly how many names of recusants the magistrates sent to the Privy Council in 1584. The entire extant city records of Norwich, which are nearly complete for the period, mention only three Catholic recusants during the forty-five-year reign of Elizabeth. Another two were mentioned in correspondence from the Privy Council, but their cases left no trace in city records. The recusants Anne Houlet and Richard Lasher, known only through Privy Council correspondence, do not appear to have been people of great substance. Two of the cases in the city records concerned the Dutch Strangers Spyuwyn and de Walle, both marginal to Norwich society and politics. The third case mentioned in the city records was the only one to concern a substantial member of East Anglian society. The recusant Henry Hobart, from a prominent Norfolk family, was examined by clerical authorities, not civic ones. He appears to have never been held in the city's custody, although his illicit books were burnt by Norwich clergy in the marketplace. Despite the presence of well-known Catholic gentry in East Anglia associated with the Duke of Norfolk and the failed Norwich plot of 1570, the Norwich magistrates never once punished a Catholic recusant of elevated social standing or reported on one to higher authorities throughout all of Elizabeth's reign.

While the magistrates did not punish the socially prominent for religious infractions and tried not to punish religious infractions at all, this reluctance to punish did not extend to the realm of social and moral behavior. There the magistrates did not spare the rod or tolerate different codes of conduct. Whereas they routinely tried to overlook or turn away from variations in religious practice, their census of the poor in 1570 was designed to make the problems of urban society and the characteristics of the poor fully visible and tractable.

Patrick Collinson is correct to highlight the role of Protestantism in giving shape to the specific campaign for social and moral discipline in Elizabethan Norwich. As Ian Archer has argued for Elizabethan London, the willingness to generalize discipline across social and gender lines distinguished the Protestant-inspired regulation of social and moral behavior from earlier efforts to discipline offenders more thoroughly.[166] The Norwich magistrates punished both men and women for sexual misconduct, even prostitution. They also punished those higher on the social ladder, including at least nine citizens whom they disenfranchised and at least four ministers.[167] One of the disenfranchised citizens also lost his position as a common councilor. Puritanism and the presence of Puritan ministers and prophesying surely played a role in crafting these new modes of authority and order in Norwich, but the magistrates' new regulation of society had no counterpart in their handling of religion.

-⊰ ⊱-

Conclusion

BELIEF AND BELONGING — CIVIC IDENTITY
IN REFORMATION NORWICH

Despite the seeming contradiction between fervor and forbearance, the drive for order and the practice of religious toleration could coexist in Elizabethan Norwich because they depended on different dynamics. The magistrates' toleration of spiritual diversity depended upon their ability to compartmentalize religion and distinguish its practice from other political concerns. Their campaign for moral and social order constituted what Patrick Collinson has called the "sacralisation of the town, which now became self-consciously a godly commonwealth, its symbolic and mimetic codes replaced by a literally articulated, didactic religious discipline."[1] Yet, as originally Protestant as this might have been in inspiration and cultural effect, the new discipline in Norwich entailed no specific confessional affiliation.

There is no evidence that the Norwich magistrates singled out suspected Catholics for moral and social correction in the Elizabethan era. Nor did their rhetoric of disorderly behavior, moral failing and physical degeneracy reflect anti-Catholic stereotypes. Anti-Catholicism in the first decades of Elizabeth's reign depicted English and foreign Catholics as implacable, devious and powerful enemies to be feared. In this sense, they were seen as equal players on the cosmic and temporal stage.

If, as Richard Helgerson suggests, John Foxe's martyrology succeeded in popularizing the image of a Protestant England locked in struggle with the papal Antichrist until the end of time, this apocalyptic battle between good and evil was perceived as a balanced one in this world.[2] Soon enough, the English colonization of Ireland, the Iberian fall from power, and then the social and scientific developments of the eighteenth and nineteenth centuries would recast this religious difference in new ways, counterposing Catholics to Protestants as worldly inferiors.[3] However, in Elizabethan Norwich, the magistrates employed a discourse of deviance that was rich with Protestant ideas of rectitude but not yet affected by the associations English Protestants would increasingly make between Catholicism and the proclivity to disorder, disobedience and dissipation.

Norwich ministers might have encouraged and inspired the magistrates to try to create a "godly commonwealth," but the magistrates punished offenders, expelled vagrants and organized the correction of the poor all on their own. As I have shown throughout this study, the Norwich magistrates understood that they were part of a larger cosmos, a larger world and a larger realm, but they also cherished their civic identity and autonomy. The magistrates of sixteenth-century Norwich understood the Reformation from this point of view, situated, as they were, in a complex and multifaceted world. If Protestant theologians and propagandists such as Foxe saw Catholics as minions of the Antichrist in cosmic and international struggles, Norwich magistrates adopted a more local view in their governance. In their corner of the world, they could accept Norwich's Catholics—and Protestant nonconformists, too—as members of the urban community. From their own experience and the institutional memory of urban upheaval going back into the last century they found good reasons to do so.

Most historians have construed the English Reformation as a religious revolution, some explaining it as driven by the state politics of religion, while others describe it as a more popularly rooted spiritual movement. Even some of the leading local studies of the Reformation frame their examination of religious change almost exclusively in these terms, limiting their field of

vision to what seems an inevitable and irreconcilable confrontation between Protestantism and Catholicism.[4] Although Christopher Haigh's insistence on speaking only of "Reformations," in
the plural, is chiefly directed at distinguishing England from the
Continent and thus detaching what he sees as England's funda-
mentally state-directed reforms from any real change in popular
spirituality and worldview, I would like to use the concept of
plural "Reformations" in a different way.[5]

Norwich seems to have experienced the religious upheavals of
the sixteenth century in ways different from other communities,
but this difference cannot be accounted for only in terms of relative commitments to Protestantism or Catholicism. Rather, the
Reformation changes in Norwich must be understood in relation
to, and as part of, other institutions and practices of urban life.
Communities in England and on the Continent experienced different Reformations because their social, political, cultural and
economic lives mattered and could not just be washed over by a
totalizing or "universal" religion. Even, and perhaps especially,
Catholicism, so often depicted by Protestant propagandists as a
monolith directed from Rome, was, in fact, practiced and understood in very different ways in different societies. Protestantism
could be no different.

The Reformation took its specific shape in Norwich, in large
part, because of the city magistrates' success at containing religious discord and tolerating religious difference. The Norwich
magistrates' practice of religious toleration did not reflect an incipient liberalism or respect for individualism. If Patrick Collinson's conclusion that "the middle age of the Reformation was often accompanied by the tightening grip of oligarchies which used
religion as a prime instrument of social control and self-advance-
ment" too thoroughly conflates religion and politics, his perception of an oligarchic order infused with Protestantism still accurately describes the magistrates' position in Norwich.[6]

The Norwich magistrates practiced religious toleration not to
respect the beliefs of dissenters, but as part of a strategy to prevent outside intervention and keep civic authority in their own

hands. To some extent, their success depended on a little good fortune. During Mary's reign, for example, the Bishop of Norwich did not inquire too closely into heresy in his own Cathedral city; if Bishop Hopton had focused more of his attention on the city, then the period of Mary's reign and much of what followed would have been very different. But it is impossible to explain the success and duration of their mode of governance solely as a function of good luck.

The effectiveness of their strategy of toleration depended on the magistrates' skill at defusing conflict and fending off the inquiries of outside powers. After the debacle of Wolsey's seven-year-long intervention and mayor Edward Rede's brush with Thomas More in the aftermath of Thomas Bilney's controversial execution in 1531, the magistrates consistently avoided punishing religious nonconformists in the mayor's court while at the same presenting a compliant face to the Church hierarchy and central government.

The success of magisterial toleration also required a sense of civic identity that distinguished residents who belonged to the community from outsiders who did not. "Aliens," as even English people from outside the city were called, were always liable to be treated more severely by the magistrates for their religious infractions than Norwich residents. But civic identity also had an internal component with substance beyond the simple contrast with outsiders.

Civic identity bound the magistrates together when they were religiously divided between Catholics and Protestants, from Henry VIII's reign to the early years of Elizabeth's, and then again when they differed in their Protestantism. During Mary's reign, civic unity prevailed over any temptations Norwich residents may have felt to inform on Protestant neighbors. The only person delated to the authorities was Simon Miller, the outsider from King's Lynn. Tellingly, the two Norwich residents who perished at the stake had to incriminate themselves publicly, one in church and the other at the first's execution.

As we have seen, the magistrates worked to cultivate civic

identity and unity in Norwich ever since their experience with the dangers of factionalism in the mid-fifteenth century. In Patrick Collinson's depiction of the close relationship between magistrates and ministers embodied in the St. Andrew's seating arrangement of 1607, we can see not only a magisterial commitment to Protestantism, but also a mimetic representation of the social order, similar to those formerly displayed in pre-Reformation pageantry.

Most historians have understood traditional civic rituals to have been victims of the official Reformation's assault on the worship of saints and Catholic ceremony. Undeniably, the official Reformation abrogated many traditional holy days and pageants. But such ritual display had always served multiple purposes, and not simply a narrowly defined religious one. The same could be true for the new forms of Protestant worship, as the seating of the Norwich magistrates together with the leading ministers in St. Andrew's church indicates.

The magistrates were required to cancel some rituals and change others by directives emanating from Westminster, as were all other communities across England. But this does not explain how they went about altering their civic calendar and institutions. The magistrates revived and reinvented civic ceremonies throughout the Reformation era, removing prohibited religious elements whenever necessary and preserving the social, political and economic functions of ritual whenever possible. For these reasons, they also invented many of their own ceremonial events. In addition to those discussed in Chapter 3, the magistrates were apparently one of the few communities in England to have an annual thanksgiving service commemorating the defeat of the Spanish Armada every year after 1588.[7] On some occasions, as we have seen, they also held festivities for lesser events that hardly seem worthy of celebration.

The Reformation in Norwich produced many changes in the city's politics and culture. Most traditional feast days ceased to be observed and, as Patrick Collinson has suggested for English towns generally, a new "coercive discipline" supplanted the "charmingly roundabout fashion of" creating order through "'pastime' and instinctive ritual and carnival." This religiously driven change is what Ronald Hutton has characterized as "the fall of Merry England." But, as I have argued, these changes have largely been overstated in terms of religious difference and underappreciated in respect to local communities and their political life. Religion was never all-encompassing. Because the Norwich magistrates had come to understand that religion was not the only game in town, they were able to play their own hand so well.

Appendixes

⊰ APPENDIX 1 ⊱

Aldermen in Office in 1524 and 1535

Aldermen in office in 1535 (Harcocke sermon)

Thomas Bauburgh	William Layer	Robert Rugge
Richard Catlyn	Robert Leche	Nicholas Sotherton
John Curat	Reginald Little-	Augustine Styward
Robert Ferrour	prowe	Nicholas Sywhat
Henry Fuller	Thomas Necton	Thomas Thetford
Robert Green	Thomas Pykerell	Ralph Wilkins
Thomas Grewe	Edward Rede	Edmund Wood
William Haste	William Rogers	
Robert Hemmyng	William Roone	

Aldermen in office 1535 who were in office in 1524 (Wolsey's solution)

Thomas Bauburgh	Reginald Little-	Edward Rede
Robert Ferrour	prowe	William Roone
Robert Green	Hamon Linsted	Nicholas Sywhat
Robert Hemmyng	Thomas Pykerell	Ralph Wilkins

Aldermen in office in 1535 who had been common councilors in 1524

Richard Catlyn	Robert Leche	Edmund Wood
Thomas Grewe	Augustine Styward	

SOURCE: Timothy Hawes, ed.

⊰ APPENDIX 2 ⊱

Aldermanic Wills Written
1530-January 1547

Richard Corpusty: NCC 334–36 Attmere, written September 9, 1540.
Robert Ferrour: NCC 211 Mingay, written November 10, 1542.
Robert Green: NCC 386 Attmere, written March 22, 1540.
William Haste: PCC 19 Crumwell, written January 16, 1536.
Robert Hemmyng: NCC 127 Hyll, written April 8, 1541.
Robert Jannys: PCC 3 Thower, written April 20, 1530.
William Layer: PCC 19 Crumwell, written October 31, 1537.
Robert Long: NCC 27 Alpe, written January 14, 1530.
Nicholas Osbern: PCC 29 Alenger, written April 15, 1541.
Thomas Pykerell: PCC F 5 Alen, written September 10, 1545.
Edward Rede: PCC F 27 Pynnyng, written October 25, 1544.
William Rogers: PCC 12 Tashe, written March 10, 1543.
William Roone: NCC 79 Godsalve, written July 21, 1535.
Nicholas Sotherton: PCC 21 Alenger, written October 20, 1540.
Thomas Thetford: NCC 273–80 Hyll, written March 26, 1546.
John Trace: PCC F 16 Pynnyng, written July 12, 1544.
Ralph Wilkins: PCC 28 Hogen, written July 13, 1535.

Testators who committed their souls to the "holy company
of heaven" and/or provided for Masses

Corpusty	Jannys	Roone
Ferrour	Long	Sotherton
Green	Osbern	Thetford
Haste	Pykerell	Ward
Hemmyng	Rede	Wilkins

Testators who also mentioned a specific patron saint

| Ferrour | Hemmyng | Roone |
| Haste | Long | Wilkins |

Testators who did not commit their souls to saints or provide for Masses

| Rogers | Trace |

⊰ APPENDIX 3 ⊱

Aldermanic Wills Written in the Reign of Edward VI

Henry Dunham: NCC 16 Walpoole, written August 29, 1552.
Thomas Greenwood: NCC 230 Lyncolne, written August 26, 1550.
Thomas Grewe: NCC 342 Wymer, written January 20, 1549.
Hamond Linsted: NCC 230 Corant, written June 5, 1551.
Felix Puttock: NCC 188 Beeles, written July 9, 1550.
Richard Suckling: NCC 185 Lyncolne, written September 17, 1551.
John Tasburgh: PCC 26 Tashe, written May 13, 1553.
Edmund Wood: PCC F.19 Populwell, written October 31, 1548.

*Testators who committed their souls to the "holy company
of heaven" and/or provided for Masses*

NONE

Testators who also mentioned a specific patron saint

NONE

Testators who committed their souls only to God

Grewe	Suckling
Linsted	Tasburgh

Testators who commited their souls to no one

Dunham

Testators who mentioned Christ

Greenwood	Puttock	Wood

Aldermanic Wills Written in the Reign of Mary

John Balle: PCC 8 Ketchyn, written November 24, 1554.
Richard Catlyn: NCC 96 Jagges, written August 28, 1558.
Thomas Cock: NCC 290 Jerves, written August 8, 1558.
Thomas Codde: NCC 431 Colman, written October 12, 1558.
Henry Fuller: NCC 360 Beeles, written August 3, 1556.
Thomas Gray: NCC 102 Jerves, written July 24, 1557.
John Howse: PCC 74 Noodes, written October 24, 1558.
Robert Leche: NCC 128 Goldingham, written September 20, 1557.
Thomas Malby: PCC F.11 Welles, written October 15, 1558.
Thomas Marsham: NCC 150 Hustings, written September 11, 1557.
Alexander Mather: PCC 25 Mellershe, written November 17, 1555.
Nicholas Sywhat: NCC 43 Ingold, written May 2, 1558.
Geoffrey Ward: PCC 26 Chaynay, written August 3, 1558.

*Testators who committed their souls to the "holy company
of heaven" and/or provided for Masses*

Catlyn	Fuller	Marsham
Cock	Howse	Mather
Codde	Malby	

Testators who also mentioned a specific patron saint

NONE

*Testators who did not commit their souls to saints or
provide for Masses*

Balle	Leche	Ward
Gray	Sywhat	

⊰ APPENDIX 5 ⊱

Aldermen Who Died in the 1558–59 Influenza Epidemic

John Atkins: no will survives.
Thomas Cock: NCC 290 Jerves, written August 8, 1558.
Thomas Codde: NCC 431 Colman, written October 12, 1558.
Thomas Gray: NCC 102 Jerves, written July 24, 1557.
John Howse: PCC 74 Noodes, written October 24, 1558.
Thomas Malby: PCC F.11 Welles, written October 15, 1558.
Alexander Mather: PCC 25 Mellershe, written November 17, 1555.
Robert Rugge: NCC 447 Colman, written December 24, 1558.
Nicholas Sywhat: NCC 43 Ingold, written May 2, 1558.
Geoffrey Ward: PCC 26 Chaynay, written August 3, 1558.

⊰ APPENDIX 6 ⊱

Offenses Punished in the Mayor's Court, 1540–41 to 1580–81

The sources for the figures given in the following table are: NRO MCB 1540–1549, MCB 1549–1555, MCB 1555–1562, MCB 1562–1569, MCB 1569–1576 and MCB 1576–1581. The table was prepared by Corey Hollis.

The count of social and moral cases in the mayor's court encompasses all appearances for which punishment or correction was typically applied. This includes all of the categories discussed on p. 216, such as "evil rule" and stealing. It excludes all cases concerning directly religious disputes of the type treated throughout this book and also all civil and other cases that typically resulted in orders for recompense, such as debt actions and bastardy cases for child support. The years are given by mayoral term, which began on the Tuesday before Midsummer.

Two categories are marked with an asterisk (*), "runaways" and "counseling." The first is concerned with runaway servants and apprentices. The second includes those who "counseled" servants or apprentices to commit misdeeds.

Offenses Punished by the Mayor's Court, 1540–41 to 1580–81

	Vagrancy	Theft	Evil rule	Run-aways*	Disobedience	Fighting/scolding	Sexual misconduct	Harboring	Counseling*	Gaming	Drunkenness	Misuse/abuse	Misbehavior/disorder	Miscellaneous	Total crimes per year
							1540–41 TO 1557–58								
1540–41	0	1	0	0	4	0	1	0	0	1	0	0	0	0	7
1541–42	1	0	0	0	1	1	1	0	0	0	0	1	0	1	5
1542–43	0	1	0	0	1	1	0	0	0	0	0	0	0	0	3
1543–44	0	0	0	0	2	0	0	0	0	0	0	0	2	0	4
1544–45	1	0	0	1	3	0	1	1	1	0	0	0	2	2	12
1545–46	0	0	0	0	0	1	0	0	0	0	0	1	2	0	4
1546–47	3	0	0	0	3	0	1	0	0	0	0	0	0	1	8
1547–48	2	1	0	0	2	0	0	0	0	1	0	1	1	2	9
1548–49	1	2	0	1	10	4	4	0	0	3	0	0	3	2	30
1549–50	1	0	0	0	2	0	3	1	0	2	0	0	1	0	11
1550–51	0	0	0	0	2	0	2	0	0	0	0	0	0	2	6
1551–52	0	1	0	0	0	0	0	0	0	0	0	0	1	3	4
1552–53	0	0	0	0	1	0	2	0	0	0	0	0	0	1	4
1553–54	0	0	0	0	1	0	1	0	0	0	0	0	0	0	2
1554–55	0	1	0	0	2	0	1	0	0	0	0	0	1	0	4
1555–56	0	0	1	0	1	0	0	0	0	7	0	0	0	0	10
1556–57	2	2	0	0	0	0	0	0	0	2	0	0	0	2	8
1557–58	0	1	0	0	0	0	1	0	0	0	0	0	2	2	6
TOTAL	11	10	1	2	34	7	17	2	1	16	0	3	15	18	137
AVG/YR	0.6	0.6	0.1	0.1	1.9	0.4	0.9	0.1	0.1	0.9	0.0	0.2	0.8	1.0	7.6
							1558–59 TO 1569–70								
1558–59	0	1	0	0	2	2	5	0	0	0	0	1	0	8	19
1559–60	3	1	2	0	1	1	5	0	0	1	0	0	0	2	16
1560–61	0	7	0	0	0	1	5	0	0	1	0	0	1	0	15

															TOTAL
1561–62	2	4	1	3	3	1	6	1	0	0	0	0	1	3	25
1562–63	8	2	6	3	1	2	4	0	0	0	0	1	0	3	30
1563–64	7	3	1	0	0	0	0	0	0	0	0	1	1	1	14
1564–65	5	5	6	2	1	0	0	1	1	0	0	0	0	8	27
1565–66	12	3	4	2	2	3	2	0	0	0	0	0	0	2	30
1566–67	18	14	5	1	0	3	0	2	0	1	0	0	0	4	47
1567–68	12	19	10	1	1	2	2	0	0	0	0	0	2	3	53
1568–69	22	21	10	11	3	2	2	2	1	1	0	0	4	2	77
1569–70	28	16	6	2	6	3	1	1	1	1	0	6	3	12	87
TOTAL	117	96	51	25	20	20	30	6	2	4	0	9	12	48	440
AVG/YR	9.8	8.0	4.3	2.1	1.7	1.7	2.5	0.5	0.2	0.3	0.0	0.8	1.0	4.0	36.7

1570–71 TO 1580–81

															TOTAL
1570–71	22	14	12	5	7	0	3	0	0	3	0	0	1	3	70
1571–72	8	10	2	7	5	1	1	0	1	0	0	0	0	4	39
1572–73	6	21	16	2	5	2	1	0	1	0	0	3	3	4	61
1573–74	2	16	8	0	1	0	0	0	0	1	0	1	1	2	31
1574–75	7	12	8	3	7	2	1	1	0	0	0	1	1	2	44
1575–76	3	16	7	4	6	2	1	3	0	3	0	1	1	2	48
1576–77	4	22	8	2	4	3	2	0	2	1	0	0	0	6	54
1577–78	7	14	3	4	4	2	6	3	2	1	4	1	1	8	60
1578–79	10	18	6	2	7	2	3	1	0	2	3	1	1	13	69
1579–80	12	13	8	3	3	0	4	1	0	0	0	5	5	6	55
1580–81	0	17	13	4	4	2	6	0	2	2	4	5	5	7	64
TOTAL	81	173	91	36	53	16	28	9	6	9	11	13	19	57	595
AVG/YR	7.4	15.7	8.3	3.3	4.8	1.5	2.5	0.8	0.5	0.8	1.0	1.2	1.7	5.2	54.1

															TOTAL
GRAND TOTAL	209	279	143	63	107	43	75	17	9	22	11	25	46	123	1,172
AVG/YR	5.1	6.8	3.5	1.5	2.6	1.0	1.8	0.4	0.2	0.5	0.3	0.6	1.1	3.0	28.6

Reference Matter

⊰ NOTES ⊱

Introduction

1. Haigh, *Reformation and Resistance*; Haigh, *English Reformations*; Scarisbrick, *Reformation*; Brigden, *London*.

2. The term magistrates is taken to mean the mayor and aldermen of the city unless otherwise noted. McClendon, "Norwich Aldermen," a typescript giving the names, dates of service and occupations (where known) of aldermen who served between 1517 and 1603 is available at the Norfolk Record Office.

3. On Norwich, see Pound, *Tudor and Stuart Norwich*, p. 28, and Dyer, *Decline*, p. 72. Dyer gives a higher figure of 9,250 for the population of Norwich, but I have chosen to accept Pound's figure of 8,500, given his extensive consideration and reconsideration of the evidence from the 1524–25 subsidy returns. See also Friedrichs, p. 20; Rappaport, p. 61.

4. Rappaport, p. 61; A. G. R. Smith, pp. 9, 166; Collinson, *Birthpangs*, p. 33; Cornwall, *Wealth*, p. 64. See also Beier and Finlay, eds., and Harding.

5. These towns had populations of about 7,600, 6,800, 5,750 and 5,660, respectively. Dyer, *Decline*, appendices 2, 4, 5; Clark and Slack, eds., pp. 1–56; Clark and Slack, pp. 46–61.

6. Pound, "Social and Trade Structure," p. 49, gives the number of taxpayers as 1,414; Dyer, *Decline*, appendices 2 and 4. For a more extensive comparison of Norwich's tax burden to that of other towns, see also Hoskins, p. 92, for a table of taxes paid by London and the 25 leading provincial towns in the subsidies of 1523–27.

7. See Pound, "Social and Trade Structure," p. 51, table I; Cornwall, *Wealth*, pp. 64–70.

8. Pound, "Social and Trade Structure," pp. 52, 55–63; see esp. table VI, p. 60.

9. Hudson and Tingey, eds., 1: lviii–lxiii. An abstract of the charter appears on pp. 31–36. From 1404, the city was known as the county of the City of Norwich.

10. Norwich was divided into four great wards and each of those was subdivided into three petty wards. The great wards and their petty wards were as follows: Conisford (North Conisford, South Conisford and Berstreet); Mancroft (St. Stephen, St. Peter and St. Giles); Wymer (West Wymer, Middle Wymer and East Wymer) and Northern (Coslany, Colegate and Fyebridge). For a discussion of the distribution of population, occupations and wealth in the city in the sixteenth century, see Pound, "Government and Society," pp. 7–8, 10–12, 18–22, 28–30 and appendix 1. Aldermen were not required to live in the petty ward which they represented since most of their duties were not associated with any specific location. Thus, it was not uncommon for a man to serve different wards during the course of his aldermanic tenure.

11. Common councilors were also elected by ward: the term of office was one year, and representation was proportional. Each year in Passion Week Conisford ward elected 12 councilmen, Mancroft 16, Wymer 20 and Northern 12. Councilmen were expected to represent the ward from which they were elected and residency in that ward was required. Unlike the aldermen, members of the Norwich common council wielded little civic authority. The council only met when called to the city Assembly by the mayor, and thus did not have an independent existence. Even in the Assembly, the council's possibilities for action were limited, for it only had the power to approve or reject legislation presented by the aldermen. Councilmen had no authority to propose measures for consideration. Hudson and Tingey, eds., 1: lxvi–lxix; Evans, p. 34. Clark and Slack, p. 129, have noted that during the sixteenth century, common councils in a number of communities that included Norwich, "increasingly lost control of civic administration to aldermanic cliques which met more frequently and had added to their old civic status by their new prestigious and powerful positions as justices of the peace."

12. These calculations are based on the information provided in Hawes, ed., pp. xxix–xxxvii. The number of men who served is smaller than the number of elections since on a few occasions a man who left office was later reelected.

13. A fourth court, the sheriff's court, which handled debt actions, was of waning significance in the sixteenth century.

14. See Pound, "Government and Society."

15. As in other communities that contained a significant ecclesiastical institution, jurisdictional disputes and citizens' jealousies about the powers of outsiders were often heated during the Middle Ages. Perhaps the best known example of hostility between a town and an ecclesiastical institution is at Bury St. Edmunds, where citizens and monks of the abbey feuded throughout the Middle Ages. See Goodwin; Lobel, *Borough*; Gottfried.

16. See below, pp. 46–47. For other clashes, see Tanner, *Church*, pp. 145–46, 152–54.

17. York was the only other provincial capital with a similarly large number of parishes, with between 40 and 50 in the early sixteenth century. Bristol and Exeter had fewer than 20 each. Hudson and Tingey, eds., 2: cxxiii; Tanner, *Church*, pp. 2, 4, 57–84, 118, 205–10; Skeeters, p. 2.

18. Tanner, *Church*, pp. 119–20, 126–29. While bequests to parish churches and clergy remained popular right up to the Reformation, those to the friaries declined significantly after 1517.

19. Tanner, ed., *Heresy Trials*, pp. 8, 22, 27, 43–50.

20. Tanner, *Church*, p. 163; Houlbrooke, "Persecution," pp. 308–26; Houlbrooke, *Church Courts*, pp. 222–23, 225–26.

21. See, for example: Dickens, *English Reformation*, pp. 191–92; Clark, *English Provincial Society*, pp. 57–59. For caveats, see Zell and Alsop. A recent critique is in Duffy, pp. 504–23.

22. Sheppard; Haigh, *English Reformations*, p. 200.

23. Dickens, "Early Expansion," p. 197; Haigh, *English Reformations*, p. 197; Palliser, *Reformation in York*; Collinson, *Birthpangs*, p. 41.

24. Haigh, "Recent Historiography," p. 24; Haigh, *English Reformations*, pp. 197–98; Dickens, "Early Expansion," pp. 197–99; Collinson, *Birthpangs*, pp. 36–40.

25. Collinson, *Puritan Movement*, pp. 169–78; also see PRO SP 15/12/27, a letter from Edward Gascoigne to the Earl of Leicester dated October 15, 1564, which describes the Norwich prophesyings.

26. Pound, ed.

27. Hill; Wrightson and Levine; Hunt.

28. Skeeters, p. 1.

29. Ibid., pp. 38–56.

30. Cross, *Church*, pp. 77–78; MacCulloch, *Suffolk*, pp. 154–55, 179; Duffy, p. 381; Brigden, *London*, p. 290; Rex, p. 98.

31. Brigden, *London*, pp. 429–30.

32. Phillips, pp. 90–94, 117–18.

33. Hughes, *Reformation*, 2: 274.

34. Collinson, *Birthpangs*, p. 33; Brigden, *London*, pp. 608–12, 625–27; R. D. Smith, p. 104.

35. See, for example: Elton, *Reform*; Starkey; Ives; Bernard; Warnicke.

36. Clark, "Reformation," and Clark, *English Provincial Society*, pp. 38–41, 57–60.

37. See below, pp. 80–81.

38. See Appendix 1.

39. Tittler, *Architecture*, pp. 154–55; Cozens-Hardy and Kent, plates III–IV.

40. Hudson and Tingey, eds., 1: lxxix, cvi–cix.

41. Hudson and Tingey, comps., pp. 110–28; Hudson and Tingey, eds., 1: 348–53.

42. The historical consciousness shown by Norwich's magistrates was not unique. When London's rulers were deciding whether to aid the Privy Council in its move against Protector Somerset in the fall of 1549, the haberdasher George Tadlowe reminded the common council that rebellion against Henry III had cost the City its liberties. Similarly, at the 1587 elections for sheriff when several candidates had refused to serve, Recorder William Fleetwood reminded them how Edward II had seized the City's liberties when a mayor had declined to attend commissions of oyer and terminer. Archer, pp. 27, 41.

43. Haigh, "Recent Historiography," pp. 1–18. Also see O'Day, chapter 6, and Patrick Collinson's evaluation of the debate, "England," esp. pp. 81–85.

44. *English Reformation.*

45. Many of these conclusions came from Dickens's work on popular religion in Yorkshire; see his *Lollards.*

46. Dickens, *English Reformation,* p. 108.

47. J. F. Davis, *Heresy,* pp. 1–2, 5, 149. Also see Oxley and Cross, *Church.*

48. Elton, *Policy;* Clark, *English Provincial Society.*

49. Scarisbrick, *Reformation,* p. 1.

50. Haigh, *Reformation and Resistance.*

51. Whiting, pp. 259, 268.

52. Duffy, pp. 1–6. The quotations appear on pp. 2, 4.

53. Haigh, "Recent Historiography," p. 32.

54. Watt; Lake, "Deeds." The quotations appear on pp. 277, 283. See also Collinson, *Birthpangs;* Brigden, *London;* MacCulloch, *Later Reformation.*

55. Brigden, *London,* p. 456.

56. Ibid., pp. 179–87, 320–24.

57. Ibid., p. 157.

58. Lake, "Calvinism," esp. p. 200; Kishlansky.

59. Brigden, *London,* pp. 3, 4, 378, 413. Joseph Ward has offered a revealing example of how the expectation of division and conflict can hide other responses to religious change from view. Whereas Brigden has looked at the grocers' company religiosity only insofar as it appeared to provide a welcome home for some prominent evangelicals, Ward examines the religious diversity of the company and therefore is able to show us that members with seemingly incompatible religious views maintained their corporate identity throughout the period. See his *Metropolitan Communities,* chapter 5.

60. Skeeters, pp. 1, 45–46, 149.

61. Collinson, *Birthpangs*, pp. 35–36.

62. Some of the most important contributions to this debate are: Clark and Slack, eds.; Clark and Slack, *English Towns*; Dobson; Phythian-Adams, "Urban Decay"; Phythian-Adams, *Desolation*; Phythian-Adams, "Urban Undulations," Palliser, "Crisis"; Palliser, *Tudor York*. Palliser's book, a more wide-ranging study, includes a chapter on the Reformation in York.

63. Clark and Slack, *English Towns*, esp. pp. 59–60, 145–47, 149–50. Also see the recent and very interesting work of Robert Tittler, *Architecture*, a study of changing modes of authority among urban elites as expressed in the increased construction and acquisition of town halls coincident with the Reformation.

64. See, for example: Dyer, "Growth"; Bridbury; Kermode.

65. Collinson, *Birthpangs*, pp. 35–36, 58–59.

66. Sacks, *Widening Gate*, p. xvii.

67. Clark, "Crisis," quoted in Archer, p. 2; Rappaport, p. 4.

68. Archer, pp. 39–49.

69. Sommerville, pp. 12, 15. In his list of "three recurring factors in pre-industrial secularization," Sommerville also includes "printing presses, which could propagate these views." The impact of the printing press in this regard is not clear in Norwich.

70. Ibid., pp. 9–11, 15, 61, 182.

71. Oberman, p. 13.

72. MacCulloch, "Archbishop Cranmer."

73. Scribner, "Preconditions."

74. Abray, "Confession."

75. Oberman, p. 29.

76. Benedict.

77. Ibid., pp. 65–66.

78. Scribner, "Preconditions," pp. 33–34.

79. Grell and Scribner, eds., p. ix.

80. Elton, "Persecution," quoted in Grell, "Introduction," in Grell and Scribner, eds., p. 12.

81. Ralph Houlbrooke has noted that "the Norwich mayor's court books tell us far more about the currents of unorthodox opinion in the city in the years 1534–47 than do the consistory court act books which cover the same period." Still, I expected to find some evidence of popular religious conflict in those records for that and other periods, but did not. See Houlbrooke, *Church Courts*, p. 230. For studies that describe cases of unorthodoxy and conflict in Norwich, see Houlbrooke, "Persecution," which analyzes the most important cases during Henry's reign. For other

references to cases in Norwich, see Elton, *Policy*, pp. 135–39, 306; Tanner, *Church*, pp. 163–64; J. F. Davis, *Heresy*, pp. 84–85, 101–2.

1. Feuds and Factions

1. Storey, p. 217; Gwyn, p. 119.

2. Thomson, p. 52; Jacob, p. 391; Hudson and Tingey, eds., 1: lx–lxi; Evans, chapter 2, esp. p. 26.

3. I have not found mention of any similar oversights in discussions of towns and their charters in the fifteenth century. See, for example, Reynolds, pp. 160–87, and Thomson, p. 52.

4. Hudson and Tingey, eds., 1: lxxx–lxxxi.

5. Ibid., 1: lxxxi–lxxxii, 320–24.

6. Jacob, pp. 388–89; Owen, ed., pp. 395–404; Reynolds, pp. 181–87; Storey, pp. 228–30.

7. Hudson and Tingey, eds., 1: 93–96.

8. Ibid., 1: 333–34.

9. They were John Querdling, John Hauke, John Bylagh, Thomas Fishlak and John May. McRee, "Religious Gilds," p. 85; Hudson and Tingey, eds., 1: 331.

10. Storey, p. 219; McRee, "Religious Gilds," p. 86, n. 56.

11. On St. George's guild in the sixteenth century, see below, pp. 121–29.

12. A united peerage successfully deprived Gloucester of the title of regent that he had wanted during Henry's minority. Lander, pp. 193, 310, 314; Storey, pp. 30–31.

13. Lander, p. 178.

14. Hudson and Tingey, eds., 1: 337–38.

15. McRee, "Religious Gilds," p. 86.

16. Ibid., p. 86, n. 57.

17. Storey, p. 220.

18. Ibid., p. 220.

19. Hudson and Tingey, eds., 1: xii.

20. Tanner, *Church*, pp. 25, 143.

21. Ibid., pp. 144–45.

22. Rye, "Riot," pp. 73–83.

23. Ibid., pp. 17–32; Hudson and Tingey, eds., 1: xiv–xv.

24. Campbell, pp. 12–13.

25. Tanner, *Church*, pp. 141, 145.

26. Blomefield, 3: 143–44; Hudson and Tingey, eds., 1: xc; Tanner, *Church*, pp. 146, 150.

27. Hudson and Tingey, eds., 1: 325–26; Tanner, *Church*, p. 147.

28. Lander, p. 183.

29. Two letters written by the Duke from around this time survive among the city records. In the first he urged city leaders, to whom he presumably was writing, to show favor to Wetherby "which standeth in favor of our good lordship." The second expressed irritation that Wetherby had not been shown required consideration and reiterated the Duke's support for him. It also warned that if such consideration were not immediately forthcoming, "we will it be reformed in such wise as shall be none ease to you as far as law and conscience requireth." Hudson and Tingey, eds., 1: 347.

30. Storey, p. 221; Tanner, *Church*, p. 148.

31. Hudson and Tingey, eds., 1: 350–51; Storey, pp. 222–23.

32. Storey, p. 223.

33. Hudson and Tingey, eds., 1: 340–41, 343–46.

34. Tanner, *Church*, p. 151.

35. Hudson and Tingey, eds., 1: xci, 354–55.

36. Ibid., 1: xci, 341–43; Tanner, *Church*, p. 151; Storey, pp. 223–24.

37. A jury declared that, in addition to the Prior's lands inside city walls, Magdalen Hospital, the hamlets of Trowse, Lakenham, Bracondale, Eaton, Trowsemyllgate and the Benedictine nunnery at Carrow were not part of the county of the city. Hudson and Tingey, eds., 1: lxxxii, 328.

38. Sir John Clifton served as the city's warden until 1446. Henry VI then appointed Thomas Catteworth, a citizen and former mayor of London, and also a citizen of Norwich, in his place. Hudson and Tingey, eds., 1: 342; Cozens-Hardy and Kent, p. 25; Storey, p. 224.

39. Suffolk was elevated to Marquis in 1444 and to Duke in 1448. Lander, pp. 181–87.

40. It is not clear how many of the individuals fined in 1443 paid those charges.

41. Blomefield, 3: 144–55; Hudson and Tingey, eds., 1: lxxxvii–xcix, 37–40, 325–28, 338–56; Storey, pp. 217–25, Tanner, *Church*, pp. 146–52; McRee, "Religious Gilds," pp. 82–90.

42. Hudson and Tingey, eds., 1: 353–54; Tanner, *Church*, p. 153.

43. No author of the account is given. Other documents relating to the 1430's and 1440's were also entered into the "Book of Pleas," whose compilation began around 1454. The "Book of Pleas" was composed chiefly of legal proceedings in the city's history dating back to the twelfth century. For a table of contents of both books see Hudson and Tingey, comps., pp. 92–103, 110–28.

44. Hudson and Tingey, eds., 1: 348–53, 354–55.

45. Ibid., 1: 350–52.

46. These fairs do not appear to have been successful. The number of traders who came declined during the reign of Richard III and the early

years of Henry VII's. Storey, p. 225; Hudson and Tingey, eds., 1: 40–43; 2: cxxxvi, 75–76.

47. Blomefield, 3: 175. Tanner, *Church*, p. 145, n. 21, notes that Blomefield's account is the only extant evidence for the precise details of this dispute, although an entry in the city records for this period indicates that something like this happened.

48. Guy, *Cardinal's Court*, p. 69.

49. C. G. Bayne, ed., p. clxi.

50. Spynke himself had probably died in 1503; in any case he ceased to serve as the Prior of Norwich after that time. Atherton et al., eds., p. 760.

51. Guy, *Court of Star Chamber*, pp. 1–5. The quotation appears on p. 2.

52. According to Guy, *Cardinal's Court*, pp. 51–53, "[s]ufficiency of documentation makes it possible to discover the principal 'real' matter behind 473 of the dated Wolsey cases." He has divided these cases into the following five categories: riot, rout, unlawful assembly, forcible entry, trespass and related offenses (292); maintenance and champerty (where a third enters a lawsuit on behalf of the plaintiff or defendant and uses extra-legal means to influence the course of the proceeding), corrupt verdicts, embracery (illegally influencing a jury), perjury and subornation, abuse of legal procedure (44); corruption of royal and franchisal officers (28); municipal and trade disputes (17); and a miscellaneous category that "derived some coherence from the actual or potential violence alleged by most plaintiffs in their bills" (92). The group of municipal and trade disputes was further subdivided: municipal disputes (8), trade disputes with the exception of engrossing, forestalling, regrating (6) and engrossing, forestalling and regrating (3). On the municipal and trade disputes see also C. G. Bayne, ed., pp. clx–clxv.

53. The chronicler of Wolsey's life, George Cavendish, noted Wolsey's hard work and evenhandedness in Star Chamber. Cavendish wrote that the Cardinal did at "divers times go into the Star Chamber, as occasion did serve, where he spared neither high nor low, but judged every estate according to their merits and deserts." Cavendish, p. 25.

54. NRO AB 1510–1550, f. 47r.

55. NRO Press 9, Cases f and g.

56. NRO Press B, Case 9, Shelves f and g, "Documents Relating to Litigation Between the City and Various Parties."

57. NRO MCB 1510–1532, p. 146; Hudson and Tingey, eds., p. cxxxviii.

58. See, for example, NRO AB 1510–1550, ff. 87–101 *passim*; NRO MCB 1510–1532, p. 138. In the fall of 1523, the Assize judges recommended that the citizens of Norwich accept Wolsey's compact, but still "the commons in any wise would not consent" to it. NRO AB 1510–1550, ff. 99v, 99r; NRO PMA 1491–1553, f. 138r.

59. Hudson and Tingey, eds., 2: 370.

60. A manuscript copy of the compact may be found in NRO Press Case 9, Shelf g. See also *Evidences Related to the Town Close*, pp. 27–36, 62–64; Hudson and Tingey, eds., 1: cix–cx; 2: cxxxvii–cxxxix; Tanner, *Church*, p. 153.

61. Guy, *Cardinal's Court*, pp. 68–69. Guy notes, p. 162, n. 124, that letters patent were never enrolled and suggests that the dispute over financial responsibility for those fees was the most likely reason.

62. *Evidences Related to the Town Close*, pp. 62–67.

2. Handling Heresies

1. NRO MCB 1510–1532 *passim*. See also Houlbrooke, *Church Courts*, pp. 222–28; Tanner, *Church*, pp. 162–66.

2. Thomas Necton was one of three men who stood surety when his brother was released from the Fleet in 1528. On Robert Necton, see Guy, *Public Career*, pp. 108, 168; J. F. Davis, *Heresy*, pp. 45, 54, 59–60, 64; Dickens, *English Reformation*, p. 52; Brigden, *London*, pp. 115, 118, 121–22, 180, 196; Skeeters, pp. 37–38; Haigh, *English Reformations*, pp. 60, 63–65 and John Fines, "Biographical Register," pt. 1, p. N1. Fines's typescript is available at the Institute for Historical Research in London, and at Stanford University's Green Library. The register has also been published; see Dickens, "Early Expansion," p. 191, n. 12.

3. Haigh, *English Reformations*, p. 58.

4. Bridgen, *London*, pp. 151–52.

5. On Nix, see *DNB*; Houlbrooke, *Church Courts*, esp. pp. 21–22, 29–30, 223–24, 226–27; MacCulloch, *Suffolk*, chapter 4 *passim*.

6. BL Cotton Cleopatra E V, ff. 389r–390v. While the recipient of this letter has generally been taken to be the Duke of Norfolk, Ralph Houlbrooke has suggested that the letter might have been written to Archbishop Warham. See his "Persecution," p. 313, n. 30.

7. BL Cotton Cleopatra E V, ff. 389r–390v.

8. MacCulloch, *Suffolk*, pp. 153–54.

9. Guy, *Thomas More*, p. 169; J. F. Davis, "Trials"; Marius, *Thomas More*, p. 346; Haigh, *English Reformations*, p. 67.

10. Guy, *Thomas More*, p. 169.

11. Gee and Hardy, comps., pp. 133–37.

12. *L&P*, 5: #569. Henry's new title had been granted with the caveat "only so far as the law allows," and a sizable minority had voted against extending that rank on the King. Rex, p. 15.

13. Marius, *Thomas More*, p. 397.

14. *L&P*, 5: #522, #560.

15. Guy, *Thomas More*, pp. 170–71.

16. *L&P*, 5: #560.

17. Ibid., 5: #560.

18. Ibid., 5: #569.

19. Marius, *Thomas More*, p. 399.

20. See Appendix 2.

21. Duffy, chapter 15. See also Zell and Alsop.

22. This conclusion also receives some support from an examination of the nineteen surviving wills of aldermen who served between 1530 and 1547, but who wrote their testaments after the death of Henry VIII. Seven apparently Catholic testators called on the saints in the preambles and an eighth bequeathed a string of rosary beads to his daughter, while five wills indicate Protestant testators. The remaining six offer no ready clue as to the testators' religious affiliation. Interpreting these wills written after 1547 to gain information about aldermen serving between 1530 and 1547 is even more treacherous than reading wills from that period. One must pay close attention to the religious and political climate at the time each will was written in order to sound out possible influences on the testator.

23. When Richard Green died in 1541, he called upon "the blessed company of heaven" in the preamble to his will, but also consigned his soul to "our redeemer and savior Jesus Christ by the merits of his blessed passion I trust to be saved." Such phraseology has often been taken to indicate reformist or Protestant sentiments by historians analyzing will preambles. But Eamon Duffy has recently argued that such an expression was equally consistent with traditional Catholic piety, maintaining that Catholics too acknowledged the fundamental role of Christ in their religion and that such a sentiment was not the exclusive preserve of Protestants. Duffy, pp. 507–9.

24. NRO AB 1510–1550, ff. 152r, 153v. In 1488, the city had become a second founder of the friary and in 1499, the city exempted the friars from all tolls. Tanner, *Church*, p. 157.

25. *L&P*, 12(2): #1177.

26. Hudson and Tingey, eds., 2: cxxxix; Lehmberg, pp. 81–82; Houlbrooke, "Refoundation," pp. 507–39; Hudson and Tingey, comps., p. 122.

27. *L&P*, 14(1): #905(5); Hudson and Tingey, eds., 1: 44.

28. NRO AB 1510–1550, f. 179r; PMA 1491–1553, f. 186v.

29. *L&P*, 13(2): #282; 15: #831(72).

30. Head, *Ebbs*, pp. 274–76.

31. Skeeters, pp. 34–57; Brigden, *London*, pp. 320–40; Clark, "Reformation," pp. 115–22.

32. 25 Henry VIII, c. 8. Houlbrooke, *Church Courts*, pp. 216–17, 222, 228–30.

33. *L&P*, 7: #779, #796; Elton, *Policy*, pp. 136–37.

34. NRO Quarter Sessions Minute Book 1511–1541, ff. 139v–r. The chronology of the remainder of Isabells's life in the records is somewhat confusing. The date of his appearance in Quarter Sessions is given in those records as 37 Henry VIII (1545–46). This must be an error, as Isabells was dead by that time. It seems more likely that he appeared in 1534. Compounding the confusion about his life is the fact that two identical wills were proved in the NRO NCC for him. The first, 302–305 Hylll, in February 1540 and the second, 245 Whytefoot, in February 1544. Again, it seems likely that probate of a will in 1540 indicates his recent death.

35. NRO MCB 1534–1540, pp. 13–15; see also Houlbrooke, "Persecution," p. 312.

36. On the role of the Mass in late medieval Catholicism see Brigden, *London*, pp. 12–18; Duffy, pp. 91–130. The quotation appears on p. 91.

37. See NRO MCB 1534–1540, p. 21, and NRO MCB 1534–1549, f. 8r, where the case is recorded again with only minor variations.

38. Fairfield, pp. 39–40. Barret would embrace the Marian restoration of Catholicism and remain a Catholic for the rest of his life. Houlbrooke, "Refoundation," p. 522.

39. In 1538, Thakker was indicted for treason for criticizing the King's Council and recent religious reforms. He escaped punishment, although on what grounds is not clear. Elton, *Policy*, p. 306.

40. In 1532, for example, Thomas Harding was put to death in Lincoln diocese for possession of an English Bible. Harding had abjured heretical opinions some years before. After he was observed reading a book in the woods outside Chesham, hostile neighbors searched his house, unearthing the Bible. They turned him over the Bishop Longland for trial. Haigh, *English Reformations*, p. 51.

41. NRO MCB 1540–1549, p. 320. The court's hope proved misplaced, as Gilmyn reappeared before magistrates in 1547 having publicly expressed controversial religious sentiments. See below, pp. 115–16.

42. Houlbrooke, *Church Courts*, p. 215; Cressy, p. 2; Duffy, p. 41.

43. NRO MCB 1534–1549, f. 22r.

44. Duffy, pp. 405, 430.

45. Slavin, ed., p. 150.

46. Guy, *Tudor England*, pp. 179–80.

47. Houlbrooke, *Church Courts*, pp. 229–30.

48. Slavin, ed., p. 146.

49. NRO MCB 1534–1540, p. 108; NRO MCB 1534–1549, f. 56v; NRO MCB 1540–1549, pp. 322, 323, 327–28. Rede's will was proved in February 1551, NCC 190 Corant. On Godsalve, see Swales, p. 33; Bindoff, ed., 2: 221, the entry about his son John Godsalve; Tanner, *Church*, p. 54.

50. NRO MCB 1534–1540, pp. 106–7; NRO MCB 1534–1549, f. 25v; NRO REG (Bishops' Registers)/30, "Tanner's Index," n.p.

51. Elton, *Policy*, p. 306.

52. NRO MCB 1534–1540, pp. 124–25.

53. Houlbrooke, "Refoundation," pp. 510–12.

54. Elton, *Policy*, pp. 16–18; Moreton, p. 32. A copy of Harcocke's offending sermon may now be found at the PRO E36/153, ff. 23–25. On Harcocke's later career in Norwich, see NRO REG/30. Harcocke was presented to St. Michael Coslany by the Marian Bishop of Norwich, John Hopton. See also Baskerville, p. 219. Harcocke's will was proved in the PCC in March 1563, 13 Chayre.

55. Gee and Hardy, comps., pp. 303–19.

56. Brigden, *London*, pp. 320–40. On persecution under the Act elsewhere, see Haigh, *English Reformations*, p. 165, and MacCulloch, *Suffolk*, pp. 164–65.

57. Cressy, pp. 4–10.

58. Hughes and Larkin, eds., 1: 270–76. The quotation appears on p. 276.

59. NRO MCB 1534–1540, p. 156.

60. NRO MCB 1540–1549, p. 21.

61. The 1543 Act for the Advancement of True Religion, 34 & 35 Henry VIII c. 1, restricted access to the English Bible among women and the lower orders, although women of gentle or noble status were exempt from its provisions.

62. NRO MCB 1534–1549, f. 51v; NRO MCB 1540–1549, p. 323; Houlbrooke, "Persecution," p. 311; Moreton, pp. 34–35. The exact day of the hearing and court action is not clear in the records. The manuscript records are not dated. Hudson's and Tingey's reprint of the entry from NRO MCB 1540–1549 is dated June 27, 1546, but mistakenly puts Corpus Christi for that year, the date of the offense, on July 1. Hudson and Tingey, eds., 2: 172. It is thus not clear whether Breten, Gifford and Grey served the entire month imprisonment stipulated for a violation of the Act for the Advancement of True Religion. The text of the court record makes it seem their case was heard and they were released very promptly after the offense.

63. Moreton, pp. 75–76; *L&P*, 16: #349, #351, #420, #424. Moreton asserts that civic as well as diocesan authorities were responsible for the apprehension of Walpole. But other than Chancellor Miles Spenser, the only other person named in the records was Thomas Godsalve, who was the diocesan registrar and not a Norwich civic official.

64. Bale, *Actes*, part 2, sigs. O3v–O5r. Blomefield, 3: 215, quotes *Actes* and provides no additional evidence. Also see Fairfield, p. 190, n. 78.

65. For the civic careers of Corbet and Rugge, see Hawes, ed., pp. xi, 43, 133.

66. Corbet, who lived in the hamlet of Sprowston north of Norwich, would be instrumental in the arrest of one of the two city Protestants to die in the Marian burnings. See below, pp. 175, 177. When he died in January 1559, he provided for Masses to be said for his soul and those of his parents. Bindoff, ed., 1: 699. When Robert Rugge penned his will in December 1558, he did not leave money for Masses, but he called on "the celestial company of heaven," and declared that he died "in the true faith of the holy Catholic church." NCC 447 Colman.

67. See Appendix 1.

3. Symbolism Without Saints

1. Phythian-Adams, *Desolation*, p. 270; Phythian-Adams, "Urban Decay," pp. 176–78. Also see Dyer, "Growth," p. 61; McRee, "Unity," p. 203; Clark and Slack, *English Towns*, p. 131.

2. See, for example, *English Reformation*, p. 31, where Dickens asserts that "the Catholic party lost the struggle in England not simply because they temporised with Henry VIII but also because, in an age when an increasing number of men were reading and thinking for themselves, the intellectual slackness of popular medieval religion played into the hands of Protestant critics." Also see pp. 80–81.

3. Phythian-Adams, *Desolation*, pp. 188, 275–78.

4. Duffy, pp. 395–98. See also Scarisbrick, *Reformation*, chapter 2; Haigh, *English Reformations*, p. 36.

5. Clark and Slack, *English Towns*, pp. 143, 149.

6. Hudson and Tingey, eds., 2: xcvii. On grain prices in the 1520's, see Clay, 1: 40.

7. A. G. R. Smith, p. 436.

8. Pound, "Social and Trade Structure," pp. 58–59.

9. John Walter and Keith Wrightson have argued that "it was of crucial importance for the maintenance of the social order that dearth was not only met, but was *seen* to be met by action on the part of the authorities." See "Dearth," p. 41.

10. Johnson, p. 144. Most of the contents of the "Mayor's Book" is printed in this article. See also Hudson and Tingey, comps., p. 54; Hudson and Tingey, eds., 2: 161; Galloway, ed., p. lviii.

11. MacCulloch, *Suffolk*, p. 298. Norwich does not appear to have been the site of major disturbances associated with the Amicable Grant of 1525, Wolsey's ill-fated and extra-Parliamentary attempt to raise money for war against France. The most serious commotions took place in Suffolk. Fletcher, *Tudor Rebellions*, pp. 13–15.

12. Hudson and Tingey, eds., 2: 116–18.

13. According to Hudson and Tingey, eds., 1: cviii, city sergeants' "duties largely consisted in overseeing the markets of all kinds of victuals and seeing that all the regulations were being carried out." See also Hawes, ed., p. 128.

14. Hudson and Tingey, eds., 2: 163–65.

15. Allen, "Administrative and Social Structure," pp. 23–27; Hudson and Tingey, eds., 2: 119–20.

16. NRO MCB 1534–1540, p. 66; NRO MCB 1534–1549, f. 20v. Utberd proclaimed, "I have bought myself freeman of Norwich; it cost me 40s. paid down. I would that I had my money in my purse again for by my faith the guild hall is so ordered that I shall have [12] false harlots that give me [12]s. for a red herring skin."

17. Pound, "Social and Trade Structure," p. 58; *L&P*, 12(2): #404.

18. Phythian-Adams, "Urban Decay," pp. 176–77.

19. The petition appears in NRO AB 1510–1550, ff. 120v–r and NRO PMA 1491–1553, ff. 149v–r. Extracts have been transcribed and printed in Harrod; N. Davis, ed., pp. xxvii–xxx; Nelson, *Medieval English Stage*, pp. 119–21.

20. The "Old Free Book" was one of the books of historical records kept by the corporation. See above, pp. 16–17.

21. The list is printed in Harrod, pp. 8–9, and Hudson and Tingey, eds., 2: 230. See also Nelson, *Medieval English Stage*, pp. 120–21, 129. Nelson maintains that these pageants were chiefly associated with the celebration of Corpus Christi.

22. In Coventry, the guilds provided men to parade with weapons and banners wearing armor to the Great Fair each year on Fair Friday. The city also owned armor that was used in pageantry or for military purposes, as in 1553 when the mayor refused to proclaim Queen Jane and ordered the city walls garrisoned. R. W. Ingram, ed., pp. xxiii, liii.

23. See above, p. 51, n. 37.

24. On the concept of invented traditions, see Hobsbawm and Terence, eds., esp. Hobsbawm's introduction, pp. 1–14.

25. Hudson and Tingey, eds., 2: 120–21; NRO AB 1510–1550, f. 145v.

26. Cressy, pp. 5–6.

27. Slavin, ed., pp. 143–51; Cressy, pp. 4–5; Gee and Hardy, comps., pp. 269–74, esp. pp. 270–71.

28. Quoted in Cressy, pp. 4–5.

29. Hudson and Tingey, eds., 2: 75.

30. NRO AB 1510–1550, f. 179v; PMA 1491–1553, f. 186v.

31. See above, pp. 71–72.

32. NRO AB 1510–1550, f. 185r; Hudson and Tingey, eds., 2: 123–24.

33. Hughes and Larkin, eds., 1: 301–2. London's Midsummer watch, which had a military element similar to St. Mary Magdalen's day in Norwich, was suppressed by the Crown in 1539, because of concerns about security. Archer, pp. 84, 94; Hutton, p. 76.

34. Nelson, *Medieval English Stage*, pp. 127–28.

35. On the origin and cultural significance of Corpus Christi, see Rubin.

36. In 1537, however, the grocers' guild did not perform its customary Corpus Christi day pageant. It is not clear whether the entire occasion was canceled or whether the grocers did not participate that year. Galloway, ed., p. 340.

37. Hudson and Tingey, eds., 2: 230, 278–96; Nelson, *Medieval English Stage*, pp. 128–29.

38. See Hudson and Tingey, eds., 2: lv, 312, where the c. 1543 order for the procession is mistakenly dated "c. 1453."

39. See above, p. 72; Galloway, ed., pp. xxx, 15.

40. In 1543, the city Assembly also formally created a new guild of hatters. Hudson and Tingey, eds., 2: 381–82.

41. Galloway, ed., pp. 3–4, 339–41; Tanner, *Church*, pp. 68–73; Hudson and Tingey, eds., 2: 296–310.

42. Hudson and Tingey, eds., 2: 296–97.

43. Duffy, pp. 410–11.

44. The grocers' and worsted weavers' guilds have extant records, which chiefly record expenditures and the results of company elections. See Galloway, ed., pp. lxvi–lxvii and appendix IV; NRO Second Book of the Worsted Weavers 1511–1638.

45. Hudson and Tingey, eds., 2: 310–11, lists guild days. The worsted weavers and members of St. Luke's guild were to attend their annual guild Mass at Norwich Cathedral and the tanners at St. Swithin's parish church, rather than the chapel of St. John, although no reason was given.

46. Hudson and Tingey, eds., 2: 297.

47. Kempe was suspended in Mary's reign for his marriage, which presumably took place after 1549 when Parliament authorized the marriage of priests. He returned to the Common Hall for one year in 1558 and disappears from local records after that. No further information about his theology is available. See above, pp. 82–83; NRO AB 1510–1550, f. 200v; NRO Chamberlains' Accounts 1541–1549, ff. 52r, 104r, 158r, 198v, 231r, 261r, 240r, 322r; NRO Chamberlains' Accounts 1551–1567, ff. 8v, 29v, 47v, 67v, 147v; NRO MC 16/1, 390 X 1, "Reverend J. F. Williams's Notes on ACT Books," pp. 13–14, 62; NRO MC 16/12, 390 X 3, "Rev. J. F. Williams's Notes on the Deprived Marian Clergy," n.p.; NRO SUN/3, Register Book of Diocesan Miscellanea, which contains a list of deprived

married clergy, and is reproduced in Baskerville, p. 53; Rev. J. F. Williams, "Married Clergy," p. 93. Williams's notes are invaluable, as the consistory court act books they calendar are in too poor condition to be consulted in manuscript. In 1559, Kempe was involved with the city's purchase of the former Greyfriars' land from the Duke of Norfolk. Assembly minutes for August 30, 1559, note that "[t]his day is sealed with the common seal of the town a letter of attorney made to Mr. Doctor Barret and John Kempe clerk to take possession of the Greyfriars to the use of the city." NRO AB 1551–1568, f. 119v.

48. Tittler, *Architecture*, pp. 89–97. The quotation appears on p. 93.

49. According to Galloway, ed., pp. xxx–xxi, 23, the nave of the Blackfriars' hall measured 125' by 70', as opposed to the Guildhall, which was 30' by 36'.

50. Hutton, p. 67.

51. A good pre-Reformation example is McRee, "Unity," which describes and analyzes changes made to the St. George's day celebration in Norwich during the fifteenth century.

52. Cressy, p. 67, has noted that in the 1540's one of Henry VIII's advisers, Sir Richard Moryson, tried to convince the King to hold an annual triumph celebrating the abolition of papal authority in England. While his recommendation was dismissed at the time, "within half a century its principle had become common practice."

53. Nelson, *Medieval English Stage*, p. 124; Galloway, ed., pp. 340–41.

54. Elizabeth Woodville, the Queen of Edward IV, and Richard III had received similar treatment when they visited Norwich in the fifteenth century. See Blomefield, 3: 173, 174, 176, 193; Nelson, *Medieval English Stage*, p. 122.

55. Scarisbrick, *Henry VIII*, p. 353.

56. I have found no references to any such ceremonies in the following volumes: Clopper, ed., pp. 30–31; R. W. Ingram, ed., pp. 143–48; Wasson, ed., pp. 134–35 (Exeter), 227–28 (Plymouth); J. J. Anderson, ed., pp. xv, 21–23; Johnston and Rogerson, eds., 1: 263–66.

57. Scarisbrick, *Henry VIII*, pp. 433–49; Guy, *Tudor England*, pp. 189–91.

58. NRO MCB 1540–1549, p. 218.

59. Galloway, ed., p. 12; Nelson, *Medieval English Stage*, p. 124.

60. Hudson and Tingey, eds., 2: 171; Nelson, *Medieval English Stage*, p. 124. Nelson notes that by May 17, the feast of St. George had already been celebrated and the grocers' records reveal that Corpus Christi had been observed, too. This left only the Whit Monday celebration on the calendar at the time the magistrates made their resolution.

61. On Norwich's role in supplying Henry's forces for the Scottish and French campaigns, see also NRO MCB 1540–1549, pp. 109, 203; "Letter

from the Duke of Norfolk"; "Letter from the Mayor"; "Letter from Henry VIII." The letter from Henry VIII is actually from 1544.

62. Galloway, ed., p. 347, maintains that the Treaty of Greenwich "was celebrated with 'triumphs' in towns all over England," but I have been unable to find any references to such festivities in the *REED* volumes for Chester, Coventry, Devon (Exeter and Plymouth), Newcastle and York.

63. Wasson, ed., pp. 230–31, 449.

64. Guy, *Tudor England*, p. 192; see also Scarisbrick, *Henry VIII*, pp. 458–64.

65. For the impact in London, see Brigden, *London*, pp. 356–67.

66. Again, I have found no references to such a celebration in Chester, Coventry, Devon (Exeter and Plymouth), Newcastle or York.

67. NRO Chamberlains' Accounts 1537–1547, quoted in Nelson, *Medieval English Stage*, p. 125; Galloway, ed., p. 17.

68. Wasson, ed., p. 232. Another celebration there later in the year honored Edward Seymour's defeat of the Scots at Pinkie Cleugh in September 1547.

69. Nelson, *Medieval English Stage*, p. 125; Galloway, ed., pp. 20, 339; Hudson and Tingey, eds., 2: 168.

70. NRO PMA 1491–1553, f. 239r; Cornwall, *Revolt*, p. 224.

71. Beer, *Northumberland*, pp. 101–2, and on Somerset's policy toward Scotland, Bush, chapter 2. In *Tudor England*, pp. 218–19, John Guy notes that England was not completely dominated in the treaty negotiations: it managed to demand 400,000 crowns (£133,333) for the surrender of Boulogne, a greater sum than Henri II of France had wanted to pay for the return of the city.

4. Protestantism Without Purity

1. Phillips, pp. 90–94, 117–18.

2. Thomas Codde, Robert Rugge and Thomas Cock all wrote Catholic wills in 1558. Codde and Cock, besides calling on the saints, made provisions for Masses. Furthermore, Codde was vilified as a "popish knave" on his election in 1549 by a defendant in the mayor's court. See below, p. 140. Rugge wrote his will in the earliest days of Elizabeth's reign and realized that it would be fruitless to make intercessory provisions, but nevertheless declared that he died "in the true faith of the holy Catholic Church." Henry Crook openly proclaimed his support for the restored Mass in 1553. While it might be argued that Crook's declaration merely represented an attempt to ingratiate himself with the new regime, he was the only alderman to make such a public statement, suggesting that his support was sincere. On the wills of Codde, Cock and Rugge, see below, pp. 180–81.

3. Haigh, *English Reformations*, p. 169.

4. Brigden, *London*, pp. 426–27.

5. NRO MCB 1540–1549, p. 374; see above, p. 76.

6. Brigden, *London*, pp. 429–30; Haigh, *English Reformations*, p. 169; Hutton, p. 81.

7. NRO MCB 1534–1549, ff. 52r–53v; MCB 1540–1549, pp. 402–3.

8. Parker's brother was Thomas Parker, who became an alderman in 1559. On Parker's career see MacCulloch, *Suffolk*, pp. 138–39, 154, n. 90, 162–63.

9. See below, pp. 138–39. King was deprived for marriage under Mary, by which time he was also rector of Great Fransham and Winterton, in Norfolk. NRO MC 16/1, 390 X 1, "Reverend J. F. Williams' Notes on ACT Books," pp. 13–14, 27, 43, 59; NRO MC 16/12, 390 X 3, "Rev. J. F. Williams' Notes on the Deprived Marian Clergy," n.p.; NRO SUN/3, Register Book of Diocesan Miscellanea, which contains a list of deprived married clergy, and is reproduced in Baskerville, pp. 52–53; Rev. J. F. Williams, "Married Clergy," p. 87. On Williams's notes, see above, p. 103, n. 47.

10. NRO MCB 1540–1549, pp. 403–4.

11. Hawes, ed., pp. 12, 16, 19, 33, 57, 126, 129, 132, 172.

12. Thomas, pp. 74–75; Brigden, *London*, pp. 433–35; Duffy, p. 460.

13. NRO MCB 1540–1549, p. 417 and NRO Norwich Sessions Depositions, Book 1A, ff. 108v–109r; Rye, ed., *Depositions*, appendix II, and pp. 48–49 where depositions concerning Swetman are printed. Rye raises the question whether these depositions were taken preliminarily to meetings of Quarter Sessions or the mayor's court. The personnel of these two courts overlapped, as the Sessions were staffed by the mayor and Justices (aldermen who had previously served as mayor). He concludes that more minor offenses would have been heard in the mayor's court, while serious ones (like treasonable words) would have been sent on to the Privy Council. When referring to documents from Rye's volume, I will note when a deposition resulted in a case heard in one of those courts. On Thomas Rose, see Pratt, ed., 8: 581–90. Rose stayed at the home of "Sir John Robster," who was perhaps John Robsart. On Robsart, see below, pp. 125, 127.

14. 1 Edward VI c. 14. The full text of the Act is printed in Gee and Hardy, comps., pp. 328–57; Kreider, pp. 190–191. Hospitals were exempted from the provisions of the Act.

15. The Edwardian Chantries Act was not the first action taken against intercessory institutions. Near the end of the first session of the 1545 Parliament, Henry VIII's government had introduced its own chantries bill. The measure, 37 Henry VIII c. 4, suppressed only selected institutions. It

denounced the patrons of intercessory institutions, who, the Act argued, had dissolved establishments in their control for purposes inconsistent with the foundations' original religious intent. To ameliorate this intolerable situation, the Act ordered the seizure into the King's hands all such institutions that had been privately endowed between February 4, 1536, and December 25, 1545. The statute also allowed the King to instruct his commissioners to seize any such institutions whose incumbents were found to be remiss in carrying out the charitable purposes intended by the founders. The greatest motivation for these selected suppressions was Henry's desperate need for revenues with which to continue the wars against France and Scotland, an intention stated in the Act's preamble. Kreider, chapter. 7.

16. Strype, *Works*, 18(2): p. 402.

17. Blomefield, 4: 201–202, 205–206.

18. NRO AB 1510–1550, f. 248v. The exception to this order was the money belonging to St. George's guild, which was to be used to help the poor.

19. The former alderman Thomas Brygges drafted his will in 1564, the same year in which it was proved. He committed his soul to God and Christ and also called on "the congregation in heaven," indicating Catholic convictions. NCC 68 Marten.

20. NRO MCB 1540–1549, pp. 427, 432, 433. The Dobleday and Derme case is also recorded in NRO MCB 1534–1549, f. 53r.

21. Le Bachery was the most influential guild in Norwich until the mid-fifteenth century, because of the close ties many of its members had to the city government. The guild became entangled in the political disturbances of the time, and citizens complained that its members bore responsibility for many of their troubles. Le Bachery disappeared from the records after 1443, when it is presumed to have merged with St. George's. Grace, ed., p. 8; Tanner, *Church*, p. 77. See also Clark and Slack, p. 129, on the role of religious guilds for urban ruling groups.

22. It is not clear why the guild received such a charter. It may have been the King's reward for members' outstanding service at Agincourt, or guild members might have requested it and had a suitably distinguished membership to obtain one. See Grace, ed., p. 9 and pp. 28–29, where the charter is printed.

23. Ibid., pp. 12–13; Hudson and Tingey, eds., 1: xcix; 2: cxli; McRee, "Religious Gilds."

24. The celebration of the feast day was postponed if guild day fell during Holy or Easter Weeks.

25. On the guild celebration, see Grace, ed., pp. 15–21; Galloway, ed., pp. xxvi–xxix; McRee, "Unity," pp. 195–98.

26. Some religious guilds survived elsewhere; see Whiting, p. 111.

27. NRO Minutes of St. George, p. 167.

28. Ibid., p. 182. For the original oath see Grace, ed., p. 29.

29. NRO Minutes of St. George, pp. 167–69.

30. Hawes, ed., pp. 71, 126, 154. This was not simply a case of flight from office; McClendon, "'Against God's Word,'" pp. 353–69, esp. pp. 355–56.

31. NRO MCB 1540–1549, p. 431.

32. NRO AB 1510–1550, f. 242r; PMA 1491–1553, f. 224v–r. NRO Minutes of St. George, p. 170, notes Quasshe's initial sole refusal and then the disenfranchisement of all three.

33. NRO AB 1510–1550, f. 242r. Eviction from the guild meant automatic dismissal from all liberties and franchises of the city. Grace, ed., pp. 39–43; Hawes, ed., pp. xiv–xv.

34. NRO AB 1510–1550, ff. 247v–r. Robsart and Clere served as Justices of Norfolk, and Robsart was also appointed a county sheriff in November 1547. They do not seem to have taken up Quasshe's case in any official capacity. Clere had been active on at least one diplomatic mission under Henry VIII, and in 1549 helped the Marquis of Northampton in his attempt to suppress Kett's rebels. See: *Lists & Indexes*, p. 88; Conford; MacCulloch, *Suffolk*, pp. 78, 232–33, appendices II and III; Bindoff, ed., 1: pp. 651–52.

35. NRO MCB 1540–1549, pp. 437–439.

36. NRO Minutes of St. George, p. 182.

37. NRO AB 1510–1550, ff. 261v–r. The material here is out of date order and the year is erroneously written as 4 Edward VI. NRO PMA 1491–1553, f. 235v, the clean version of the Assembly record of this meeting only contains Quarles's submission and the entry about Tompson's refusal to submit.

38. NRO Minutes of St. George, p. 182.

39. NRO AB 1510–1550, f. 264v; PMA 1491–1553, f. 236r.

40. Both represented the Northern ward, Quarles from 1552 to 1554 and Tompson from 1553 to 1554.

41. NRO MCB 1540–1549, p. 447.

42. Ibid., p. 454.

43. Ibid., p. 475.

44. Ibid., p. 476.

45. NRO AB 1510–1550, ff. 247v–r; NRO PMA 1491–1553, ff. 226v–r.

46. Hutton, p. 82, suggests that the feastmakers' refusal stemmed from their desire to see the traditional ceremony reinstated. But a close reading of local evidences makes such a conclusion less tenable.

47. NRO Minutes of St. George, pp. 175, 177–78.

48. There is insufficient evidence about Quarles and Tompson to con-

sider their motives in refusing to cooperate with the guild in more detail.

49. Although the mayor and aldermen agreed to give Watson a position, he never took one up. This story is told in more detail in Elton, *Policy*, pp. 138–41 (the quotation appears on p. 139), and in Houlbrooke, *Church Courts*, pp. 230–31. See also NRO MCB 1534–1540, pp. 152–53. Watson probably received a Bachelor's degree in canon law from Oxford in 1528, and was a Steward to Archbishop Cranmer during Edward VI's reign. Strype, *Memorials*, pp. 450, 610; *DNB*; Foster, 4: 1583; Beer, "'The commoyson.'"

50. Clere was dismissed from the Norfolk bench under Mary, when the Queen cleansed the commission of the peace of Edwardian Protestant appointees. Watson was arrested as a Protestant heretic, but fled England for the Continent. See below, pp. 155, 160–61.

51. NRO MCB 1540–1549, p. 474, and printed in Hudson and Tingey, eds., 2: 174. For other dimensions of Quasshe's refusal that concerned his standing in the civic community see McClendon, "'Against God's Word,'" pp. 366–67.

52. For Quasshe's continuing troubles with the mayor and aldermen, see NRO MCB 1549–1555, pp. 117, 134, 148, 149; NRO MCB 1555–1562, p. 183; Rye, ed., *Depositions*, pp. 27, 43–44 (where Quasshe is misidentified as an alderman), 71–72 (which must be misdated, as Quasshe's will had been proved by June 1563). Quasshe paid a hefty £100 fine to the city for the restoration of his liberties in December 1554, although half was later returned. NRO AB 1551–1568, f. 4r, and NRO PMA 1491–1553, f. 245v, contain records of the disenfranchisement. NRO AB 1551–1568, ff. 54r, 58v, 64v, 68v, 77r, and NRO PMA 1553–1583, ff. 19r, 22v, 24r, 27v, 33v for the restoration of his liberties.

53. Quasshe's will (PCC 18 Chayre) was proved 10 May 1563.

54. See Appendix 3.

55. Duffy, chapter 15.

56. Further evidence can be found in the wills of the seventeen men who served as aldermen during Edward's reign but wrote their wills after the King's death in 1553. Ten of the seventeen wills were written during Mary's reign. Of those ten, six preambles either called on the saints, provided for anniversary Masses or expressed faith in the "holy Catholic Church." None of the remaining four contained those traditional elements or made any intercessory provisions. Seven wills were drafted during Elizabeth's reign. Five testators committed their souls to Christ and made no invocations to the saints, while the sixth dedicated his soul to God alone. The seventh testator, Henry Crook, who made his will in 1565, did not dedicate his soul at all. But during Mary's reign, he had publicly rejoiced at the return of the Mass.

57. Duffy, pp. 450, 460–61.
58. NRO MCB 1540–1549, p. 445.
59. Ibid., pp. 454–55.
60. Ibid., p. 455.
61. Ibid., p. 467.
62. Ibid., p. 468; Hughes and Larkin, eds., 1: 432–33.
63. On King's probable religious affiliation, see below, pp. 138–39.
64. NRO MCB 1540–1549, p. 478.
65. Ibid., p. 493; NRO SUN/3; Baskerville, p. 227. From 1548, Curston received an annual pension of £6.
66. NRO MCB 1540–1549, p. 502.
67. Ibid., p. 512.
68. On Wood, see above, p. 131.
69. NRO MCB 1540–1549, p. 538.
70. Ibid. On Floraunce see NRO SUN/3 and Baskerville, p. 210. Floraunce, blind by 1555, received an annual pension of £4 11*d*. after the chantry's suppression.
71. Hughes and Larkin, eds., 1: 416–17, 417–18.
72. NRO MCB 1534–1549, f. 54 (a)r.
73. Ibid.
74. NRO DCN 47/1, Dean and Chapter Ledger Book, c. 1538–1562, f. 71. None of the tracts are extant.
75. NRO MCB 1534–1549, f. 55r; NRO DCN 47/1, f. 71. The letter, which was dated March 13, 1549, is also printed in L'Estrange, ed., pp. 171–75. On Salisbury, see above, pp. 78–80; Houlbrooke, ed., *Letter Book*, p. 42; Houlbrooke, "Refoundation," pp. 510–12, 513, 522, 527, 536; MacCulloch, *Suffolk*, pp. 186–187.
76. NRO DCN 47/1, f. 71.
77. NRO Dean and Chapter Ledger, ff. 73v–74r. William Rogers drafted a distinctly Protestant will in 1542, in which he renounced "all my good works." See above, p. 69.
78. NRO MCB 1534–1549, ff. 58r, 59v, 62r.
79. Ibid., f. 59r.
80. Dickens, *English Reformation*, pp. 252–53; Brigden, *London*, pp. 462–64, 468–69; Haigh, *English Reformations*, pp. 176–77.
81. NRO MCB 1534–1549, f. 59r.
82. Houlbrooke, *Church Courts*, p. 245; Sheppard, p. 48. On his deprivation see below, p. 172.
83. 2 & 3 Edward VI c. 21. Gee and Hardy, comps., pp. 366–68. SUN/3; Baskerville; Williams, "Married Clergy."
84. NRO MCB 1534–1549, f. 63v.

85. 2 & 3 Edward VI c. 1; Gee and Hardy, comps., pp. 358–66; Whiting *passim*.

86. NRO MCB 1534–1549, f. 66v.

87. Ibid., ff. 65r–66v. Colby would also be deprived for marriage in Mary's reign. See below, p. 172.

88. See, for example, Fletcher, *Tudor Rebellions*, pp. 65–66; Dickens, *English Reformation*, p. 246; Haigh, *English Reformations*, p. 175.

89. Fletcher, *Tudor Rebellions*, p. 66; Beer, "'The commoyson,'" pp. 82, 92–93; Cornwall, *Revolt*, pp. 149–51.

90. For contemporary treatments of the rebellion see Beer, "'The commoyson'"; Neville. It is not clear whether "'The commoyson,'" written by Nicholas Sotherton, is an eyewitness account, as some writers assert. Alexander Neville was secretary to Matthew Parker, and this account was drafted many years after the rebellion. Diarmaid MacCulloch discusses the problematic nature of these accounts in *Suffolk*, p. 300. Among the modern accounts are Russell; Fletcher, *Tudor Rebellions*, pp. 54–68; Cornwall, *Revolt*; Land; MacCulloch, "Kett's Rebellion"; Cornwall, "Kett's Rebellion."

91. Fletcher, *Tudor Rebellions*, p. 62.

92. Land, pp. 45–46.

93. NRO MCB 1534–1549, f. 67v.

94. Ibid., ff. 67v–r.

95. Fletcher, *Tudor Rebellions*, pp. 120–23, the list of Kett's demands; Land, p. 56. The identity of Thomas Aldrich is uncertain. Although Cornwall, *Revolt*, p. 149, and Land, p. 57, identify him as the man who was mayor of Norwich in 1516, that Thomas Aldrich died in 1528–29. Cozens-Hardy and Kent, pp. 39–40. Nicholas Sotherton's identification suggests a different man. Beer, "'The commoyson,'" p. 82.

96. Sir John Cheke, the reforming humanist who served as a tutor to King Edward before his accession, distinguished between "white-livered Cities," by which he meant Norwich, where he believed that the rebels were not resisted but favored, and a city like Exeter, "which being in the midst of rebels, unvictualled, unfurnished, unprepared for so long a siege, did nobly hold out the continual and dangerous assault of the rebel," pp. 28–29.

97. NRO MCB 1534–1549, f. 67r.

98. Beer, "'The commyson,'" p. 88.

99. Ibid., p. 89.

100. Russell, p. 156; Fletcher, pp. 57–60.

101. Hudson and Tingey, eds., 1: cxi, 44–45.

102. NRO Terry's Charity Book 1547–1614, n.p., notes "that Mr. Hom-

erston, alderman," had been "kept as a prisoner among the rebels in the commotion time and there slain."

103. NRO MCB 1549–1555, p. 3. On such distaste for the gentry, see MacCulloch, *Suffolk*, pp. 305–6.

104. NRO MCB 1549–1555, p. 2.

105. Ibid., p. 3.

106. Rye, ed., *Depositions*, pp. 18–22 *passim*, 25.

107. NRO PMA 1491–1553, f. 239r. The day was observed for over a century afterwards. NRO Chamberlains' Accounts 1603–1625 *passim*; Cornwall, *Revolt*, p. 224; see also above, p. 109.

108. NRO MCB 1549–1555, pp. 15–16.

109. Ibid., p. 90. The entry is not dated, but appears to come from around February.

110. Ibid., p. 103.

111. Dickens, *English Reformation*, p. 172, calls Rich "unprincipled," while Brigden, *London*, p. 365, labels him "redoubtably conservative." See also Bindoff, ed., 3: 192–95.

112. Brigden, *London*, pp. 497–511.

113. Ibid., pp. 508–11.

114. NRO MCB 1549–1555, p. 110.

115. Fylby's deposition can be found among the Sessions depositions, where she testified on February 28. Her testimony thus resulted in a mayor's court case. Rye, ed., *Depositions*, p. 23.

116. Rugge had been forced to resign as part of the central government's effort to "make a fresh start out of the confusion which Kett's rebellion had revealed." MacCulloch, *Suffolk*, p. 78.

117. NRO MCB 1549–1555, pp. 99–100. Thirlby served on a commission in Norwich in 1552. MacCulloch, *Suffolk*, p. 78, n. 82.

118. NRO MCB 1549–1555, p. 192.

5. The Quiet Restoration

1. Loades, pp. 98–102; Haigh, *English Reformations*, p. 206; Brigden, *London*, pp. 530–31; Dickens, ed., pp. 79–80.

2. Gee and Hardy, comps., pp. 373–76.

3. For a more extensive treatment of the restoration of Catholicism, see, for example, Loades, chapters 3, 8.

4. NRO MCB 1549–1555, p. 329.

5. Loades, p. 274.

6. Garrett; Brigden, *London*, p. 561. Brigden has noted the difficulty in identifying Londoners with certainty.

7. Blomefield, 3: 266.

8. NRO MCB 1549–1555, p. 294. The quotation about Hallybred is

taken from an October 31 letter to the court from the Privy Council, which is discussed below.

9. NRO MCB 1549–1555, p. 284. This could have been the same Bonyng who complained about Thomas Rose in Edward's reign. See above, pp. 133–34.

10. NRO MCB 1549–1555, p. 291. William Derne might have been the same man cited for throwing stones through the window of St. Andrew's church in 1548. See above, pp. 119–20.

11. NRO MCB 1549–1555, p. 294.

12. Hughes and Larkin, eds., 2: 390; APC, 4: 321.

13. Perhaps his appearance before the Privy Council was sufficient to convince Hallybred to conform to the new religious directives. Ralph Houlbrooke has labeled Hallybred as one of the "conservative conformists" at the Cathedral during Mary's reign. See his "Refoundation," pp. 512–13, 518–19, 522, where the priest is called Hallybred alias Stokes.

14. Tuddenham's will, written and proved in 1557, committed his soul to the Virgin and saints and provided for anniversary Masses. NCC 153 Hustings.

15. NRO MCB 1549–1555, p. 295.

16. In fact, it was never heard in the mayor's court. Walter Rye, ed., Depositions, pp. 39–40. On these depositions, see above, p. 118, n. 13.

17. Four members of the Sotherton family had served in city government, including Nicholas Sotherton who had been mayor in 1539. Perhaps this Richard Sotherton was the same one who would become a common councilor in 1557, despite his brushes with the mayor's court. Hawes, ed., p. 142.

18. NRO MCB 1549–1555, p. 314.

19. APC, 2: 178; Houlbrooke, "Refoundation," p. 521; Strype, Memorials, pp. 450, 610.

20. Bindoff, ed., 3: 560.

21. See below, pp. 172–73.

22. NRO MCB 1549–1555, p. 319; APC, 4: 394. While in exile, Watson published Aetiologia, an account of his incarceration. See also Garrett, pp. 322–23; Bale, Scriptores, pp. 729–30; and above, pp. 125–29. Watson's will, PRO PCC 31 Chaynay, was proved in 1559. I owe the reference to Bale to Tom Freeman.

23. A good brief summary of the rebellion and review of the motives of the rebels can be found in Fletcher, Tudor Rebellions, pp. 69–81.

24. Rye, ed., Depositions, pp. 56–58.

25. On the life and career of Thomas Howard, see Head, Ebbs.

26. NRO MCB 1549–1555, p. 332.

27. See above, pp. 75–76; DNB; Venn and Venn, eds., 1(1): 96.

28. NRO MCB 1549–1555, pp. 333–34. Barret ultimately embraced the Marian restoration of Catholicism and according to Houlbrooke, was rewarded with a prebend at the Cathedral in 1558. In his will, written and proved in 1563, Barret declared "that I believe as the holy Catholic Church doth believe and teach and hath ever believed and taught." Houlbrooke, "Refoundation," p. 521; NCC 119 Knightes.

29. Rye, ed., *Depositions*, p. 55. The text of Wharton's examination is printed in full in Galloway, ed., pp. 34–35. The clerk taking down Wharton's deposition referred to Mary as "by grace of God Queen of England France and Ireland Defender of the Faith and in earth under God chief Head of the Church of England and Ireland." Mary had rejected the title of Supreme Head of the church at the end of 1553, finding it an affront to her loyalty to the Roman church. Perhaps its inclusion in the May 1554 deposition was the court clerk's small gesture of defiance against the new religious regime.

30. NRO MCB 1549–1555, pp. 352, 354; Galloway, ed., pp. 33–34.

31. Corbet resigned as Recorder in 1550, but was granted an annual fee of 4 marks by the corporation to act for the present Recorder whenever he was absent. Bindoff, ed., 1: 698.

32. NRO MCB 1549–1555, p. 382.

33. Ibid., pp. 392, 394.

34. Gee and Hardy, comps., p. 382.

35. 1 & 2 P&M c. 8. Gee and Hardy, comps., pp. 385–415.

36. Galloway, ed., pp. 343–44.

37. Haigh, *English Reformations*, p. 214; Hutton, p. 98.

38. NRO Minutes of St. George, pp. 201, 203.

39. Ibid., p. 187, also printed Galloway, ed., pp. 26–27.

40. For a fuller treatment of the reinventions of St. George's guild and a consideration of the revival of rituals in the Reformation era, see McClendon, "A Moveable Feast."

41. Galloway, ed., pp. 38–43, 392.

42. The details are sketchy, but it is known that the corporation paid the city waits for music at the celebration. Galloway, ed., pp. 38, 392. Galloway holds that London and many other cities and towns in England celebrated the victory of St. Quentin, but I have found no references to any such festivity in the *REED* volumes for Chester, Coventry, Exeter and Plymouth (Devon), Newcastle or York.

43. Guy, *Tudor England*, pp. 247–48; Slack, *Impact*, pp. 69–78; Loades, pp. 312–14.

44. Tittler, *Reign of Mary*, pp. 63–64.

45. Loades, p. 385.

46. See, for example, Brigden, *London*, p. 593.

47. On the concept of concord, see MacCulloch's helpful "Archbishop Cranmer."

48. Gee and Hardy, comps., p. 384.

49. Haigh, *English Reformations*, pp. 230–31; Brigden, *London*, pp. 606–14.

50. In Norwich diocese, Bishop William Alnwick's investigations uncovered about sixty Lollards in 1428–29. Three were burnt in 1428 and the rest were permitted to abjure and do penance. This was sufficient, apparently, to cripple heresy in the diocese until the early sixteenth century. In Kent in 1511, the Archbishop of Canterbury William Warham presided over the burning of five Lollards and the recantations of about thirty more, which also seems to have curtailed heresy there for over a decade. Haigh, *English Reformations*, p. 53.

51. Loades, p. 272; Haigh, *English Reformations*, p. 230.

52. Brigden, *London*, p. 613; Dickens, *English Reformation*, p. 293. Dickens suggests that the enthusiasm with which Bonner reportedly took to the task of disciplining heretics could "be interpreted as rough but well-meaning attempts to frighten the less resolute offenders and so save them from the flames."

53. Haigh, *English Reformations*, p. 231; Brigden, *London*, pp. 607–13.

54. See, for example, the narrative of Joyce Lewes of Mancetter in the diocese of Coventry and Lichfield, who was turned over to ecclesiastical authorities by her husband. Richard Woodman from Warbleton, Sussex, was betrayed to officials by his brother. Foxe, 8: 332–38, 401–5. I am grateful to Tom Holien for bringing these examples to my attention.

55. The biblical translator John Rogers was the first to die under the heresy law, executed on February 4. Five people in Suffolk went to the stake two weeks before the Queen's own death. Haigh, *English Reformations*, pp. 230, 233.

56. Houlbrooke, *Church Courts*, p. 232. John Hopton, formerly Queen Mary's personal chaplain, was nominated to the see of Norwich in 1554, when Thomas Thirlby was translated to the diocese of Ely.

57. Gee and Hardy, comps., p. 381; Rev. J. F. Williams, "Married Clergy," p. 85; Houlbrooke, *Church Courts*, pp. 181–82; Haigh, *English Reformations*, p. 227.

58. A fourteenth man, Henry Symond, the fourth prebendary at the Cathedral since 1548, may also have been deprived. NRO REG/30, "Tanner's Index"; NRO MC 16/12, 390 X 3, "Reverend J. F. Williams' Notes on the Deprived Marian Clergy." On Williams's notes see above, p. 103, n. 47. See also NRO SUN/3, Register Book of Diocesan Miscellanea, which contains a list of deprived married clergy and of pensioned religious. Much of that has been reproduced in Baskerville.

59. This figure is based on the list of city parishes in Campbell, pp. 23–24.

60. Houlbrooke, *Church Courts*, pp. 166–67, notes that seventeen parishes were summoned to the consistory in 1555. Houlbrooke must not include St. Andrew's, which was also called on that occasion. See NRO MC 16/1, 390 X 1, "Reverend J. F. Williams' Notes on ACT Books," pp. 59–62.

61. NRO Quarter Sessions Minute Book 1553–1556, f. 24v.

62. NRO MCB 1555–1562, pp. 113, 134.

63. Foxe, 8: 380–81.

64. Dunning was actually the co-Chancellor of the diocese, sharing the post with Miles Spenser, who had been appointed by Richard Nix in 1531. Spenser was the sole occupant of that post under Nix and his successor William Rugge, and appears to have held it jointly after Rugge's 1550 resignation.

65. Foxe, 8: 427–29.

66. Wolman's recantation can be found among Foxe's papers: BL Harleian 421, f. 154. On Richard Crashfield and Thomas Carman, see Foxe, 8: 398–400, 462–66, 781. For Wolman's will (NCC 160 Colman), see Farrow, ed., *Index . . . 1550–1603*, p. 185.

67. Foxe, 8: 381.

68. Hughes, *Reformation*, 2: 274. According to Hughes, Foxe identified 273 Marian martyrs. Of those narratives, 102 described the apprehension of the victims. Sixty (58.82%) were captured by lay justices and constables, while 13 (12.74%) were turned over by friends or family. Twelve (11.76%) had already been in prison before the revival of the heresy laws; 8 (7.84%) were seized through their own public actions and 7 (6.86%) detentions were a result of clerical initiative. One (0.98%) person had been turned in by someone hoping for a reward and another's (0.98%) arrest had been directly ordered by the Privy Council.

69. Loades, pp. 274–75.

70. Houlbrooke, *Church Courts*, p. 237.

71. Ibid., pp. 232–37.

72. See above, p. 113.

73. See Appendix 4.

74. Evidence from the wills of the fourteen aldermen who served during Mary's reign and wrote their wills during Elizabeth's suggests the continuation of religious diversity. Henry Crook's preamble committed his soul to God alone, but we know of his public support for the Mass during Mary's reign. Robert Rugge penned his will in the first month of Elizabeth's rule. Rugge undoubtedly realized the futility of providing for Masses, but he noted in his lengthy preamble that he died "in the true faith of the holy Catholic Church." William Mingay, alderman from 1556 until his death in 1565, selected Miles Spenser, the

well-known conservative Chancellor of Norwich, as the supervisor for his will. MacCulloch, *Suffolk*, p. 184, has noted the "conservative associations" of Mingay, who was also the diocesan registrar. One testator, Richard Davy, wrote no preamble and the other ten wills also contain elements that place them within the Elizabethan mainstream.

75. Bindoff, ed., 2: 254.

76. A brief review of the landholdings of Balle and Corbet can be found in Bindoff, ed., 1: 374–75, 698–99.

77. Houlbrooke, "Refoundation," p. 522; above, n. 28.

78. See, for example, Brigden, *London*, pp. 593–98.

79. Skeeters, pp. 132–33.

80. Brigden, *London*, pp. 602–3, 606, 624. A few of London's martyrs were put to death elsewhere; see table 6, pp. 608–12.

81. Pound's figures suggest that Norwich's population dipped from about 8,500 in 1525 to about 8,000 in 1570. London's population, on the other hand, climbed from about 50,000 in 1500 to about 70,000 in 1550. Pound, *Tudor and Stuart Norwich*, pp. 28, 125; Rappaport, p. 61, n. 1.

82. Ward, *Metropolitan Communities*.

83. Dickens, *English Reformation*, p. 293.

84. Brigden, *London*, pp. 613–14.

85. Ibid., pp. 321, 626.

86. Ibid., p. 626.

87. Ibid., pp. 626–27.

88. Ibid., p. 627.

89. Ibid., p. 628.

6. Fervor and Forbearance

1. On Parkhurst's life and career see Houlbrooke, ed., *Letter Book*, pp. 17–57.

2. Guy, *Tudor England*, p. 258; Haigh, *English Reformations*, pp. 238–39; A. G. R. Smith, p. 108.

3. Haigh, *English Reformations*, pp. 242–48; Duffy, pp. 569–77.

4. Gee, pp. 252–69, provides a list of clergy deprived between 1558 and 1564.

5. Haigh, *English Reformations*, p. 243.

6. Slack, *Impact*, pp. 70–72, 127–28.

7. NRO Press D, Case 17, Shelf b, "Mayor's Book."

8. See Appendix 5.

9. Hawes, ed., pp. 40, 133, 145.

10. Haigh, *English Reformations*, p. 270.

11. NCC 128 Goldingham (Leche); NCC 20 Marten (Crook); NCC 187 Marten (Mingay).

12. PCC 18 Chayre (Quasshe); NCC 167 Cowlles (Blome). See also above, p. 117.

13. PCC 6 Sheffeld.

14. PCC 13 Lyon; Houlbrooke, ed., *Letter Book*, pp. 41, 53, 118.

15. Churchwardens' accounts for St. Stephen's for 1568–69 note no expenditure for the washing of the surplice, indicating that Leeds did not wear one as prescribed in the Act of Uniformity. Rump, ed., pp. 34–38.

16. When Robert Watson returned to Norwich in 1554, where he got in trouble for his refusal to attend Mass, he was staying at the home of Thomas Beamond, either the man who became alderman in 1560 or his father. See above, pp. 160–61.

17. Haigh, *English Reformations*, p. 243; MacCulloch, *Suffolk*, pp. 182–83.

18. Gee, pp. 281–82, contains a list of institutions made after the deprivations, on which no one from Norwich appears. Ralph Houlbrooke, *Church Courts*, p. 245, has noted that although Norwich diocese was comprised of about 1,200 parishes, only about 500 clergy subscribed to the royal Supremacy in 1559. For the subscription book for Norwich diocese see Lambeth Palace Library, CM xiii, #57.

19. NRO Minutes of St. George, p. 214; Galloway, ed., p. 159. On the significance of the decision to allow the dragon to remain a part of the annual procession, see McClendon, "A Moveable Feast."

20. The Norwich Grocers' guild noted in its records that there was "no solemnity" in 1559 after they had recorded payments for the Corpus Christi procession since 1556. Galloway, ed., p. 44. The celebration of Corpus Christi continued in several places into the 1580's; Cressy, p. 25.

21. NRO Chamberlains' Accounts 1551–1567, f. 147v. In 1559–60, the city purchased a Prayer Book for the Common Hall, as well as a surplice for Kempe; f. 177r.

22. Rye, ed., *Depositions*, pp. 65–66. On these depositions, see above, p. 118, n. 13.

23. Rye, ed., *Depositions*, p. 66.

24. Ibid., pp. 66–67.

25. NRO MCB 1555–1562, pp. 513–15, 518–19, 522–23.

26. Rye, ed., *Depositions*, p. 78.

27. MacCulloch, *Suffolk*, pp. 83–104, 187–89.

28. Ibid., p. 186.

29. Houlbrooke, ed., *Letter Book*, pp. 41, 42, 44; Houlbrooke, *Church Courts*, pp. 207–8; Houlbrooke, "Refoundation," p. 511.

30. Houlbrooke, "Refoundation," p. 522.

31. Houlbrooke, ed., *Letter Book*, p. 27.

32. MacCulloch, *Suffolk*, pp. 164, 185–87, 191.

33. Houlbrooke, ed., *Letter Book*, pp. 20–24.

34. Quoted in MacCulloch, *Suffolk*, p. 185.

35. Houlbrooke, ed., *Letter Book*, p. 44.

36. Collinson, *Puritan Movement*, chapters 1, 2; Houlbrooke, ed., *Letter Book*, p. 44.

37. Collinson, *Puritan Movement*, p. 80.

38. Houlbrooke, ed., *Letter Book*, p. 45.

39. Ibid., pp. 40–41, 45; Houlbrooke, *Church Courts*, pp. 208, 255; Houlbrooke, "Refoundation," p. 522.

40. L'Estrange, ed., pp. 67–68; NRO DCN 29/1, Dean and Chapter *Liber Miscellaneorum*, ff. 27v–43r. In response to the findings of the 1569 visitation, Parkhurst issued injunctions to the Cathedral chapter in 1570 or 1571. As Houlbrooke points out, *Church Courts*, p. 208, although they sought to establish rigorous discipline at the Cathedral, they were hardly comprehensive, making no reference, for example, to regular preaching by the prebends. Houlbrooke compares Parkhurst's injunctions unfavorably to those issued by Bishop Robert Horne to Winchester Cathedral in the early 1560's. See NRO DCN 47/3, Dean and Chapter Ledger Book 1565–1631, ff. 53r–54r, printed in L'Estrange, ed., pp. 18–21.

41. Houlbrooke, *Church Courts*, p. 252.

42. On the Northern Rebellion, see Fletcher, *Tudor Rebellions*, pp. 82–96.

43. Houlbrooke, *Church Courts*, pp. 246, 248, 250–51; Houlbrooke, ed., *Letter Book*, p. 175, n. 374; NRO VIS 1/3, Diocesan Visitation Records (1569), n.p.

44. Houlbrooke, ed., *Letter Book*, p. 175–79, 212; Houlbrooke, *Church Courts*, p. 251.

45. See, for example, Parkhurst's mishandling of two matrimonial cases; Houlbrooke, ed., *Letter Book*, pp. 30–31.

46. Houlbrooke, *Church Courts*, p. 254.

47. Houlbrooke, ed., *Letter Book*, pp. 121–22, 188.

48. Ibid., p. 222.

49. McIntosh; Spufford, "Puritanism"; Archer, p. 249.

50. Slack, *Impact*, p. 128.

51. Pound, *Tudor and Stuart Norwich*, p. 55; Pound, "Social and Trade Structure," p. 61.

52. Moens, pp. 17–18; NRO Book of Orders for Strangers, ff. 16r–18v; Hudson and Tingey, eds., 2: 332–33; Allison, pp. 61–62.

53. Pound, *Tudor and Stuart Norwich*, 57–59. Relations between the residents of Norwich and the Strangers were strained for some time, and there were few attempts to teach the manufacture of the New Draperies to the English for many years. Pound argues, however, that by the 1580's,

the Norwich textile industry "had been restored to the position of pre-eminence it had occupied earlier in the century."

54. Houlbrooke, *Church Courts*, appendix 3.

55. Wrightson, p. 157 and pp. 149–82 on the more general problem of order; Herrup, p. 54.

56. See Appendix 6. These figures are based on the examination of NRO MCB 1540–1549, NRO MCB 1549–1555, NRO MCB 1555–1562 and NRO MCB 1562–1569.

57. Herrup, p. 40.

58. Brigden, "Youth," p. 49.

59. Collinson, "A Mirror," pp. 296–97.

60. Collinson, *Puritan Movement*, pp. 51, 169–78. See also PRO SP 15/12/27, a letter from Edward Gascoigne to the Earl of Leicester dated October 15, 1564, which describes the Norwich prophesyings. For other Puritan clergy who were in Norwich from the 1570's, including John More, "the apostle of Norwich," see Collinson, *Puritan Movement*, pp. 127, 129, 141, 149, 202–4; Peel, ed., 1: 143–47. For Leeds, see above, n. 15, and for his preaching before the corporation, see NRO Chamberlains' Accounts 1551–1567, ff. 228r, 335v, 336r; NRO Chamberlains' Accounts 1580–1589, ff. 33r, 65v–r, 96(a)r, 109r, 267v, 270r; NRO Chamberlains' Accounts 1589–1602, ff. 16r, 60r, 102v, 131r, 159r, 186r, 212v. The accounts for 1568–1579 are lost.

61. NRO MCB 1569–1576, p. 70.

62. NRO MCB 1562–1569, p. 13.

63. Ibid., p. 591.

64. NRO MCB 1555–1562, p. 394.

65. Appendix 6.

66. NRO MCB 1540–1549, pp. 235–36.

67. Ibid., p. 79.

68. Ibid., p. 452.

69. Ibid., p. 61.

70. NRO MCB 1555–1562, p. 132.

71. NRO MCB 1549–1555, p. 76.

72. NRO MCB 1555–1562, p. 37.

73. Ibid., p. 211.

74. Ibid., p. 225.

75. Ibid., p. 367.

76. Ibid., pp. 394, 417.

77. Ibid., p. 444.

78. NRO MCB 1569–1576, p. 74. On Bownd, see Collinson, *Puritan Movement*, pp. 186, 377, 378, 436–37.

79. NRO MCB 1569–1576, pp. 5, 12, 15, 23.

80. NRO MCB 1562–1569, p. 192; NRO MCB 1569–1576, p. 43.

81. NRO MCB 1562–1569, pp. 297, 466.

82. NRO MCB 1555–1562, pp. 548, 550.

83. NRO MCB 1562–1569, pp. 91, 281.

84. NRO MCB 1569–1576, p. 31.

85. NRO AB 1551–1568, ff. 146v, 148r, 158r, 175v. In March 1570 Kyndersley was back before the Assembly apparently in connection with a debt or fine in another matter. He claimed he was unable to pay the money and made "humble request to have some relief." The Assembly then ordered the city foreign receiver (the officer responsible for monies taken in on admission to the freedom) to give Kyndersley 100s. so that he could pay the city Chamberlain what he owed. NRO AB 1568–1585, f. 18v. Cases of disenfranchisement have not been included in the total number of cases considered, as they did not appear in the mayor's court books.

86. Archer, pp. 248–52. The quotation appears on p. 252.

87. Evans, p. 7.

88. The will of Robert Kyndersley, draper, was proved in 1574. Farrow, ed., *Index . . . 1550–1603*, p. 101.

89. Collinson, *Birthpangs*, p. 55.

90. Ibid., p. 55.

91. McGrath, p. 101.

92. N. Williams, *Thomas Howard*, pp. 179–82.

93. Ibid., p. 183; *APC*, 7: 362.

94. N. Williams, *Thomas Howard*, pp. 185–88.

95. Houlbrooke, ed., *Letter Book*, p. 41.

96. McGrath, p. 106.

97. See above, pp. 208–9.

98. Houlbrooke, ed., *Letter Book*, p. 177.

99. Ibid., pp. 45–46.

100. McGrath, pp. 103–5; Guy, *Tudor England*, p. 277.

101. Haigh, *English Reformations*, p. 259.

102. Houlbrooke, ed., *Letter Book*, p. 212.

103. NRO Quarter Sessions Minute Book, 1571–1581, f. 4v.

104. Pound, *Poverty*, p. 66.

105. Ibid., p. 24.

106. Pound, ed.; Pound, *Tudor and Stuart Norwich*, p. 125.

107. NRO Mayor's Book of the Poor, n.p.; NRO AB 1568–1585, ff. 39r, 40v.

108. Pound, *Poverty*, pp. 63–64.

109. See Appendix 6.

110. NRO MCB 1569–1576, p. 127.

111. Ibid., p. 622.

112. NRO MCB 1576–1581, p. 482.

113. Ibid., p. 262.

114. NRO MCB 1569–1572, p. 285.

115. NRO MCB 1576–1581, p. 212.

116. Ibid., p. 486.

117. Ibid., p. 514.

118. Ibid., pp. 557, 559.

119. Ibid., p. 729.

120. NRO MCB 1569–1576, p. 429.

121. NRO MCB 1576–1581, p. 78.

122. Ibid., p. 294; for another example, see also ibid., p. 378.

123. Ibid., p. 569.

124. Ibid., p. 576.

125. Collinson, *Religion*, p. 141.

126. On More and the Norwich Puritans see Collinson, *Puritan Movement*, pp. 51, 127, 186–87.

127. In November 1591 the city Assembly noted how the minister had "wholly employed his time in taking pains and travail by study to preach and teach God's Word diligently and painfully in this city to the comfort and edifying of divers good and godly people, and hath thereby brought his body to great weakness," and granted him the profits of a lease of property in nearby Heatheld. NRO Chamberlains' Accounts 1580–1589, ff. 33r, 65v–r, 96r, 109r, 159v, 267v, 207r; NRO Chamberlains' Accounts 1589–1602, ff. 16r, 60r; NRO AB 1585–1613, f. 98v. More preached twice before the corporation in 1581–82. Thomas Roberts also preached before the corporation in 1579 and 1580–81. See also NRO Clavors's Book 1550–1601, ff. 77v. Also see Ellis Bate's and John Aldrich's wills, PCC 49 Pyckeryng and PCC 27 Tirwhite.

128. NRO Mayor's Book for the Poor, n.p.

129. Pound, *Tudor and Stuart Norwich*, pp. 132–33, tables 10.5, 10.6.

130. Pound, ed., p. 7.

131. Houlbrooke, ed., *Letter Book*, p. 44.

132. For a fuller treatment of this episode, see Collinson, *Puritan Movement*, pp. 191–92; Houlbrooke, ed., *Letter Book*, p. 46.

133. Collinson, *Puritan Movement*, p. 192.

134. Ibid., pp. 202–4.

135. A. H. Smith et al., eds., 1: 236–37.

136. NRO MCB 1576–1581, p. 59. Holland may have been the same man who would be listed in a Puritan survey of unfit ministers from 1586, where he was noted as "ignorant, a maintainer of seven sacraments, suspected of conjuring." Peel, ed., 2: 147.

137. A. H. Smith et al., eds., 1: 237.

138. Collinson, *Puritan Movement*, p. 203.

139. NRO MCB 1576–1581, p. 122; on Seman see above, pp. 201–2.

140. NRO MCB 1576–1581, p. 518.

141. NRO MCB 1582–1587, pp. 42, 52.

142. A. H. Smith, *County*, pp. 213–16.

143. A. H. Smith et al., eds., 2: 274–76.

144. Ibid., 2: 275–76.

145. Ibid., 2: 276.

146. L'Estrange, ed., pp. 79–80; A. H. Smith, *County*, pp. 201–2.

147. NRO MCB 1582–1587, p. 362. Crask, who would become mayor in 1623, has been described by John Evans as an "ardent Puritan." Evans, p. 86.

148. A. H. Smith, *County*, p. 52.

149. NRO Norwich Chamberlains' Accounts 1580–1589, f. 162r; NRO MCB 1582–1587, p. 387; MacCulloch, *Suffolk*, p. 215, n. 78.

150. Gee and Hardy, comps., pp. 485–92. On official reaction to the escalating problems associated with Catholicism in the 1580's see McGrath, chapter 8, and A. H. Smith, *County*, pp. 133–36.

151. *APC*, 15: 368.

152. NRO MCB 1587–1595, p. 251. This page is bound out of sequence in this volume and appears after p. 228.

153. Ibid., p. 308.

154. Ibid., p. 540.

155. *APC*, 21: 144–45.

156. Collinson, *Birthpangs*, pp. 55–56.

157. Collinson, "Magistracy," p. 445.

158. Collinson, *Religion*, pp. 141–42, 188.

159. See my discussion of Brigden's *London* in the Introduction, above, pp. 21–24. See also the comment of Palliser, *Age of Elizabeth*, p. 381: "The idea, dominant in England since 1689, that religion and politics can be separated, would have seemed very dangerous to Tudor men and women of every religious persuasion."

160. Collinson, *Puritan Movement*, p. 188.

161. NRO Norwich Quarter Sessions Minute Book, 1571–1581, f. 144v; NRO MCB 1576–1581, pp. 386, 392; Johnson, p. 149; A. D. Bayne, p. 206.

162. Johnson, p. 150.

163. Ibid., p. 151; A. D. Bayne, p. 206, which gives Cole's residence as Ipswich. An entry in the mayor's court book for January 15, 1589, notes that the undersheriff of Norfolk "did request [the mayor] and his brethren the aldermen to have license to burn in the Castle ditch one Francis Ket *alias* Knight . . . for denying the deity of Christ," which indicates that Ket probably came from Norfolk. NRO MCB 1587–1595, p. 229. This page is bound out of sequence after p. 250.

164. Browne, pp. 36–43; White, pp. 44–66, esp. pp. 45–49. In an April 19, 1581, letter to William Cecil, now Lord Burghley (Browne, pp. 37–38), Bishop Freke recounted the activities of the Brownists, of which he had learned "upon complaint made by many godly preachers."

165. MacCulloch, "Archbishop Cranmer."

166. Archer, pp. 248–52.

167. In addition to John Gorney, Thomas Steward and Robert Kyndersley, at least six more citizens were disenfranchised during the Elizabethan period. See NRO AB 1568–1585, ff. 126r, 249r; NRO AB 1585–1613, ff. 76r, 134r; NRO MCB 1582–1587, p. 307. For examples involving ministers, see NRO MCB 1576–1581, pp. 185, 359–60, 408, 413, 427.

Conclusion

1. Collinson, *Birthpangs*, p. 55.

2. Helgerson, pp. 254–83.

3. Linda Colley, for example, has shown that in the eighteenth century, Catholicism was seen as "un-British." See p. 19 and her discussion of the role of anti-Catholicism in the formation of British identity, pp. 20–25.

4. For example, Brigden, *London*; Whiting.

5. Haigh, *English Reformations*, esp. pp. 12–13, 288–89, 295.

6. Collinson, *Birthpangs*, p. 56.

7. NRO MCB 1587–1595, p. 191; NRO AB 1585–1613, f. 51r; Cressy, p. 120. The service continued at least to the end of Elizabeth's reign; see Galloway, ed., pp. 95, 99, 101, 103, 105, 107, 114, 119, 122. The Armada's defeat was also noted in the "Mayor's Book"; Johnson, p. 151.

⊰ BIBLIOGRAPHY ⊱

Manuscript Sources

Norwich, Norfolk Record Office

CORPORATION RECORDS

Books of the Proceedings in the Norwich Mayor's Court
Mayor's Court Book, 1510–1534.
Mayor's Court Book, 1534–1540.
Mayor's Court Book, 1534–1549.
Mayor's Court Book, 1540–1549.
Mayor's Court Book, 1549–1555.
Mayor's Court Book, 1555–1562.
Mayor's Court Book, 1562–1569.
Mayor's Court Book, 1569–1576.
Mayor's Court Book, 1576–1581.
Mayor's Court Book, 1582–1587.
Mayor's Court Book, 1587–1595.
Mayor's Court Book, 1595–1603.
Mayor's Court Book, 1603–1615.

Assembly Minute Books
Assembly Minute Book, 1510–1550.
Assembly Minute Book, 1551–1568.
Assembly Minute Book, 1568–1585.
Assembly Minute Book, 1585–1613.

Folio Books of the Proceedings of the Municipal Assembly
Proceedings of the Municipal Assembly, 1491–1553.
Proceedings of the Municipal Assembly, 1553–1583.
Proceedings of the Municipal Assembly, 1583–1587.

Quarter Sessions Minute Books
Minute Book of Quarter Sessions, 1511–1541, 1542–1550, 1553–1556.

Minute Book of Quarter Sessions, 1571–1581.
Minute Book of Quarter Sessions, 1581–1591.
Minute Book of Quarter Sessions, 1591–1602.

Sessions Records: Interrogations and Depositions
Sessions Records Book, 1549–1554.
Sessions Records Papers, 1553–1561.
Sessions Record Book, 1561–1567.
Sessions Record Book, 1563–1572.

Chamberlains' Accounts
Chamberlains' Account Book, 1537–1547.
Chamberlains' Account Book, 1541–1550.
Chamberlains' Account Book, 1551–1567.
Chamberlains' Account Book, 1580–1589.
Chamberlains' Account Book, 1589–1602.
Chamberlains' Account Book, 1602–1625.

Books of the Clavors' Accounts
Clavors' Book of Accounts, 1550–1601.

Books of the Poor
Mayor's Book of the Poor, 1571.

Books Relating to Charitable Donations
Terry's Charity Book, 1547–1614.
Rogers' Gift Book, 1553–1605.
Head's Charity Book, 1569–1673.

Great Hospital Account Rolls
Great Hospital Account Rolls, 1548–1575 (26 rolls).

St. George's Guild Books and Rolls
St. George's Account Rolls, 1491–1592 (7 rolls).
Minutes of St. George's Guild, 1452–1602.

Worsted Weavers' Books
Second Book of the Worsted Weavers, 1511–1638.

DIOCESAN RECORDS

Register Book of Diocesan Miscellanea (SUN/3).
Register Books of Wills Proved in the Consistory Court, 1513–1618.
Tanner's Index to the Institution Books (REG/30).
Visitation Book, 1569 (VIS 1/3).

Dean and Chapter Records
Agreement Between City and Priory, 1520 (DCN 89/8).
Agreement Between City and Priory, 1523 (DCN 89/10).

Copy of Agreement Between City and Priory, 1517 (DCN 89/5).
Dean and Chapter Ledger Book, c. 1538–1562 (DCN 47/1).
Dean and Chapter Ledger Book, 1565–1631 (DCN 47/3).
Grant of Tombland by Prior, 22 May 1523 (DCN 89/9).
Liber Miscelleaneorum (DCN 29/1).

Parish Records
Churchwardens' Accounts
St. Gregory, 1574–1771 (PD 59/54).
St. John Maddermarket, 1556–1592 (PD 461/48).
St. Margaret Westwick, 1552–1600 (PD 153/42).
St. Peter Mancroft, 1580–1654 (PD 26/71).

OTHER MANUSCRIPTS

Agreement Between City and Prior, 1519–1521.
Articles of Cardinal Wolsey Respecting Prior's Jurisdiction as to Right
    of Sanctuary, 1520.
Book of Order for Strangers, 1564–1643.
Book of Pleas.
Complaint of Prior Against Citizens, 1500.
Liber Albus.
Mayor's Book.
MS Ecclesiastical History of Norwich (MS 4914.T133E).
MS History of Norwich to 1716 (MS 453.7133A).
Norfolk Sessions Papers, 1583, Bradfer-Lawrence Collection, VIb (III).
Reverend J. F. Williams' Index to SUN/3.
Reverend J. F. Williams' Notes on ACT Books, 1544–1555,
    1577–1592, 1595–1602 (MC 16/1, 390 X 1).
Reverend J. F. Williams' Notes on Marian Clergy (MC 16/12, 390 X 3).

London, British Library

Additional MSS 5524, 48101.
Additional Charter 26723.
Cotton MS Cleopatra E iv, E v.
Cotton MS Vespasian F ix, F xiii.
Harleain MS 368, 416, 421.
Landsdowne MS 981.

London, Lambeth Palace Library

Carte Antique et Miscellanee, xiii.

London, Public Record Office

Exchequer, King's Remembrancer, Ecclesiastical Documents (E 135).

Exchequer, King's Remembrancer, Lay Subsidies (E 179).
Prerogative Court of Canterbury, Will Registers (PROB 11).
State Papers, Henry VIII (SP 1).
State Papers, Edward VI (SP 10).
State Papers, Mary I (SP 11).
State Papers, Elizabeth I (SP 12).
State Papers, Addenda, Edward VI–James I (SP 15).

Other Sources

Publishers are listed only for twentieth-century works.

Abray, Lorna Jane. "Confession, Conscience and Honour: The Limits of Magisterial Authority in Sixteenth-Century Strassburg." In Ole Peter Grell and Bob Scribner, eds., *Tolerance and Intolerance in the European Reformation*. Cambridge, Eng.: Cambridge University Press, 1996, pp. 94–107.

"Account of the Company of St. George in Norwich from Mackerell's History of Norwich, MS. 1737." *Norfolk Archaeology*, 3 (1852): 315–74.

Acts of the Privy Council of England. Ed. John Roche Dasent. 9 vols. London: HMSO, 1890–1907.

Agnew, Jean-Christophe. *Worlds Apart: The Market and the Theater in Anglo-American Thought, 1550–1750*. Cambridge, Eng.: Cambridge University Press, 1986.

Allen, Bruce Halliday. "The Administrative and Social Structure of the Norwich Merchant Class, 1485–1660." Ph.D. dissertation, Harvard University, 1951.

Allison, K. J. "The Norfolk Worsted Industry in the Sixteenth and Seventeenth Centuries." *Yorkshire Bulletin of Economic and Social Research*, 13 (1961): 61–77.

Alsop, J. D. "Religious Preambles in Early Modern English Wills as Formulae." *Journal of Ecclesiastical History*, 40 (1989): 19–27.

Anderson, J. J., ed. *Newcastle upon Tyne*. Records of Early English Drama. Toronto: University of Toronto Press, 1982.

Archer, Ian W. *The Pursuit of Stability: Social Relations in Elizabethan London*. Cambridge, Eng.: Cambridge University Press, 1991.

Atherton, Ian, Eric Fernie, Christopher Harper-Bill and Hassell Smith, eds. *Norwich Cathedral: Church, City and Diocese, 1096–1996*. London: Hambledon, 1996.

Baker, Donald C. "When Is a Text a Play? Reflections upon What Certain Late Medieval Dramatic Texts Can Tell Us." In Marianne G. Briscoe and John C. Coldewey, eds., *Contexts for Early English Drama*. Bloomington and Indianapolis: Indiana University Press, 1989, pp. 20–40.

Bale, John. *The Actes of Englysh Votaryes*. The English Experience: Its Record in Early Printed Books Published in Facsimile, no. 906. 1560; rpt. Amsterdam: Theatrum Orbis Terrarum, Ltd., 1979.

―――. *Scriptores Illustrium Maoiris Brytannie Catalogus.* Vol. 9. London, 1557.

Baskerville, G. "Married Clergy and Pensioned Religious in Norwich Diocese, 1555." *English Historical Review*, 48 (1933): 43–64, 199–228.

Bayne, A. D. *A Comprehensive History of Norwich.* Norwich, 1869.

Bayne, C. G., ed. *Select Cases in the Council of Henry VII.* Selden Society, 75 (1958).

Beer, Barrett L. "'The commoyson in Norfolk, 1549': A Narrative of Popular Rebellion in Sixteenth-Century England." *Journal of Medieval and Renaissance Studies*, 6 (1976): 73–99.

―――. *Northumberland: The Political Career of John Dudley, Earl of Warwick and Duke of Northumberland.* Kent, Ohio: Kent State University Press, 1973.

Beier, A. L., and Robert Finlay, eds. *London, 1500–1700: The Making of a Metropolis.* London: Longman, 1986.

Benedict, Philip. "*Un Roi, Une Loi, Deux Foix*: Parameters for the History of Catholic-Reformed Co-existence in France, 1555–1685." In Ole Peter Grell and Bob Scribner, eds., *Tolerance and Intolerance in the European Reformation.* Cambridge, Eng.: Cambridge University Press, 1996, pp. 65–93.

Berlin, Michael. "Civic Ceremony in Early Modern London." *Urban History Yearbook*, 1986: 15–27.

Bernard, G. W. "The Fall of Anne Boleyn." *English Historical Review*, 106 (1991): 584–610.

Bindoff, S. T., ed. *History of Parliament: The House of Commons, 1509–1558.* 3 vols. London: Secker and Warburg for the History of Parliament Trust, 1982.

Block, Joseph S. *Factional Politics and the English Reformation, 1520–1540.* Woodbridge, Suffolk, UK: Boydell Press, 1993.

Blomefield, Francis. *An Essay Towards the Topographical History of the County of Norfolk.* 11 vols. London, 1805–1810.

Brewer, J., J. Gardiner and R. Brodie, eds. *Letters and Papers, Foreign and Domestic, of the Reign of Henry VIII, 1509–1547.* 21 vols. London: HMSO, 1862–1932.

Bridbury, A. R. "English Provincial Towns in the Later Middle Ages." *Economic History Review*, 2nd ser., 34 (1981): 1–24.

Brigden, Susan. *London and the Reformation.* Oxford: Clarendon Press, 1989.

―――. "Youth and the English Reformation." *Past and Present*, 95 (1982): 37–67.

Brown, Andrew. *Popular Piety in Late Medieval England: The Diocese of Salisbury, 1250–1550.* Oxford: Clarendon Press, 1995.

Browne, John. *History of Congregationalism and Memorials of the Churches in Norfolk and Suffolk.* London, 1877.

Burke, Peter. *Popular Culture in Early Modern Europe.* New York: Harper and Row, 1978.

Burton, William. *Seven Dialogues Both Pithie and Profitable.* London, 1606.

Bush, M. L. *The Government Policy of Protector Somerset.* Montreal: McGill-Queen's University Press, 1975.

Campbell, James. "Norwich." In Mary D. Lobel and W. H. Johns, eds., *Historic Towns.* Vol. 2. Oxford: Lovell Johns, Ltd., 1975, pp. 1–25.

Cavendish, George. *The Life and Death of Cardinal Wolsey. Two Early Tudor Lives.* Ed. Richard S. Sylvester and Davis P. Harding. New Haven: Yale University Press, 1962.

Cheke, John. *The Hurt of Sedicion.* London, 1549.

Clark, Peter. "A Crisis Contained? The Condition of English Towns in the 1590s." In Peter Clark, ed., *The European Crisis of the 1590s: Essays in Comparative History.* London: G. Allen & Unwin, 1985, pp. 44–66.

———. *English Provincial Society from the Reformation to the Revolution: Religion, Politics and Society in Kent, 1500–1640.* Hassocks, Eng.: Harvester, 1977.

———. "Reformation and Radicalism in Kentish Towns, c. 1500–1553." In W. J. Mommsen, ed., *Stadtbürgertum und Adel in der Reformation: Studien zur Sozialgeschichte der Reformation in England und Deutschland.* Stuttgart: Klett-Cotta, 1979, pp. 115–22.

——— and Paul Slack. *English Towns in Transition 1500–1700.* London: Oxford University Press, 1976.

———, eds. *Crisis and Order in English Towns, 1500–1700: Essays in Urban History.* London: Routledge and Kegan Paul, 1972.

Clay, C. G. A. *Economic Expansion and Social Change: England, 1500–1700.* 2 vols. Cambridge, Eng.: Cambridge University Press, 1984.

Clopper, Lawrence M., ed. *Chester.* Records of Early English Drama. Toronto: University of Toronto Press, 1979.

Coleman, D. C. *The Economy of England, 1450–1750.* London: Oxford University Press, 1977.

Colley, Linda. *Britons: Forging the Nation, 1707–1837.* New Haven: Yale University Press, 1992.

Collinson, Patrick. *The Birthpangs of Protestant England: Religious and Cultural Change in the Sixteenth and Seventeenth Centuries.* Basingstoke, Hampshire, Eng.: Macmillan, 1988.

———. *The Elizabethan Puritan Movement.* Berkeley: University of California Press, 1967.

————. "England." In Bob Scribner, Roy Porter and Mikulás Teich, eds., *The Reformation in National Context*. Cambridge, Eng.: Cambridge University Press, 1994, pp. 80–94.

————. "England and International Calvinism, 1558–1640." In Menna Prestwich, ed., *International Calvinism, 1541–1715*. Oxford: Clarendon Press, 1985, pp. 197–224.

————. "Magistracy and Ministry: A Suffolk Miniature." In Patrick Collinson, *Godly People: Essays on English Protestantism and Puritanism*. London: Hambledon, 1983, pp. 445–66.

————. "A Mirror of Elizabethan Puritanism: The Life and Letters of 'Godly Master Dering.'" Ibid., pp. 289–324.

————. *The Religion of Protestants: The Church in English Society, 1559–1625*. Oxford: Oxford University Press, 1982.

Cornford, Barbara. "The Cleres of Ormesby." *Yarmouth Archaeology*, 1 (1982): n.p.

Cornwall, Julian. "Kett's Rebellion: A Comment." In Paul Slack, ed., *Rebellion, Popular Protest and the Social Order in Early Modern England*. Cambridge, Eng.: Cambridge University Press, 1984, pp. 63–67.

————. *Revolt of the Peasantry, 1549*. London: Routledge and Kegan Paul, 1977.

————. *Wealth and Society in Early Sixteenth Century England*. Basingstoke, Eng.: Macmillan, 1988.

Cozens-Hardy, Basil, and Ernest A. Kent. *The Mayors of Norwich, 1403–1835: Being Biographical Notes on the Mayors of the Old Corporation*. Norwich: Jarrold and Sons, Ltd., 1938.

Craig, Hardin. *English Religious Drama of the Middle Ages*. Oxford: Clarendon Press, 1955.

Cressy, David. *Bonfires and Bells: National Memory and the Protestant Calendar in Elizabethan and Stuart England*. Berkeley: University of California Press, 1989.

Cross, Claire. *Church and People, 1450–1660: The Triumph of the Laity*. Atlantic Highlands, NJ: Humanities Press, 1976.

————. *Urban Magistrates and Ministers: Religion in Hull and Leeds from the Reformation to the Civil War*. Borthwick Papers, no. 67. York: University of York Press, 1985.

Davis, John F. *Heresy and Reformation in the South-East of England, 1520–1559*. London: Royal Historical Society, 1983.

————. "The Trials of Thomas Bylney and the English Reformation." *Historical Journal*, 24 (1981): 775–90.

Davis, Natalie Zemon. "The Reasons of Misrule." In *Society and Culture in Early Modern France*. Stanford, Calif.: Stanford University Press, 1975, pp. 97–123.

———. "The Sacred and the Body Social in Sixteenth-Century Lyon." *Past and Present*, 90 (1981): 40–70.

Davis, Norman, ed. *Non-Cycle Plays and Fragments*. London: Oxford University Press for the Early English Text Society, 1970.

Del Villar, Mary. "The Staging of the Conversion of Saint Paul." *Theatre Notebook*, 25 (1970): 64–68.

Dickens, A. G. "The Early Expansion of Protestantism in England 1520–1558." *Archiv für Reformationgeschicte*, 78 (1987): 187–221.

———. *The English Reformation*. 2nd. ed. London: Batsford, 1989.

———. *Lollards and Protestants in the Diocese of York, 1509–1558*. London: Oxford University Press for the University of Hull, 1959.

———, ed. "Robert Parkyn's Narrative of the Reformation." *English Historical Review*, 62 (1947): 58–83.

Dobson, R. B. "Urban Decline in Late Medieval England." *Transactions of the Royal Historical Society*, 5th ser., 27 (1977): 1–22.

Duffy, Eamon. *The Stripping of the Altars: Traditional Religion in England, c. 1400-c. 1580*. New Haven: Yale University Press, 1992.

Dures, Alan. *English Catholicism, 1558–1642*. London: Longman, 1983.

Dutka, Joanna. "Mystery Plays at Norwich: Their Formation and Development." *Leeds Studies in English*, n.s., 10 (1978): 107–20.

Dyer, A. D. *The City of Worcester in the Sixteenth Century*. Leicester: Leicester University Press, 1973.

———. *Decline and Growth in English Towns, 1400–1640*. Houndsmill, Basingstoke, Hampshire: Macmillan, 1991.

———. "Growth and Decay in English Towns, 1500–1700." *Urban History Yearbook*, 1979: 60–72.

Elton, G. R. "Persecution and Toleration in the English Reformation." In W. J. Sheils, ed., *Persecution and Toleration*. Oxford: Blackwell for the Ecclesiastical History Society, 1984, pp. 163–88.

———. *Policy and Police: The Enforcement of the Reformation in the Age of Thomas Cromwell*. Cambridge, Eng.: Cambridge University Press, 1972.

———. *Reform and Reformation: England, 1509–1558*. Cambridge, Mass.: Harvard University Press, 1977.

Evans, John T. *Seventeenth-Century Norwich: Politics, Religion and Government, 1620–1690*. Oxford: Clarendon Press, 1979.

Evidences Related to the Town Close Estate, Norwich. Norwich, 1887.

Fairfield, Leslie. *John Bale: Mythmaker for the English Reformation*. West Lafayette, Ind.: Purdue University Press, 1976.

Farrow, M. A., ed. *Index of Wills Proved in the Consistory Court of Norwich, 1370–1550*. 3 vols. Norfolk Record Society, 16 (1943–1945).

———. *Index of Wills Proved in the Consistory Court of Norwich, 1550–1603*. Norfolk Record Society, 21 (1950).

Fines, John. "A Biographical Register of Early English Protestants and Others Opposed to the Roman Catholic Church 1525–1558." Unpublished typescript.

Fitch, Robert. "Norwich Pageants: The Grocers' Play." *Norfolk Archaeology*, 5 (1859): 8–31.

Fletcher, Anthony. *Tudor Rebellions*. 3rd ed. London: Longman, 1983.

Foster, Joseph. *Alumni Oxiensis: Members of the University of Oxford, 1500–1714*. 4 vols. Oxford, 1891–92.

Foxe, John. *The Acts and Monuments of John Foxe*. Ed. Rev. Josiah Pratt. 8 vols. London, 1877(?).

Frere, Walter Howard. *The Marian Reaction in Relation to the English Clergy: A Study of the Episcopal Registers*. London, 1896.

Friedrichs, Christopher R. *The Early Modern City, 1450–1750*. London: Longman, 1995.

Galloway, David, ed. *Norwich, 1540–1642*. Records of Early English Drama. Toronto: University of Toronto Press, 1984.

Garrett, Christina Hallowell. *The Marian Exiles: A Study in the Origins of Elizabethan Puritanism*. Cambridge, Eng.: Cambridge University Press, 1938.

Gee, Henry. *The Elizabethan Clergy and the Settlement of Religion 1558–1564*. Oxford, 1898.

——— and William John Hardy, comps. *Documents Illustrative of English Church History Compiled from Original Sources*. London, 1896.

Goodwin, A. *The Abbey of St. Edmundsbury*. Oxford: Blackwell, 1931.

Gottfried, Robert S. *Bury St. Edmunds and the Urban Crisis, 1290–1539*. Princeton, NJ: Princeton University Press, 1982.

Grace, Mary, ed. *The Records of St. George's Gild in Norwich, 1389–1547: A Transcript with an Introduction*. Norfolk Record Society, 9 (1937).

Green, Mrs. J. R. *Town Life in the Fifteenth Century*. 2 vols. New York and London, 1894.

Grell, Ole Peter. "Introduction." In Ole Peter Grell and Bob Scribner, eds., *Tolerance and Intolerance in the European Reformation*. Cambridge: Cambridge University Press, 1996, pp. 1–12.

———, Jonathan Israel and Nicholas Tyacke, eds. *From Persecution to Toleration: The Glorious Revolution and Religion in England*. Oxford: Clarendon Press, 1991.

Guy, J. A. *The Cardinal's Court: The Impact of Thomas Wolsey in Star Chamber*. Hassocks, Eng.: Harvester, 1977.

———. *The Court of Star Chamber and Its Records to the Reign of Elizabeth I*. Public Record Office Handbooks, no. 21. London: HMSO, 1985.

———. *The Public Career of Sir Thomas More*. Brighton, Sussex: Harvester, 1980.

———. *Tudor England*. Oxford: Oxford University Press, 1988.

Gwyn, Peter. *The King's Cardinal: The Rise and Fall of Thomas Wolsey*. London: Barrie and Jenkins, 1990.

Haigh, Christopher. *English Reformations: Religion, Politics and Society Under the Tudors*. Oxford: Oxford University Press, 1993.

———. "The Recent Historiography of the English Reformation." In Christopher Haigh, ed., *The English Reformation Revised*. Cambridge, Eng.: Cambridge University Press, 1987, pp. 1–18.

———. *Reformation and Resistance in Tudor Lancashire*. Cambridge, Eng.: Cambridge University Press, 1975.

———, ed. *The Reign of Elizabeth I*. Athens, GA: University of Georgia Press, 1985.

Harding, Vanessa. "The Population of London, 1550–1700: A Review of Published Evidence." *London Journal*, 15 (1990): 111–28.

Harris, Barbara J. "A New Look at the Reformation: Aristocratic Women and Nunneries, 1450–1540." *Journal of British Studies*, 32 (1993): 89–113.

Harrod, Henry. "A Few Particulars Concerning Early Norwich Pageants." *Norfolk Archaeology*, 3 (1852): 3–17.

Hawes, Timothy, ed. *An Index to Norwich City Officers, 1453–1835*. Norfolk Record Society, 52 (1989).

Head, David M. *The Ebbs and Flows of Fortune: The Life of Thomas Howard, Third Duke of Norfolk*. Athens, GA: University of Georgia Press, 1995.

Helgerson, Richard. *Forms of Nationhood: The Elizabethan Writing of England*. Chicago: University of Chicago Press, 1992.

Herrup, Cynthia B. *The Common Peace: Participation and the Criminal Law in Seventeenth-Century England*. Cambridge, Eng.: Cambridge University Press, 1987.

Hill, Christopher. *Society and Puritanism in Pre-Revolutionary England*. London: Secker and Warburg, 1964.

Hobsbawm, Eric, and Terence Ranger, eds. *The Invention of Tradition*. Cambridge, Eng.: Cambridge University Press, 1983.

Hoskins, W. G. "English Provincial Towns in the Early Sixteenth Century." In Peter Clark, ed., *The Early Modern Town: A Reader*. London: Longman, 1976, pp. 148–67.

Houlbrooke, Ralph. *Church Courts and the People During the English Reformation, 1520–1570*. Oxford: Oxford University Press, 1979.

———. "The Persecution of Heresy and Protestantism in the Diocese of Norwich Under Henry VIII." *Norfolk Archaeology*, 35 (1972): 308–26.

———. "Refoundation and Reformation, 1538–1628." In Ian Atherton, Eric Fernie, Christopher Harper-Bill and Hassell Smith, eds., *Norwich Cathedral: Church, City and Diocese, 1096–1996*. London: Hambledon, 1996, pp. 507–39.

————, ed. *The Letter Book of John Parkhurst Bishop of Norwich Compiled During the Years 1571–5.* Norfolk Record Society, 43 (1974–75).

Hudson, William, and John C. Tingey, eds. *The Records of the City of Norwich.* 2 vols. Norwich: Jarrold and Sons, Ltd., 1906–10.

————, comps. *Revised Catalogue of the Records of the City of Norwich.* Norwich, n.d.

Hughes, Paul L., and James F. Larkin, eds. *Tudor Royal Proclamations.* 2 vols. New Haven: Yale University Press, 1964–69.

Hughes, Philip. *The Reformation in England.* 2 vols. London: Hollis and Carter, 1951–53.

Hunt, William. *The Puritan Moment: The Coming of Revolution in an English County.* Cambridge, Mass.: Harvard University Press, 1983.

Hutton, Ronald. *The Rise and Fall of Merry England: The Ritual Year, 1400–1700.* Oxford: Oxford University Press, 1994.

Ingram, Martin. "From Reformation to Toleration: Popular Religious Cultures in England, 1540–1690." In Tim Harris, ed., *Popular Culture in England, c. 1500–1850.* New York: St. Martin's Press, 1995, pp. 95–123.

————. "Religion, Communities and Moral Discipline in Late Sixteenth- and Early Seventeenth-Century England: Case Studies." In Kaspar von Greyerz, ed., *Religion and Society in Early Modern Europe, 1500–1800.* London: German Historical Institute, 1984, pp. 177–93.

Ingram, R. W., ed. *Coventry.* Records of Early English Drama. Toronto: University of Toronto Press, 1981.

Ives, E. W. *Anne Boleyn.* Oxford: Blackwell, 1986.

Jacob, E. F. *The Fifteenth Century, 1399–1485.* Oxford: Oxford University Press, 1961.

James, Mervyn. "Ritual, Drama and the Social Body in the Late Medieval English Town." In Mervyn James, *Society, Politics and Culture: Studies in Early Modern England.* Cambridge, Eng.: Cambridge University Press, 1986, pp. 16–48.

Jessopp, A. *Visitations of the Diocese of Norwich, A.D. 1492–1532.* Camden Society, n.s., 43 (1888).

Johnson, Goddard. "Chronological Memoranda Touching the City of Norwich." *Norfolk Archaeology,* 1 (1846): 140–66.

Johnston, Alexandra F., and Margaret Rogerson, eds. *York.* Records of Early English Drama. 2 vols. Toronto: University of Toronto Press, 1979.

Jones, Norman L. *Faith by Statute: Parliament and the Settlement of Religion, 1559.* London: Royal Historical Society, 1982.

Kermode, Jennifer. I. "Urban Decline? The Flight from Office in Late Medieval York." *Economic History Review,* 2nd ser., 35 (1982): 178–98.

Kishlansky, Mark. "The Emergence of Adversary Politics in the Long Parliament." *Journal of Modern History*, 49 (1977): 617–40.

Konnert, Mark W. *Civic Agendas and Religious Passion: Châlons-sur-Marne During the French Wars of Religion, 1560–1594*. Kirksville, MO: Sixteenth Century Journal Publishers, 1997.

———. "A Tolerant City Council? Châlons-sur-Marne During the Wars of Religion." *Proceedings of the Western Society for French History*, 16 (1989): 40–47.

———. "Urban Values Versus Religious Passion: Châlons-sur-Marne During the Wars of Religion." *Sixteenth Century Journal*, 20 (1989): 387–405.

Kreider, Alan. *English Chantries: The Road to Dissolution*. Cambridge, Mass.: Harvard University Press, 1979.

Lake, Peter. "Calvinism and the English Church, 1570–1635." In Margo Todd, ed., *Reformation to Revolution: Politics and Religion in Early Modern England*. London: Routledge and Kegan Paul, 1995, pp. 179–207.

———. "Deeds Against Nature: Cheap Print, Protestantism and Murder in Early Seventeenth Century England." In Kevin Sharpe and Peter Lake, eds., *Culture and Politics in Early Stuart England*. Stanford, Calif.: Stanford University Press, 1993, pp. 257–75.

Land, Stephen K. *Kett's Rebellion: The Norfolk Rising of 1549*. Totowa, NJ: Rowman and Littlefield, 1977.

Lander, J. R. *Government and Community: England, 1450–1509*. Cambridge, Mass.: Harvard University Press, 1980.

Lehmberg, Stanford E. *The Reformation of Cathedrals: Cathedrals in English Society, 1548–1603*. Princeton, NJ: Princeton University Press, 1988.

L'Estrange, John. *Calendar of the Freemen of Norwich from 1317 to 1603*. Ed. Walter Rye. London, 1888.

———, ed. *The Eastern Counties Collectanea: Being Notes and Queries on Subjects Relating to the Counties of Norfolk, Suffolk, Essex and Cambridge*. Norwich, 1872–73.

"Letter from the Duke of Norfolk, at Kenninghall, to the Mayor of Norwich, Requiring Men to Be Raised to Resist the Malice of the Scots, 1542." *Norfolk Archaeology*, 1 (1846): 32–34.

"Letter from Henry VIII Requiring Forty Able Men, with Bows, Arrows, & c. to Assist Him in the Invasion of France; with Proceedings of the Mayor, & c. Relative Thereto, 1533." *Norfolk Archaeology*, 1 (1846): 36–38.

"Letter from the Mayor, & c. to the Duke of Norfolk, with the Replies Concerning 40 Men to Be Levied in Norwich, Trimmed with Harness, & c., and sent to Yarmouth, 1542." *Norfolk Archaeology*, 1 (1846): 34–36.

List of Sheriffs for England and Wales from the Earliest Times to AD 1831. Ed. E. A. Fry. Lists & Indexes, no. 9, London, 1898.

Loades, D. *The Reign of Mary Tudor: Politics, Government and Religion in England, 1553–58.* 2nd ed. London: Longman, 1991.

Lobel, M. D. *The Borough of Bury St. Edmunds.* Oxford: Clarendon Press, 1935.

MacCulloch, Diarmaid. "Archbishop Cranmer: Concord and Tolerance in a Changing Church." In Ole Peter Grell and Bob Scribner, eds., *Tolerance and Intolerance in the European Reformation.* Cambridge, Eng.: 1996, pp. 199–215.

———. "Kett's Rebellion in Context." In Paul Slack, ed., *Rebellion, Popular Protest and the Social Order in Early Modern England.* Cambridge, Eng.: Cambridge University Press, 1984, pp. 39–62.

———. "Kett's Rebellion in Context: A Rejoinder." Ibid., pp. 68–76.

———. *The Later Reformation in England, 1547–1603.* London: Macmillan, 1990.

———. *Suffolk and the Tudors: Politics and Religion in an English County 1500–1600.* Oxford: Oxford University Press, 1986.

Marius, Richard. *Thomas More: A Biography.* New York: Knopf, 1984.

Martin, J. W. "The Protestant Underground Congregations of Mary's Reign." *Journal of Ecclesiastical History,* 35 (1984): 519–38.

McClendon, Muriel C. "'Against God's Word': Government, Religion and the Crisis of Authority in Early Reformation Norwich." *Sixteenth Century Journal,* 25 (1994): 353–69.

———. "Discipline and Punish? Magistrates and Clergy in Early Reformation Norwich." In Eric Josef Carlson, ed., *Religion and the English People 1500–1620: New Voices/New Perspectives.* Kirksville, MO, forthcoming.

———. "A Moveable Feast: Saint George's Day Celebrations and Religious Change in Early Modern England." *Journal of British Studies,* 39 (1999): 1–27.

———. "Norwich Aldermen, 1517–1603." Norfolk Record Office typescript.

McGrath, Patrick. *Papists and Puritans Under Elizabeth I.* London: Blandford, 1967.

McIntosh, Marjorie K. *A Community Transformed: The Manor and Liberty of Havering, 1500–1620.* Cambridge, Eng.: Cambridge University Press, 1991.

———. "Local Change and Community Control in England, 1465–1500." *Huntington Library Quarterly,* 49 (1986): 219–42.

McRee, Ben R. "Religious Gilds and Civic Order: The Case of Norwich in the Late Middle Ages." *Speculum,* 67 (1992): 69–97.

———. "Unity or Division? The Social Meaning of Guild Ceremony in Urban Communities." In Barbara A. Hanawalt and Kathryn L. Reyerson, eds., *City and Spectacle in Medieval Europe.* Minneapolis: University of Minnesota Press, 1994, pp. 189–207.

Midmer, Roy. *English Medieval Monasteries, 1066–1540: A Summary*. Athens: University of Georgia Press, 1979.

Moens, William John Charles. *The Walloons and Their Church at Norwich: Their History and Registers 1565–1832*. London, 1887–88.

Moreton, C. E. *The Townshends and Their World: Gentry, Law, and Land in Norfolk, c. 1450–1551*. Oxford: Clarendon Press, 1992.

Muir, Edward. *Civic Ritual in Renaissance Venice*. Princeton, NJ: Princeton University Press, 1981.

Neale, J. E. "The Elizabethan Acts of Supremacy and Uniformity." *English Historical Review*, 65 (1950): 304–32.

Nelson, Alan H. *The Medieval English Stage: Corpus Christi Pageants and Plays*. Chicago: University of Chicago Press, 1974.

———. "Some Configurations of Staging in Medieval English Drama." In Jerome Taylor and Alan H. Nelson, eds., *Medieval English Drama: Essays Critical and Contextual*. Chicago: University of Chicago Press, 1972, pp. 116–47.

Neville, Alexander. *The History of the Rebellion in Norfolk in the Year MDXLIX: Which Was Conducted by Robert Kett, a Tanner by Trade at Wymondham*. Norwich [c. 1750].

Oberman, Heiko. "The Travail of Tolerance: Containing Chaos in Early Modern Europe." In Ole Peter Grell and Bob Scribner, eds., *Tolerance and Intolerance in the European Reformation*. Cambridge, Eng.: Cambridge University Press, 1996, pp. 13–31.

O'Day, Rosemary. *The Debate on the English Reformation*. London: Methuen, 1988.

Owen, Dorothy M. *The Making of King's Lynn: A Documentary Survey*. London: Oxford University Press for the British Academy, 1984.

Oxley, J. E. *The Reformation in Essex to the Death of Mary*. Manchester: Manchester University Press, 1965.

Palliser, D. M. *The Age of Elizabeth: England Under the Later Tudors, 1547–1603*. 2nd ed. London: Longman, 1992.

———. "Civic Mentality and Environment in Tudor York." *Northern History*, 18 (1982): 78–115.

———. "A Crisis in English Towns? The Case of York, 1480–1640." *Northern History*, 14 (1978): 108–25.

———. "Popular Reactions to the Reformation During the Years of Uncertainty, 1530–1570." In Felicity Heal and Rosemary O'Day, eds., *Church and Society in England: Henry VIII to James I*. London: Macmillan, 1977, pp. 35–56.

———. *The Reformation in York, 1534–1553*. Borthwick Papers, no. 40. York: St. Anthony Press, 1971.

———. *Tudor York*. Oxford: Oxford University Press, 1979.

————. "Urban Decay Revisited." In J. A. F. Thomson, ed., *Towns and Townspeople in the Fifteenth Century*. Gloucester: Alan Sutton, 1988, pp. 1–21.

Peel, Albert, ed. *The Seconde Parte of a Register: Being a Calendar of Manuscripts Under That Title Intended for Publication by the Puritans About 1593, and Now in Dr. Williams's Library, London*. 2 vols. Cambridge, Eng.: Cambridge University Press, 1915.

Phillips, John. *The Reformation of Images: Destruction of Art in England, 1536–1660*. Berkeley: University of California Press, 1973.

Phythian-Adams, Charles V. "Ceremony and the Citizen: The Communal Year at Coventry, 1540–1550." In Peter Clark and Paul Slack, eds., *Crisis and Order in English Towns, 1500–1700: Essays in Urban History*. London: Routledge and Kegan Paul, 1972, pp. 57–85.

————. *Desolation of a City: Coventry and the Urban Crisis of the Late Middle Ages*. Cambridge, Eng.: Cambridge University Press, 1979.

————. "Dr. Dyer's Urban Undulations." *Urban History Yearbook* (1979): 73–76.

————. "Urban Decay in Late Medieval England." In Philip Abrams and E. A. Wrigley, eds., *Towns in Societies: Essays in Economic History and Historical Sociology*. Cambridge, Eng.: Cambridge University Press, 1978, pp. 159–85.

Pound, John F. "Clerical Poverty in Early Sixteenth-Century England: Some East Anglian Evidence." *Journal of Ecclesiastical History*, 37 (1986): 389–96.

————. "Government and Society in Tudor and Stuart Norwich, 1525–1675." Ph.D. dissertation, University of Leicester, 1974.

————. *Poverty and Vagrancy in Tudor England*. 2nd ed. London: Longman, 1986.

————. "The Social and Trade Structure of Norwich, 1525–1575." *Past and Present*, 34 (1966): 49–69.

————. *Tudor and Stuart Norwich*. Chichester, Eng.: Phillimore, 1988.

———— and A. L. Beier, "Debate: Vagrants and the Social Order in Elizabethan England." *Past and Present*, 71 (1976): 126–34.

Pound, John F., ed. *The Norwich Census of the Poor, 1570*. Norfolk Record Society, 40 (1971).

Rappaport, Steve. *Worlds Within Worlds: Structures of Life in Sixteenth-Century London*. Cambridge, Eng.: Cambridge University Press, 1989.

Rex, Richard. *Henry VIII and the English Reformation*. New York: St. Martin's Press, 1993.

Reynolds, Susan. *An Introduction of the History of English Medieval Towns*. Oxford: Clarendon Press, 1977.

Rigby, S. R. "Urban Decline in the Later Middle Ages: Some Problems in Interpreting Statistical Data." *Urban History Yearbook*, 1979: 46–59.

Rubin, Miri. *Corpus Christi: The Eucharist in Late Medieval Culture.* Cambridge, Eng.: Cambridge University Press, 1991.

Rump, A. E., ed. "Account Books of St. Stephen's Church and Parish, Norwich." *The East Anglian: or Notes and Queries,* n.s., 8 (1899–1900): 34–38, 70–72, 109–11.

Russell, Frederic William. *Kett's Rebellion in Norfolk.* London, 1859.

Rye, Walter. "The Riot Between the Monks and Citizens of Norwich in 1272." *Norfolk Antiquarian Miscellany,* 2 (1883): 17–89.

———, ed. *Depositions Taken Before the Mayor & Aldermen of Norwich, 1549–1567: Extracts from the Court Books of the City of Norwich, 1666–1668.* Norwich: Agas H. Goose, for the Norfolk and Norwich Archaeological Society, 1905.

———, ed. *The Visitation of Norfolk, 1563, 1589 and 1613.* Harleain Society Publication, 32 (1891).

Sabean, David Warren. *Power in the Blood: Popular Culture & Village Discourse in Early Modern Germany.* Cambridge, Eng.: Cambridge University Press, 1984.

Sachse, William L., ed. *Minutes of the Norwich Court of Mayoralty, 1630–1631.* Norfolk Record Society, 15 (1942).

Sacks, David Harris. "Celebrating Authority in Bristol, 1475–1640." In Susan Zimmerman and Ronald F. E. Weissman, eds., *Urban Life in the Renaissance.* Newark, DE: University of Delaware Press, 1987, pp. 187–223.

———. "The Demise of the Martyrs: The Feasts of St. Clement and St. Katherine in Bristol, 1400–1600." *Social History,* 11 (1986): 141–69.

———. *The Widening Gate: Bristol and the Atlantic Economy, 1450–1700.* Berkeley: University of California Press, 1991.

Saunders, H. W. *A History of the Norwich Grammar School.* Norwich: Jarrold and Sons, Ltd., 1932.

Savage, William. *The Making of Our Towns.* London: Eyre and Spottiswoode, 1952.

Scarisbrick, J. J. *Henry VIII.* Berkeley: University of California Press, 1968.

———. *The Reformation and the English People.* Oxford: Blackwell, 1984.

Scribner, R. W. "Civic Unity and the Reformation in Erfurt." In R. W. Scribner, *Popular Culture and Popular Movements in Reformation Germany.* London: Hambledon, 1987, pp. 185–216.

———. "Cosmic Order and Daily Life: Sacred and Secular in Pre-Industrial German Society." Ibid., pp. 1–16.

———. "Preconditions of Tolerance and Intolerance in Sixteenth-Century Germany." In Ole Peter Grell and Bob Scribner, eds., *Tolerance and Intolerance in the European Reformation.* Cambridge, Eng.: Cambridge University Press, 1996, pp. 32–47.

———. "Ritual and Reformation." In R. W. Scribner, *Popular Culture and Popular Movements in Reformation Germany*. London: Hambledon, 1987, pp. 103–22.

———. "Why Was There No Reformation in Cologne?" Ibid., pp. 217–42.

Seaver, Paul S. *The Puritan Lectureships: The Politics of Religious Dissent, 1560–1662*. Stanford, Calif.: Stanford University Press, 1970.

Sheppard, Elaine M. "The Reformation and the Citizens of Norwich." *Norfolk Archaeology*, 38 (1981): 44–56.

Skeeters, Martha C. *Community and Clergy: Bristol and the Reformation, c. 1530-c. 1570*. Oxford: Oxford University Press, 1993.

Slack, Paul. *The Impact of PLAGUE in Tudor and Stuart England*. Oxford: Oxford University Press, 1985.

———. *Poverty and Policy in Tudor and Stuart England*. London: Longman, 1988.

Slavin, A. J., ed. *Humanism, Reform and Reformation in England*. New York: Wiley, 1969.

Smith, A. Hassell. *County and Court: Government and Politics in Norfolk, 1558–1603*. Oxford: Clarendon Press, 1974.

———, Gillian M. Baker and R. W. Kenny, eds. *The Papers of Nathaniel Bacon of Stiffkey*. 2 vols. Norfolk Record Society, 46, 49 (1978–83).

Smith, Alan G. R. *The Emergence of a Nation State: the Commonwealth of England, 1529–1660*. 2nd ed. London: Longman, 1997.

Smith, J. Challenor C. *Index of Wills Proved in the Prerogative Court of Canterbury, 1383–1558*. British Record Society, 10–11 (1895).

Smith, Richard Dean. "Social Reform in an Urban Context: Colchester, Essex, 1570–1640." Ph.D. dissertation, University of Colorado, 1995.

Smith, S. A., comp. *Index of Wills Proved in the Prerogative Court of Canterbury, 1558–1583*. Ed. Leland L. Duncan. British Record Society, 18 (1898).

———. *Index of Wills Proved in the Prerogative Court of Canterbury, 1584–1604*. Ed. Edward Alexander Fry. British Record Society, 25 (1901).

Sommerville, C. John. *The Secularization of Early Modern England: From Religious Culture to Religious Faith*. Oxford: Oxford University Press, 1992.

Spufford, Margaret. *Contrasting Communities: English Villagers in the Sixteenth and Seventeenth Centuries*. London: Cambridge University Press, 1974.

———. "Puritanism and Social Control?" In Anthony Fletcher and John Stevenson, eds., *Order and Disorder in Early Modern England*. Cambridge, Eng.: Cambridge University Press, 1985, pp. 41–57.

Stacy, John. *A Topographical and Historical Account of the City and County of Norwich*. London, 1819.

Starkey, D. R. *The Reign of Henry VIII: Personalities and Politics*. London: Collins and Brown, 1985.

Stokes, E., comp. *Index of Wills Proved in the Prerogative Court of Canterbury, 1605–1619*. British Record Society, 43 (1912).

Storey, R. L. *The End of the House of Lancaster*. 2nd ed. Gloucester: Alan Sutton, 1986.

Strype, John. *Memorials of Cranmer*. London, 1840.

——. *Works*. 19 vols. Oxford, 1820–24.

Swales, T. H. "The Redistribution of the Monastic Lands in Norfolk at the Dissolution." *Norfolk Archaeology*, 33 (1966): 14–44.

Tanner, Norman P. *The Church in Late Medieval Norwich, 1370–1532*. Toronto: Pontifical Institute of Medieval Studies, 1984.

——, ed. *Heresy Trials in the Diocese of Norwich, 1428–31*. London: Royal Historical Society, 1977.

Thomas, Keith. *Religion and the Decline of Magic*. London: Weidenfeld and Nicolson, 1971.

Thompson, E. P. "The Moral Economy of the English Crowd in the Eighteenth Century." *Past and Present*, 50 (1971): 76–136.

Thomson, John A. F. *The Transformation of Medieval England, 1370–1529*. London: Longman, 1983.

Tittler, Robert. *Architecture and Power: The Town Hall and the English Urban Community, c. 1500–1640*. Oxford: Clarendon Press, 1991.

——. "The Emergence of Urban Policy, 1536–58." In Jennifer Loach and Robert Tittler, eds., *The Mid-Tudor Polity, c. 1540–1560*. London: Macmillan, 1980, pp. 74–93.

——. "The End of the Middle Ages in the English County Town." *Sixteenth Century Journal*, 18 (1987): 471–87.

——. *The Reign of Mary I*. 2nd ed. London: Longman, 1991.

Tyacke, Nicholas. "Anglican Attitudes: Some Recent Writings on English Religious History, from the Reformation to the Civil War." *Journal of British Studies*, 35 (1996): 1–23.

Underdown, David. *Fire from Heaven: Life in an English Town in the Seventeenth Century*. New Haven: Yale University Press, 1992.

Urlin, Ethel L. *Festivals, Holy Days and Saints' Days: A Study in the Origins and Survivals in Church Ceremonies and Secular Customs*. London: Simpkin, Marshall, Hamilton, Kent and Co., Ltd., 1915.

Venn, J., and J. A. Venn, eds. *Alumni Cantabrigiensis, Part I: From the Earliest Times to 1751*. 4 vols. Cambridge, Eng.: Cambridge University Press, 1922–24.

von Friedburg, Robert. "Reformation of Manners and the Social Composition of Offenders in an East Anglian Cloth Village: Earls Colne, Essex, 1531–1642." *Journal of British Studies*, 29 (1990): 347–85.

Walter, John, and Keith Wrightson. "Dearth and the Social Order in Early Modern England." *Past and Present*, 71 (1976): 22–42.

Ward, Joseph P. *Metropolitan Communities: Trade Guilds, Identity, and Change in Early Modern London*. Stanford, Calif.: Stanford University Press, 1997.

———. "Religious Diversity and Guild Unity in Early Modern London." In Eric Josef Carlson, ed., *Religion and the English People, 1500–1620: New Voices/New Perspectives*. Kirksville, MO, forthcoming.

Warnicke, Retha M. "The Fall of Anne Boleyn Revisited." *English Historical Review*, 108 (1993): 653–65.

Wasson, John M., ed. *Devon*. Records of Early English Drama. Toronto: University of Toronto Press, 1986.

Watson, Robert. *Aetiologia Roberti Watsoni*. N.p., 1556.

Watt, Tessa. *Cheap Print and Popular Piety, 1550–1640*. Cambridge, Eng.: Cambridge University Press, 1991.

White, B. R. *The English Separatist Tradition: From the Marian Martyrs to the Pilgrim Fathers*. London: Oxford University Press, 1971.

Whiting, Robert. *The Blind Devotion of the People: Popular Religion and the English Reformation*. Cambridge, Eng.: Cambridge University Press, 1989.

Williams, J. F. "The Married Clergy of the Marian Period." *Norfolk Archaeology*, 32 (1961): 85–95.

Williams, Neville. *Thomas Howard Fourth Duke of Norfolk*. London: Barrie and Rockliff, 1964.

Wrightson, Keith. *English Society, 1580–1680*. London: Hutchinson, 1982.

——— and David Levine. *Poverty and Piety in an English Village: Terling, 1525–1700*. New York: Academic Press, 1979.

Wrigley, E. A., and R. S. Schofield. *The Population History of England, 1541–1871: A Reconstruction*. Cambridge, Eng.: Cambridge University Press, 1981.

Zell, Michael. "The Use of Religious Preambles as a Measure of Religious Belief in the Sixteenth Century." *Bulletin of the Institute of Historical Research*, 50 (1977): 241–53.

ᴥ INDEX ᴥ

In this index an "f" after a number indicates a separate reference on the next page, and an "ff" indicates separate references on the next two pages. A continuous discussion over two or more pages is indicated by a span of page numbers, e.g., "57–59." *Passim* is used for a cluster of references in close but not consecutive sequence.

Library of Congress Cataloging-in-Publication Data

McClendon, Muriel C.
   The quiet Reformation : magistrates and the emergence of
Protestantism in Tudor Norwich / Muriel C. McClendon.
        p.   cm.
   Includes bibliographical references and index.
   ISBN 0-8047-3513-1 (hardcover : alk. paper).
      1. Reformation—England.   2. Protestantism—England.
3. England—Church history.   I. Title.

BR375.M26   1999
274.26'1506—dc21   98-37996
                                                        CIP

This book is printed on acid-free, recycled paper.

Original printing 1999
Last figure below indicates year of this printing:
08   07   06   05   04   03   02   01   00   99